New Perspectives in German Political Studies

General Editors: **William Paterson OBE** is Honorary Professor in German and European Politics at the University of Aston and Chairman of the German British Forum.

Charlie Jeffery is Professor of Politics at the University of Edinburgh.

Germany remains a pivotal country in Europe. It is Europe's biggest economy, continues to play a central role in the European Union, and has a growing significance in international security politics based on its strategic location at the centre of Europe and its evolving role as a provider of security in Europe and beyond. All this is nuanced by the legacies of a turbulent recent history: the two World Wars, the Holocaust, Germany's division after World War II and its unification in 1990.

New Perspectives in German Political Studies has been designed as a platform for debate and scholarship on contemporary Germany. It welcomes contributions from political science, international relations, political economy and contemporary history. It follows on from the success of the earlier series on New Perspectives in German Studies, co-edited by William Paterson and the late Professor Michael Butler.

Titles include:

Ed Turner
POLITICAL PARTIES AND PUBLIC POLICY IN THE GERMAN LÄNDER
When Parties Matter

Timo Fleckenstein
INSTITUTIONS, IDEAS AND LEARNING IN WELFARE STATE CHANGE
Labour Market Reforms in Germany

Alister Miskimmon, William E. Paterson and James Sloam (*editors*)
GERMANY'S GATHERING CRISIS
The 2005 Federal Election and the Grand Coalition

Anne Fuchs
PHANTOMS OF WAR IN CONTEMPORARY GERMAN LITERATURE, FILMS AND DISCOURSE
The Politics of Memory

Beverly Crawford
POWER AND GERMAN FOREIGN POLICY
Embedded Hegemony in Europe

Dan Hough, Michael Koß and Jonathan Olsen
THE LEFT PARTY IN CONTEMPORARY GERMAN POLITICS

Roger Woods
GERMANY'S NEW RIGHT AS CULTURE AND POLITICS

Christian Schweiger
BRITAIN, GERMANY AND THE FUTURE OF THE EUROPEAN UNION

Matthew M.C. Allen
THE VARIETIES OF CAPITALISM PARADIGM
Explaining Germany's Comparative Advantage?

Gunther Hellmann (*editor*)
GERMANY'S EU POLICY IN ASYLUM AND DEFENCE
De-Europeanization by Default?

Charles Lees
PARTY POLITICS IN GERMANY
A Comparative Politics Approach

Ronald Speirs and John Breuilly (*editors*)
GERMANY'S TWO UNIFICATIONS
Anticipations, Experiences, Responses

James Sloam
THE EUROPEAN POLICY OF THE GERMAN SOCIAL DEMOCRATS
Interpreting a Changing World

Margarete Kohlenbach
WALTER BENJAMIN
Self-Reference and Religiosity

Henning Tewes
GERMANY, CIVILIAN POWER AND THE NEW EUROPE
Enlarging Nato and the European Union

Wolf-Dieter Eberwein and Karl Kaiser (*editors*)
GERMANY'S NEW FOREIGN POLICY
Decision-Making in an Interdependent World

Ruth Wittlinger
GERMAN NATIONAL IDENTITY IN THE TWENTY-FIRST CENTURY
A Different Republic After All?

Chantal Lacroix
IMMIGRANTS, LITERATURE AND NATIONAL INTEGRATION

Gerard Braunthal
RIGHT-WING EXTREMISM IN CONTEMPORARY GERMANY

New Perspectives in German Political Studies
Series Standing Order ISBN 978–0–333–92430–3 hardcover
Series Standing Order ISBN 978–0–333–92434–1 paperback
(*outside North America only*)

You can receive future titles in this series as they are published by placing a standing order. Please contact your bookseller or, in case of difficulty, write to us at the address below with your name and address, the title of the series and the ISBN quoted above.

Customer Services Department, Macmillan Distribution Ltd, Houndmills, Basingstoke, Hampshire RG21 6XS, England

Political Parties and Public Policy in the German Länder

When Parties Matter

Ed Turner
Lecturer in Politics, Department of Politics and International Relations, Aston University, UK

First published 2011 by
PALGRAVE MACMILLAN

Palgrave Macmillan in the UK is an imprint of Macmillan Publishers Limited, registered in England, company number 785998, of Houndmills, Basingstoke, Hampshire RG21 6XS.

Palgrave Macmillan in the US is a division of St Martin's Press LLC, 175 Fifth Avenue, New York, NY 10010.

Palgrave Macmillan is the global academic imprint of the above companies and has companies and representatives throughout the world.

Palgrave® and Macmillan® are registered trademarks in the United States, the United Kingdom, Europe and other countries

ISBN 978-0-230-28442-5   hardback

This book is printed on paper suitable for recycling and made from fully managed and sustained forest sources. Logging, pulping and manufacturing processes are expected to conform to the environmental regulations of the country of origin.

A catalogue record for this book is available from the British Library.

Library of Congress Cataloging-in-Publication Data

Turner, Edward, 1977–
   Political parties and public policy in the German Länder : when
   parties matter / Ed Turner.
      p. cm.
   Includes bibliographical references and index.
   ISBN 978–0–230–28442–5 (alk. paper)
     1. Political parties–Germany–States. 2. Political planning–
   Germany–States. 3. Political parties– Germany–States–Case studies.
   4. Political planning– Germany–States–Case studies. 5. State
   governments–Germany. I. Title.

JN3971.A988T87 2011
324.243–dc22   2011012478

10   9   8   7   6   5   4   3   2   1
20   19 18 17 16 15 14 13 12 11

Printed and bound by CPI Group (UK) Ltd, Croydon, CR0 4YY

Contents

List of Tables

Acknowledgements

This book is the culmination of several years' work on German politics, and could not have been written without a great deal of support from friends, family, and colleagues.

I am extremely grateful to both the Economic and Social Research Council, and subsequently the University of Birmingham, for financial support.

I am also very grateful to officials, politicians and other professionals who took time out of hectic schedules to discuss the issues addressed in this study.

Colleagues and friends at Birmingham University's Institute for German Studies provided a great deal of help. Special thanks are owed to William Paterson and Thomas Poguntke for reading sections of the manuscript and offering very helpful advice.

Thanks are also due to Otto Wurbs, Adelheid Mallach and Nadine Müller for putting me up (and putting up with me!) while I was undertaking fieldwork, as well as providing many useful suggestions and impulses. Nadine Greulich was also very kind and hospitable. Antonia Bance generously looked after my commitments in Oxford while I was away on fieldwork. Especially in the early years, my friends Siobhan McAndrew and Rick Muir were a frequent source of guidance, entertainment, inspiration and delay to progress!

My interest in policy change at the sub-national level in Germany developed during a spell at the Geschwister-Scholl Institute in Munich in 1998–99. I am particularly grateful to Florian Bieberbach, Florian Sipek, Christoph Moosbauer, Ulrike Boesser, and Nikolaus Gradl for their camaraderie during this time, and for demonstrating the deep-rooted convictions on which sub-national political engagement can be based.

Particular thanks are due to Charlie Jeffery, for his help in the early stages of this study, and to Simon Green throughout, for never-ending patience in dealing with a recalcitrant colleague, and keeping faith in him until the bitter end.

On a personal as well as a professional note, I owe a debt of thanks to Dan Paskins, Bill Turner, and particularly Anneliese Dodds, for discussing the ideas in this study, proof-reading beyond the call of duty, and much more besides. I am also very grateful to Frank Pattison for turning me Germanophile.

The editorial team and all the production staff at Palgrave Macmillan have been wonderful and I am indebted to them for all their patient assistance.

Finally, a debt of thanks is due to my parents. In different ways, they prompted and fostered my interests in both academic study and politics, and it is a source of sadness that they will not see this book. It does not do them justice.

Preface

All translations, unless otherwise stated, are by the author. Where there is a reference to the 'Statistisches Bundesamt' or 'Statistisches Landesamt', this refers to the relevant statistical office's publicly available data sets. Official publications (such as official records of laws, regulations and decrees, and stenographic reports of parliamentary sessions) are publicly available and are referred to in the text but not separately in the Bibliography. Election results and details of government composition are available from the relevant state government and state election officer.

1
Introduction: Partisan Influence Upon Public Policy in Decentralised Polities

The question of whether parties matter – the extent to which parties exert an exogenous influence upon public policies – is a central one for the study of Politics. Debate upon it has raged in the discipline for generations (Hibbs 1977; Tufte 1978; Garrett and Lange 1986; Blais et al. 1993; Schmidt 1995, 1996; Garrett 1998; Boix 1998), yielding inconclusive, and at times contradictory, results. No less striking are analyses of state activity that do not acknowledge the possibility of partisan influence upon public policy. For instance, Genschel and Zangl (2007), in their discussion of 'stateness', do not discuss this potentially significant determinant of what states do. Other recent work, considering the extent of convergence on Anglo-Saxon, liberalised economic models, either does not discuss, or downplays, the impact of parties (Streeck and Thelen 2005).

Where partisan influences upon public policy have been explicitly examined, the analysis has tended to be quantitative in nature, in particular focusing on levels of public expenditure. This brings clear advantages – notably comparability of data, and the facilitation of research into a large number of cases, giving rise to generalisable conclusions. However, there are several ways in which such research may be insufficient.

First, the most important features of public policy change may have nothing to do with public expenditure, and be hard to capture in terms of numbers (save by quantitatively coding qualitative changes). For example, the degree of selection or the method of assessment in an education system might be affected by a government's partisan composition, yet is unrelated to the level of expenditure. Kittel and Obinger (2003, p.40) remind us of the importance of programme design, and make a compelling case for the use of qualitative research to capture this in consideration of parties' influence upon public policy.

Secondly, in understanding whether policy changes are due to partisan orientation, or other factors, the researcher needs to drill down into specific policy choices, and evaluate what prompted them. For instance, a rise in welfare expenditure might appear to be the result of the election of a left-leaning

1

government; however, it might be that both are due to an exogenous event, such as a rise in unemployment (with the change in the population prompting more votes for the left, as well as higher welfare expenditure). As Hicks and Swank put it, there is a risk of some quantitative research 'courting biased findings by omitting variables that may be correlated with included variables' (1992, p.658).

Thirdly, research measuring policy change by looking at the level of public expenditure may prove too sensitive to changes in the dependent population. For instance, if unemployment increases, as it did in 1980s Britain, spending on welfare also increases, but that may not reflect higher levels of benefit for individuals, or a shift to an expansionist welfare policy by the government of the day (Allan and Scruggs 2004).

The literature upon partisan influence also has a significant gap: discussions of partisan influence upon public policy have tended, barring a few studies of US federalism (e.g. Erikson et al. 1989), to focus on exclusively on the nation-state level. Although such a focus is perfectly understandable, it gives us an incomplete picture. As Watts notes, some 23 nations count as federal states (on a strict definition), encompassing around 40% of the world's population (Watts 1999, p.xi). In these federal states, at least, an exclusive focus upon the national level will tend to neglect partisan influence upon any areas of policy where sub-national levels of government have autonomy. There is a further, interesting puzzle about partisan influence in federal states. Scholarship on federalism often asks if the existence of federal structures has a particular influence upon policy (for instance, inhibiting the development of a welfare state, or curbing public spending). Such analyses tend not to consider the impact of parties upon public policy in federal states, but this may be a mistake: it is not obvious that a federal state dominated by governments of the left would necessarily curb public spending, for instance.

This study attempts to fill two major gaps in the literature, namely the dearth of qualitative research into the influence of parties upon public policy, and the shortage of consideration of the sub-national level in assessing partisan influence. It undertakes a qualitative study of partisan influence upon public policy at a sub-national level in a major western polity, Germany. In doing so, it attempts to complement the existing literature on partisan influence, which has pursued a quantitative approach focused upon the national level.

The introduction is split into two sections. The remainder of this chapter sets the book in context, firstly by reviewing the *do-parties-matter?* debate in Political Science, and then considering some of the reasons why parties might not, contrary to expectations, have such a profound, exogenous influence on public policy. Thereafter, the chapter considers the dynamics of decentralised policy-making, looking in particular at whether federalism will spawn territorial policy variation of a particular sort, and how parties might fit into this picture. Chapter 2 then brings discussion back to Germany, examining the way public policy is made at the regional level in Germany, and reviewing earlier attempts to consider ways in which parties attempt to shape it.

1.1   The *do-parties-matter?* debate in political science

In a seminal paper, Manfred Schmidt spells out a number of key propositions which underpin what he terms the 'partisan hypothesis', namely that 'a major determinant of variation in policy choices and policy outputs in constitutional democracies is the party composition of government' (Schmidt 1996, p.155).

Amongst the most important of these propositions are that parties represent social constituencies with distinctive preferences, and parties' policy orientations mirror these preferences; and moreover, that governments are capable of implementing policies that are chosen by incumbent parties (ibid., p.156). These claims are by no means uncontroversial: after all, social change is often held to have weakened the distinctiveness of parties' social constituencies (Mair 2008), and there are now a wealth of constraints upon the ability of national-level policy-makers to change policy (arising for instance from globalisation, competitive pressures and the power of organisations such as the European Union).

Schmidt (1996, p.156) also notes that the extent to which the partisan composition of government can shape policy depends upon a number of variables: the distribution of power in parliament, institutional arrangements, and the extent to which a country's economy is vulnerable to international markets. For instance, partisan effects would be greater in a relatively closed economy, where power is strongly concentrated within an executive in a unicameral legislature. In contrast, in an open economy, with power dispersed vertically and horizontally, we would expect government composition to have less impact upon policy choices.

The number of empirical studies finding conformation of the partisan hypothesis outnumbered, by some distance, those which did not (Blais et al. 1993; Schmidt 1996), at least until the end of the 20th century. Starting with data ranging from 1960 to 1975, Cameron (1978) considered the relationship between government revenues as a proportion of gross domestic product (GDP) and the electoral base of left-wing parties, and found a significant, positive correlation: left-wing governments were associated with higher spending increases. In a similar vein, Hibbs (1977) found that governments of the left pursued policies that tended to reduce unemployment at the expense of inflation, whereas the opposite policy trade-off was pursued by governments of the right.

Although this view was not universally shared (e.g. Rose 1980), subsequent analysis continued to detect significant partisan influence upon public policy. Castles and McKinlay (1979), in an influential study, considered the relationship between different levels of welfare development and three political factors (federalism, type of leadership, and the ideological dominance, or otherwise, of right-wing parties). They found that the political dominance of right-wing parties did indeed lead to lower levels of welfare development, refuting views which suggested welfare development was largely a function of social modernisation – although federalism was found to be a significant inhibitor of welfare development. Castles (1982) developed this line of enquiry, finding a powerful correlation between the growth in public expenditure and the electoral strength of parties of the left – a view confirmed by Corina et al. (1982) in the same volume.

Further important contributions to this debate were made by Garrett and Lange (1986, 1991). In an investigation of economic performance in the 1970s, when countries confronted the problem of 'stagflation' (economic stagnation and high inflation), they assessed the impact of domestic political structures upon economic performance (Garrett and Lange 1986). Their key finding was that economic growth was significantly higher when the political power of the left was combined with strong and centrally organised trade unions (the requirements of 'corporatism'). In the absence of left parties in government, strong trade unions would pursue immediate gains, through industrial militancy, at the expense of growth in the medium term.

Garrett and Lange (1991) developed this finding. Although evidence for expansionist economic policies in circumstances of corporatism was limited, they ascertained that 'economic strategies in corporatist political economies have combined traditional welfarist concerns with interventionist government industrial, investment, and labor market policies designed to promote competitiveness and flexible adjustment' (p.563). Taken together, these findings suggest that, at least in the 1970s and 1980s, parties could make a difference in key areas of economic policy, albeit far more when combined with strong, centralised trade unions. Alvarez et al. (1991) demonstrate that the flip-side is true for parties on the right: they could, and did, pursue different economic strategies, and were able to do so successfully if trade unions were weak and divided.

Swank (1988) examined governments' domestic expenditure over the time periods 1960–73 and 1973–80. He found that, in the earlier period, there was quite strong confirmation for the 'partisan hypothesis', and that governments of the left and the centre routinely spent more than governments of the right. In the latter period, the gap narrowed somewhat, as parties' room for manoeuvre was circumscribed by the economic circumstances of the time. During both time frames, the strength of unions and working-class protest also affected spending levels. Unsurprisingly, party politics was a determinant of spending policy choices – but not their sole determinant, and its influence upon them was contingent upon social and economic circumstances.

Hicks and Swank (1992) developed a further refinement of the partisan hypothesis, finding that, in terms of state expenditure, governments of the political centre are more likely to have higher welfare spending than those of the right. More surprisingly, they are also likely to have higher expenditures than left governments – a result Hicks and Swank explain through the greater likelihood of leftist governments pursuing full-employment policies, reducing the level of reliance upon welfare transfers. They also find that higher voter turnout exerts upward pressure upon welfare expenditure (as poorer voters make their presence felt in the electoral process), and that the shape of the political opposition plays a role (for instance, a centrist government will spend more on welfare if it faces a strong leftist opposition).

Garrett (1998), in an important contribution, revisited the possibility of partisan influence upon public policy in circumstances of globalisation. His conclusions were far-reaching: parties of the left retained the ability to develop national economic policies to reduce inequality, and indeed often had strong incentives to do so, in particular to support those who had been affected by market dislocations. Boix (1998) similarly identifies distinctive supply-side policies that can be and are pursued by governments of the left and of the right, even though globalisation has reduced the ability of the left to pursue a distinctive demand-side agenda.

All these studies, and many more, provide confirmation of Schmidt's 'partisan hypothesis', which, to recap, is the claim that the party composition of government is a major determinant of policy choices and outputs. None claims that the party in government is the only variable to affect public policies, nor that its importance as a variable will be constant. There are, however, a number of alternative viewpoints that place far less emphasis on the partisan composition of government in shaping policies, and these are discussed in the next section.

1.2   Alternatives to partisan influence

As we recall, Schmidt (1996) notes that, for the partisan hypothesis to hold, political parties need to pursue distinctive policies. Yet this claim has been challenged in a number of recent works (Mair 2008).

Some authors suggest that partisan influence upon public policy has diminished due to *partisan convergence*, that is, parties no longer seeking to pursue distinctive policy agendas. This may be due to an inexorable drift to the political centre, as predicted, albeit in quite particular circumstances, by Downs (1957), in order to maximise the electoral appeal to the median voter.

Partisan convergence might also occur if there is a breakdown in the size or the coherence of the social groups on which parties previously focused their electoral appeals, such as unionised, manual workers in the case of social democratic parties, or church-going Catholics, for Christian democratic parties (Mair 2008, p.219). Parties' shift away from particularist appeals to such groups will partly be prompted if, following the title of Rose and McAllister's well-known book (1986), 'Voters begin to choose', and the connection between membership of a social group and partisan affiliation is weakened. As Mair puts it, 'It is beyond dispute that ... parties have become electorally more catch-all ... . In part ... this is the inevitable result of social change' (2008, p.219). In addition, parties have increasingly tended to cast their appeal more widely, learning 'to be more attractive to those segments of the electorate which were once seen as beyond the pale. ... In other words, it is not only that the vote has become more free-floating and available, but so also have the parties themselves, with the result that political competition has become characterised by the contestation of socially inclusive appeals in search of support from socially amorphous electorates' (ibid., pp.219–20). In this area also, a study into the sub-national level will be useful in elucidating trends. Research has tended to focus on national parties and national elections but it might be hypothesised that, confronted with greater social homogeneity at a regional level, and a greater proximity to policy-seeking grassroots members, partisan convergence would be more limited below the level of national politics.

Parties might also find that their ability to change public policy is constrained by 'path dependence' (Pierson 2000). Levi (cited in Pierson 2000, p.252) defines the concept thus:

> Path dependence has to mean, if it is to mean anything, that once a country or region has started down a track, the costs of reversal are very high. There will be other choice points, but the entrenchments of certain institutional arrangements obstruct an easy reversal of the initial choice.

The notion of 'path dependence' originated in economics – with the argument, in contrast to the neo-classical orthodoxy, that markets will not always clear at an optimal outcome (Arthur 1989, 1990; Mokyr 1991). Instead, errors can be made at first, and these are 'locked in' through a process of positive feedback. So, for instance, manufacturers of typewriters persisted in using the QWERTY keyboard, even though it was less efficient than the Dvorak alternative (David 1985), and equally the VHS video cassette persisted in favour of the apparently superior Betamax system (Arthur 1990).

In our case, we are not so much interested in policy choices which happen to be sub-optimal (after all, parties' view of what is optimal will differ depending on their political standpoint), but instead in the extent to which path dependence constrains their room for manoeuvre; their ability to change policies in the direction which, all other things being equal, they would ideologically favour.

To illustrate this, we might consider the area of welfare benefits. Pierson (1996), in a discussion of welfare policy, found that the right-wing governments of Ronald Reagan and Margaret Thatcher were unable to implement radical cutbacks in benefits as might have been expected:

> Even in Thatcher's Britain, where an ideologically committed Conservative Party has controlled one of Europe's most centralized political systems for over a decade, reform has been incremental rather than revolutionary, leaving the British welfare state largely intact. In most other countries the evidence of continuity is even more apparent (p.174).

The reason for this, Pierson finds, is that '... Today's policymakers operate in an environment fundamentally shaped by policies inherited from the past' (p.179). In particular, once groups in society receive certain benefits, interest groups will form to defend them and there is likely to be a substantial electoral cost to retrenchment, so that, in the area of welfare policy at least, change will be incremental at most.

Pierson's findings are by no means universally supported. For instance, Clayton and Pontusson (1998) believe that he understates the extent to which parties of the right were able to undertake retrenchment of the welfare state. First, they point out that measuring overall welfare 'effort' by looking at the proportion of GDP spent is misleading, as it is very responsive to external factors, such as growth in unemployment – confirming a point made earlier in this introduction. In fact, the recession of the 1980s and the expenditure increases associated with serving a larger number of claimants served to mask substantial welfare cuts. Secondly, they highlight the importance of programme design, contending that, for instance, a shift to means-tested benefits and the privatisation of public services can constitute retrenchment, but may not be captured by spending data. Again, this emphasises the value of a qualitative assessment of public policy change.

Just as with the partisan hypothesis above, the counter-hypothesis that partisan policy change will be limited owing to path dependence will not be confirmed entirely: just as few would anticipate an immediate transformation of public policy owing to the presence of a new government, so the hypothesis of path dependence suggests policy change will be incremental, rather than non-existent. Our purpose here is to understand the *extent* to which the past and the financial and political costs of deviating from set policy paths, constrain party politicians in the realisation of their policy goals. Here, too, a focus on the sub-national level is useful, giving the opportunity to consider whether historical development trajectories are as important at the regional level as they are at the national level in accounting for policy stability.

Critics of those who see the partisan complexion of a government as being a major factor in shaping policy change often point to the openness of an economy as being a major constraint upon policy change (Keohane and Nye 1989). Indeed, even exponents of the partisan hypothesis argue that, the more open an economy, the less parties can make a difference (Schmidt 1996, p.156). There are three principal arguments here (Garrett and Lange 1991, pp.542–3). First, Keynesian policy instruments, often associated with left parties in government, which involve the macroeconomic stimulation of domestic demand are significantly harder to pursue in an open economy, as they may simply lead to a surge in imports or balance of payments deficits. Secondly, financial market integration has the potential to undermine such efforts almost instantly. Thirdly, with growing exposure to international trade, governments of all political colours face pressure to liberalise their markets in order to attract inward investment. This leads to downward pressure on levels of taxation, regulation and public spending, even where this is anathema to governments of the left.

There are, however, two reasons to be sceptical of such claims. The first challenges the assumption that all countries' economies are equally open and thus subject to the same ubiquitous pressures. However, as Garrett (1998) convincingly demonstrates, this is not the case, and in fact there are stark variations between industrialised countries both with regards to their exposure to international trade and the degree of capital mobility. Secondly, the classical demand-management instruments which are no longer available to left-wing governments do not constitute the totality of national economic policy, and indeed significant variations remain possible on the supply side (Garrett and Lange 1991; Boix 1998; Garrett 1998).

For our purposes, there are two important points to draw out here, which are investigated in this study. First, it is not obvious whether international economic integration necessarily poses the same level of constraint upon policy-makers at the sub-national level as at the national level. Even though regional actors had little scope, in integrated national economies, to pursue regional demand-management strategies (we don't, after all, hear of Keynesianism on a regional level very often!), it is quite possible to believe that international economic integration reduces regions' scope for higher levels of taxation, spending, and labour market regulation. Moreover, central governments, as a result of these pressures, may restrict the fiscal or regulatory capacity of sub-national politicians, not wishing them to disadvantage the national economy in a competitive market. These possibilities demand investigation.

Secondly, the focus upon questions of economic policy in consideration of the partisan hypothesis neglects other important areas of policy where parties have fundamentally different views, such as on the role of the family, or the relationship between church and state (Schmidt 1996, pp.168–9). Indeed, if parties' ability to shape economic policy declines, they might seek to achieve a distinctive policy profile by pursuing divergent strategies in other policy areas.

Further grounds for scepticism of the partisan hypothesis can broadly be grouped under the headings of *institutional and constitutional inertia*. As Schmidt notes (1996, p.156), the partisan hypothesis assumes that 'governments are capable of implementing the policies that were chosen by incumbent parties'. However, there are several ways in which governments are constrained – to varying degrees – in doing this.

First, it is often assumed that the civil service will be immediately responsive to a new government's demands. But, to follow the popular German saying, 'Politicians come and go, but the civil service stays'. The civil service might lack the capacity to deliver large programmes of policy change, or it might lack the will. In particular if there is a high level of political appointment of the civil service combined with employment protection, any new government faces the unenviable task of persuading ideologically hostile bureaucrats to implement its policies (Lees 2000, pp.37–8).

Secondly, constitutional and legal constraints will have a key bearing upon the ability of partisan actors to implement their policies. Lijphart (1999) contrasts the constitutional arrangements of different types of democracies (Table 1.1).

Table 1.1   Majoritarian vs. Consensus democracy (adapted from Lijphart 1999, pp.3–4)

Majoritarian democracy	Consensus democracy
Concentration of executive power in single-party, majority cabinet	Executive power-sharing in broad, multi-party coalition
Executive-legislative relationship dominated by the executive	Balance of power between legislature and executive
Two-party system	Multi-party system
Majoritarian electoral system	Proportional electoral system
Pluralist interest groups with free-for-all competition	Coordinated and 'corporatist' interest groups aiming at compromise and coordination
Unitary and centralised government	Federalism and decentralised government
Concentration of legislative power in a unicameral system	Division of legislative power between two equally strong but differently constituted houses
Flexible constitutions which can be amended by a simple majority	A rigid constitution that can only be amended by a super-majority
No system of judicial review	Laws subject to judicial review by a supreme or constitutional court
Central bank dependent on the executive	Independent central bank

Majoritarian democracies are likely to see a higher degree of partisan influence, both because more spheres of policy are amenable to political control (such as monetary policy), but also because institutions such as a powerful second chamber, a restrictive constitution backed up by a powerful constitutional court, and in particular a system of federalism, will all restrict a government's ability to act.

Although Lijphart focuses on the national level, such constraints are no less important for regional and local governments. In particular, their degree of constitutional autonomy and the extent to which they can exercise influence over the central government are likely to be significant to determining the scope partisan actors at the sub-national level have to pursue their policy goals.

There are four conclusions that can be drawn from this short exposition of literature concerning the partisan hypothesis. First, we can see that, although there is a strong body of literature in support of the partisan hypothesis, there are also good reasons to believe that counterveiling pressures will, in some circumstances, also be very important: investigation of the degree of partisan influence upon public policy, and the circumstances when it is greatest or most restricted, is vital. Secondly, we can see a bias in existing studies towards socio-economic areas of policy, yet in some polities parties may well be divided along quite different lines. Thirdly, quantitative literature dominates explorations of the partisan hypothesis to date, yet qualitative research has something significant to add. Finally, we see a strong focus on the national level, but investigation of the sub-national level is important as well.

This study aims to shed light on all of these areas.

1.3   The dynamics of decentralised policy-making

So far, this chapter has considered whether parties matter. Next we need to turn our attention to whether *federalism* matters. This can be considered in two ways.

First, many political scientists have addressed the question of whether federalism will affect public policies pursued in a nation-state. Famously, Riker (1975) is noted for his scepticism on this point, suggesting that, save for delaying national legislation, the impact will be limited. Riker believes that it is the underlying distribution of preferences, not political structures, that will determine policy choices. This view has been robustly and successfully challenged by Rose-Ackerman (1981) and institutionalist scholars (e.g. Tsebelis 2002), who see institutional arrangements as having a profound impact upon public policies, both because institutions such as federalism will *shape* political views, and also because different decision rules can lead to different decision outcomes.

Secondly, scholars of federalism often consider whether the existence of federalism is likely to shape a nation's public policy in *particular* ways. For instance, Hicks and Swank (1992) argue that federalism has been anathema to welfare state development, and Huber et al. (1993) confirm this view, finding that the greater number of veto points in a federal system allow actors hostile to a welfare state's development to resist its expansion. More broadly, Weingast (1995) contends that federalism restricts the scope of state economic activity, and provides a secure foundation for the functioning of markets.

On the other hand, some scholars oppose the view that federalism invariably leads to a smaller, more market-driven state. Manow (2005) argues that, in some circumstances, federalism can have expansionary consequences, and exemplifies this with reference to the German welfare state. Such a view is supported by Pierson (1995, pp.457–8), who notes that, in some cases, component territories in a federation might press central government to intervene to solve certain collective action problems amongst units of a federation, thus widening the scope of state activity. Obinger et al. (2005a, p.38) see two reasons why federalism can obstruct welfare retrenchment: firstly, sub-national actors may become veto points, resisting reductions in entitlements. Secondly, as they baldly put it, 'vertical power separation means more democracy': there will be more elections, and politicians will be loath to propose unpopular acts of retrenchment and risk incurring voters' wrath at the ballot box.

Fritz Scharpf (1988) highlights the possibility that federal states, characterised by 'bargaining' rather than 'problem-solving' relationships between component sub-national units, may end up with sub-optimal policy choices because of the 'joint decision trap'. This 'trap' concerns the fact that the *de facto* requirement for unanimity for constitutional issues means in a number of policy areas that the only decisions that can be reached are at those of the 'lowest common denominator', where there is complete agreement. Even if some actors recognise that a particular outcome is sub-optimal, they will be reluctant to change the rules of the game, believing that this could harm them in the future. As a result, in Scharpf's view, federalism can be associated with the entrenchment of harmful compromises on the rules of political decision-making.

Scholars of federalism in divided societies also debate its impact in those circumstances, with some, such as Bunce (1999), arguing that it will fuel the flames of ethnic conflict, while others (Stepan 1999) consider it to be an essential ingredient in successful, multi-ethnic states.

Those who disagree with Riker, contending that federalism can impact upon public policy, specify different mechanisms at work. Sometimes these are associated with a particular normative standpoint. For example, Jeffery discusses the notion, which originated in the United States, of 'laboratories of democracy':

> A theoretically powerful argument in favour of allowing greater territorial variation is that of regions as 'laboratories of democracy'. There is a tradition of argument in the US that the existence of the states as fifty separate locations for policy-making promotes a 'competition of ideas' which fosters innovation, benchmarks alternative approaches and diffuses good practice (Jeffery 2002, p.177).

Particular benefit can be gained from testing policies in regions, without the necessity of nationwide roll-out (although of course this can be achieved by regional or local pilots in a unitary policy); the tailoring of policies to local circumstances; and the facilitation of feedback and institutional learning (ibid., p.179).

In his discussion, Jeffery draws upon examples of laboratories of democracy from economic policy and social policy. In the case of economic policy, this centres upon regions trying to 'find the right niche for the regional economy amid global economic flows' (ibid., p.181). In particular, regions work to develop the right kind of local incentive to attract inward investment: '... the new regionalism is about a shift from the demand-side to supply-side economic intervention and has to varying degrees come to shape regional economic policy debates in the US, Germany and Canada' (ibid., p.181). The impact of federalism on encouraging policy laboratories in social policy is more debatable, but there is still some evidence that federal states attempt different policies, testing different ideas and tailoring them to local need (ibid., pp.186–7).

If 'laboratories of democracy' represents a positive normative view of the decentralisation of decisions upon public policy, the idea of a 'race to the bottom' potentially represents a negative standpoint. The 'race to the bottom' occurs when states engage in competition to maintain a competitive advantage over other states, be it in the field of regulation (for instance of labour markets or the environment) or government activity (with states seeking to under-cut each other's levels of taxation). There is a particular twist to this in the field of social policy, with states not only seeking to reduce their expenditure in order to keep taxes low, but also wanting to avoid becoming 'welfare magnets', which attract poor people with their more generous rates of benefit (Peterson 1995, p.121). Such a view is popular amongst those who see federalism as anathema to welfare development.

Empirical examination of the 'race to the bottom' hypothesis has yielded mixed results. For instance, in the field of welfare policy, although evidence of vast population moves to chase the highest level of benefits is lacking, policy-makers do appear to factor competitive calculations, as well as anxieties about welfare migration, into their decisions on benefits (Schram and Soss 1998; Brueckner 2000; Rom 2006). In the field of environmental regulation, to take another example, Vogel (2000) finds that there is little evidence of decentralisation of policy decisions undermining environmental regulation (and indeed it has on occasion led to its strengthening); the competitive advantages attached to lower levels of environmental regulation are relatively small and do not outweigh the perceived disbenefits. In the case of labour market regulation, evidence again suggests that there can be downward regulatory competition in a decentralised polity, but that need not be the case: it will depend upon the preferences of the actors involved, and also whether there is any likely competitive advantage from a more regulated labour market (Barenberg 2000). In a detailed study of the Canadian federation, Harrison expresses scepticism towards the 'race to the bottom' narrative:

> The clearest lesson from this volume is that provinces within the Canadian federation are not completely at the mercy of destructive provincial competition ... Rather, corporate taxes continue to increase steadily while subsidies to business have fallen, environmental standards are stable ..., minimum wages continue to increase. ... That is not to say that provinces do not face a less extreme version of a race to the bottom ... that prompts them to set standards or taxes lower than they would have done in the absence of mobility of capital, goods and individuals (Harrison 2006b, p.257).

Green and Harrison (2006, p.193) identify the intriguing possibility of a 'race to the middle' dynamic, in which 'politicians seek to stay in line with other provinces in order to show voters that they have struck a reasonable balance between generosity ... and the economic imperatives of business'. More commonly, there are a number of mechanisms which are classed as a 'race to the top'. Vogel (2000) identifies a 'California effect' in environmental regulation, whereby powerful companies sometimes identify that an upward shift in standards will give them an advantage over competitors; this was named after the case of California, which varied its air quality standards upwards, only for Congress to follow suit and increase national regulations to the same level. Of course, this sort of 'race to the top' might be more associated with larger jurisdictions, with large internal markets. Rom (2006, p.253) finds that, in the case of education spending, those states with higher spending, 'are willing to increase educational spending, perhaps to increase their competitive edge, in a race to the top in demand side policy'.

Even in the area of social policy, a 'race to the top' is not inconceivable. Keating notes that this is sometimes in evidence in the United Kingdom, following devolution, as 'citizens become aware of better services elsewhere and demand the same of their elected representatives' (2010, p.15).

Rodden (2003a) has influentially argued that the effect of federalism upon public expenditure and service provision depends upon the nature of fiscal arrangements. If sub-national units are responsible for raising their own taxes, they will indeed seek to keep spending, and thus tax rates, low. However, if expenditure is funded primarily by intergovernmental transfers and government grants, expenditure can actually be driven up: 'by breaking the link between taxes and benefits, mere expenditure decentralization might turn the public sector's resources into a common pool that competing local governments will attempt to overfish' (Rodden 2003a, p.497). German fiscal federalism is sometimes cited as an example of such a trend (e.g. Seitz 2000; Rodden 2003b), whereby states face little incentive to widen their tax base by increasing efficiency, as these gains will simply be redistributed to other, less efficient states.

In sum, we can observe a tremendous debate in political science about the likely impact of federalism upon public policy. It seems that, almost by turns, federalism can lead to downward or upward convergence of levels of taxation, regulation and spending; it is associated in turn with welfare states that are either under-developed, or especially resistant to cutbacks. It produces politicians seeking benevolently to provide the most generous level of public services, those who aim to be precisely in the mid-range of such provision, or paranoid souls looking to keep benefits down to avoid welfare recipients pitching up in their states. The circumstances in which each phenomenon applies vary according to the structure and history of the federation, as well as the area of policy under discussion.

Yet in all this discussion, political parties rarely merit a mention. For instance, when Rom (2006) considers the dynamics of education spending in the US and finds divergent trends, he sees no need to test a partisan hypothesis. In discussion of the possibilities of a 'race to the bottom' (or, for that matter, a 'race to the top'), the role that partisan actors might play is also neglected. Yet public policy change relies upon partisan action, and it is, at any rate, not implausible that party politicians respond to pressures resulting from federalism in different ways: for instance, politicians of the right may be more willing to yield to downward regulatory pressure, while politicians of the left may be attracted to growth theories that point to the benefits of higher levels of regulation. The discourse of 'laboratories of democracy' assumes rather technocratic lesson-drawing ('laboratories of public policy practice' might be an appropriate designation), yet here, too, partisan actors might step into play: 'laboratories of social democracy', or 'laboratories of conservatism' might hold, whereby politicians are keen to draw lessons from the practice of political soul-mates.

If we find, in this study, that parties *do* matter at a sub-national level, it will at any rate caution scholars against far-reaching conclusions about the impact of federalism, and make a strong case for tempering such claims with the possibility of partisan influence.

In all of this, the history and design of the specific federal system clearly matters. Stepan (1999) influentially distinguished between different types of federalism along three dimensions:

1. Between *coming together, holding together,* and *putting together* federalism (ibid., pp.22–3). 'Coming together' federal states, such as the US, pooled their sovereignty so as to achieve greater security and other collective goals. 'Holding together' federal states, such as India, Belgium and Spain, by contrast, saw the centre pass some sovereign to constituent states in order to keep their countries together as a democracy. 'Putting together' federalism refers to those federations, such as the USSR, where a non-democratic, centralising power constructs a polity of states that might otherwise have been sovereign and independent.
2. Between *demos-constraining* and *demos-enabling* federalism (ibid., pp.25–9). 'Demos-constraining' federalism sees states act as a significant impediment upon the centre, characterised in particular by weak federal parties, strong over-representation of smaller component units in the second chamber nationally, a second chamber with large policy scope, and strong powers reserved for states. 'Demos-enabling' federalism, by contrast, is characterised by strong federal parties, no over-representation of smaller territories in the second chamber nationally, a second chamber with limited powers, and few residual powers for states.
3. Between *symmetrical* federalism, where all components of a territory have the same power, and *asymmetrical* federalism, where this is not the case (ibid., pp.29–32).

To this we can add some other important features of the institutional design of federal states. In particular, Leibfried et al. (2005, p.339) distinguish between inter-state (or 'dual') federalism and intra-state (or 'cooperative' federalism). They find that the latter is significantly more conducive to the growth of welfare states than the former. Of particular consequence, as noted above, is the nature of *fiscal decentralisation*, that is, which functions have to be paid for by the centre, and which by states (Oates 1999; Rodden 2003a).

In Chapter 3, we will review the precise nature of German federalism's institutional framework. The point here is simply that, in seeking to identify the likely influence of federalism upon public policy (that is, the way in which federalism matters), we need to be very clear what sort of federalism we are talking about.

1.4   Conclusion

In this introduction, we have very briefly sketched two major controversies in political science: the *do-parties-matter?* debate, which seeks to understand the impact of political parties upon public policy, and the *does-federalism-matter?* debate (admittedly, not often so characterised), which seeks to understand what systematic impact federalism might have upon public policy. Surprisingly, these debates are rarely linked: discussion of whether parties matter focuses, more often than not, upon the national rather than sub-national level, and discussions about the policy impact of federalism tends to neglect the role that might be played by political parties.

In its focus upon the influence of parties upon public policy at a sub-national level, this study contributes to filling these gaps. The study examines whether, and under what circumstances, partisan actors at a state level can influence policies, and when instead they find themselves stymied, be it by path dependence, bureaucratic intransigence, legal barriers, the economic logic of globalisation, or indeed by binding policy 'logics' arising from federalism like the 'race to the bottom'.

2
Do Parties Matter in the German Länder? Theoretical and Practical Challenges, Past Attempts at Exploration, and a New Approach

Having set the scene for examination of the impact of political parties at the sub-national level, this chapter discusses the specifics of the German case. It examines previous studies of German federalism, identifying gaps in that research, explains the rationale for case selection, and spells out clear hypotheses and counter-hypotheses which are investigated in subsequent chapters.

2.1 Why Germany?

But first of all, why Germany? As will be discussed in Chapter 3, Germany's federalism is unique. Initially, German federalism served the process of nation-building (and thus fitted into the 'coming together' category). After the Second World War, where Germany's new federal settlement was negotiated between the occupying powers and German actors, the clear aim was to limit the power of the political centre (thus making German federalism 'demos-constraining'). German federalism is also symmetrical in its formal powers, although in practice the ability of different Länder to shape policy varied. This gave rise to an odd hybrid system, memorably described by Hesse (1962) as a 'unitary federal state'. On the one hand, Germany lacked the territorial diversity of such federations as Switzerland or India, who needed political decentralisation to hold them together; equally, the Länder enjoyed certain constitutionally guaranteed areas of policy supremacy in contrast to such unitary states as France or the UK. Of particular importance is the second chamber (the Bundesrat), in which governments of the Länder are represented, and through which they have an influence on any federal legislation that impacts upon them. Although there is symmetry in the formal powers of the Länder, there is a sharp asymmetry between different areas of policy, with some being the exclusive responsibility of the federal government, others the sole responsibility of the Länder, and others still being the subject of negotiation, with shared jurisdiction.

This makes Germany an interesting test-bed for the ability of parties to influence public policy. Land governments enjoy some constitutionally enshrined autonomy, but competence over swathes of public policy is contested. Moreover, in the circumstances of heightened territorial diversity since Germany's reunification in 1990, the federal settlement has come under growing pressure, with greater pressures for policy variation (Jeffery 1999). This provides the opportunity to examine a federal system subject to a high level of dynamism and contestation. In this context, it is unlikely that the extent of parties' influence upon public policy can be gleaned simply from a formal analysis of their powers.

The literature on German federalism is vast, and federalism's shape is a source of constant debate in German public life. Much attention, on the part of politicians, scholars and journalists, has been devoted to the political and legal structures that sustain federalism, the changing nature of federalism over time, elections in the Länder, differences in prosperity between the Länder, and so on (Benz 1999; Seitz 2000; Jeffery 2005; Sturm 2006). There are frequent declarations that federalism is 'in crisis', and there is a lively debate over the possibility of a reform of federalism, variously either to ensure greater or more meaningful devolution of power to the Länder, or to render the complex structures of federalism more efficient (Fischer and Hüttmann 2001; Münch 2001). Moreover, a great deal of consideration has been given to questions of coalition formation – the choice of coalition partners and the nature of their interaction and compromises (Jun 1994; Lees 2000).

Following Schmidt (1980), two competing hypotheses can be constructed (and are developed below). The first, the 'political hypothesis', suggests that different political parties advance sharply differing views in a range of areas of public policy and succeed in implementing these contrasting visions, leading to a variation in policies being pursued, according to the partisan composition of governments. Set against this is the second hypothesis, the 'political null hypothesis', whereby policies do not diverge – or where such divergence occurs, but is not attributable to the partisan composition of the government. These hypotheses are examined in relation to sub-national Land-level governments in Germany. As the last chapter suggested, either hypothesis is plausible, with, on the one hand, most studies of the '*do-parties-matter?*' question confirming that parties do have an exogenous influence upon policy. On the other hand, some works find significant constraints upon partisan action, and scholars of federalism detect effects of federal structures which apply across governments of different political colours. As will be demonstrated in Chapter 4, in several areas of policy the programmes of the two largest political parties diverge sharply, which would lead us to expect the political hypothesis to be confirmed. On the other hand, a measure of convergence between Christian Democratic and Social Democratic parties has been noted (e.g. Seeleib-Kaiser et al. 2005). Moreover, due to the 'interlocking' nature of German policy-making, the room for manoeuvre of state-level politicians is heavily circumscribed (Scharpf 1988). Indeed, Wilhelm Hennis, in his influential essay originally published in 1956, claimed the Länder were nothing more than 'autonomous administrative provinces', and stated that there could be no more 'Christian Democratic road-building' than 'Social Democratic water supply' (Hennis 1968, cited in Reutter 2008, pp.22–3).

Furthermore, an element of 'path dependence' might be expected to undermine partisan influence upon policy choices: varying preconditions and histories of public policy development in different Länder provide different incentives for policy-makers to change, or leave in place, those policies (Pierson 2000). These factors can lead parties in government to pursue policies which deviate from what would be expected of parties of that political colour.

This chapter first of all considers existing studies of partisan influence upon public policy in the Länder. It then sets out the approach deployed in this study to discern the extent of partisan influence, setting out the rationale for a qualitative method. The following two sections explain the choice of Länder and of policy areas as case studies. Finally, specific hypotheses are developed which are the subject of examination over the following chapters.

2.2 Existing studies of party influence on public policy in the Länder

The most significant attempt to address the degree of partisan influence upon public policy for the German Länder across a range of policy areas was by Manfred G. Schmidt in a 1980 study (Schmidt 1980). He notes that, at the level of political rhetoric, the differences could hardly appear greater. The CDU suggested that SPD-led Land governments would dismantle the social market economy and attempt to create a 'socialist society' (well aware, against the background of the Cold War, of the pejorative connotations of this term). By contrast, the SPD claimed that CDU-led governments would threaten social peace, the welfare state, the rule of law (*Rechtsstaat*) and the new *Ostpolitik* (Schmidt 1980, p.1).

As noted above, Schmidt compares two hypotheses: the 'political hypothesis', which suggests that the difference in policies pursued by Land governments is due to the composition of the government (and specifically whether it is led by Social Democrats or Christian Democrats); and the 'political null hypothesis', which suggests that there is either little or no difference between the policies of governments of different parties, and where there is a difference, it is due to other factors (such as the socio-economic position of a Land, or the relative strength of different social classes), rather than the composition of the government (ibid., p.7). In fact,

Schmidt's 'null hypothesis' contains a variety of different claims, ranging from the 'end of ideologies' thesis, with all parties having become 'catch-all parties', through to the 'federalism-theory null-hypothesis' (ibid., p.18), which suggests that any differences in policy are driven mainly by the relative wealth of the Land in question. Three factors are held to dampen the possibility, and size, of partisan impact – the relatively limited ability of the state apparatus, *vis-à-vis* the private economy, to 'steer society'; the situation of *Politikverflechtung* (interlocking policy-making) between the federal government and the Länder, which reduces the possibility of the Land governments to pursue autonomous paths; and the preponderance of coalition governments in the Länder which restrict the ability of the major coalition partner to determine policy.

Schmidt considers four main areas of policy – education policy, the size and nature of the public sector, interior policy, and policies aimed at disadvantaged groups (such as psychiatric provision and integration of people with disabilities). The general conclusion of the study is that there is greater support for the political hypothesis than for the political null hypothesis – in other words, the composition of the government does indeed affect policy outcomes. In the field of education policy, the sector is better resourced under SPD-led governments than under CDU-led ones; in addition, the policies pursued display a greater level of egalitarianism, with more support for comprehensive schools (*Gesamtschulen*), secularisation, and paid training vacations for employees. Differences are also noticeable in the treatment of disadvantaged groups (Schmidt 1980, pp.129–31). In other areas, the differences tend to be less pronounced, with Schmidt arguing that the farther the policy area is from the conflict between labour and capital (which he later relates to the level of influence and interest trade unions have in a policy area), and the greater the influence of the market economy, the lesser the difference. As a consequence, in interior policy (where he considers the *Radikalenerlass* – the decision to ban from state employment those with a history of involvement in extra-parliamentary opposition), and in economic policy at times of crisis, there is no appreciable difference in the policies pursued (with the exception of a more liberal interpretation of the *Radikalenerlass* in SPD-governed Bremen).

According to Schmidt, the differences between the parties in distributional conflicts tend to be least in evidence when there is a zero-sum game involved – both major parties are adverse to major distributional conflict – and they are more prevalent when there are extra resources to be distributed. Schmidt also argues that a change of government does not automatically lead to a change of policy. Rather, 'the political composition is most clearly felt under specific political conditions: namely when the SPD had a political predominance in the party system, when it was the leading government party for an uninterrupted and lengthy period, so that it has time for its personnel to conquer the bureaucracy ... and when it was clearly ahead of the CDU in terms of votes' (ibid., p.131). Politics (or rather, the party composition of the government) matters, but most substantially under these conditions.

The importance of having time to capture the civil service is also emphasised by Lees, in his discussion of red-green coalitions in Germany. In general, he argues that:

> The Federal Republic's policy-making environment is characterised by the penetration of the civil service by the mainstream political parties, who placed appointees at all levels of the administration. At the same time, this resulted in the reciprocal effect whereby the parties' own ideological profile was shaped by the technocratic discourse of the civil service (Lees 2000, pp.37–8).

This proved particularly obstructive for the Greens, for three reasons. Obstructive civil servants would be locked into an 'iron triangle' alongside the coalition partner and interest groups; they might be SPD members and thus nominal allies, making them harder to retire, and the more senior ones could protect sympathetic underlings. The Greens would also need to find civil servants of sufficient calibre to be able to take over (ibid., p.38). Not all these difficulties would apply to a better-established political party – finding potential alternative civil servants would be easier, and the difficulty of getting rid of 'nominal allies' would not exist were there a change of all parties in government. However, links between existing civil servants and interest groups, as well as the sheer difficulty of removing German civil servants following a change of government, could certainly be expected to generate a certain amount of 'policy stickiness' following a change of government.

Clearly, given the changing nature of German federalism, most notably due to reunification in the intervening period, the conclusions Schmidt draws may no longer be valid. Two recent trends have been discerned. First, there appear to be growing asymmetries in German federalism (Münch 1999; Luthardt 1999). Secondly, there has been an apparent recentralisation of power, with the Länder increasingly responsible merely for the implementation, and less the autonomous formulation of policy (Klatt 1999). These trends are attributable to domestic, European and international factors. Developing this argument, we might expect that the poorer Länder, due to their greater financial dependence on the federal government and other external funders, such as the European Union, enjoy far less ability to shape their policies than their more prosperous counterparts. This would particularly affect the Länder in the former East (the 'new' Länder). We might thus expect that Land governments have a far greater ability to effect policy change in the richer, western Länder than in the poorer ones, and in particular than in the eastern ones. This possibility will be explored further later in the chapter. At the same time, since Schmidt's study, the influence of the Länder through the Bundesrat has grown, with a rise in the proportion of laws requiring Bundesrat assent (Lhotta 2004, p.157); again, it will be useful to assess whether the use of this power in the Bundesrat has been primarily territorial or partisan in character.

Following Schmidt (1980), three further studies very explicitly examine the question of partisan influence upon public policy in the Länder. Jutta Stern (2000) examines education policy across time, counterposing the 'partisan hypothesis' with the alternatives of economic, institutional or social factors instead being the strongest determinant of policy (ibid., pp.44–7). She confirms Schmidt's finding of the importance of partisan influence upon policy:

> The role of the parties ... is confirmed even under the conditions of the overall economic situation of the 1990s as an important source of political influence. ... In the overall scheme of developments it is appropriate to speak of the primacy of politics (ibid., p.310).

Bernhard Payk (2009) also discusses education policy in the Länder, this time in the light of responses to the Programme for International Student Assessment (PISA) study of educational attainment published in 2001. Payk's quantitative study meticulously codes a range of potential policy developments, seeking to understand whether the external shock of PISA led to partisan convergence, or whether differences between parties continued to be important. Although in some areas of education policy (notably newer issues without a history of partisan division, such as the merit of external inspection of schools) there were no partisan divisions (ibid., p.278), in half of the areas investigated profound partisan impacts upon policy are clear, and Payk concludes:

> For education policy it could be shown that 'New Public Management' Modernisation did not lead to a 'depoliticisation' of this area of policy: parties do still matter (ibid., p.282)

Hildebrandt and Wolf (2008a) produced an edited volume, in which experts in 15 different areas of policy (not just public policy – political structures, such as the inclusion of direct democratic instruments, are also examined) consider different determinants of policy in the Länder, highlighting the possible influence of socio-economic factors in each Land, the partisan composition of the government, the legacy of past choices, political institutions, the power resources of different social actors, and international influence (Hildebrandt and Wolf 2008b, p.16). In their conclusion, Wolf and Hildebrandt (2008) find that explanatory variables for policy outcomes vary sharply between different policy areas. For instance, party politics remains an important determinant of education and Higher Education policy, although intriguingly, in contrast to Stern's finding, spending on schools is lower under Social Democratic than Christian Democratic governments. By contrast, path dependency is highlighted as being important in explaining some aspects of police organisation, and economic policy, and the presence of agricultural interest groups is found to slow adoption of environmental measures (ibid., pp.364–5). This study certainly marks an important development in considering the determinants of public policy in the Länder, although the brevity of discussion of each policy area necessarily precludes the detailed examination of mechanisms of policy change. Although Wolf and Hildebrandt draw inferences, these are insufficient to support their robust conclusions about the precise causes of particular policy outcomes.

Detterbeck and Jeffery (2008), in a recent discussion, detect a number of trends in the relationship between party organisations and federalism. First and foremost, they find a growing level of autonomy between Land organisations of parties. This is related to the growing regionalisation of party competition, as well as territorial pressures for policy divergence. However, national ideological profiles of parties still lend them a certain ideological coherence across the territory: policy is 'fine-tuned to specific Land circumstances' (ibid., p.84). Moreover, parties retain quite a high degree of vertical integration, with continued cooperation between the different tiers of party organisation, not least because of the strong incentives, in cooperative federalism, for parties to attempt to reach agreement internally and act cohesively (ibid., p.76). Detterbeck and Jeffery present a convincing case for looking at the impact of party organisation at the Land level in discussions of German federalism and party policy.

There have been further studies which touch upon the same area. For instance, Jun (1994) looks at coalition formation, although his analysis stops at the point at which the party leaders 'sign on the dotted line' of the coalition agreement. This is still important in understanding the extent to which policy-makers at a Land level set themselves particular challenges, which they attempt to realise during the parliamentary term. Even in the phase of coalition negotiations (which he notes have a tendency to bracket difficult issues – cf. ibid., p.79), he finds confirmation for the view that Land politicians may aspire to achieve radical policy shifts in certain areas. At the same time, they are by no means autonomous actors, even at this stage:

> Party competition in the FRG [Federal Republic of Germany] has to be considered against the background of the intermeshing of, above all, financial, economic and cultural relations between the federal and state governments. The whole structure of the political system of the FRG is the starting point for the development of the party systems in the

Länder and thus for the formation of coalitions. There are dynamic relations between elections to the Landtage [Land-level legislatures], coalition formation, and federal politics (ibid., p.92).

Downs (1998) studies sub-national coalitions in international comparison. His starting point is a different one – he finds it hard to square the view that federalism enhances democracy with the 'opaque and indirect link between election outcomes and who actually forms the government' (ibid., p.8). So, although one of his key questions is whether electoral competition at a sub-national level really matters, Downs discusses this in terms of the mechanics of the choice of coalition partner and the extent to which regional politicians are autonomous, rather than looking at policy choices and outcomes. Certainly, both questions are interesting at the level of the Länder, indeed, perhaps more interesting than can be done justice by his single case study. The linkage between electoral behaviour and coalition outcome is often clarified by *Koalitionsaussagen* before an election – statements by the parties about whom they will seek to form a coalition with – though this does not prevent seemingly 'perverse' outcomes.[1] Downs' view – that the Länder are more autonomous than many regions in other federal systems, while interesting, avoids the question posed in this study – even given the autonomy of Land politicians and their interest in pursuing autonomous policies, to what extent can they in fact achieve substantive policy change as a result of their political convictions?

2.3   A new analytical approach

Apart from filling a significant gap in the recent literature, which will be of value to those involved in the study of federalism, of policy-making and of German Studies, a study of the Länder, as opposed to policy outcomes at the national level, also brings with it the methodological advantage of being able to compare different sets of outcomes in the same time frame (Schmidt 1980, p.3). Notwithstanding that there are fluctuations in the budgetary resources available to the different Länder at any given time (in

---

[1]To give but two examples: in the 1997 election to the Hamburg *Bürgerschaft*, the SPD lost its overall majority, with significant gains for the CDU – a rightward shift, it would be considered. Yet this forced the resignation of the distinctly centrist Hamburg SPD mayor, Henning Vorscherau, who was replaced by the more left-leaning Ortwin Runde (SPD), and the SPD was also forced to take on a Green coalition partner – thus, at odds with the electorate's shift, the coalition appeared to shift somewhat to the left (Brunner and Walz 1998). Equally, Henning Scherf's (SPD) statement that he would resign as mayor of Bremen were the CDU to become the largest party in the *Bürgerschaft* would likely have led to an SPD/Green, in place of a grand coalition (Roth 2004). However, such odd courses of events are relatively unusual.

particular between east and west), differences in policies pursued between the Länder are not entirely reducible to the background economic or social context, as could be the case with consideration of changes of government at the federal level. This study is an application of the 'Method of Difference' (Mill 1950), which involves, ideally, cases which vary in only one causal condition. This is difficult to create in the social sciences, although Skocpol has maintained it can be realised through comparing cases over time (Skocpol, 1979).[2] Examining case studies within one country, rather than undertaking a cross-national comparison, also helps overcome the problem of equivalence of concepts which can bedevil other comparative studies (Hakim 2000).

Whereas the approach taken in Schmidt's seminal (1980) study was largely quantitative, and analysed several areas of policy across all Länder, this study's focus on just three Länder and three areas of policy allows for the exploration of mechanisms which enable, or prevent, policy change. This adds to the insights from quantitative research, as it enables a sharper distinction to be drawn between territorially and politically underpinned decisions and shifts in policy. By contrast, quantitative research struggles to elucidate what drives policy change, and what allows policy change to be achieved, instead assessing simply whether different Länder arrive at the same destination, and whether they do so at the same pace. To continue a metaphor (borrowing from Schmidt 1980, p.134), when policy change is compared to a train journey, it is important to look not merely at the destination of Land governments, but also at the route taken, the staff employed on the train, and the reason for one route to be taken rather than another. The study attempts to trace the processes of change, rather than trying to identify causal mechanisms on the basis of cross-sectional data alone. In a sense, this is what Macintyre described as 'comparative history' (MacIntyre 1984).

The discussion above highlights two difficulties with Schmidt's 1980 study. First, there is a potentially serious problem concerning the direction of causation of policy differences. Schmidt argues that social democratic governments make a greater difference in those Länder where they have a lengthy period of strength, and in policy areas where political divisions between the parties are greatest (in his terms, those where the conflict between the interests of capital and labour is most acute). Yet it might be argued that the policies are in fact a function of territorial or socio-economic factors, especially in those areas – they are the reason for the

---

[2]For instance, Russia in 1905 was very similar to Russia in 1917, but revolution occurred in 1917 and not 1905. So it is necessary to isolate what is different between 1905 and 1917. However, this is problematic: in particular, a key difference is that 1917 Russia had already experienced 1905 Russia, whereas 1905 Russia had not.

policy, and also for the election of the SPD government. Does the party in government actually determine the policy outcome, or do the factors which determine policy outcomes also determine which party tends to win elections and then lead the government? Secondly, as Schmidt himself acknowledges (1980, p.134), the way in which government is conducted is not investigated. A closer examination of the way in which policies are made, and the mechanisms which are used to achieve change, is important in elucidating the otherwise opaque direction of causation. It is crucial to resolve whether change is driven by parties, pursuing a particular agenda set by their manifesto priorities and the will of their politicians, or whether it is driven by factors exogenous to the government, perhaps linked through formal and informal mechanisms to civil servants, with politicians merely holding the ring.

2.4 Hesse, the Saarland and Saxony-Anhalt: The diversity of German federalism

The phenomenon of 'divided government' has been widely noted by several commentators. Perhaps due to mid-term unpopularity of federal governments, or perhaps due to the electorate's desire to see adequate checks and balances on those governments, there has been a propensity for much of the post-war period to see elections in the Länder swing to the right at times of SPD-led government, and to the left at times of CDU-led government (cf. Lehmbruch 2000; Jeffery and Hough 2001; von Blumenthal 2008).

In turn, differing majorities in the Bundestag and Bundesrat have led to accusations of 'blockades', that is, the party-political obstruction of federal initiatives by representatives of the Länder in the Bundesrat. These have become more intensive since reunification, with the initial failure of Kohl's reform of the tax system in 1991/92 (cf. Lehmbruch 1998, p.169), then Oskar Lafontaine's further obstruction of tax reform in 1997, and finally the protracted obstruction of the Schröder government's reform of immigration policy in 2002 (Arndt and Nickel 2003). Of course, these difference can be over-stated – opposition resistance in the Bundesrat can peter out, or an opposition-governed Land can be 'bought off', or split off from its partners due to its divergent interests. Eastern Länder have proven particularly susceptible to diverting from the line – SPD-led Brandenburg was won over in the end to Kohl's 1991/92 reforms, while CDU-led Berlin was won around to Schröder's tax reform in 2000 (Harlen 2002). A differing propensity to be 'bought off', of course, testifies to a difference in power between the Länder, with asymmetrical ability to withstand pressure to deviate from the party line.

In addition to this consequence of 'divided government', it might be anticipated that if a Land government were of a different political colour to the federal government, it would therefore encounter an additional barrier to policy change. Given the argument that the Länder's autonomous power has declined and that of the federal government has increased, it might then be expected that CDU-led Land governments under an SPD/Green federal government might encounter difficulties in achieving policy change. This would, obviously enough, be particularly the case in policy areas where the federal government enjoyed greater influence.

Schneider argues that:

> Policy outputs vary between different politicians of the same party in different states. ... This is in part to do with the political culture of the state in question, the self-perception of the state party, its membership structure [and] the particular challenges the state faces (1997, p.425).

It is difficult to disentangle the independent influence of the character of the Landesverband (Land-level party) on policy choices from the contextual factors which, while they may influence the Landesverband's character, also have a more direct input into the policies pursued by the government.[3] However, political conflicts between a Landesverband and a Land government are by no means unknown,[4] and, even in the absence of an actual conflict, the government's perception of potential for conflict may have an impact upon the policies it pursues. As such, the links between the Land party and the government are certainly worth exploring, to see if the nature of the governing party's Landesverband impacts upon a Land government's policy choices. Schmid (1990a, 1990b) found significant variation in positions taken by the CDU Landesverbände, and it will be interesting to ascertain the extent to which these endure.

This study will therefore explore in detail the ability of Land governments led by the CDU to effect policy change under the SPD/Green federal government. This narrows down the range of potential case studies somewhat, although, given the propensity of the SPD to lose elections in the Länder when it is in government nationally, there is still a wide range of Länder from which to choose – Hesse, Brandenburg, Saxony-Anhalt, the Saarland, Thuringia, North-Rhein Westphalia, Lower Saxony and Hamburg all swung to the right in between the election of the SPD/Green government at a federal level in 1998, and its replacement by a grand coalition in 2005.

Of these Länder, Hesse, from 1999 onwards, is a particularly interesting case, and is an obvious candidate for a case study for several reasons. First,

---

[3]Indeed, Jun (1994, pp.232–4) notes that socio-structural and socio-cultural aspects of a Land (in this instance Rheinland-Palatinate) can play a role in the choice of coalition partner.

[4]Lees (2002, pp.56–9) shows how the character of the Green Party in Berlin was a major factor in the demise of the red-green coalition there.

it reflects a clear shift in the party of government. The SPD led the government over an uninterrupted period from 1945 to 1987 (albeit in a grand coalition from 1946 to 1950) and again from 1991 to 1999, in coalition with the Greens. Notwithstanding the brief interlude of CDU-led government from 1987 to 1991, the change of government in 1999 certainly reflected a departure from the norm. It is a particularly interesting case, too, considering Schmidt's observation, detailed above, that policy changes are more likely to be achieved by Social Democrats than by Christian Democrats, and in particular only when they have time to shift personnel in the ministries. Given the extended period of SPD-led government (as well as the severe restrictions on shifting personnel immediately after an election), the possibility of the CDU achieving significant policy change would appear to be slim. This did not, however, stop the election campaign being particularly contentious, with fiery rhetoric on both sides, inspired by the robustly conservative CDU leader in Hesse, Roland Koch. Although in the final days of the campaign the CDU's petition against the SPD/Green government's immigration proposals took centre stage, much of the campaign was dominated by a focus on education policy, with the accusation that, in Hesse, the SPD/Green government of the time had allowed schools to run out of control, with lessons cancelled due to a shortage of teachers and dogma coming ahead of standards (CDU Hessen 1999). Since taking office in 1999, Hesse's government, and in particular Koch himself, led the way in arguing for centre-right reforms, ranging from education, through to wide-ranging proposals on welfare policy (Annesley 2002), arguments over the direction of federalism,[5] immigration policy, European affairs, and indeed just about every aspect of policy pursued by the red-green federal government (Schumacher 2004). Nonetheless, given the previous entrenchment of the SPD in the Land, following Schmidt's hypotheses, the ability of a leader like Koch to shape policies in a state like Hessen would be rather more limited that his fiery rhetoric would suggest. A further potential constraint was that the CDU needed to go into coalition with the FDP, which might prove a moderating force. As will be shown in Chapter 5, there was little ambiguity about Roland Koch's political vision and the direction in which he wanted to take his Land politically. The question to be explored in this study is in what measure he was able to succeed.

Hesse is, of course, a relatively wealthy Land (it was the wealthiest western Land both prior to and after reunification, according to Mackenstein and Jeffery 1999, p.171). It is therefore necessary, especially given Schmidt's finding that fiscal constraints have a clear impact upon policy decisions,

---

[5]Roland Koch signed Hesse up to Bavaria and Baden-Württemberg's appeal to the Federal Constitutional Court to overturn the current arrangements for fiscal redistribution between the Länder.

to select a western Land for a case study which is less well off. Here, the Saarland seems particularly appropriate, being amongst the worst-off western Länder (and indeed having the lowest per capita financial capacity, after inter-Land equalisation: ibid., p.171). It, too, experienced a change of government in 1999, albeit following a rather more low-key election campaign and with an apparently more moderate leader, Peter Müller, at the helm. Although the Saarland had experienced CDU-led governments from 1965 to 1985, Müller came to power following 14 years of uninterrupted social democratic government, and so, again, his ability to shape policies might, under Schmidt's analysis, be restricted, at least at the outset. Moreover, the Saarland is a relatively small Land, with a population of just over a million (compared to over six million in Hesse), which might again be expected to restrict the likelihood significant changes in policy. One factor which could, however, promote rather than inhibit the ability of the government to effect change in the Saarland, unlike in Hesse, is the absence of a coalition partner. Whereas in Hesse the FDP might be expected to have a moderating influence, especially on issues on the 'liberal-authoritarian' issue dimension, in the Saarland the CDU was able to become the sole party of government, winning an overall majority in the Landtag. As will be discussed in Chapter 6, unlike the relatively conservative Hesse, the Saarland's CDU Landesverband has a reputation for moderate, centrist politics, which Peter Müller reflects. This may have had a moderating effect upon the extent to which the CDU-led government was able to, and indeed aspired to, effect radical policy change compared to its predecessor.

As a third case study, it makes sense to examine one of the new (eastern) Länder. These Länder, of course, face particularly extreme versions of the problems faced by those western Länder which were smaller, and less well off, prior to 1990. Of the eastern Länder to experience a change of government from left to right, Saxony-Anhalt saw a direct shift from a government without CDU participation to one without SPD participation. This might be expected, therefore, to make the ambitions for a shift in policy more pronounced than in Länder which shifted from SPD control to a grand coalition (as happened in Brandenburg and Mecklenburg Lower Pomerania). The SPD led the government in Saxony Anhalt from 1994, under the so-called Magdeburg model, whereby it was 'tolerated' by the PDS (from 1994 to 1998 in coalition with the Greens, and then from 1998 to 2002 on its own). The election campaign in 2002, which led to the election of a CDU/FDP coalition, focused in particular on the disastrous state of Saxony-Anhalt's economy, with its very high unemployment, crippling debt, and high level of westward emigration (see Chapter 7).

Seitz (2000) notes the very considerable disparities in the levels of debt across the Länder. Saxony-Anhalt, alongside the Saarland, had amongst the highest levels of debt at some 6,111 Euro per inhabitant at the end of the year 2002, an increase of 689 Euro over the previous 12 months

(Bundesministerium der Finanzen 2003). It is amongst the Länder facing a severe lack of sustainability in fiscal policy.

In Saxony-Anhalt, the conditions for the coalition achieving radical policy change could hardly have been less auspicious – given the combination of massive debt and a weak economy, leading to a high level of dependence on the federal government, the necessity of coalition (with the FDP), the relatively small size of the Land, and the length of the previous, SPD-led government. If the analysis finds significant policy change was possible, it would provide important support for the political hypothesis.

In sum, then, in choosing these case studies, which span an over-lapping time frame and experienced a change of government in the same direction, it has been possible to find widely divergent cases – essentially, a rich, larger, western Land, a poor, small, western Land, and an eastern Land (as with all eastern Länder, poor and relatively small).[6] This enables an assessment of the degree to which Land-level policy-making is circumscribed by a Land's size and economic situation. In each case, the period being evaluated is confined to one complete parliamentary term.

2.4 Comparing policy sectors in Germany

In his 1980 study, Schmidt examined several areas of policy. Although the selection of a wide range of policy areas is potentially attractive, it can also be suggested that a study of such ambitious scope would sacrifice depth for breadth, and would be unable to undertake a detailed examination of the mechanisms by which policy change is effected, or what obstacles hinder politicians seeking to change policy.

A variety of different policy areas, relating to different 'issue dimensions', need to be considered for several reasons. First, Kitschelt (1994), in a wide-ranging and thorough analysis, demonstrates that, while political competition in post-war West Germany may have been primarily along one issue dimension (the 'left-right' axis, posed initially over the extent of redistribution), the emergence of a post-material issue dimension in the 1970s and 1980s allowed the Greens to make a successful entry onto the political scene, with political competition being about such issues as the importance attached to preservation of the environment and the rights of minority communities. Indeed, if one considers the most bitter conflicts at the level of the Länder in recent years, many would fall outside the left-right axis, either concerning 'post-material issues' (such as debates around citizenship and immigration policy, the length of middle-school education,

---

[6]A study of Hamburg was excluded because, as a city-state, it is directly responsible for delivering more services than the other Länder, putting it in a significantly different position in some areas of policy.

the construction of new airports, or perceived 'toughness' on law and order) or revolving primarily around issues in territorial politics (such as the fiscal equalisation mechanism between the Länder). Secondly, in certain circumstances political leaders may elect, for reasons of political entrepreneurship, to emphasise issue dimensions other than the dominant one, which could then affect policy choices (McLean 2001). Lees (2000, p.14) also argues the case for more than one dimension of policy, and suggests that red-green coalitions involve selective emphasis upon the post-material dimension. Thirdly, it may be the case that political conflict has shifted, with convergence on issues relating to the economy and redistribution, but division on social questions; as a result, a focus on just one issue dimension might paint a misleading picture of the extent of convergence between parties, and could not be generalised.

The analysis of areas of policy needs to be expanded to relatively politicised areas – those where there is a clear division between the approaches of parties of the left and right. These may lie on the classical fault-line between economic liberalism and state intervention in the economy, or they may lie on Kitschelt's 'libertarian-authoritarian' issue dimension, or indeed represent conflicts on further issue dimensions which are of particular significance in the Länder. A focus exclusively on the socio-economic issues may give a misleading picture. Just as the researcher who focuses on the fiscal redistribution mechanism as a case study will doubtless find that territorial interests are foremost in the minds of the Länder, so Schmidt's focus on spending in the 1970s found significant partisan division (Schmidt 1980). However, with other issue dimensions now growing in importance, a wider range of policy areas with a greater diversity of potential conflict is needed.

Moreover, Schmidt specifically excluded from consideration areas of policy which lay outside the exclusive power of the Länder. This aspect of the choice of areas for analysis now seems outmoded. As has been widely demonstrated (e.g. Klatt 1999), the power of the federal government has crept up, at the expense of the power of the Länder, with an increasing number of policy areas shared between the federal government and the Länder, being the subject of torturous negotiations between the two, at least until the federalism reform of 2006. As a consequence, it would make sense to explore at least one policy area where the Länder are *not* the sole and undisputed authority. Given the growing number of areas of policy where power is shared, if it is discovered that a change of government can only effect a change of policy in those areas of policy where the Land has prime or exclusive authority, and that it has no impact at all upon those areas where power is shared, then here, too, that poses a serious challenge to the partisan hypothesis.

However, it is not necessarily the case that the Länder are impotent in areas where they do not enjoy policy autonomy. In his study of SPD/ Green coalitions, Lees (2000, p.33) notes how Joschka Fischer, as Hesse's environment minister, focused on achieving the stricter implementation of existing legislation. For instance, with regard to the chemical industry, he forced companies to reduce discharges into the Main by installing new equipment. It is necessary to consider whether this applies to other policy areas where the Länder do not have primary responsibility for making policy, but are in charge of its implementation. As a result, one policy area will be considered where responsibility is shared between the federal government, the Länder, and local government, and another where responsibility lies primarily with the federal government, but with part of the responsibility for implementation being delegated.

2.5   Education policy, family and childcare, and labour market policy in the Länder

Notwithstanding these comments, it also makes sense to choose one policy area where the Länder are pre-eminent in setting policy. Here, the area of education policy, which clearly falls within the responsibility of the Länder (as will be spelt out in Chapter 3), is a good choice. The study will particularly focus on policies towards general needs schools, falling firmly within the domain of Land-level competence (unlike the more complicated domain of higher education policy) and affecting a large number of citizens. As noted above, education policy, and in particular policy towards schools, had a major impact in the election campaign in Hesse (and also featured in the campaigns in the other two Länder under examination). Issues to be determined at the state level include the length of schooling (12 or 13 years); the extent of selection (or rather the extent to which comprehensive schools are supported or rejected); the length of teaching hours (with politicians, notably on the left, favouring *Ganztagsschulen* – all-day schools – in order to support working parents); the teaching of religion; and the system of examination. Chapter 4 will outline the different points of view taken by Christian Democrats and Social Democrats on issues of education policy.

Interestingly, as Lehmbruch (1998, pp.154–60) notes, education is an area of policy where the federal government has previously tried to push the Länder in a particular direction, attempting to coordinate policy and initiate reforms, especially during the period of the social-liberal coalition. Specifically, that government attempted to develop 'swiftly and in partnership ... a wide-ranging, integrated comprehensive school and university system' (Lehmbruch 1998, p.154). The main object was to see the widespread introduction of comprehensive schools. Although some of the SPD-governed Länder were cooperative, the federal government was, in general, unsuccessful at promoting these changes; at first, it tried to introduce 'trial models', but even these were blocked following a shift of power in the Federal-Länder-Commission on education after the Lower Saxony election of 1976 (ibid., p.156). The message was clear – power over educational policy would not, at least in the 1970s, be ceded to the federal government. This conclusion is supported by Schmidt's study, and it remains to be seen whether, especially in the weaker Länder, it remains the case.

A related point is that the power of the Länder to determine policy may manifest itself as the power to resist federal pressure for reform, rather than the power actively to change their own policies – this power was demonstrated by the CDU-led Länder in the 1970s in the field of education policy. It would seem particularly germane to the case studies following reunification, where the eastern Länder might be in a weaker position to resist the involvement of the Bund, owing to their financial dependence.

The politics of school-level education has gained massively in prominence since the launch of the PISA investigation into educational standards, commissioned by the OECD and extended by the federal government at the decision of the KMK (Conference of Ministers of Culture) to allow comparison between the Länder (Stanat 2002, p.1), with first results published in 2001. The results of the study were damning for the German system of education – in each of the three areas explored (reading literacy, mathematical literacy and scientific literacy), German children were significantly below the OECD average (ibid., p.8). In addition, Germany showed differences between high and low performing pupils which were far greater than average, and teachers were found not to classify those the study termed 'low performers' as such in all but 15% of cases (ibid., p.10). Of all the nations participating in the survey, Germany had the highest level of correlation between social class and achievement (ibid., p.13), lending some support to the left's arguments against selection in the German system. The divide between those pupils who spoke German at home as well as at school, and those who spoke a different language at home, was also particularly great in terms of educational standards, second only to Belgium in the extent of its division (ibid., p.14).

No less significant in terms of the political reaction they prompted were the differences in standards between the Länder (announced in 2002). Although most Länder displayed relatively similar levels of performance, at the extremities there were significant differences, with variation in performance between children in different Länder spanning the equivalent of up to two school years (ibid., pp.16–17). Of the Länder under consideration here, the Saarland and Hesse achieved middle-ranking results, while Saxony-Anhalt reached only the second bottom place in the table. Certainly, debates about the area of education policy, already polarised, were fuelled by the outcomes of the PISA study, putting all Länder under discussion under pressure to achieve significant reforms, but with sufficient disagreement about the direction to generate ample potential for party-political conflict.

As a second area of policy, as argued above, it is important to examine one of the numerous areas of policy where the Länder are forced to share power with the federal government, or implement policy decided at the federal level (albeit, often, with Bundesrat involvement). Social and welfare policy has often been highly politicised. It is, however, to a significant extent the responsibility of the federal government. Still, as Münch (1998) discussed, the Länder (and also local government) have the ability to shape some areas of policy (cf. also Matthias 2003). In particular, Roland Koch, the Minister President of Hesse, attempted to forge ahead in demanding reform, arguing for the devolution of greater powers to the level of the Länder (Annesley 2002, p.90).

In this study, it is necessary to narrow down the huge field of social policy, to focus particularly on two areas. The first is labour market policies, where there are significant differences between political parties, but at the same time where *territorial* pressures are strong (Blancke 2004; Schmid et al. 2004). As will be discussed in Chapter 4, Land governments often come under strong pressure to improve the state of labour markets, and in two of the election campaigns leading to the changes of government examined/ investigated here, the state of the Land's labour market played a significant role. There is thus a significant 'problem pressure', which Land governments are expected to address. Yet doing so is extremely challenging, owing to the large number of different actors with a stake in this area of policy: the Federal Labour Organisation, the Federal Government, the European Union, and municipalities all play a role, with social partners – trade unions and employers' representatives – also taking a keen interest. As with education policy, labour market policy was the focus of a great deal of debate as a result of a particular report. The Hartz Commission, established by Chancellor Gerhard Schröder to examine how to revitalise the German labour market, published its recommendations in 2002, giving rise to controversial and far reaching reforms in the ensuing years (Kemmerling and Bruttel 2006).

Secondly, childcare policy and policy towards families will be considered. These have been areas of significant political contestation recently, where differences emerged within the CDU (to be discussed in Chapter 4). Like labour market policy, they involve both the federal and local government, and so enable evaluation of whether a new CDU government can achieve policy change at a Land level in spite of the involvement of other (potentially politically opposed) actors. Also in common with labour market policy, there are significant differences in the existing frameworks of childcare policy, as well as expectations amongst the populations in east and west Germany, and this may be expected to affect policies pursued on a Land level.

2.6   Evaluating policy change using case studies and ideal types

The key hypothesis, as suggested above, is that, notwithstanding the considerable constraints, parties do matter at the level of the Länder. This was the central finding of Schmidt's 1980 study, and it is at least a hypothesis still worth exploring. Lijphart (1971) identifies five different 'ideal types' of case study: interpretative case studies using existing theory, hypothesis-generating case studies, case studies used to interrogate or test a theory, case-studies used to confirm a theory, and 'deviant' case studies. The case studies here fall within the third and fourth categories. In principle, Schmidt's 'political hypothesis' is here, once again, submitted to analysis (representing the fourth category of case study). However, given the changes to Germany and its federal balance since 1980, we might expect tests of Schmidt's hypothesis to generate different results, bringing the study closer to the third category of case study.

In each of the three policy areas under consideration, and for each of the three relevant Länder, the study will consider changes pursued, in relation to 'ideal types' of Christian and social democratic policies for each policy area – those policies which, other things being equal, we might expect CDU-led, and SPD-led, governments to favour. These ideal types are developed in Chapter 4. Chapter 4 also considers the parameters within which Land-level politicians operate, and the extent to which they are responsible for policy-making in the areas in question. The use of 'ideal types', or 'paradigms' of policy, which of course dates back to Max Weber, is a familiar tool in comparing policies (Esping-Andersen 1990; Seeleib-Kaiser et al. 2005). These are not approximations to the policies of any particular party, at any particular time (Esping-Andersen 1990, pp.28–9) but an attempt to conceptualise what we consider important in those policy areas, and 'clusters' of policies which may be adopted by political parties of a political family. This may, as Esping-Andersen notes (ibid., p.2) lead to a focus on qualitative, rather than quantitative choices: 'The existence of a social program and the amount of money spent on it may be less important than what it does'.

In subsequent chapters, for each of the three Länder, the political background is outlined, as are any significant parameters affecting policy-making in the Land, such as the social and economic context. The chapters also examine the background to each area of policy, the role the policy area played in the election campaign, and pledges made – either in the coalition agreement or the programme of government. Each aspect of the 'ideal type', spelt out in Chapter 4, is then considered, demonstrating the extent to which policy change occurred in each Land.

The practice of policy-making in each Land is also considered. The role of different actors – both within the government and the Landtag (government and opposition parties included), and other social actors – is examined, with a view to understanding who is in a position to promote or obstruct policy change within each policy area, and whether these catalysts, or obstacles, vary from Land to Land, and from policy area to policy area. The extent to which party organisations play a role is also discussed.

There are, in total, nine different case studies, considering in detail changes in three policy areas, in each of the three Länder in question.

For each case study, the relevant election programmes or coalition agreements are analysed, as are relevant items of legislation, both primary and secondary, and secondary documents, notably a full analysis of the regional media for each case. Where appropriate and relevant, data from the Statistical Offices of the Bund and the Länder are investigated to assess the extent to which policy change has been implemented (for instance, on the proportion of nursery places available compared to the number of children, or the number of children attending schools of a different type). To complement this, and also better understand the practice of policy-making in each Land, interviews with politicians (from the government and opposition side in the Landtag, and also in the relevant ministry) and key civil servants, as well as other actors outside the government (such as trade union representatives) were conducted. Because of the diversity of those involved, a 'free' interview format was most appropriate: the objective was to 'elicit rich, detailed materials that can be used in qualitative analysis... to find out what kinds of things are happening rather than to determine the frequency of predetermined kinds of things that the researcher already believes can happen' (Lofland 1971, p.76). Findings concerning the frequency of events were gleaned from other primary and secondary sources. Given the degree of sensitivity, interviewees were offered the opportunity to remain anonymous.

For each of the nine case studies, it is possible to consider the extent to which policy in the particular Land shifted from the social democratic to the Christian democratic ideal type, as well as understand the role different actors played, such as the *Landesverband* and *Fraktion* (party group) in the Landtag, the coalition partner (where relevant), trade unions and other social actors, and the political opposition, and to find where blockages to policy change occurred. In doing so, some tentative conclusions can be drawn about the impact of particular political institutions at the Land level. The variable geometry of Land-level political institutions has been a source of particular interest recently (Freitag and Vatter 2008; Reutter 2008), although without specific reference to the *do-parties-matter?* debate. The findings of this study will therefore provide us with a clearer understanding of how this variable geometry impacts upon policy change.

2.7   Just puppets on a string? Hypotheses on party impact

The key hypothesis to be examined in this text is the claim that parties do matter – that they are able to shape policies pursued and outcomes arrived at in the Länder.

A number of corollary hypotheses are also examined. The first such hypothesis is that the power of the Länder is greater in areas where they are exclusively responsible for policy and, rhetoric notwithstanding, far less significant in areas where the federal government retains some involvement; where it leaves the Länder responsible only for the implementation of policy; or where some responsibility for policy decisions or execution rests with local government. While this is predictable enough, it is an important caveat to any conclusion that 'parties do matter', and it is important to assess the extent to which parties can 'make themselves matter' in areas which do not fall neatly under their control. One would, based on this hypothesis, expect parties to be able to shape policies and their outcomes in the field of education policy. They would have less ability to do so in childcare, family and labour market policy. The extent to which they are still able meaningfully to shape policies in these areas will have a significant impact upon the extent to which the political hypothesis – that is, the view that parties do matter – is still valid.

The second hypothesis is that the Saarland and, in particular, Saxony-Anhalt will be less able autonomously to shape policy than Hesse, due to their economic weakness, and, especially in the case of Saxony-Anhalt, their dependence upon the federal government for subsidies and for the co-financing of any policy initiatives. Schmidt found this to be the case in his 1980 study, but contemporary literature suggests that these asymmetries in the extent to which Land governments can effect policy change will be far starker in this, more recent, time frame (Münch 1999; Luthardt 1999).

A third hypothesis is that the CDU's ability to implement its policy objectives will be hampered by its participation in a coalition government in Saxony-Anhalt and Hesse, with the obvious caveat that this will only be the case in areas where the two coalition partners disagree. Schmidt found in 1980 that this was a significant determinant of the extent to which a Land government could change the direction of policies; Wolf (2006, p.265) found that, in the case of education policy, the FDP had a significant effect upon spending patterns, being associated with a higher level of expenditure when it was a part of the government. Schmidt further suggested that the interaction of the two coalition partners, and the extent to which the FDP can act as a check upon the CDU in these two coalitions, will further affect the extent to which policy change occurs (a point confirmed by Jun 1994, pp.155–6).

Finally, in particular in the case of Hesse, and to a lesser extent in the other two cases, the long history of SPD-led government would, according to Schmidt (and also later to Lees 2000), act as a curb on the ability of the CDU-led government to change policy, due to the presence of a core of civil servants appointed by the SPD, potentially hostile to the new government's policy agenda.

Against this, there is the political 'null hypothesis' – that the presence of particular parties in government at the Land level is not the determinant of policies chosen. As discussed, this may be because of characteristics of the Land in question: for instance, labour market policy choices will be shaped by the extent and nature of unemployment, and this may affect policies chosen as much as the political colour of the party of government. It may be because certain policy choices are costly, and the Land does not have the resources to pursue them, or equally, because the Land decides to make sacrifices in its chosen policy field in order to access federal government funding.

Alternatively, as noted in Chapter 1, path dependence may restrict the extent of partisan impact upon public policy. To recap, theorists of path dependence note that policy-makers will sometimes be locked into sub-optimal policies, as the cost of changing path will be greater than the cost of remaining on the same trajectory. For the purposes of this study, we are not so much concerned with the locking in of sub-optimal policies: in policy choices in education, childcare and labour market policy, normative standpoints will significantly affect what is considered to be optimal. We are, though, concerned with why policy-makers might persist in allowing policies they regard as sub-optimal to endure. For instance, as will be shown in Chapter 5, in Hesse the Koch government inherited a network of comprehensive schools which had been created by previous SPD-led governments. To reorganise the school system and replace the comprehensive schools with selective alternatives – which might well have reflected the Koch government's policy preferences – could meet opposition from affected parents, teachers and pupils, and this might be an obstacle to policy change, both because interest groups have formed to protect existing institutions, and also expectations of interested actors are shaped by the prevailing institutions and policies.

In sum, this study provides an insight into whether or not parties matter at the level of the Länder. It considers whether or not the victorious men and women, on the night of a Land election, really have the ability to affect the lives of those who installed them, or whether they are mere 'puppets on a string', hemmed in by territorial needs (the socio-economic position of their Land, or the policy legacy they've inherited), an all-powerful federal government, and an uncooperative bureaucracy. This dilemma, not fully explored since Schmidt's pathbreaking study in 1980, goes to the heart of German federalism – it begs the question of whether the partisan element of federalism really matters.

3
Contemporary German Federalism

As discussed in the previous chapter, policy-making in German federalism is characterised by considerable complexity in the division of power between the federal government and the Länder; it is also a system characterised by constant vertical and horizontal negotiation, underpinned by a social and economic structure that has changed significantly since reunification. The aim of this chapter is thus to give us a clear picture of the framework within which partisan actors in the German Länder act.

The first part of this section spells out the division of powers between the federal government and the Länder, with a view to understanding what powers the Länder have, and thus what resources are available to a newly-formed Land level government. The second section discusses political structures within the Länder, assessing the extent to which differences can shape the ability of partisan actors to shape policy. The third section outlines the substantial shifts in German federalism that have taken place since reunification, and in particular questions whether it is correct to speak of a move from 'cooperative' to 'competitive' federalism. The fourth section discusses the changing nature and role of political parties in German federalism. Finally, a brief explanation of recent reforms to German federalism is provided, while noting that these fell narrowly outside the time frame of the case studies analysed here.

3.1 The formal division of powers in German federalism

The division of powers between the federal government and the Länder is defined by the Basic Law (*Grundgesetz*). The key principle is that, where not otherwise specified, powers are held by the Länder (Art. 70 GG). As will be seen, however, this has led to the erosion of the power of the Länder over time, with the federal government enjoying increasing influence. There are four types of legislation spelt out in the Basic Law (cf. Rudzio 2003, p.377):

Ausschliessliche Bundesgesetzgebung (exclusively federal competencies):
This includes primarily foreign affairs (though now with the caveat that the

Bundesrat's consent is required for European treaties), defence, currency, federal railways, post and air transport, rules on cooperation between federal government (*Bund*) and Länder on protection of the constitution, and crime (Art. 71 and 73 GG);

Konkurrierende Gesetzgebung (competing legislation): These fall into the competencies of the Länder as long as the Bund has not previously legislated: and include such areas as criminal and civil law, justice, economy, labour law, social affairs, travel, environment, health. (Art. 72, 74, 74a GG);

Gemeinschaftsaufgaben (joint tasks): These are areas where the Bund assists the Länder in the fulfillment of their duties, including laws covering the civil service, universities, media, protection of nature, immigration and registration (Art. 75 GG);

Ausschliessliche Landesgesetzgebung (exclusively Land competencies): Culture, schools, police, local government and all other, non-listed areas (Art. 70 GG).

In addition to their direct responsibilities, Land governments are represented in the Bundesrat (sometimes translated as the 'Federal Council'). The number of votes each Land enjoys is weighted according to population, but in such a way that smaller Länder enjoy disproportionately large representation, so that, for instance, Bremen, with a population of 660,000 in 2001 had three votes, whereas the population of 18,000,000 in North-Rhine Westphalia was represented by six votes. The Land governments, through the Bundesrat, enjoy three roles (Schmidt 2003, pp.57–9):

- The support of two-thirds of the members in the Bundesrat, as well as two-thirds of members of the Bundestag, is required to amend the Basic Law;
- Legislation which directly affects the interests of the Länder, which has tended to be over half of all bills and most domestic ones of importance, require the support of a majority of members of the Bundesrat;
- Legislation which does not affect the interests of the Länder can still be delayed if the Bundesrat objects. A 'conciliation committee' of Bundesrat and Bundestag is formed, and if agreement is not reached, the Bundestag can be required to vote again, with a two-thirds majority required to overturn the Bundesrat's objection, if a two-thirds majority voted against the proposal in the Bundesrat.

The representatives of a Land government are required to vote 'as one' in the Bundesrat, and coalition agreements normally stipulate abstention if there is disagreement.

It is further worth noting that German federalism often has a sharp distinction between responsibility for legislation, and responsibility for execution of policy: the Bund has relatively few agencies of its own (such as the army, the federal water administration and others); often, agencies which fall primarily under its jurisdiction are also reliant upon cooperation with the Länder, such as the Federal Finance Administration (*Bundesfinanzverwaltung*), or more commonly still, in areas where the Bund legislates, the Länder are responsible for implementation.

Initially in the Basic Law, there was an assumption that the Bund and Länder had different sources of income which financed their expenditure, and had budgets independent of each other (Rudzio 2003, p.382). However, this is flatly contradicted by the Basic Law's commitment to the harmonisation (or latterly, 'equivalence') of standards of living, and, in any case, the picture has become far more complex, with a growth in the number of joint tasks, where legislation is agreed by Bundestag and Bundesrat, and financed jointly, or by the federal government. It is also worth noting that, in its executive role, local government plays an important role, though unlike the Länder, it is in no position to have a veto over legislation or the extension of its responsibilities (except where such powers result from the constitutions of the Länder).

While some taxes are directly allocated specifically to one level of government (such as customs and the most important consumer taxes going to the Bund, Länder having control over vehicle and wealth taxes, and local government receiving business and property taxes), the largest part of tax income is divided according to the tax distribution key (*Steuerverbund*), where federal laws and the Basic Law decide on their division between the three levels. The introduction of the Steuerverbund was specifically designed in order to prevent particular levels of government becoming entirely dependent upon particular, fluctuating sources of income.

The power of the Bund over certain areas of policy was greatly expanded with the 1969 finance reform, which introduced the co-financing of Land and municipal responsibilities. Co-financing need not operate exclusively in the domain of joint tasks; it can also fund action in relation to economic responsibilities which threaten the national economic picture, threaten to promote economic inequality, or which are necessary to support economic growth. Examples include programmes on building works, public transport, housing construction, hospital finance, and various investment programmes to generate economic growth or environmental provision. This undermines Länder competencies, not least as the desire to gain federal subsidies may diminish the willingness to alter proposals in the Bundesrat.

A final power of the Bund is its ability, granted under Article 109 of the Basic Law, to intervene in the interests of economic stability, such as by pursuing an anti-cyclical economic policy. Heavily informed by Keynesian economics, this was introduced in response to the 1966/67 recession, and further eroded the fiscal autonomy of the three layers of government (ibid., p.388).

3.2   Politics within the Länder

For each of the Länder considered in this study, there is a discussion of the particularities of its institutional arrangements, inasmuch as they will affect the ability of Land-level politicians to shape policy after a change of government. The Länder do, however, share a number of common features in their political systems; they have a Land constitution, and a legislature (Landtag), which usually agrees Land-level legislation in two readings, with a committee phase in between. According to Article 28 of the Basic Law, all Länder have to reflect the 'republican, democratic state governed by justice of this Basic Law'. Land-level law, in areas of federal competence or constitutional matters, is overridden by federal law.

Areas of variation within the Länder include the extent of direct democracy; methods by which the government is formed (for instance, whether each Minister requires the approval of the Landtag in a secret ballot, or just the Minister President); the rules on recalling the government (with a mixture of positive and negative votes of confidence being available); whether the Minister President has the explicit power to determine the parameters of policy; and the role of the Land's constitutional court. There are also variations in the electoral systems in each Land, which may affect the likelihood of the government being formed of one party (Rudzio 2003, pp.367–71; Mielke and Reutter 2004). The Land government also retains responsibility for local government – again, there are variations in the structure, although there has been a shift in recent years towards the model of directly elected mayors (Rudzio 2003, pp.404–9). As will be discussed for each of the case studies, although legal responsibility for the execution of many federal policies lies with Länder, this in turn is often passed to the local level, where directly elected and legitimated local government, with a constitutionally enshrined right to self-administration (Article 28 of the Basic Law), is able to have an input. The federal government is thus often reliant on the Länder in policy implementation, but in turn the Länder have to rely on municipalities, which may present a constraint to policy-makers. A particular issue explored in interviews with Land-level actors is whether the party composition of local government makes a difference to the nature of cooperation and the ease with which policy change can be effected, especially in the light of growing party penetration of local government (Rudzio 2003, p.101).

Freitag and Vatter (2008) undertook a detailed analysis of variation in the political structures of the Länder using the Lijphart's framework outlined in Chapter 1. They found (ibid., pp.311–16) significant variations in Land-level political structures, notably in the degree of disproportionality in electoral systems, the nature of party competition and the format of government, the relationship between legislature and executive and the power of local government. There were also important variations in the extent of direct-democratic instruments, although a trend towards greater power was noticeable across the country. By contrast, only modest variations are visible in the power of constitutional courts in the Länder (p.315) and in the ease of constitutional reform (p.314). The different models of interest group mediation, as well as the power of central banks, were not considered.

Pulling these points together, Freitag and Vatter draw a number of conclusions. In what they term the 'consociational-democratic versus centralised' dimension (considering the type of cabinet, the degree of decentralisation, the electoral system and the number of parties), the western Länder (other than the city-states) and Saxony are rather more majoritarian in character than the city-states and the eastern Länder, which appear to have a more consensual distribution of power (ibid., p.322). On their 'judicial division of power' dimension (covering the process of constitutional amendment and the power of the constitutional court), there is a high level of constraint upon power (akin to Lijphart's consensus democratic ideal type) across the Länder, although Bavaria sees a greater level of constraint upon power than most Länder, and Schleswig-Holstein and Baden-Württemberg are notably less constrained. On the third dimension identified, 'executive jurisdiction' (covering the degree to which the executive is constrained by the legislature and by direct democratic instruments), again the overall pattern amongst the Länder is one of constraint upon executive power, but with some variations attributable to different levels of direct democracy: Bavaria, Lower Saxony, Rhineland-Palatinate and Schleswig-Holstein have the highest levels of constraint upon the executive, with Baden-Württemberg, Hesse and North-Rhine Westphalia having the lowest (ibid., p.322). In seeking to explain these variations, the history of a Land's occupation, be it by the US (attaching high importance to decentralisation and the judiciary) or the British (lower importance to both) is partially informative; there are also patterns to be seen amongst the eastern Länder (ibid., p.325). However, they also find that particular turns of events, and 'critical junctures' are significant (ibid., p.326).

3.3   The challenge of reunification – from cooperative to competitive federalism?

Since reunification, Germany has become significantly more diverse, and less equal. This has placed tensions on its federal system, which have been thoroughly explored in the academic literature (see, amongst others, Jeffery 1999; Benz 1999; Sturm and Zimmermann-Steinhart 2005; Jeffery 2005).

The concept of the 'unitary federal state' (*kooperativer Bundesstaat*, a phrase coined by Konrad Hesse in 1962), referred to the establishment of the mechanisms described above, which ensured that any transfer of power from the Länder to the Bund was accompanied by a growth in the power of the representatives of the Land governments in the Bundesrat. This allowed the progressive generation of a single legal framework, which reflected the interest of economic actors in harmonisation of law across the Federal Republic, while also allowing the creation of comparable standards of living across it.

This latter possibility is related to the concept of the *Sozialstaat* (literally, 'social state'). For Benz (1999), this had two key concepts: the underwriting of risk through social insurance, and the generation of social justice, understood here as the provision of 'a minimal level of provision of public services and economic prosperity across all areas'. There is a rejection implicit in German cooperative federalism that citizens of deprived areas should not be encouraged due to the deprivation to move to a more prosperous area, in contrast to the US, but rather should have the state step in to ensure change (as will be discussed in Chapter 4, in relation to decentralisation of labour market policy, this is now coming under challenge). The aim of achieving 'social justice' led to a combination of mechanisms, such as the common tasks and different grants alluded to above, which were intended to contribute to development of infrastructure in the less prosperous areas of the state, as well as the construction of the fiscal equalisation mechanism, which was intended to generate a roughly equal division of tax revenue for the Länder, regardless of their exact income.

This process of centralisation of power on the one hand, alongside the extension of the powers of the Länder through the Bundesrat on the other, has been criticised by Scharpf, who argued that this awkward process restricted the possibility of state action, with a tendency to policy stagnation (cf. for instance Scharpf 1994). The reasons for this were, firstly, that the actors were only able to agree on policies which did not distribute costs and benefits with excessive inequality; secondly, the nature of party competition in the Bundestag and the various Landtage and equivalents meant that parties had to be seen to represent the interests of their particular Land (or those of the Bund), rather than attempt to achieve optimal policy outcomes.

Benz (1999) rejects Scharpf's argument that such stagnation is necessarily present in German federalism – rather, he argues that it applies only when, firstly, economic growth is sufficiently low that the richer Länder, through the process of redistribution, actually have to lose money, as opposed merely to failing to gain. At times of high economic growth, provided there is agreement on the consensus of the Sozialstaat, there will be an acceptance of inequality in the division of resources in the interests of the poorer Länder; however this acceptance greatly declines in times of lower economic growth, when the richer Länder are forced by redistribution to sacrifice existing resources, rather than merely standing still. Secondly, the pursuit of the interests of the particular Land by the parties involved, rather than the pursuit of an optimal policy aim, ignores the possibility of parties providing a mechanism for compromise. In fact, Benz argues that, for most of the post-war period, the nature of German parties, being both nationally organised (with the exception of the CSU) and programmatically moderate, as well as providing an arena for negotiation between Bund and Länder, meant that they were an integrating factor in German politics. In addition, the presence of the FDP in many Land governments as well as, with one brief interregnum, the federal government, provided an integrative factor in many cases between government and opposition (cf. also Lehmbruch 2000).

However, since reunification, things have changed in three ways: firstly, there are far greater economic disparities between the Länder, meaning that the level of redistribution between the Länder in order to see a comparable standard of living across Germany has increased (Seitz 2000). Secondly, Germany entered a recession, exacerbating tensions concerning distributional conflicts. Thirdly, party systems at a Land level have become far more diverse (Lehmbruch 2000).

This has had two effects. Firstly, there has been a push, in particular from some of the more prosperous, southern Länder, to move away from cooperative federalism, towards a more 'competitive' model, with fewer elements of redistribution (Adelberger 2001). Secondly, the cohesion of party blocs in the Bundesrat has weakened, with representatives of the Länder increasingly voting along lines of territorial, rather than partisan interest (Jeffery 2005).

These combined pressures to act in a way motivated primarily by territorial, rather than party interest, may reduce the extent to which a change of government at a Land level will affect policy choices, and specifically that Land's conduct in the Bundesrat – pointing to a declining validity of the 'political hypothesis' stipulated in the introduction. Moreover, the growing disparities between the Länder will lead to differences in their ability to enact policy change in two ways. Firstly, and most obviously, richer Länder will have more policy options at their disposal than their poorer counterparts. Secondly, poorer Länder may be more reliant on external funding, and may allow their policies to be steered by conditions set by the external funder.

Although trends towards territorialisation are readily identified, there is a lively debate about the extent to which it holds (Jeffery 2005). In a major study looking at reaction by the Länder on a verdict of the Federal Constitutional Court giving them the power to regulate the wearing of headscarves by such public servants as teachers, von Blumenthal (2009) finds confirmation of a growing tendency towards 'territorialisation'. She ascertains that socio-cultural differences between Länder, as well as socioeconomic ones, following Jeffery, are of growing importance. However, this should not be overstated, because partisan structures, constitutional requirements and also a strong public preference for unitary solutions (ibid., p.278) are also all of significance. This study should therefore give us some insights into the extent of 'territorialisation' of German federalism.

A further change faced by Land-level governments since the 1980s, and particularly since reunification, has been the growth in the power of the European Union (EU). On the surface, closer European integration will potentially weaken the position of Land-level governments, because they are not formally represented in the core institutions of the EU, and because of the loss of control over some areas of policy to the EU level. Benz (1999, pp.72–6) argues that, in fact, through changes negotiated to Article 23 of the Basic Law, the power of the Länder has been strengthened: in areas where the Länder enjoy sole competence, one of their representatives can chair the delegation to the Council of Ministers, and they are in a position to force the federal government to adopt their position, if it is agreed by a two-thirds majority. Additionally, the Länder have an important 'blackmail power', in their ability to threaten to block European treaties, or other measures requiring unanimity at a European level. These powers may only be relevant to Land governments occasionally; however, the growing power of the EU has had a direct impact upon them, through the ability, especially for poorer Länder, to receive funds from European programmes, such as the European social fund. As will be seen in relation to labour market policy, in particular, this can be of assistance to Land-level governments in realising their policy goals, although the parameters for funding streams are set down at a European level, and so they do not have complete autonomy in generating uses for such funds.

3.4   Political parties and German federalism

As noted above, German political parties have been an important factor in achieving horizontal and vertical coordination in German federalism (Haas et al. 2008). Nonetheless, with pressures towards greater 'territorialism' in German federalism, we would expect a shift in parties' role, becoming more assertive in representing the interests of their territories; rather than mediating territorially founded conflicts, they would instead pursue such conflicts.

Detterbeck and Renzsch (2003, p.265) find just such a development:

> In the 1990s, there has been a tendency towards increased political autonomy of regional party organizations in terms of policies, coalition building and electoral appeal. Regional politicians have facilitated the regionalization of party competition by agreeing to form incongruent coalitions or by playing the 'regional advocate's card' in election campaigns.

However, somewhat incongruously, this territorialisation of politics has been matched by changes in party organisation only to a limited degree.

Looking ahead, they foresee a gradual erosion of parties' ability to perform the function of vertical integration (ibid., p.266).

The role of parties in the German federal system can be divided three-fold: between their role at a federal level, the role in the Länder, and the role in the relationship between the two levels of government (Haas et al. 2008).

In circumstances of greater territorialisation, we would expect a change in the pattern of parties' interaction at the federal level. In the past, as discussed in Chapter 2, the federal government would expect hostility from the Bundesrat where the opposition enjoyed a majority there, while support would be anticipated where the same parties enjoyed power in both Bundestag and Bundesrat. Benz (2003; cited in Haas et al. 2008, p.20) sees four reasons why this will be eroded: greater regionalisation within parties as a result of growing economic and social disparity between the Länder; more diversity within the party systems of the Länder (cf. also Detterbeck and Renzsch 2008); the growing variety of governments in the Länder, together with more frequent changes of government due to higher electoral volatility; and the regionalisation of political conflict as a result of the forces of globalisation and Europeanisation.

We would also expect territorialisation to have an impact upon the parties within the Länder. Here, we would expect to see different policies being pursued by the same party in different Länder. Such a view is confirmed by Debus (2008), who finds quite significant variations between the programmatic orientations of the same party in different Länder, both in respect of economic and social policy.

Finally, some expectation of change would be expected in the role parties play in between the two levels of government. Haas et al. (2008), in their discussion of this issue, focus almost entirely on the issue of federal influence upon Land elections. They highlight disagreement in the literature: on the one hand, there are those who see a decline in the influence of the popularity of the federal government upon Land elections (e.g. Jeffery and Hough 2001), due to the growing importance of territorial issues, as well as the greater willingness of Land politicians to distance themselves from their parties nationally. On the other hand, some (e.g. Burkhart 2007; also von Blumenthal 2008) find that federal influence upon Land elections has actually grown, or at least remains the primary determinant of election results in the Länder. The dynamic relationship between party politics at the federal and the Land level can certainly be more widely conceived than this: for instance, in the extent to which politicians of the same party from different Länder are able to reach agreement in horizontal negotiation arenas, such as the KMK.

This study will shed light upon the changing role of parties in German federalism in three ways: firstly, it will consider whether Land-level party organisations appear to be exerting an exogenous influence upon policy choices in the Länder. Secondly, it will assess whether different policy choices are pursued by CDU-led governments in different Länder in a similar time frame, supporting the view of growing territorialisation of federalism. Thirdly, in those areas where both the federal government and the Länder are involved in making policy (notably labour market policy), we will be able to assess whether Land-level politicians appear to give primacy to Land or partisan interests in their interaction in the Bundesrat.

3.5   Reform of German federalism

In spite of the pressures discussed above, the institutional architecture of German federalism remained largely the same for the period under discussion here. Adelberger (2001) considered that the attempts to reform failed because the poorer Länder had sufficient votes in the Bundesrat to block any reform they would lose from, including any which 'imposed greater competition of jurisdictions against Länder with greater resources'. The institutional architecture of cooperative federalism continued to exist, even if the richer Länder were anything other than conciliatory in the tone they took towards it.

There were two major attempts at reform during this period, however. The first was the 'Federalism Convention', jointly chaired by Franz Müntefering, the SPD Chairman, and Edmund Stoiber, the CSU Chairman and Minister President of Bavaria, which negotiated with representatives of the federal government, the Bundestag, and the Länder, as well as involving academic experts. Negotiations took place throughout 2004, but ultimately failed. The ostensible reason given for the convention's failure was continued disagreement over education policy: the CDU-led Länder, in particular Bavaria and Hesse, were unwilling to accept any deal which did not give them total control over education (Benz 2005). Scharpf, in a convincing analysis, argues that, in fact, this was only partially the case, and the succession of decisions from the Federal Constitutional Court enhancing the power of the Länder meant that the *status quo* of German federalism was moving towards the aspirations of the Länder anyway; moreover, the weaker Länder were successful in resisting changes which would be to their detriment, rather as Adelberger predicted they would (Scharpf 2005).

The second reform was successful: in summer 2006, both Bundestag and Bundesrat agreed to a number of changes to federalism (though they did not consider amendments to fiscal federalism and the equalisation mechanism, which were postponed to a later phase of discussion). The key aim was to 'disentangle' decision-making, facilitating policy change and enhancing accountability: as a result, the Länder sacrificed a veto in some areas of policy, in return for greater authority over others. In particular in the areas of environmental policy, higher education, special care facilities, and licensing regulations, the power of the Länder increased (Hrbek 2007). This reform came into effect on 1st September 2006, after the end of each of the parliamentary terms considered here, so it did not shape the context in which the Land-level politicians acted. However, reference will be made, where relevant, to their involvement in discussions of federalism reform.

In sum, three particular conclusions are of relevance to this study. Firstly, it is clear that German federalism has become more complex, with a greater number of formal and informal arenas for policy-making, since Schmidt's 1980 study – this makes a focus on mechanisms, rather than just outcomes of policy-making processes, indispensable. Secondly, the view that federalism has become increasingly asymmetric, with the poorer Länder, notably in the east, massively dependent on the Bund, has gained in currency since Schmidt's 1980 study. Thirdly, as Jeffery (2005) argues, there are growing pressures for the Länder to act in a way determined by territorial, rather than party interests (a 'new territorialism'). In the light of these points, we might expect the political hypothesis to have weakened in favour of the territorial counter-hypothesis, and the ability to effect policy change may vary between the different Länder, depending on their degree of wealth.

4
Education, Family and Childcare, and Labour Market Policies at a Land Level

This chapter sets out the background to each area of policy examined here, providing relevant history, setting out the legal framework in which the Länder are able to influence policy and detailing what other institutions are involved. It then derives two paradigms, or ideal types, of Land-level policies in each area, setting out what might be expected of a CDU-led government, and an SPD-led government. These provide the 'yardstick' against which to consider policies pursued by the Land government under consideration in future chapters.

4.1   Education policy

As noted in Chapter 3, this area of policy falls under the sole jurisdiction of the Länder, under Article 70 of the Basic Law (Münch 2005). This section will examine the history of education policy in the post-war federal republic, and it will be demonstrated that this area of policy has long been rich in conflict. Disputes have at times proven extremely bitter, going to the heart of ideological differences between the parties.

As discussed in Chapter 2, the PISA study into educational achievement found very significant differences in policy outcomes – measured in terms of educational achievement – between the Länder. This has led, on the one hand, to a great intensity of interest in the policy area, with it sometimes playing a significant role in Land-level election campaigns; and on the other hand, to a debate about the 'division of labour' between the federal government and the Länder, with some of the Länder demanding greater autonomy in education provision, while the SPD-led federal government emphasised the need for greater coordination.

4.1.1   The legal context of German educational policy

There is a significant body of legislation in Germany surrounding education policy, which affects the ability of the Länder, as well as the federal government, to change policies.

The end of the second world war did not 'wipe the slate clean' of previous educational laws. With the exception of laws which were obviously inspired by the Nazis, the 'Reich education law' (*Reichsbildungsrecht*) continued from 1945, and then existed alongside further laws passed by the Länder after 1949, at times carrying on into the latter half of the 1950s (Reuter 1998, p.35). The Basic Law, passed in 1949, generally confirmed through Article 30 the assumption that the Länder were to be responsible for education policy. It also confirmed the assumption that the state could and should regulate (or 'supervise') schools (with Art. 7, Sec. 1 of the Basic Law mirroring exactly the relevant passage of the Weimar Constitution). Subsequent suggestions that references to 'supervision' (*Aufsicht*) in the Basic Law imply a restriction on the state's ability to control schools, or to greater powers being given to local government, have not found support (ibid., p.37).

The Basic Law's Art. 6, Sec. 2 also impacts/affects policy: 'The care and upbringing of children is the natural right of parents and a duty primarily incumbent upon them'. This has been the source of controversies where parents have confronted the state with regard, for example, to confessional choice of school. For instance, the Catholic Church attempted to use this provision to force the Länder to offer a choice of schools, to include confessional schools. More recently, this clause has been used to restrict the possibility of selection, instead entrenching the right of German parents to choose which sort of school their children attend (ibid., p.37).

Reuter identifies three aspects of education law in Germany derived from the Basic Law (ibid., pp.38–9):

- Right of entry to institutions: A right to attend educational institutions, or to a fair method of selection if these are oversubscribed;
- Right to development: A right to develop ability and interests, and to be able to acquire the necessary skills and knowledge that modern society demands;
- Right to participation in institutions: A right to participatory structures in educational institutions and involvement in decision-making processes.

Furthermore, the Basic Law has, at various stages, helped to clarify the relationship between the federal government and the Länder. For instance, Art. 77, Sec. 11 makes the federal government primarily responsible for the economy, which has been taken to mean that it is also responsible for the works-based part of professional education.

Over the course of the history of the federal republic, a strong tendency towards the judicialisation of education policy has been noted (ibid., pp.43–4). In the early years, the Länder passed a plethora of different laws (often in a piecemeal form), covering, by the end of the 1950s, school organisation, school administration and supervision, school financing, attendance rules and laws covering private schools. Moreover, regulations extended into areas as detailed as timetables, grading, examinations and even school newspapers! In the 1970s, many areas of education law were challenged under the 'democracy and rule of law' provisions of the Basic Law; these in turn led to greater levels of legislation in areas which had previously been governed by decree, though the courts were willing to allow the Länder long periods in which to implement changes. The fundamental tenets of the Basic Law were also used by both parents and schoolchildren in order to challenge a variety of educational reforms (such as the introduction of sex education, politics as a subject, and different year-group categories), though in general the Federal Constitutional Court held that the Basic Law was not intended to be a measure for comparing the value of different school systems (ibid., p.45).

A modest impact on German education policy-making has also been made by the growth of European Economic Council (EEC) (now EU) competences, even though education is a policy area clearly devolved to nation-states. As early as 1968, the decision was taken to allow free movement of workers within the EU, and a later (1977) decision on school education for children of travelling workers specified that education for the children of travelling workers had to be provided, together with local children, with support for their mother tongue and also education about their native country. This specification was later extended to foreign workers (see Reuter 1998, p.50). Perhaps even greater anathema to German policy-makers was the subsequent stricter interpretation of provisions surrounding free movement of workers, with regard to the mutual recognition of qualifications. In 1986, the European Court ruled that Baden-Württemberg had to offer a position as a trainee teacher (*Referendar*) to a British citizen who had passed the relevant German teachers' examination (ibid., p.52). Although there is still an exception for head teachers, foreign citizens have a right to be considered for teaching posts, as well as positions at German universities.

In sum, then, it can be seen that German education, in the fields of university, school, tertiary and adult education, operates within a tight legal framework. This operates on two levels: first, the huge number of laws, decrees and regulations in the field of school education passed by the Länder, or stemming either from federal or Land legislation. This makes the process of policy change in the field of education at best a slow and rather cumbersome process, and at worst completely obstructed. Secondly, litigants can use the general provisions for the 'free and democratic basic order' in the Basic Law in order to challenge actions of governments in this field. Although on occasion this has been used to assert 'positive' rights and generate educational reform, more commonly it has been used to obstruct proposed reforms.

As a result, although Land level governments enjoy a relatively high degree of autonomy in developing education policy, there are some existing legal constraints, notably those set down by the Basic Law, as well as a body of prevailing legislation within each Land which provide significant impediments to change.

4.1.2 German education policy since the Second World War – continuity with little change?

Thränhardt (1990, pp.177–8) observes that unity, central responsibility and hierarchical oversight have remained general principles of German education policy since the Second World War. Notwithstanding at times heated debates at the foundation of the Federal Republic, during the profound political challenges in the 1960s, and the current heated debate over standards following the PISA study, the system's foundations have escaped significant amendment.

It is also argued by Thrändardt (1990, p.181) that there is, given the autonomy of the Länder with regard to education policy, a surprising lack of regional variation, in contrast to other federal systems like Switzerland and the United States. Indeed, attempts to promote diversity have proven unpopular. He traces this back to two aspects of political culture – the national unity movement in the 19th century, and the legacy of the Prussian state which took over two-thirds of the Reich's territory and set up a centralised administration. Another explanation for this uniformity which is at least convincing would be the practical one that any lack of comparability inhibits freedom of movement when looking for work. The qualifications taken by pupils are also generally nationally comparable. When there are minor deviations (such as the special examination on Bavarian history in Bavaria) these cause public consternation or bafflement. However, as was illustrated by the failed 2004, and successful 2006, reforms to federalism, most Länder do not favour handing further power to the federal government, instead choosing to agree on education policy topics, through consensus-based cooperation mechanisms.

Strengthening the role of the Land government, within each Land, school organisation is quite centralised. The *Bildungsrat*, which was a joint decision-making body set up by the Länder) made proposals for greater school autonomy and far-reaching decentralisation, but this led to its winding-up in 1974 (Baden-Württemberg refused to extend its contract through the Bundesrat), and only part of the recommendations could even be published. Parent and pupil participation has had only a limited impact upon the statist character of education policy. In the southern Länder, participatory bodies including pupils and parents have not been influential, while even in those Länder where they are stronger (such as Hamburg and North-Rhein Westphalia), they only affect local decisions within the wider context set by the Land government (ibid., p.180).

One result of this combination of desire for unity, but lack of competences of the federal government, has been the establishment of vertical and horizontal cooperation (Reiter-Mayer 2005). The 'Conference of Education

Ministers' (KMK) has had over 1,000 agreements translated into Land law. The KMK operates on a system of unanimity, whereby the representatives of the Land governments agree to introduce common laws and regulations. At first, not all KMK agreements were translated into law (as they are not, of course, binding on Landtage, who are completely written out of these processes of cooperation) – not a single Landtag implemented daily sport lessons decreed in 1955, and the Bavarian Landtag subsequently declined to implement the decision to begin the school year at Easter (in fact, all the other Länder subsequently adopted the Bavarian Autumn arrangement). Indeed, the problem of the deparliamentarisation of decision-making is often alluded to (and was recognised by the federal government in 1978: cf. Thränhardt 1990, p.184). Further problems with this method of policy-making include a lack of clarity about the political responsibility for decisions which have been taken, and the confusion of political lines of accountability for decisions.

The KMK has on some views become a bureaucratic instrument itself. Burchkardt, quoted in Thränhardt (1990, p.182), said that 'No federal law could be devised with such perfection and have such a centralised effect as these agreements'. However, the principle of unanimity can hinder joint decisions and in particular amendments to prevailing agreements, with party-political disagreements also causing further obstruction (ibid., pp.182–3).

Thränhardt (1990, p.188) argues that the first phase in the history of post-war German education policy can be found in the period of occupation and then the foundation of the federal republic, from1945 to 1953. The left wanted egalitarian reform, its main supporters being left-wing parties, unions, the adult education teachers' federation (*Volksschullehrerverbände*) and also the American military government. They argued that the traditional class school system should be abolished, as it was held responsible for the success of *Führerprinzip* (deference to the Nazi leader, Hitler) and for the arrogance of elites. By contrast, the right, comprising in the main the CDU/CSU, the universities, which had been purged of critical elements in 1933 and so were dominated by those who at least had acquiesced in the Nazi period, and grammar school teachers, opposed such reforms, instead giving support to more 'elitist' and confessional forms of education, in particular resisting changes to the three-tier system of education. The support of the CDU/CSU for more conservative positions certainly paid off: it led to the electoral success of the CDU/CSU, FDP and other right-wing parties in Schleswig-Holstein, Berlin and Hamburg in the period 1951–1953, with different conceptions of education policy proving a decisive factor in those elections. Equally, unusual coalitions involving the SPD, BHE (a party of expellees from the former German territories to the east) and the FDP came together in Baden-Württemberg and Bayern against confessional education (*Bekenntnisschule*) as favoured by the CDU/CSU.

From 1953 to 1963, the three-tier system consisting of *Hauptschule* ('secondary modern school', *Realschule* ('middle-tier school'), and *Gymnasium* ('grammar school') was introduced in all the Länder. It attempted to cater for the three different levels of academic ability, with parents, in the first instance, deciding which school was appropriate for their offspring. In 1955 it was cemented in the Düsseldorf Agreement between the Länder, a relatively early example of the Länder's willingness to harmonise policies on a voluntary basis (ibid., p.190). Further conservative elements of education policy were also retained: school fees existed in some Länder where neither Americans nor the SPD had prevented them (indeed, they existed in North-Rhein Westphalia up to the 1960s).

The period from 1964–1973 was one of 'education boom and euphoria' (Thränhardt 1990, pp.191–5). Initially, a relatively slow expansion took place compared to other western nations. But in 1964 the KMK appeared to endorse the expansion of education, demanding 'The education of the individual up to the summit of his abilities'. There was also criticism of the relatively low level of German educational expenditure. Debates in the field of education policy were spurred on by academic literature, which noted the low proportion of children from Catholic, working-class and rural backgrounds at grammar schools (and also girls). The relatively poor situation of Catholic children proved a challenge to Catholic politicians in the CDU/CSU, who were often the strongest defenders of differentiation by ability (Schmid 1990a).

The change of government of 1966, leading to a grand coalition at a federal level, moved things forward – apart from primary schools in North-Rhine Westphalia, confessional schools now largely came to an end, and the full division of school organisation into year groups was made possible by extension of the school system (Thränhardt 1990, p.195). Even in Bavaria, the end of confessional schools was brought about by pressure from the threat of referendums organised first by the FDP, then the SPD. There were two consequences of this development. On the one hand, the abolition of confessional schools across the federal republic aided the expansion of education, enabling far more schoolchildren to reach a level at which they could achieve qualifications. It also brought about the end (or at least a softening) of the conflict over religious education, which had proved so greatly divisive, both between left and right, and especially within the bourgeois elements of society (the FDP having been hostile to confessional schools).

The next change of government at a federal level, in 1969, brought about an SPD-FDP coalition, which proclaimed its desire to extend the reforms, with further expansion of education provision, echoing demands coming from the 1968 student protests. More support for schoolchildren after the end of compulsory education was introduced, and greater financial support was put in place for students, agreed at a federal level under the terms of the 'Federal Educational Support Law' (*Bundesausbildungsfördungsgesetz,* or *Bafög* for short, also the colloquial name given to student financial support), in 1971. In addition, SPD-led Länder, such as Hesse, introduced some comprehensive schools (*Gesamtschulen*), in moves regarded with some scepticism by the CDU, which favoured, at most, more limited pilots with teaching of children of mixed ability (Schmid 1990a, pp.307–9).

By the mid-1970s, however, this consensus had once again begun to erode (Thränhardt 1990, pp.196–9), with some Länder, such as Bavaria, and conservative elements more generally, becoming sceptical about the merits of further reform, and feeling it had gone too far. This view gained resonance after the oil price crisis and the economic decline it heralded, led to greater distributional conflicts. In this context, education could be expanded, but only at the expense of other areas of government expenditure, or of higher taxes. In the 1970s, there were greater conflicts over the further introduction of comprehensive schools – whereas the SPD-governed Länder wanted to continue to implement the concept, or at least to conduct permanent pilots, the CDU wanted to end any trials as soon as possible (although often did not close the schools affected once they had been set up).

There was also conflict over the issue of whether to introduce initial, non-selective years at the start of secondary education (known in different variants as the *Orientierungsstufe* or the *Förderstufe*): such models were favoured by the left, as they ameliorated the perceived negative effects of division according to ability, while the right felt they introduced comprehensive education by the back door and was far more sceptical. Conflicts between Christian and Social Democrats were also present in this period over the extent of applied subjects, to be combined with traditional ones, in grammar schools – their more widespread introduction was favoured by the left, but opposed by the CDU/CSU.

In general, there was a consistent growth in the numbers taking higher qualifications like the *Abitur* (school-leaving exam for pupils at grammar school). More pupils started to take the Abitur without going on to university. There were further arguments between left and right over the content of politics and social studies curricula, for instance with a dispute over whether to teach 'military' or 'peace' education (ibid., p.168). The at times heated conflict over personnel (with for instance the *Berufsverbot* – legislation barring those with a politically radical past from the teaching profession) were ameliorated as it was shown that the effort put into enforcing them was not matched by results. Major divisions continued over personnel policy in schools and universities, with the parties in government in the Länder intervening to 'carve up' posts.

The next major challenge to education in Germany was posed by the fall of the Berlin wall, and specifically by reunification (Phillips 1995). East Germany had a radically different system, where there was no differentiation according to ability until the 'extended upper school' (*erweiterte Oberschule*), which followed from the ten-year general polytechnical school (ibid., p.247). Immediately after reunification, a decision had to be taken whether to mirror the educational system in the 'old' republic, or to adopt a different, or hybrid system. The decision was taken by the then Federal Education Minister, Jürgen Möllemann (FDP), to go for a model as close as possible to the western one, though taking 'dove-tailing' (*Verzahnung*) as the preferred image, rather than, say, absorption. The Länder chose somewhat different types of school according to their political complexion (the only SPD-governed Landtag, Brandenburg, opted not to have a Hauptschule, instead allowing grammar schools and *Realschulen* to co-exist alongside comprehensive schools); Mecklenburg Lower Pomerania chose to have some comprehensive schools alongside the three main types of school in the west. Saxony-Anhalt and Thüringia went for a variation on the western system, with a *Sekundarschule*, with different streams within it (corresponding to those pursued by pupils at the Hauptschule and Realschule in other Länder), alongside grammar schools. Saxony went for a differentiated *Mittelschule* alongside the grammar schools (cf. Phillips 1995, p.245). Brandenburg was the only eastern Landtag to introduce 13 years of school leading up to the Abitur, with the other Länder opting for 12. Alongside this structural reorganisation, there was a perceived need for an increase in teacher training, as well as the release of those members of the teaching profession who were perceived to have been compromised by the old regime (the criterion being used tending to be collaboration with the *Stasi*, or holding higher party office, rather than simple party membership – Phillips 1995, p.249; Döbert 1997). On account of the history of children learning together for longer, before being differentiated by ability in the east, as well as the emphasis on 'equality' there, it might be expected that this will feed into the preferences of the population there, and potentially constrain the choices of CDU politicians in setting education policies.

As discussed in the introductory chapter, the PISA study of educational attainment brought education policy to the forefront of German public debate (Winkler 2005b). Reactions to the study were strongly coloured by different conceptions of education policy, however (Payk 2009). For instance, the CDU-led governments of Hesse and Bavaria argued for the retention of rigorous and early differentiation between different levels of ability. By contrast, Edelgard Bulmahn, the SPD Federal Education Minister, argued that PISA showed that 'Germany is world-class only in the social selection of children', and this had to be broken down once and for all with more support for all-day education (Spiegel, 12th May 2003).

Secondly, the debate over standards quickly translated into one over the scope of federalism, with the Bavarian Culture Minister, Hans Zehetmaier, with some support from his CDU colleagues, demanding an end to the joint task of education, in order to allow the Länder to go their own way without federal interference, while Edelgard Bulmahn argued that the challenge of PISA was to renew vertical and horizontal cooperation, with a national programme to raise standards (Spiegel, 26th February 2003).

4.1.3　Party positions on education policy: Two paradigms

From the picture painted above, two conclusions can be drawn. First, the variations in school systems at the Land level are not mainly, or even primarily, borne of the structural features of the Land, but rather of politics: different visions of education policy, underpinned by different values. Polarisation in Land-level education policy, and often bitter debates about school structure, demonstrate significant differences between politicians of different parties about what education policies should be pursued. We might expect, in the cases looked at here, the new CDU-led governments want to initiate significant policy change.

Secondly, however, the differences in education policy in the Länder reflect different histories, and have resulted in significant variations in school systems. As a result, this will significantly shape the context in which Land-level policy-makers have to operate, and a degree of path dependence (as discussed in Chapter 1) might be anticipated. In education policy, this is most obviously the case in relation to school structure: if a network of comprehensive schools has been created, a coalition of parents, teachers and pupils will (provided it is not obviously failing) have a stake in its continuation and will be likely to oppose a programme of school closures or aggressive reorganisation. This should temper our expectation of change in education policy as a result of a change of government.

The differences between political parties are immediately apparent when the party programmes in force at the time are consulted (e.g. CDU 1994; SPD 1997). The CDU programme's discussion of education begins with reference to the *Leistungsprinzip* ('Principle of merit', or 'principle of performance'): 'Equality of opportunity cannot be achieved by levelling down. ... The *Leistungsprinzip* demands that high performance is both demanded of individuals and is supported, and that everyone gets appropriate recognition for his performance' (CDU 1994, p.22). The implicit contrast here is with an alleged lack of interest in performance, and levelling down, by educationalists of the 1968 generation (Thurn 2004). Alongside the *Einheitsschule*, or 'one size fits all' school, one of the favoured derogatory terms of CDU education politicians is *Kuschelpädagogik* (the 'educational philosophy of cuddling'), with the assumption that children should just be supported, rather than challenged, and that 'everyone must have prizes'.

The programme goes on to make some substantive demands:

> We support streamlining educational curricula and pathways, shortening education times and differentiating what is offered. We support a

school system divided by ability, which recognises the differences in interest and ability. ... We want to retain the Hauptschule alongside the Realschule and the grammar school as independent educational courses with a different profile and qualifications. ... With the transition to a secondary school, alongside the wishes of parents, the recommendation of the school has to be given greater weight. ... It is the job of the school to provide general education and core knowledge. We support legally protected Protestant and Catholic religious education in our schools. Alongside this, religious education for members of other religious communities must be possible. We support all-day education/provision on a voluntary basis in all forms of school (CDU 1994, pp.22–3).

This stands in stark contrast to the SPD's programme:

Education has a value of its own for personal development. [It] must be open for everyone. Pupils ... are to be financially supported so that they can go their professional way regardless of the income of their parents. ... We want to offer all-day schools. We want more involvement of those affected including in decisions about which educational pathway to choose, and greater educational freedom in educational institutions. ... We want to couple the transmission of knowledge with social learning, in order to counteract competitive pressures from the world of work. Social democratic education policy wants to support, rather than select. We want schools which offer a variety of educational opportunities and qualifications, recognise the different interests and abilities of pupils, encourage them in a differentiated way, and so create more equality of opportunity. The comprehensive school is best suited to implementing our educational aims (SPD 1989, pp.30–1).

This gives us several elements of an ideal type, or paradigm (which fits comfortably with the history of the German education system outlined above): on the Christian democratic side, there should be a school system strongly differentiated by ability, and on the social democratic side there should be more comprehensive schools. Christian democrats will be insistent upon the provision of religious education of a Protestant or Catholic nature, and will allow other religions to be involved, but with a different status. Social democrats may deviate from this model; they have no explicit commitment to it. The Christian democratic paradigm places greater emphasis on core knowledge, whereas social democrats emphasise greater flexibility for teachers and pupils in curriculum content. This also has an impact upon testing arrangements: the Christian democratic paradigm will include more centralised testing, the social democratic paradigm will have less centralised testing, and greater discretion for individual teachers. The Christian democratic insistence on the *Leistungsprinzip* places a greater emphasis on testing, and performance more generally, than does the SPD's programme.

We can add to this different views of the role of the federal government in education policy, as discussed above in relation to parties' reactions to the PISA study. The Christian democratic paradigm emphasises the Länder having complete control over education policy, while coordinating where necessary, whereas the social democratic paradigm envisages a greater role for the federal government.

The SPD has a particular commitment to removing financial barriers to education. We might expect this to be reflected in the provision of *Lernmittelfreiheit* (the free provision of learning materials, notably school books). In several CDU-led Länder, such as Lower Saxony, North-Rhine Westphalia, and Baden-Württemberg, plans to reduce or remove the Lernmittelfreiheit were attacked by the SPD opposition (GEW 2008 provides a summary of provision). The CDU has sometimes been more sceptical about this. In an interview with the author, one CDU Education Minister stated: 'And [on this subject] I get very moralistic, and I say someone who doesn't want to buy his kid books, won't want to buy him shoes either, and then they can call for the state as well. Parents have a duty, regardless of how well or badly off they are, to buy books, we can't ask the state for everything' (Interview N).

On the Christian democratic side, all-day schools will only be supported if the afternoon elements are not compulsory, whereas there are no such caveats on the social democratic side. This also has an impact upon staffing arrangements: if the afternoon component of all-day schools is *optional*, there is no necessity for it to be provided by teachers, and indeed it might give children whose parents choose to take them home for the afternoon a disadvantage if it is. By contrast, the social democratic model of the all-day school, which integrates teaching and other activities throughout the day, will involve teachers in the afternoon (taz, 25th March 2008). As will be discussed in Chapter 5, any involvement of non-teachers in delivering education can encounter stiff resistance from trade unions.

The desire to shorten the period of education, referred to in the CDU's programme, gave rise to significant attempts at reform in a number of Länder during the period from 1999 onwards, and specifically the project to reduce the number of years of schooling prior to the Abitur from 13 to 12. Whereas in Saxony-Anhalt, an SPD-led government extended the time taken to reach the Abitur from 12 to 13 years in the 1990s (cf. Traeger 2005), several Land governments (including some SPD-led ones) went in the other direction by the late 1990s, starting, as is discussed in Chapter 6, with the Saarland. Pressure to reduce the time taken to reach the Abitur came particularly from employers, and the project was pursued with some vigour by CDU educational politicians. The SPD was altogether more cautious, at one point arguing that individual schools should decide on the length of time taken to reach the Abitur (Spiegel, 23rd April 2001). This issue played a role in a number of Land election campaigns; for instance, in Hesse in 2008, the SPD demanded a return to the Abitur being taken after 13 years, and the CDU's reduction to 12 years before the Abitur was taken was criticised in the Hamburg election campaign of 2008 as well (Focus, 5th March 2008). As a result, a shift to reaching the Abitur after 12 years is included in the Christian democratic paradigm. The higher 13-year period before reaching the Abitur is included in the social democratic paradigm, recognising however that this is not the consistent view of SPD-led governments.

The commitment to the *Leistungsprinzip* and the recognition of achievement in the CDU's programme leads to consideration of the method of grading in schools. Payk (2005), in his construction of 'ideal types' of education policy, places numerical grading of pupils' attainment from year 1 in the ideal type of Christian democratic education policy, along with grading of behaviour and teamwork. By contrast, his social democratic paradigm does not grade behaviour and teamwork, and supplements numerical grades with individual comments. This will be adopted for the paradigms in this study (with particular social democratic reluctance to introduce numerical grading for very young children), and it will be shown, in each of the cases discussed here, that grading is indeed an issue for education policy affected by ideological standpoints. The same applies to repetition of years (Payk 2005, p.23; Thurn 2004). In Germany, it is possible for a pupil who obtains poor grades to fail a year, and have to repeat it. This is often viewed critically by social democratic politicians. For instance, Andrea Ypsilanti, the SPD's candidate for Minister President, demanded an end to the practice in Hesse's election campaign of 2008; Ute Erdsiek-Rave, the SPD's Education Minister in Schleswig-Holstein, spoke of a 'moth-eaten relic in education', and of 'squandering of life' (Focus, 6th May 2008). Norbert Seller, the SPD's education spokesperson in Baden-Württemberg (a CDU-led Land in favour of retaining the practice), stated that it was 'educationally outdated and expensive' (SPD-BW 2008). By contrast, CDU-led Länder have been reluctant to see the practice blocked completely, suggesting it would lead to children doing whatever they fancied, and that repetition could sometimes be beneficial for children (Focus, 6th May 2008).

Finally, the paradigms differ in relation to the expectations of relationships with trade unions, and in particular with the GEW (*Gewerkschaft Erziehung und Wissenschaft*), the largest, education trade union, counting over 250,000 members, and affiliated to the DGB (the German Trade Union Confederation). The GEW has been a consistent supporter of measures counted here as part of the social democratic paradigm. For reasons to be discussed further in the section 3 of this chapter, we would expect SPD-led governments to retain closer links to trade unions than their CDU-led counterparts, all the more so in a domain of policy where the GEW's demands for particular policies went way beyond the levels of remuneration of its members, and into ideologically polarised issues in education policy. There are several other unions involved in representing German teachers, often specific to particular types of school, and also whether or not the teachers in question enjoy the status of *Beamte* (Traeger 2005). Naturally, we would expect less disagreement between CDU-led governments and unions more supportive of the Christian democratic education policy paradigm.

Pulling these different elements together, we reach two policy paradigms summarised in Table 4.1, and it will be against these that education policy change in the Länder will be analysed.

Table 4.1   Two paradigms of education policy

Social democratic paradigm	Christian democratic paradigm
Comprehensive education (or if unacceptable, late and flexible selection)	Early and rigid selection, with limited movement between types of school
Any selection based on parental choice	Selection based on tests/teacher assessment
High level of individual teacher discretion over curriculum content and testing	Centralised tests and examinations
Abitur after 13 years	Abitur after 12 years
Extensive pupil choice of subject	Limiting of pupil choice
Compulsory, integrated all day education	Half-day education with possibility of extension
Teachers provide education all day	Some supervision undertaken by volunteers/unqualified helpers
Limited reliance on grading	High reliance on grading
Grading only in secondary school	Grading from year 1
No grading of behaviour and teamwork	Grading of behaviour and teamwork
Limited repetition of years in event of poor performance	High level of repetition of years in event of poor performance
Free provision of school books	Parental contribution towards school books
No compulsory Religious Education (RE)	Compulsory RE
Non-Christian RE provided	No non-Christian RE provided
Opposition to Länder having exclusive control over policy	Support for Länder having complete control over policy
Partnership with trade unions	Limited involvement with unions

4.2 Childcare and family policy in Germany

4.2.1 Background and Land-level competence

As discussed in Chapter 2, like labour market policy, family policy – and in particular childcare policy – is an area where all three tiers of government share some responsibility. This section will, first, give some relevant history and background to childcare policy, sketch the legal framework making it clear what the Länder can do, and will then introduce the Christian democratic and social democratic policy paradigms operating in family policy.

As Hagemann (2006, pp.219–20) puts it, 'For working mothers, unified Germany, at least its western regions, remains a developing country'. She notes the low labour-market participation of women with children: although 61% of married women aged between 20 and 59 are in employment in Germany, only 38% of married women with children under 12 are in employment; 'In no other European country do so many women leave the labour market when they become mothers' (ibid., p.220). Amongst those who do return to work, part-time employment is predominant, with only 5% of working mothers of those aged 0 to 3 in western Germany working full-time, and 10% of those with children aged 3 to 6 (ibid., p.220). This policy has come under challenge, in part because of declining birth-rates, in part because of industry's desire not to lose women's skills to the labour market (Evers et al. 2005; Hagemann 2006).

Until the mid-1960s, institutional childcare provision was viewed with some suspicion in western Germany, with the family being viewed as the main unit for rearing children. Nursery facilities, such as there were, tended to be provided by the not-for-profit sector, notably by organisations close to the Catholic and Protestant Churches, and also the union movement. Almost all were open for half a day only. Hagemann argues that 'The chief opponents of the expansion of childcare and all-day schools in West Germany were the Catholic Church, the CDU, the CSU, and conservative Christian interest groups ... [They] continued to argue that such a policy would alienate children from the family and threaten the very substance of its child-rearing potential' (Hagemann 2006, p.235).

There was some shift in the 1970s and 1980s, with the expansion of nursery education in particular, although it – alongside regular schools – continued to be provided for only half a day (and thus was incompatible with both parents working full-time). There remained no social consensus about the desirability of pre-school and after-school provision, however, and this was barely available (Dienel 2002, p.116).

This picture was radically different in the German Democratic Republic (GDR): 'Public childcare was the condition for resocialisation according to the model of the working mother, and it was accordingly extended, including for children of school age' (ibid., p.115). Crèches also played a significant role in the GDR, including an 'educational' role, although that

Table 4.2   Available places in childcare institutions: % of children for whom a place was available

	Western Länder				Eastern Länder			
	1986	1990	1994	1998	1989	1990	1994	1998
Creches for children aged 0–3	1.6	1.8	2.2	2.8	56.4	54.2	41.3	36.3
Nursery schools	69.3	69.0	73.0	86.8	112[1]	97.7	96.2	111.8
After-school childcare institutions	3.0	3.4	3.5	5.9	60.6	32.4	22.6	47.7

Source: Dienel 2002, p.119

was focused more on conforming to collective norms than developing individuality and creativity (ibid., p.117).

Reunification obviously brought significant change to both parts of Germany, as their starting points in institutional childcare provision differed radically (see Table 4.2). A common legislative framework governing childcare (the *Kinder- und Jugendhilfegesetz*, KJHG, 'Child and Youth Support Law') came into effect in 1990, and, in 1992, a legal entitlement to a nursery place, according to need, was agreed, to come into force on 1st January 1996. The change was agreed alongside amendments to abortion laws, where there were also radically different starting points in the two parts of Germany. The legal entitlement led to an extension of childcare in western Germany, with around 600,000 new places being created, although the majority of these provided only four hours of provision per day (Dienel 2002, pp.118–19).

The KJHG (more properly known as Book 8 of the Social Code) continues to govern childcare provision. It provides the entitlement to services to support children, young people, and parents, and its guiding principles include prevention, integration and participation in the provision of services and benefits for young people. In a case in 1997, the Federal Constitutional Court ruled that the focus of childcare was still welfare-related, and therefore legitimated the involvement of the federal government, whereas a purely educational role would have strengthened the authority of the Länder (OECD 2004, p.28). The principle of subsidiarity applies in welfare provision: the family is the smallest social institution, and superior bodies may only carry out tasks if the lower unit is unable to on its own; this also governs institutional relations, so that public bodies should

---

[1]This refers to spare capacity in the eastern Länder.

only provide childcare provision where voluntary bodies cannot (ibid., p.29).

Book 8 of the Social Code – as federal legislation – grants some latitude to the Länder. They can pass further laws or decrees on such topics as the parental fees for childcare, staffing, parental participation and other issues. The Code also stipulates that local government units (districts, or *Landkreise*, and cities, or *kreisfreie Städte*) have to establish a youth welfare office, which organises provision locally (ibid., pp.32–4). There is a wide variety of regulations amongst the Länder, with no two Länder being the same; the extent of regulation and of charging, and the organisation of provision, all vary (ibid., pp.34–5), as does the extent to which childminders, as an alternative to institutional provision, are used and regulated (ibid., p.80).

Responsibility for paying for nursery provision varies from Land to Land. The highest proportion of funding comes in each case from local authorities; it is in some cases supplemented by individual Land governments, who in 1999 contributed up to 51% of the cost – though some Länder placed all responsibility for meeting costs at a local level (ibid., p.140). Because in the 'city-states' of Hamburg, Bremen and Berlin the Land government is also the relevant local authority, it pays all the public contribution. In addition, in each case (apart from the Saarland, which will be discussed in detail in Chapter 6), a parental contribution to the cost is made, amounting to an average of around 20% in the eastern Länder, and 23% in the west. It does not exceed 3–4% of household income, with parents on social assistance receiving the service free of charge (Evers et al. 2005, pp.200–1). Finally, an average of around 10% of the cost is met by the providers themselves, in the case of voluntary provision, such as the relevant churches. The role of private, commercial (i.e. profit-making) providers in nursery school provision is very small – in most Länder they cannot receive public subsidies and therefore would not be able to compete with the not-for-profit sector (ibid., p.200).

As can be seen from this summary, therefore, childcare provision is an example of a policy area subject to interlocking policy-making, with the Land governments playing a significant role, but still one requiring the involvement of a variety of other actors, including the federal government, local government, and the providers. The radically different starting points, different levels of influence of the Catholic Church, and also different histories of provision, will obviously be expected to shape the parameters within which Land-level policy is set; we might anticipate a high degree of path-dependency, notably in contrasting provision between eastern and western Germany (Hagemann 2006).

Although other policies towards families are largely the responsibility of other actors (Dienel 2002; Gerlach 2004; Opielka 2004), Land governments can play some, albeit limited, role. Gerlach (2004, pp.126–9) identifies a number of opportunities for this:

- Implementation of federal laws through the overall responsibility for policy implementation that the Länder enjoy;
- Using exclusive competencies in educational and cultural policy, as well as opportunities in areas of competing legislative competency (cf. Chapter 3);
- Provision of money to families on top of that coming from the federal government (although this is restricted by budgetary pressures and the constitutional guarantee to ensure comparable standards of living).

Examples of action that can be taken – aside from the provision of institutional childcare – include supplementary childcare payments, family advice and education, support for families, support for family holidays, building of family housing, and support for foundations, for example those which help families who find themselves in difficult circumstances.

4.2.2 Party positions on childcare and family policy: Two paradigms

As mentioned above, there were significant disagreements in the post-war period between politicians of the CDU and of the SPD on childcare and family policy, both in the degree of acceptance of institutionalised childcare, and in the view of the family that this reflected. Looking at the party programmes in place throughout the time period of this study (1999–2006), there are significant differences, although the CDU's view had certainly evolved since the 1950s. The CDU programme included a section entitled 'Supporting family and marriage' (CDU 1994). Key statements included:

- 'Marriage is the guiding principle of the community of man and woman. It is the best foundation for the common responsibility of mother and father in bringing up children' (p.16).
- 'We want to realise a legal entitlement to a nursery place, so that children have encouragement, support and contact with other children. In particular we support private initiative and nursery schools in independent, not-for-profit schools' (p.17).
- 'We stand for women and men being able to combine family and work better. Many women and increasingly also men provisionally or completely devote themselves to work in the family and bring up children. That means security and protection for the children. ... We Christian Democrats want a stronger recognition of the performance of family work' (p.18).

Although there is therefore support for childcare provision, the emphasis (in these and other sections) is strongly on making the world of work flexible, to allow time off for parents – predominantly mothers – to look after children, rather than to facilitate full-time employment. There is no reference to pre-nursery childcare.

The SPD's programme over this period contained significant differences (SPD 1989). Key statements included:

- 'Still, dominant culture is shaped by men. ... Women are allotted the private sphere, house work and bringing up children, and the role that women have played in history is played down or falsified' (pp.20–1);
- A desire to reduce working times for *all* workers (p.21);
- 'Nursery schools and all-day schools are amongst the prerequisites which make work and family compatible for women and men' (p.21);
- 'All forms of partnership have an entitlement to protection and legal security; none must be discriminated against, including same-sex partnerships' (p.22).

This constitutes a different view of the family; the SPD places a greater emphasis on the ability of women to work alongside looking after children, as well as to return to work after a phase of looking after children; and there is no expressed scepticism about state, rather than independent provision. An issue not covered in either programme is the cost of childcare, although free childcare is a long-standing aspiration of several SPD Land parties. The CDU is also sceptical about any *disadvantaging* of parents who choose to look after their children at home *vis-à-vis* those who go to work, which could speak against complete ending of fees. As will be discussed in section 3, concerning labour market policy, the SPD is also less sceptical about regulation than the CDU. From these statements, two ideal types of childcare and family policy are proposed at Land level, and set out in Table 4.3 below.

Table 4.3   Two paradigms of childcare and family policy

Social democratic paradigm	Christian democratic paradigm
Provision free for all	Provision only available at cost
Subsidised provision starts at age 0	Subsidised provision starts at age 3
Subsidised provision extensively available	Subsidised provision available where demand exists
Provision in formal institutions	Flexible methods of provision
Close regulation of childcare institutions	Light-touch regulation of childcare institutions
No preference about types of family unit	Support for 'traditional' family

Seeleib-Kaiser et al. (2005) argue that the CDU's policy paradigm towards families has shifted, with greater support for external childcare provision (albeit a private model). The Christian democratic paradigm stated above does explicitly support some childcare provision. However, aside from the matter of the precise form of provision, the Christian democratic paradigm includes the CDU's scepticism about institutional support for children aged under three, and also its disagreement with the assumption that women should work, rather than be at home caring for children. This study is therefore a good opportunity to see whether the shift identified by Seeleib-Kaiser et al. is reflected at the Land level, closer to the grassroots membership than federal politicians.

The relevance of this debate within the CDU about the role of the family was emphasised with a conflict on a federal level, shortly after the end of the time frame being considered here. When Ursula von der Leyen, the CDU's federal family minister, proposed a legal entitlement to childcare for children aged 1–3, some CDU and CSU politicians, as well as representatives of the Catholic Church, reacted angrily. Jörg Schönbohm, the CDU Chairman in Brandenburg, accused von der Leyen of belittling women who chose not to go to work (Spiegel, 21st February 2007); and Bishop Mixa of Augsburg said that von der Leyen was turning women into baby-making machines, damaging children and families, and fetishising households where both parents worked (Spiegel, 22nd February 2007). The CSU successfully insisted that there should be the possibility, in future legislation, of childcare vouchers being accompanied by cash payments to parents who chose not to avail themselves of childcare facilities, in a move strongly criticised by the SPD, who called it a 'stove supplement' (Spiegel, 25th May 2007).

This does, therefore, appear to be a contested domain within the CDU, and it will be helpful to understand what difference its participation in government at a Land level makes to policy in this area: whether a shift towards the traditional CDU paradigm is evident, or whether its paradigm has in fact changed.

4.3   Labour market policy

4.3.1   Background and Land-level competencies

In contrast to education policy, where the Länder are clearly in the driving seat, labour market policy sees competence shared. As will be discussed, it primarily resides with the federal government and its agency, the Federal Labour Organisation (which was renamed the Federal Labour Agency in 2004). However, the Land governments, municipalities, and also the European Union, all play a role.

As will be demonstrated for each of the Länder discussed, although their competence in labour market policy is limited, they are under significant pressure to act – and the issue of the labour market featured quite strongly in election campaigns in Saxony-Anhalt and the Saarland (as well as, to a more limited degree, in Hesse). Schmid and Blancke have undertaken extensive research on labour market policy at the Land level (cf. Blancke and Schmid 1998; Blancke 1999; Schmid and Blancke 2001; Blancke 2003; Blancke 2004; Schmid et al. 2004). They argue:

> High unemployment in some Länder means that their governments hardly have any choice but to become active in labour market policy, as low unemployment is considered an indicator of 'good politics'. However, it has to be noted that the financial parameters for active labour market policy by the Länder are very limited, and the measures of the Länder can in no way replace those of the federal government and the Federal Labour Organisation (Blancke and Schmid 1998, pp.8–9).

Blancke distinguishes between employment policy (which includes fiscal and finance policies performing macroeconomic steering, as well as certain regulations which have an impact on the labour market, such as protection from dismissal) and labour market policy in a narrower sense. The latter includes the regulation of compensatory payments following unemployment (passive labour market policy) and 'all the measures which selectively influence the relationships between demand and supply, and firm-level and above-firm level labour markets – active labour market policy – for instance through employment placement, qualification, retraining and similar measures' (Blancke 2004, p.61).

Blancke notes the possibility for influence on employment policy by the Länder is limited, although they are of course able to introduce proposals through the Bundesrat. It is however the role of the federal government to propose legislation in this area, which is agreed by the Bundestag (most relevant legislation is to be found in Book 3 of the Social Code). Administration of unemployment benefit, and job placement for those in receipt of it, was a matter for the Federal Labour Organisation, prior to the Hartz reforms from 2003 onwards, when the picture got more complicated. Yet even in these circumstances, there are a number of possibilities for Land influence on labour market policy (Blancke 2004, pp.62–7):

- Some influence can be exercised through the Bundesrat (though whether or not the consent of a majority of the Bundesrat is required depends on the legislation in question);
- The Länder (as well as local government) can invest, and create jobs in the public sector;
- The Länder can get involved in the implementation of federal programmes, for instance supporting cooperation between labour offices and regional companies;

- Legislative opportunities exist where the federal government chooses not to legislate (although in practice creating binding commitments is undesirable, because of budget pressures);
- The Federal Social Assistance Law (prior to the Hartz reforms and the merger of unemployment and social assistance) gave the Länder, alongside local government, some capacity to get involved, especially if they brought in additional funding;[2]
- Although the federal government is responsible for negotiations with the European Union, detailed planning and implementation of EU-led programmes, from such funding streams as the European Social Fund, often falls to Land governments.

Amongst the active measures that can be undertaken are:

- Supply-side measures, such as qualification and training measures, to ensure that the workforce meets the needs of employers. These are often targeted at groups particularly at risk of unemployment, or those who are already unemployed;
- Demand-side measures, such as job creation schemes and wage subsidies/ 'top-ups' in different forms;
- Infrastructure measures, such as active job placement programmes, and support for infrastructure and coordination (Blancke 2004, pp.85–95).

Job creation schemes – that is, those creating jobs in the so-called 'Second Labour Market' (publicly funded jobs, as opposed to the 'First', or regular, labour market) – have come in for significant criticism since the 1990s. The stated aim of such measures tended to be reintegration into the regular labour market, and on some accounts they failed to achieve much success in this regard (ibid., pp.86–7). However, such schemes (notably the 'ABM', or *Arbeitsbeschaffungsmassnahmen* – 'job creation measures') have played a major role in several Länder, notably in the east. As will be discussed in Chapters 5, 6, and 7, in each of the cases studied here, the CDU expressed considerable doubts about such job creation schemes and the second labour market in its Land election programmes, considering them acceptable only for small groups for a short period.

---

[2]The Länder had a keen interest in this, until the merger of social and unemployment assistance at the start of 2005. If they supported local authorities in getting recipients of social assistance back into the labour market for a period, these recipients would become entitled to unemployment assistance again, and would cease to receive social assistance. Social assistance was administered and financed by municipalities, unemployment assistance by the Federal Labour Organisation. Accordingly, the municipalities would save money – which could reduce their need for funding from the Land government (cf. Blancke 2004, p.69).

By contrast, wage top-ups, known as *Kombilohn*, have not been used anything like as widely as ABM, although numerous different models have been tested (cf. Blancke 2004, pp.112–30; Forschungsverbund 2000; Forschungsverbund 2001; FES 2003). The best-known of these was the 'Mainz model', which subsidised employees' social insurance contributions in low-paid work, provided this was remunerated at the level of the sectoral wage agreement (*Tarif*) or the regular local level, and the employee had been out of work for six months previously. In general, although some SPD-led Land governments (most notably that in Rheinland-Palatinate) have experimented with wage top-ups of this nature, the SPD, and in particular those closest to the trade union movement within it, have been sceptical about the encouragement of a low-pay sector by this or other means; this scepticism is all the stronger if the low-wage sector undermines sectoral wage agreements, and if there is a sense in which companies are being paid to undermine them (Blancke 2004, p.119). To such sceptics, at the most, support for workers' social insurance payments would be acceptable. In more recent pronouncements, SPD politicians have been more supportive of wage subsidies, but only in combination with a minimum wage, which was vehemently opposed by most sections of the CDU (Die Zeit, 2nd January 2006). The CDU is altogether more supportive of the idea of wage top-ups, and more comfortable with the notion of a low-paid sector. Indeed, this was one of the toughest points of disagreement between CDU and SPD politicians in coalition negotiations in Saxony-Anhalt in 2006 (Interview M).

Josef Schmid and various collaborators (for instance Schmid et al. 2004, pp.163–8) have divided the different Länder by their labour market policies as falling into the following categories:

- 'Push' Länder: these are those Länder with a high level of innovation and active intervention in labour market policy, intensive coordination with labour market and economic actors, and a high level of expenditure;
- 'Pull' Länder: these are the Länder with middling to low innovation and levels of intervention in labour market policy, low levels of coordination with other actors, and low levels of spending; expenditure is strongly targeted on groups at high risk of unemployment;
- 'Stay' Länder: these are the Länder with low levels of innovation and depth of involvement, low levels of coordination, and high levels of targeting on specific groups, but with significant levels of spending.

Western SPD-led Länder are predominant amongst the 'push' Länder, western CDU-led Länder are predominant among the 'pull' Länder, and the poorer western Länder and eastern Länder (regardless of the party in government) are predominant amongst the 'stay' Länder (cf. also Baum et al. 2004).

A major series of reforms were undertaken in Germany following the report of the Hartz Commission in 2002 (von Berchem 2005; Kemmerling and Bruttel 2006; Malik 2008). Amongst its features were the creation of temporary work agencies, tighter definitions of suitable work and more flexible sanctions regimes, tax and benefit incentives to take on low-paid work, internal reorganisation of the Federal Labour Organisation, and, of particular significance, the merger of unemployment assistance and social assistance. Previously, those who had been in work with a sufficient contributions history received unemployment benefit at a rate of up to 67% of previous income for up to 32 months; they then shifted onto unemployment assistance, which was paid for an unlimited duration at a level of up to 53%. Those without sufficient contributions history, or who were not available for work, received social assistance, from the local authority, at a subsistence level. Following the Hartz reforms, after a period on unemployment benefit, all recipients moved onto a new transfer payment, called 'unemployment benefit 2' (ALG 2), set at a subsistence level.

These reforms all required the consent of the Bundesrat, and so in the forthcoming chapters, the stance of the three Länder on these reforms is examined, in as much as it is relevant to the paradigms of labour market policy set out below, and where the negotiations fell within the parliamentary term under consideration.

One particular dispute between SPD and CDU politicians concerned responsibility for job placement activity. The SPD favoured, and the federal government initially proposed, a model which gave the Federal Labour Agency complete responsibility for all job placements. By contrast, the CDU/CSU proposed to give full responsibility to municipalities (under the supervision of the Länder). The outcome was a compromise, with – in most areas – placement being shared by joint bodies set up by municipalities and the Federal Labour Agency, but with some municipalities (so-called *Optionskommunen*) taking full responsibility (cf. Malik 2008, pp.3–5). A handful of areas continued to have responsibility divided between the Federal Labour Agency and the municipality, without the formation of a joint body, because agreement on the appropriate model could not be reached The debate over responsibility for job placement activity reflects conflict more generally over the desirability of cooperative or competitive elements of federalism (cf. Sturm 2006), and the possible impact of decentralisation of responsibility for welfare more generally (Peterson 1995), with parties of the left being more sceptical of decentralisation than those of the right.

4.3.2 Social democratic and Christian democratic paradigms of labour market policy

In contrast to education policy, it is not straightforward to set down clear, universally applicable fault-lines in labour market policy at a Land level, and studies of this area (Blancke and Schmid 1998; Blancke 2004; Schmid et al. 2004; Malik 2008) have all found significant variation. The policies of CDU-led and SPD-led Länder are not always distinct, nor do CDU-led Länder, or SPD-led Länder, always pursue the same agenda. However, as outlined in the introduction, these paradigms are not approximations of actual positions taken by particular governments, but *ideal types*, and it can be seen from the above discussion that there is a pattern in positions taken by the CDU, and the SPD, at a Land level. To start with, the SPD places greater emphasis on active labour market instruments than the CDU, and it is more cautious about promoting a low-pay sector and wage top-ups (at least in the absence of a minimum wage); and the CDU is more in favour of decentralisation of responsibility for labour market policy.

In its party programme in force during the period in question, the SPD states:

> The right to work is a human right. It is the duty of a democratic and social state, governed by justice, to ensure full employment. Unemployment is not an individual risk which can be insured against, but a socially caused problem which has to be solved politically. ... We want to finance jobs, not unemployment (SPD 1989, pp.27–8).

The SPD's programme confines itself to quite general aspirations. The tone of the CDU's programme over the same period is rather different, and it provides more detail:

> We are aiming for full employment. ... The best policy for the labour market is the creation of long-term, competitive jobs by investment. ... Structural change and labour market policy go hand in hand. A successful labour market policy is decentralised and flexible. In all labour market measures the aim has to be followed of offering the highest possible number of unemployed people a job, and strengthening the incentives for a move into a regular job. ... We demand that social partners recognise the special character of ABMs [job-creation measures] and agree to special, lower pay rates. That also applies to opportunities for the long-term unemployed: introductory pay agreements are necessary which facilitate payment below the regular pay agreement (CDU 1994, p.47).

We can expect, then, support for payment below the level of sectoral wage agreements to come from the CDU side, and an acceptance of a low-wage sector in order to create jobs (something viewed with suspicion by social democrats). In addition, CDU-led Länder can be expected to be more inclined to leave job creation to the market, and to emphasise the need for swift integration in the first labour market (whereas the SPD's programme does not exclude long-term subsidised labour; indeed, this is an implicit requirement if the right to work is a human right, and it is the job of politics to realise it). The CDU-led Länder are more likely to pursue policies within the 'pull' category of labour market policy, whereas the SPD-led Länder will likely fall closer to the 'push' category. The 'stay' category might be expected of CDU-led Länder with high levels of unemployment.

It is also suggested in the CDU's programme that increases in pay should be related to increased productivity, and there should be greater flexibility in determining wage rates for different sectors. There is no such reference in the SPD's programme, which states:

> Autonomy in setting wage rates is a central part of democracy. We will defend it against every attack. Sectoral wage agreements, which secure and strengthen the legal position of individual workers, give rise to a need for trade unions with an ability to strike (SPD 1989, p.51).

Here, too, the tone is markedly different in the CDU's document; there is a commitment to securing social peace and social partnership (between employers' representatives and trade unions), but it sits alongside support for 'privatisation, the reduction of subsidies, [and] deregulation' (CDU 1994, p.33).

We can, then, add a commitment to some labour market deregulation and deviation from sectoral wage agreements to the Christian democratic paradigm, by contrast with the social democratic one. Finally, the relationship between the government and trade unions can be included in the alternative paradigms. The CDU has a labour wing (and indeed German Christian democracy, in common with that of the consociational democracies, has some tradition of its own trade unions), but we would expect employers' organisations to be treated as equal social partners (van Kersbergen, 1995). By contrast, SPD-led Länder might be expected to have a closer relationship to trade unions, in the light of their party programme. Armingeon (1989) found this confirmed: 'Data from the 1981 elite survey ... showed no severe programmatic differences between the leaders of the SPD and those of the DGB [German Trade Union Confederation] and its affiliates. The major line of attitudinal cleavage runs between the SPD and the unions on the one side, and the Christian Democratic parties (CDU/CSU) and business elites on the other' (Armingeon 1989, p.11).

Pulling these differences together, we can derive two policy paradigms which will assist us in assessing policy change – or lack of it – in the Länder examined here. These are summarised in Table 4.4.

The period from 1999, in particular, saw German social democracy change considerably. Following the resignation of Oskar Lafontaine as Federal Finance Minister and SPD Chairman, the SPD moved sharply to the right on labour market policy (Taylor-Gooby et al. 2004; Hough and Sloam 2007), and it would be right to speak of a paradigm shift. This shift was further

Table 4.4 Two paradigms of labour market policy

Social democratic paradigm	Christian democratic paradigm
Willingness to contemplate long-term subsidised state jobs	Rejection of long-term subsidised state jobs
Reluctance to subsidise private sector	Willing to subsidise private sector
Active labour market measures appropriate for general labour market	Active measures only for special needs groups (e.g. disabled, long-term unemployed) for limited period
Reluctance to create extensive low-paid sector	Encouragement of low-paid sector, e.g. through 'Kombilohn' (wage subsidies)
Rejection of localisation/decentralisation	Support for localisation/decentralisation
Rejection of deregulation	Support for deregulation
Apprenticeships and jobs-creation schemes paid at Tarif (collectively agreed) level	Apprenticeships and job-creation schemes paid at lower level
Privileged partnership with unions	Parity of partnership with social partners, or limited partnership

evidenced by the Hartz reforms of 2002 onwards. Nonetheless, in two of the three Länder discussed in this study, this shift was in its infancy at the time the CDU entered government, and in any event, these are ideal types, rather than approximations of the policies of a particular social democratic government at a particular time. The social democratic paradigm sketched above is consistent with the SPD's party programme in force during the period in question, which had not adapted to the change in the direction of the party at the level of the federal government. As a result, throughout this study the 'Social democratic paradigm' in relation to labour market policy will refer to social democracy before its recent shift towards the centre ground.

Given the preponderance of different actors involved in setting policy in this domain, as well as the radically different labour markets in the Länder considered, we might anticipate there will be some variation in the labour market policies pursued. It might also be an area where Länder with more limited budgets find themselves 'steered' in the policy direction they take by external actors, notably the federal government. However, the paradigms put forward are quite distinct, and it is interesting to see the extent to which the party composition of the government leads to actual policy change in this area.

5
The Case of Hesse 1999–2003

5.1 Background

As outlined in the introduction, Hesse was chosen as a case study for three reasons: it is a relatively large, western Land, it is amongst the wealthier Länder, and it is one which contributes to, rather than receives from, other Länder as part of the fiscal equalisation mechanism (*Länderfinanzausgleich*). It also witnessed a dramatic change of government, with a Social Democrat-led administration being replaced in 1999 by a particularly strident Christian Democrat-led one. These factors suggest that circumstances for a clear shift in policies pursued at the Land level were extremely promising.

However, there are two specific factors which mitigate against such a shift. First, as Schmidt's previous study showed (Schmidt 1980), supported by Lees' later study (Lees 2000), the long-standing SPD-led government would have been responsible for civil service appointments, and it is likely that a number of senior posts would be filled by those unsympathetic to change, and potentially in a position to obstruct it. Secondly, the CDU did not win an outright majority in 1999, instead forming a coalition with the FDP, which could be expected to prompt some deviation from the Christian democratic paradigm.

The state was created by the American occupying powers in 1945 as 'Greater Hesse', including the state of Hesse which existed in Prussian times, excluding its area to the left of the Rhine, and also the Prussian province of Hesse-Nassau. Between the foundation of the state in September 1945, and the first Land election in December 1946, there were a variety of provisional structures, culminating in an elected assembly which agreed on the Land's new constitution (Schiller 2004, p.224).

5.1.1 Social structure/Religious affiliation

As indicated in the introduction, Hesse is one of the larger German Länder, with a population of 6,098,000 at the end of 2004. Some 29% of the population live in the ten largest towns and cities, including 656,000 in Frankfurt am Main alone. The population has grown, steadily, since 1946 (Hessische Landesregierung 2006, pp.99–101). As will be discussed in Chapter 6, this contrasts particularly sharply with developments in Saxony-Anhalt, where a dramatic decline in the Land's population posed significant challenges to policy-makers. Hesse's population, in common with Germany as a whole, was gradually ageing (although not to the same, dramatic extent as in Saxony-Anhalt), causing an increase in the number of older people needing care, and a decline in the number of children of primary school age (ibid., pp.134–6).

Hesse has the highest proportion of non-German citizens of any German Land, with the exception of the city-states of Hamburg, Berlin and Bremen; non-Germans represent over 12% of the population. Turks are the largest of these groups, with around 188,000 in 2004, representing 25% of all foreign citizens (ibid., p.155).

Hesse is largely, though not overwhelmingly, a Protestant Land. According to the relevant churches, around 2.5 million Hesse residents are members of the Protestant Church, and a further 1.5 million are members of the Catholic Church, out of the overall population of 6.1 million. In comparison with the other Länder discussed in this study, it has a far lower proportion of Catholics than the Saarland, but a significantly higher proportion of church members (taking Protestants and Catholics together) than Saxony-Anhalt. Some church influence might be expected upon education policy, in particular, as a result of this.

5.1.2 Economy and fiscal position

As noted in the introduction, one reason for the selection of Hesse as a case study was that it was a relatively prosperous Land. This could impact in a number of ways upon policy-makers. The Land's prosperity could be expected to widen the range of possible policy choices through greater fiscal means but conversely, it would also lessen pressures for fiscal retrenchment which could be used as a rationale for policy change.

Hesse's GDP per inhabitant was 32,060 Euro in 2004, significantly above the federal average of 26,390 Euro, and the highest of all the Länder apart from the city-states. Its productivity was also consistently higher than the national average between 1991 and 2004 (Statistisches Bundesamt 2006, pp.68–74). Wage rates in Hesse were also the highest of any of the Länder in three surveys, undertaken in 1991, 1995 and 2004 (ibid., p.74).

Table 5.1 Unemployment in Hesse 1999–2003

Year	1999	2000	2001	2002	2003
Unemployment in %	9.4	8.1	7.4	7.8	8.8
Federal unemployment in %	11.7	10.7	10.3	10.8	11.6

Source: Statistisches Bundesamt

Unemployment in Hesse was below the federal average in the period from 1999 to 2003, as is illustrated by Table 5.1. Hesse's unemployment was below the average of western German Länder, and ranked fourth amongst these in 2003/4 (ibid., p.144).

As will be discussed later in this chapter, this is of significance in setting the background to labour market policies pursued at the Land level and through the Bundesrat. High levels of unemployment may make policymakers resistant to move in the direction of the Christian democratic paradigm.

It might be expected that a Land with this level of prosperity would be in a relatively strong fiscal position. Yet in reality, Hesse's budget was in quite a challenging position. Historically, Hesse's public spending was significantly above the average for west German Länder excluding citystates. In his 2000 study, Seitz found it to be 5,386 DM per inhabitant, the second highest of these Länder in 1996, which had an average per capita expenditure of 5,064 DM (Seitz 2000, p.193). The Land's government had persistent difficulties in submitting a budget which conformed to Article 115 of the Basic Law, which requires that new borrowing is at or below the level of investment (Spiegel, 17th January 2003). The Land government, of course, pointed to the fact that its expenditure on the fiscal equalisation mechanism between the Länder was significantly higher than its new debt: between 1999 and 2006, the Land spent 16,644 billion Euros on redistribution to the poorer Länder, while taking on 9,902 billion Euros in new credit (Hessische Landesregierung 2006, p.107). In 2002, for instance, the Land's overall expenditure was 18,121 billion Euros, of which 2,038 billion Euros went on redistribution. 9.2% of the Land's expenditure went on investment, and a further 7.9% went on debt servicing – an overall cost of 1,271.4 billion Euros, or 208 Euros per person (Landesregierung Hessen 2007).

As discussed in Chapter 3, the Länder have relatively little control over revenue raising power (and even less over fiscal redistribution, where Hesse was one of a number of Länder to challenge the mechanism before the Federal Constitutional Court), this does point to significant fiscal constraints on the state government. These were very much in evidence from 1999 to 2003.

5.1.3   Politics in Hesse

Tables 5.2 and 5.3 point to an important feature of post-war politics in Hesse: the dominance, in government, of the SPD. From 1946 to 1999, the SPD led the government for all but four years (1987–1991). However, the SPD's claim on the popular vote has not been hegemonic – at times, even when in government, it fell behind the CDU, but the SPD managed to form coalitions to retain leadership of the government. Given the relative prosperity of the Land, this might seem surprising (as discussed in the introduc-

Table 5.2 Landtag election results in Hesse 1946–2003

Year	SPD		CDU		LDP/FDP		Green		GDP/BHE		NPD		KPD	
	%	Seats	%	Seats	%	Seats	%	Seats	%	Seats	%	Seats	%	Seats
1946	44.3	42	37.3	35	8.1	6	–	–	–	–	–	–	9.7	7
1946	42.7	38	30.9	28	15.7	14	–	–	–	–	–	–	10.7	10
1950	44.4	47	18.8	12	31.8	21	–	–	–	–	–	–	4.7	–
1954	42.6	44	24.1	24	20.5	21	–	–	7.7	7	–	–	3.4	–
1958	46.9	48	32.0	32	9.5	9	–	–	7.4	7	–	–	–	–
1962	50.8	51	28.8	28	11.5	11	–	–	6.3	6	–	–	–	–
1966	51.0	52	26.4	26	10.4	10	–	–	4.3	–	7.9	8	–	–
1970	45.9	53	39.7	46	10.1	11	–	–	–	–	3.1	–	–	–
1974	43.2	49	47.3	53	7.4	8	–	–	–	–	1.0	–	–	–
1978	44.3	50	46.0	53	6.6	7	–	–	–	–	–	–	–	–
1982	42.8	49	45.6	52	3.1	–	8.0	9	–	–	–	–	–	–
1983	46.2	51	39.4	44	7.6	8	5.9	7	–	–	–	–	–	–
1987	40.2	44	42.1	47	7.8	9	9.4	10	–	–	–	–	–	–
1991	40.8	46	40.2	46	7.4	8	8.8	10	–	–	–	–	–	–
1995	38.0	44	39.2	45	7.4	8	11.2	13	–	–	–	–	–	–
1999	39.4	46	43.4	50	5.1	6	7.2	8	–	–	–	–	–	–
2003	29.1	33	48.8	56	7.9	9	10.1	12	–	–	–	–	–	–

Source: Landeswahlleiter

Table 5.3   Land governments in Hesse 1946–2007

Years	Parties in Government	Minister President
1946–1950	SPD/CDU	Christian Stock (SPD)
1950–1954	SPD	Georg August Sinn (SPD)
1954–1958	SPD/GB/BHE	Georg August Sinn (SPD)
1958–1962	SPD/GB/BHE	Georg August Sinn (SPD)
1962–1966	SPD/GDP/BHE	Georg August Sinn (SPD)
1966–1970	SPD	Georg August Sinn (SPD)
1970–1974	SPD until Dec 1970, SPD/FDP thereafter	Albert Oswald (SPD)
1974–1978	SPD/FDP	1974–1976 Albert Oswald (SPD)
		1976–1978 Holger Börner (SPD)
1978–1982	SPD/FDP	Holger Börner (SPD)
1982–1983	SPD	Holger Börner (SPD)
1983–1987	1983–1984 SPD	Holger Börner (SPD)
	1984–1985 SPD in cooperation with Greens	
	1985–1987 SPD/Green	
1987–1991	CDU/FDP	Walter Wallmann (CDU)
1991–1995	SPD/Green	Hans Eichel (SPD)
1995–1999	SPD/Green	Hans Eichel (SPD)
1999–2003	CDU/FDP	Roland Koch (CDU)
2003–2007	CDU	Roland Koch (CDU)

Source: Hessische Landesregierung

tion, all other things being equal one might expect richer Länder to tend to support the CDU, and poorer ones to support the SPD). The Land's religious composition, however, would indicate a greater propensity to elect social democrats; indeed, the strongly Catholic orientation of Hesse's CDU was one reason for the CDU's weakness in the immediate post-war period (Schiller 2004, p.228).

It is also worth noting that in the early years of the Land's development, the relative weakness of the CDU was partly due to competition on the right of the political spectrum: from the GDP/BHE (*Gesamtdeutsche Partei/ Bund der Heimatvertriebenen und Entrechteten* – 'All-German Party/Alliance of Expellees and Disenfranchised'), which represented in particular the significant population of Germans who had been expelled from the former eastern territories; the FDP, which under August-Martin Euler was a supporter of the nationalist, right wing of the FDP; and, for a brief period in the 1960s, the National Democratic Party of Germany, the NDP (ibid., p.230).

Reflecting this competition, from the 1970s onwards the CDU in Hesse, under Alfred Dregger, pursued a strongly conservative, right-wing course. Meanwhile, from 1969–1982 there was an SPD/FDP coalition at the federal level, and this was mirrored at the Land level in Hesse – in part with the aim of stabilising the coalition at a federal level (ibid., p.231).

In 1982, the FDP failed to get the 5% of votes necessary for representation in the Landtag, and the Green Party gained representation in Hesse's Landtag for the first time, assisted partly by the presence of significant environmental conflicts over infrastructure (most notably the Frankfurt International Airport runway), as well as the 'New Left' influence in university cities such as Marburg (Lees 2000, p.30; Schiller 2004, p.231). Initially, Holger Börner, the Minister President, was reluctant to embrace red-green cooperation, eventually entering a toleration arrangement, with new elections to take place in Autumn 1983. Following conflicts over the budget, the new elections were brought forward, and again results precluded the SPD heading a government without green assistance. A new cooperation agreement ensued, which – following protracted conflicts – led to the formation of an SPD/Green government, with Greens entering government for the first time in the Federal Republic's history (Lees 2000, pp.30–2). This coalition collapsed in 1987, leading to new elections and the formation of the first CDU-led government in Hesse's history, under Walter Wallmann. In turn, this government was defeated at the 1991 elections, and replaced with a further SPD/Green coalition, under Hans Eichel, which was re-elected in 1995 and governed until 1999, the start of the CDU/FDP coalition to be discussed in this chapter (Schiller 2004, p.231).

The length of social democratic hegemony might be expected to make it harder for a CDU-led government to achieve policy change. As discussed in the introduction, not only will social democratic policies be entrenched (with potential, path-dependent resistance to change coming from these policies' beneficiaries); the civil service is also likely to be occupied by those of a different political persuasion to the new government, who will be unsympathetic to policy change.

5.1.4 Political structures in Hesse

It is worth outlining in brief the distinctive variations which exist in the political system in Hesse compared to other Länder, although as is noted in Chapter 3 there are many points of commonality.

Landesverfassung

Hesse's constitution (the *Landesverfassung*) was agreed by the Land Assembly (a directly-elected predecessor of the Landtag) in 1946, and subsequently confirmed by a referendum held on 1st December 1946, alongside the Landtag election taking place on the same day. There were significant points of disagreement – notably over the nationalisation of industries (which were the subject of a separate question in the referendum) and also the possibility of a second chamber, which was supported by the CDU and LDP, but successfully rejected by the SPD and KPD as a constraint upon majoritarian government (Schiller 2004, p.226). In order to be amended, the Landesverfassung requires the agreement of 50% of the public voting in a referendum (Article 123).

The Landesverfassung contains a number of peculiarities, such as a reference to state ownership of industries in Article 41, and the retention of the possibility of the death penalty in Article 21 (which was superseded by the Basic Law). It also contains a series of commitments to human rights (Articles 1–63), some of which have proven a constraint upon policy-makers. For instance, Article 59 states:

> In all public schools and universities teaching is free of charge. ... Admission to middle, higher and high schools is only to be made dependent upon the ability of the pupil.

This was cited by opponents to plans for tuition fees proposed by the CDU-led government in 2006 (Spiegel, 4th September 2006), although the Land's highest court (*Staatsgerichtshof*) found (by a vote of 6–5) in July 2008 that the law was not in contravention of the Landesverfassung, because the provision of loans ensured those of lesser means could still study (Staatsgerichtshof Hessen, P.St. 2133, P.St. 2158).

A law banning all civil servants from wearing any religious garments (focused on the Muslim headscarf), proposed by the CDU-led government in 2004, was the subject of a similarly unsuccessful legal case, resting on the claim that it was contrary to the Landesverfassung (Staatsgerichtshof Hessen, P.St. 2016). Again by a narrow majority, the court found that this was not contrary to Article 9 (the right to religious freedom), Article 48.1 (the right to free religious practice), and Article 134 (the right of equal access to public appointment). These two high profile cases suggest that the Landesverfassung has been less of a constraint upon Hesse's policy-makers than might be expected, although the fact that both decisions were agreed with the narrowest possible majority suggests that, with a change in the Court's composition in the future, this may change.

The Landesverfassung does contain provision for elements of direct democracy, in Articles 116 and 124. One-fifth of electors can present a petition (which must be in the form of a proposed law) on matters other than those relating to budgets, taxation or pay, and this must either be agreed immediately by the Landtag, or put to a referendum. A simple majority of those voting must support the proposition for it to pass into law.

The electoral system

Hesse's electoral system has frequently been modified, in part because specifics are not spelt out in the Landesverfassung, and instead are determined by law – the Landesverfassung simply requires, in Article 75, that if there is a hurdle for representation it may not be higher than 5%. Since 1988 there has been a two-vote system, with the first vote being cast for a constituency candidate, and the second for a party, with distribution of seats occurring using the Hare-Niemeyer system: half the MdL are directly elected, and half are elected on party lists. There is no possibility of a division of seats not being proportional to votes cast (above the 5% hurdle); any 'overhanging mandates' would be compensated by an increase in the size of the Landtag until proportionality is achieved (Schiller 2004, pp.227–8; *Landeswahlgesetz Hessen*). As a consequence, this is a strict variant of proportional representation.

Civil service and local government

Local government in Hesse – as in the rest of Germany – forms part of the administration (*Verwaltung*), although at the same time it is subject to the principle of local self-administration (*Kommunale Selbstverwaltung*), which is guaranteed by Article 28, Section 2 of the Basic Law, and Article 137 of the Landesverfassung. The body of legislation regulating local government is known as the *Hessische Kommunalverfassung*, which comprises different legislation covering localities, districts, elections and elections.

In Hesse, there are 426 districts (*Gemeinden*) at the lowest level of representation – each with a directly elected mayor. Above this level, there are 21 counties (*Landkreise*), and five city districts (*Kreisefreie Städte*). In each case, there is a local council and also a directly-elected mayor, or in the case of the counties, a *Landrat* (directly-elected head of the administration). Local government is supervised by the Land government. The Land's interior ministry carries out this function for the cities of Frankfurt and Wiesbaden, and in other cases, the supervision is carried out by three *Regierungsbezirke* (government offices), based in Darmstadt, Kassel and Gießen. However, the government's role is restricted to ensuring the legal conformity of the actions of local government (Article 137.3 Landesverfassung), and protecting local administration (Article 11 of the Hessische Gemeindeordnung, and Article 10 of the Hessische Landkreisordnung).

In 2002, a referendum was held on a number of constitutional changes in Hesse, including the anchoring of the 'connexity principle' in the Landesverfassung; this provision passed, and ensures that any additional obligations passed onto local government must be fully funded (Article 137.6 Landesverfassung). This was regarded by senior local authority representatives as a significant victory (Interview T).

This structure imposes potentially significant constraints upon the Land-level government: not only must it rely on local government for the delivery of Land-level functions, but it must finance any additional obligations. In addition, there are constitutional defences of local government autonomy. The presence of directly-elected heads of the local administration, in the form of mayors and *Landräte*, as well as local councils, some of whom are inevitably of a different political colour to the Land government, could also prove an obstacle to achieving policy change.

5.1.5   Hesse's election campaign of 1999

The campaign leading to Hesse's election began a year ahead of several state elections, and followed (as Hesse elections frequently did) the federal election of 1998, which saw the election of Germany's first SPD/Green federal government. The SPD/Green government had presided over a period of economic success in Hesse, and although the government had not been without its difficulties, few expected a change of government as a result of the 1999 election: four-fifths of voters expected the SPD/Green government under Hans Eichel to be re-elected (Schmitt-Beck 2000, p.8). Hesse's Greens had experienced particular difficulties in the 1995–1999 parliament, with several high-profile resignations. The government, and especially the Social Democrats, still enjoyed quite reasonable approval ratings (notably regarding the economy): in January 1999, only 29% felt a CDU-led government would be better at solving the Land's problems, and 54% supported the continuation of an SPD/Green coalition (ibid., p.8).

There were signs, however, that this predicted outcome might be not be realised during the election campaign. The federal government had introduced proposals for dual nationality, allowing non-Germans to naturalise without forfeiting their other citizenship. A polemical campaign against this – taking the form of a petition – was launched by Roland Koch, the CDU's candidate for Minister President (perceived as a CDU hard-liner very much in the tradition of Alfred Dregger and Manfred Kanther). Although only a minority (43%) of Hesse's voters were supportive of Koch's campaign, even fewer (between a fifth and a third, depending on the exact question) were supportive of the federal government's proposal, with the FDP's proposal that dual nationality be permitted, but only up to the age of 18 (when the citizen would have to relinquish one passport or the other) enjoying significant public support (ibid., p.9).

A second area where the Land government was heavily criticised was in policy towards schools, where the cancellation of timetabled lessons owing to a lack of teachers had become a significant issue. A quarter of voters felt that school policy was the main problem for the Land, and only a quarter were satisfied with the SPD/Green government on this point (ibid., p.9); this issue is discussed more fully later in this chapter.

Thirdly, the SPD/Green federal government did not boost those parties' chances in Hesse: although Chancellor Schröder enjoyed reasonable popularity, a growing percentage (rising from 39% to 48% in the weeks before the election) felt that it had made an unsuccessful start (ibid., p.8).

The election saw a surprise victory for the CDU, although there was uncertainty until the final results were published about whether the FDP would beat the 5% hurdle (had it not done so, the SPD and Greens would have continued to have a majority). Hans Eichel still enjoyed greater support (44% to 31%) than Roland Koch as Minister President (Forschungsgruppe Wahlen 1999a, pp.46–7). There was in fact a small rise in the SPD vote (coming almost entirely at the expense of the Greens), but a larger one in the CDU vote (coming in part but not entirely from former FDP supporters). Two key factors appear to have played a role in this result. First, Roland Koch's campaign against dual nationality did appear to give his party a boost; in particular, it seemed to mobilise some support amongst working-class former SPD supporters, and also younger male voters – 64% of those who switched from the SPD to the CDU mentioned that this campaign had played a role in their decision, and the SPD's support fell amongst working-class voters (Schmitt-Beck 2000, p.13; Forschungsgruppe Wahlen 1999a). Moreover, Koch was successful in mobilising his support base – those who had supported the CDU at the federal election in 1998 – significantly better than the SPD (Schmitt-Beck 2000, p.130). Secondly, perceived failings with Hesse's schools were influential: only 13% of voters declared themselves satisfied with the Land's schools, compared to 57% who were dissatisfied, and the CDU was (albeit by a margin of only 31% to 25%) perceived as the party most able to improve them.

The decline in support for both the Greens and the FDP of course reflects the polarisation which occurred at this election (as well as the unhappy recent history of Greens in Hesse), from which the two major parties benefited. This polarisation was attributable to the strident campaign fought by Roland Koch, in particular on the issue of dual nationality.

4.1.6   Coalition negotiations and formation

The coalition negotiations in Hesse proceeded smoothly: interviewees did not mention particular difficulties in reaching agreement, and there was, in any event, little uncertainty about the outcome (the FDP having committed, during the election campaign, to form a coalition with the CDU, and having been put in a fairly weak position by its election result). The FDP gained two of the ten Cabinet positions on offer (Ruth Wagner becoming Minister for Higher Education and Art, and Dieter Posch becoming Minister for the Economy, Transport and Development). The new coalition's priorities were to change education policy, to implement a significant shift towards more conservative crime and justice policies (something the CDU had also emphasised in the election campaign), and to promote economic growth, including expansion of Frankfurt Airport, which the Greens had resisted in the previous government (Schmitt-Beck 2000, p.14). The FDP did oppose the expansion of the size of the Cabinet from eight to ten ministries, but was not in a position to prevent it (Spiegel, 15th February 1999), although it did prevent a stand-alone agriculture ministry being created, secured agreement to reduce the personnel of the *Regierungspräsidien* (regional offices of the Land government), and also reached a compromise over a shift to a centrally-set Abitur, which the CDU favoured. The CDU managed to secure the agreement of the FDP for several hard-line criminal justice measures, including an extension of stop-and-search, and the possibility of interning potentially violent demonstrators for up to six days (FR, 20th March 1999).

For the purposes of this study, the key ministerial appointments both came from the CDU: Marlies Mosiek-Urbahn, up to that point an MEP, took charge of the social affairs ministry, which included responsibility for labour market policy, and Karin Wolff, a trained teacher who had been a member of the Landtag since 1995, took over as Education Minister (SZ, 23rd October 1999). Some years later, Wolff attracted attention on a national level after coming out as a lesbian, and also for her proposal to teach the Christian account of creation in biology lessons (taz, 5th July 2007), but neither issue was mentioned by the Land-level media coverage from 1999 to 2003, or in interviews.

4.1.7   Politics in Hesse 1999–2003

A hallmark of the CDU/FDP coalition in Hesse, from 1999 to 2003, was strong, centralised leadership, coming from the Minister President and his large and powerful office (*Staatskanzlei*); this played a significant coordinating role between other ministries (Interview W). For instance, every morning a conference call took place between all the ministerial press officers, and another between the head of each minister's office (Interview V). The programme for government was set out in the coalition agreement, and this was rigidly pursued. Indeed, the government published a version of the agreement in the run-up to the 2003 election, and found that around 95% of its pledges had been realised (Hessische Landesregierung 2002, Interview W). As will be discussed below, the government introduced significant reforms, especially in education policy, but also around childcare, and launched a prominent initiative in the Bundesrat to reform social and unemployment assistance.

Between 1999 and 2003, Roland Koch's leadership was characterised by some sharp ambiguities. On the one hand, Koch was a polemicist *par excellence*, becoming the sharpest critic of the SPD/Green federal government on such issues as tax reform and the proposed immigration law (Schumacher 2004, p.235). At times, Hesse's CDU and Roland Koch in particular courted controversy for appearing close to the far right. In 2002, Koch spoke at the '*Studienzentrum Weikersheim*', which was founded by Hans Filbinger, the former Minister President of Baden-Württemberg and Military Judge in the Nazi era, who resigned from his political offices after accusations of his activities during the Nazi era came to light. Koch also wrote a foreword to a book alongside right-wing nationalist figures, such as Hans-Helmuth Knüttner, an employee of an organisation which was, according to the Office for the Protection of the Constitution, the 'most significant cultural organisation of the extreme right'. Koch stated that: 'I don't agree with everything which is in the book, but I believe that the discussion about it is valuable' (Schumacher 2004, pp.235–40). Koch also courted controversy when he compared the naming of rich Germans who could be affected by a super tax, in a speech by Frank Bsirske, leader of the Verdi trade union, to the Nazi requirement that Jewish citizens wear stars to identify them-selves. Koch subsequently apologised, and said he got carried away (Spiegel, 12th December 2002). Within Hesse's CDU Landtagsfraktion, there were other moments when the CDU looked close to the far right. Clemens Reif, a right-wing CDU MdL, heckled Tarek Al-Wazir, the Green group leader. He maintains that he said 'A student from Sanaa' (the capital of Yemen), whereas SPD and Green politicians claim to have heard 'Go back to Sanaa' (Spiegel, 4th September 2000a). Another right-wing CDU backbencher, Bernd Hamer, tabled numerous questions about Jewish immigrants, their language ability and property holdings, attracting criticism from the FDP (FR, 2nd September 2000).

The picture of Koch's government often painted in the media (and in particular the national media) of uncompromising right-wing polemicism, and a commitment to the hard right in word and deed, might on its own be misleading. For example, despite criticism from the CDU Fraktion, the government agreed to Frankfurt's participation in a pilot project to allow heroin to be prescribed to a small number of addicts, in an initiative sup-ported by the FDP (FR, 6th May 1999). In spite of initial reservations, the project was able to continue after the government agreed it had been a success (Interview V). Some interviewees cited a second example: alongside the government's decision to introduce a language test for children, with a pass necessary in order for them to join Year 1 of primary school, the gov-ernment invested significantly in extra pre-school language teaching, which had traditionally been a priority of the left (Hessisches Kultusministerium 2007a).

For the purposes of this study, therefore, this poses interesting questions. Hesse's CDU would appear to be a Landesverband strongly committed to the pursuit of a clearly conservative, Christian Democrat agenda (unlike the more moderate CDU Landesverbände in the Saarland and Saxony-Anhalt). Significant policy change could therefore be expected, and it would testify to the extent of constraints upon policy-makers if this was not apparent. At the same time, this case demonstrates that the image of a Land government might differ from the policies it substantively pursues: in particular, the desire of Hesse's CDU to appeal to right-wing voters might lead it to adopt polemical rhetoric, which might not be matched by its policies.

There was one ministerial resignation of direct relevance to two of the three areas of policy under consideration here. In January 2001, Social Affairs Minister Marlies Mosiek-Urbahn resigned from the cabinet, citing changes in her personal circumstances. She had been having an affair with a member of the Landtag, in spite of being married, and stated that she was resigning due to a 'forthcoming change in my private arrangements', and saw a 'danger for convincing presentation of the value-orientated family political aims of the Landesregierung' (Tagesspiegel, 20th August 2001). There was, however, a suspicion that Mosiek-Urbahn had struggled to win the support of the Fraktion, and was also not sufficiently engaged with Roland Koch's desire to reform social assistance (FR, 21st August 2001). An interview with a key ministry official at this time supported this view: 'She did have it harder because she wasn't an MdL, and having this base in the Fraktion is very important ... that was a hurdle she had to climb. So she was viewed more critically than other ministers who'd grown up in the Fraktion' (Interview V). Mosiek-Urbahn's replacement was Silke Lautenschläger, at 32 the youngest Minister in Germany. She was a lawyer who had been in the Landtag since 1999, and was regarded as a traditionalist, conservative politician (FR, 21st August 2001).

The government in Hesse between 1999 and 2003 was significantly overshadowed (and indeed came close to being brought down) by a party finance scandal (related to the finance scandal in the federal CDU). It emerged that leading functionaries in Hesse's CDU, including Manfred Kanther, the former Chair and Federal Interior Minister, and Casimir Prinz zu Sayn-Wittgenstein, the Treasurer, had allowed illegal donations – reaching to several million DM – to the CDU to be made over an extended period, some of which were routed through a political education academy which was close to the CDU. Koch denied all knowledge of illegality, and demanded the 'most brutal possible investigation' (Spiegel, 4th September 2000b). However, Koch stated to a journalist, in January 2000, that he 'knew of no single event outside the official book-keeping of the CDU'. Koch subsequently admitted that he knew this to be untrue (Schumacher 2004, pp.173–92). There were widespread demands for his resignation – including from CDU politicians such as Rita Süssmuth and Richard von Weizsäcker. A particular threat came from the FDP; following the scandal and Koch's admission, there was strong pressure for it to leave the coalition, either demanding a new Minister President or new elections. Indeed, both the federal FDP's General Secretary, Guido Westerwelle, and the Chairman, Wolfgang Gerhardt, supported this view, and put strong pressure on Hesse's FDP to step down from the coalition (FR, 11th February 2000). This was resisted, especially by Ruth Wagner, the Chair of Hesse's FDP and also Jörg-Uwe Hahn, the parliamentary leader; Wagner threatened to resign if she was not supported (FR, 24th February 2000). The FDP's Land executive went along with the views of Wagner and Hahn (FR, 14th February 2000). There was unanimity, too, amongst its Landtagsfraktion in support of the coalition's continuation (Interview EE). A special conference of the Land party was convened, and voted by 166 to 132 votes to continue the coalition (Schumacher 2004, p.191). Subsequently, the Head of Koch's

Staatskanzlei, Franz Josef Jung, did indeed resign over the affair, partly at the insistence of the FDP (Spiegel, 11ᵗʰ September 2000).

One particular effect of this scandal was that it brought about an even sharper polarisation than had otherwise existed between the parties in the Landtag. Norbert Kartmann, the CDU Fraktions chairman from 1999 to 2003, put it thus:

> 1999–2003 is not comparable with other times, [it was] so ferocious, polemical, defamatory, hurtful; in this time the relationships between parliamentarians suffered greatly (Interview W).

At the same time, Kartmann saw positive side-effects:

> [The scandal] made the intensity of the Fraktion's work far greater. It gave us an existential *Angst*. We worked better than ever before. It was the greatest problem we ever had, and that led to the greatest success, as a side effect (Interview W).

This episode reduced any possibility of the CDU entering into the sort of dialogue with the SPD over policy change that was seen in, for example, Saxony-Anhalt (see Chapter 7), promoting an even sharper level of polarisation than that seen before in the Landtag (which was traditionally great in Hesse – all the more so after the polemical 1999 Land election campaign).

The next election took place on 2ⁿᵈ February 2003. Obviously the party finance scandal played a role in the campaign – indeed the SPD attempted to make it a decisive issue – but it also took place at a time when the SPD/Green federal government was extremely unpopular, with 80% dissatisfied with its performance (Schmitt-Beck and Weins 2003, p.673). The CDU campaigned under the slogan: 'A lot done, a lot to do', pointing to its record on meeting its previous pledges. Roland Koch was felt by Hesse's voters to be significantly stronger on substantive issues (such as security, economic policy, labour market policy and education policy) than his SPD challenger Gerhard Bökel who, amongst those voters who had heard of him, was perceived to be more believable, honest and likeable (ibid., p.678). Koch was however favoured, by a margin of 57% to 37%, as Minister President (ibid., p.686). Fifty-two percent of voters wanted a continuation of the CDU/FDP coalition (ibid., p.679).

The result was a triumph for Roland Koch, with the CDU winning 48.8% of the votes compared to 29.1% for the SPD (a record low). As a result, Koch's CDU won an overall majority in the Landtag. Koch attempted to persuade the FDP to join an over-size coalition, but at the particular insistence of Ruth Wagner, it declined (FR, 5ᵗʰ February 2003). Koch was the first CDU Minister President of Hesse to be re-elected.

5.2   Education policy in Hesse 1999–2003

As noted above, in Hesse education was an important topic in the 1999 Landtag election campaign, as it had been in several post-war elections. The Land had seen a significant amount of polarisation in this area of policy. Although there were other phases of consolidation, during which there was less substantive disagreement between the relevant actors, there was almost certainly never a period of partisan consensus.

A hypothesis outlined in the introduction is that with a shift from left to right in government, there will be a substantive shift in education policies. Given the degree of polarisation in Hesse – both in general and particularly in the field of education – we might expect this to be confirmed.

5.2.1   Background to education in Hesse

In a detailed study of Hesse's education policies, Hepp and Weinacht, referring to the 1970s, state that:

> For years there was an intense exchange of blows in Hesse's Landtag, there was hardly a sitting of parliament which took place without a debate about education policy, such that at times the Landtag seemed like an education parliament. The damage was long-lasting, since in no other Land was the education policy climate so affected as in Hesse, the peace in schools was poisoned. '*Förderstufe*', 'comprehensive schools' and 'framework guidelines' became symbolic, sensitive terms which served as an organisational catalyst for a broad protest movement in the middle-class, conservative milieu (Hepp and Weinacht 2003, p.19).

In the early post-war period in Hesse, education minister Erwin Stein (who was put in post by the CDU) was extremely sympathetic to various liberal aspects of education – notably the 'democratisation' of education administration, involving pupils and parents, and also the ideas of the Förderstufe and the non-integrated comprehensive schools (that is, comprehensive schools with distinct 'streams', according to ability, within them). However, Stein did not manage to realise his ideals – instead, on account of the Land's economic challenges and uncertainties, as well as the lack of interest of both Volksparteien in education reform, the school structures of the Weimar republic were maintained. The SPD-led governments in the 1960s did, however, practice some mergers of primary with secondary schools, and also paid for pupils' transport – both policies which proved highly popular (ibid., p.16).

In 1967, the SPD, with support from the FDP, took some steps towards a 'modernisation' of the education system, as well as its 'democratisation'. In particular, they wanted to overcome rigid selection, and promote greater equality of opportunity, with moves towards Förderstufen across the Land,

and also the creation of more comprehensive schools; both measures which were not well-received by the CDU. The appointment of Ludwig von Friedeburg (SPD) as education minister led to even more contention: von Friedeburg was an ardent supporter of the democratisation of schools, both for its own sake and as part of a social agenda that 'only through education could the equality of opportunity that was aimed for and thus the "real-isation of social democracy" be reached' (ibid., pp.17–18). He aimed, step by step, to remove selective types of school and replace them with com-prehensives, both through the universal introduction of the Förderstufe, and the extension of comprehensive schools to become the 'regular form of school', encompassing all previous grammar schools. The government in particular favoured integrated comprehensive schools, and made clear that 'cooperative comprehensive schools' were just a step in this direction. Von Friedeburg also amended curricula in German and social science, incor-porating social critical and emancipatory theories of socialisation and pol-itics, which were not well received by the conservative opposition (ibid., pp.18–19).

Although the CDU did not win the election of 1974, it saw a large rise in its vote, in significant part as a result of the unpopularity of von Friedeburg's school reforms, and the new SPD/FDP coalition did not see him reappointed as a Minister. His successor, Hans Krollman (SPD), attempted to limit the damage, and appointed Erwin Stein – the previous CDU minister – to head a commission looking at curricula, reversing some of the most contentious changes. Krollman also introduced further har-monisation of curricula and timetable plans across school forms, con-solidated the Förderstufe – introducing a law in 1987 which intended to make it universal from 1987 – and also consolidated the position of com-prehensive schools (although from 1974 onwards no new ones were intro-duced). These changes ensured that the polarisation of education policy in Hesse continued, with the CDU bringing legal action and a mass petition against the extension of the Förderstufe (ibid., p.22). The policies were con-tinued following the formation of the first SPD/Green coalition in 1985.

With the election of a CDU/FDP government in 1987, some reversals were undertaken, notably the removal of the compulsory Förderstufe, although the FDP insisted on exemptions for certain areas. The govern-ment also aimed to amend curricula and timetables, so that they varied according to the type of school, rather than being common across them, although the further change of government, in 1991, meant that this was not fully implemented (ibid., p.24). Relations with teachers' unions, and in particular the GEW, were poor during this time, especially when the gov-ernment refused to implement a reduction in working hours which had been agreed across the public sector, leading to a strike. This policy was reversed – to little avail – five days before the election, which the CDU lost (ibid., p.25). Interestingly, a commentator at the time believed that the then education minister was consistently undermined by SPD members in the ministry: 'He can't prepare anything in peace, since social democrats are in the majority in the education ministry. Drafts for the minister reach the opposition more quickly than they do [him]' (ibid., p.31).

Polarisation continued into the period of office of the red-green coalitions from 1991 to 1999, under minister Hartmut Holzapfel (SPD), who had worked as the personal advisor to von Friedeburg (ibid., p.30). Rather than introducing major changes to the organisation of education, Holzapfel was interested in strengthening the autonomy of individual schools, and in particular allowing the 'school conference', comprising parents, teachers and pupils, to have significant decision-making power. As Holzapfel put it, 'This is the paradigm shift: this [proposed law] embodies the conviction that it is not sensible to order processes of change from the top down onto schools, but that they can only be successful if they are carried at the level of the school itself' (cited in Hepp and Weinacht 2003, p.34).

The education policy of the SPD/Green coalition from 1994 to 1999 was characterised by fiscal pressures, and the breakdown of relations between the SPD and the GEW. A growth in pupil numbers, and refusal of the government to employ extra teachers (instead increasing teachers' workload and class sizes) led to further, rancorous conflict with the GEW, and significant cancellation of lessons (ibid., pp.48–52). Interviews with those involved at the time (Interview Y, Interview AA) drew attention to the intensely personal nature of the conflict with Holzapfel – not only was Hesse's school system the subject of dissatisfaction on the part of the population, but the previously supportive teaching personnel were alienated.

In summary, then, the CDU/FDP government inherited a challenging position. The nature of the education system (with widespread Förderstufen, and a significant number of comprehensive schools) was far closer to the social democratic than to the Christian democratic paradigm, and there were serious financial and organisational problems, with the cancellation of lessons becoming a major issue in the election campaign.

On the one hand, this history might be expected to act as a constraint upon a future CDU government. For instance, closing or reforming existing schools (such as the comprehensive schools) ran the risk of opposition from parents and teachers. Therefore, some 'path-dependent' resistance to change could be anticipated. On the other hand, there was public pressure for change – in particular, for increased resources to deal with lesson cancellation.

One other feature of Hesse's education system is worth highlighting. The Land is responsible for what goes on in schools, but local authorities (the Landkreise and cities) are responsible for the fabric of schools: the buildings, caretaking and secretarial staff, and also for school planning (whether to close or merge schools, or request conversion to a different type of school). Decisions about reorganisation also needed the consent of the education ministry. The education ministry has a devolved structure, with the *Staatliche Schulämter* (State School Offices – SSÄ), in each city or Landkreis, being responsible for personnel and organisational issues and making recommendations to the ministry. This could also serve as a blockage to change – in the early 1990s, 18 out of 26 heads of the SSÄ were social democrats, compared with three Christian Democrats (Hepp and Weinacht 2003, p.31). These social democratic officials constituted a possible element of bureaucratic resistance to change, whether due to inertia or their political misgivings, as anticipated by Manfred Schmidt's study (Schmidt 1980).

5.2.2 The coalition agreement

Interviewees did mention some disagreement between the CDU and the FDP during the coalition negotiations, although their election programmes on education policy were relatively similar. In particular, the FDP was keen to oppose anything it regarded as centralisation, and supported a variety of different school forms, with impulses for change coming from the bottom up (Interview EE).

The very first chapter of the coalition agreement was entitled 'School', reflecting the prominence this had had in the election campaign, and the strong pressure to act. The agreement specifically mentioned the need to ensure timetables were fully covered, and the introduction of processes of quality control, to ensure that Hesse's children were nationally and internationally competitive (CDU and FDP Hessen 1999, p.3). Key policies in the coalition agreement included:

- A 'lesson guarantee', to ensure that all lessons currently foreseen in the model timetable took place by the end of the parliamentary term. The shortfall of around 50,000 extra lessons would be met by the creation of new jobs and various measures to increase the workload of existing teachers on a paid basis (p.3);
- A commitment to ensuring that parents took decisions on the type of school their children would go to, but with 'extra advice' offered if teachers disagreed with their choice (p.4);
- The reintroduction of numerical grades from the second half of year 2 of primary school (p.4);
- The introduction of the 'reliable half-day school', with four hours of teaching to take place in all primary schools for years 1 and 2, and five hours for years 3 and 4 (p.5);
- Extension of the possibility of the provision of childcare and activities for children, before and after core school times (p.5);
- Changing curricula to match the type of school, rather than having general curricula across all school types (p.5);

- Ending teaching in mother-tongues other than German, and redeploying staff into schools with a high proportion of children for whom German was not the first language (p.5);
- The introduction of school leaving exams across all types of school, with the eventual aim of a centralised Abitur (p.5);
- Introduction of comparative tests, with the publication of results after the first round (p.6);
- Strengthening of the *Leistungsgedanke* (emphasis on performance/ standards), with grading of homework, and grades to reflect absolute not relative standards within a class (p.6);
- Support for gifted and talented children (p.6);
- Support for those with special needs, with a statement against the presumption that mainstream education is correct for such children: 'A principle of common lessons in the normal type of school does not do justice to the need for support for the individual child' (pp.6–7);
- More cooperation between schools and companies (p.7);
- Reduction in powers of the 'school conference' compared to those of the staff meeting, and strengthening of the position of individual teachers and heads (p.8);
- Support for continued religious education (p.8);
- Ensuring there is a plurality of types of school in each district, including the possibility of selective classes as well as a Förderstufe, and providing a mechanism for school conferences (of parents, teachers and pupils) to abolish the Förderstufe (p.9).

There are several elements here which are clearly part of the Christian democrat typology of education policy. There is a particularly strong emphasis on external testing and evaluation, while aspirations on selection are slightly weaker than, for instance, in Saxony-Anhalt (see Chapter 6), reflecting the path-dependent constraints referred to above. The need for additional spending in order to fully resource schools was a particularly important element, reflecting Hesse's recent past.

5.2.3   Abitur: From 13 years to 12

A shift from Abitur in 13 years to Abitur in 12 was enabled by the first 'Law to secure the quality of Hesse's schools' (*Gesetz zur Qualitätssicherung in Hessischen Schulen*), which amended Hesse's School Law (GVBl 1999, p.384ff). This enabled grammar schools to apply to shift towards a 12-year Abitur, although only for 'pupils for whom it is appropriate not just because of their grades, but who also excel by their ability to think and speak, and through their learning and working behaviour and social competence', as Minister Wolff put it (FR, 14th January 2003). Although the law was opposed by the SPD/Green opposition, this particular aspect did not feature strongly in their parliamentary criticisms of the policy (Plenar-protokoll 1999, pp.293–309).

At the very end of the parliament, Minister Wolff made it clear that she would switch to a 12-year Abitur at all the grammar schools in Hesse (FR, 14th January 2003), with an aim of introducing it universally by 2009. Up to that point, only 18 grammar schools requested, or attempted to make use of this possibility (Hessische Landesregierung 2002, p.21). This extension was opposed by the SPD (Quanz 2003). Minister Wolff justified the decision not to switch to a 12-year Abitur sooner with reference to lesson cancellation: she claimed that, in the previous context, a 12-year Abitur in Hesse would, in fact, have reflected just eleven years of teaching, because of the cancellation of so many lessons (FR, 13th September 2001).

5.2.4   Changes to selection

There were two main changes to selection introduced in this period: first, reforms to the Förderstufe, and secondly amendments to the curriculum, which made it reflect streaming by ability in schools.

The controversial issue of the Förderstufe was addressed in 1999 by the first 'Law to secure quality' (GVBl 1999, p.384ff). This law gave the school conference, involving teachers, pupils and parents, the opportunity to decide (at Hauptschulen, Realschulen and comprehensive schools) whether or not there should be a Förderstufe. This matter was taken out of the hands of local government, which previously would have been able to veto such a change. For the SPD, Lothar Quanz criticised this, partly as an attack on local government, and partly in principle, calling it a 'return to the school discussions of the early 1970s' (FR, 20th May 1999). Moreover, the new law required that, by 2002/3, there would be a full choice of school forms in each area covered by a city or Landkreis from the 5th year onwards, provided there was sufficient need (Hessische Landesregierung 2002, p.30).

The practical impact of this change was limited, however. The number of Förderstufen, apart from those in comprehensive schools, is listed below:

Table 5.4   Number of Förderstufen and pupils in Förderstufen in Hesse 1999–2004

Year	No. of Förderstufen	No. of pupils in Förderstufen
1999–2000	135	17,633
2000–2001	134	17,731
2001–2002	130	17,274
2002–2003	126	16,041
2003–2004	122	14,843

Source: Statistisches Landesamt

On a related issue, rules around the role of parents in taking decisions about the type of schools a child should attend were amended, in line with the coalition treaty outlined above. Parents could initially take the decision on what type of school their child was suited to, and if the primary school disagreed, then the parents were offered 'extra advice'; if the child proved unsuitable, the staff meeting could take a decision to send the child to a different form of school by the end of the 5th year. Provisions in the School Law were amended by the 1999 law to facilitate this, and a decree was also passed in 2000 (Hessische Landesregierung 2002, p.30). Again, this change was opposed by the SPD, which felt it 'disempowered' parents (FR, 20th May 1999). Norbert Kartmann (the CDU's Fraktionvorsitzender in the Landtag) supported the change: 'The state gets the chance to break off mistaken educational pathways and to say "That's over"' (FR, 15th May 1999).

Curricula were amended, so that they varied according to the type of school, on 1st August 2000, and the model timetable was also amended according to the type of school. The new timetables came into effect for school year 2002/3 (Hessische Landesregierung 2002, p.18). This sharpened the distinction between the schools for children of different ability, and could make it harder for children to switch between different types of school.

Given the controversy in Hesse's history, as well as the commitment in the coalition agreement to ensure access to all forms of school – including selective schools – it is perhaps surprising that the Land government did not significantly reduce the number of comprehensive schools, which stayed remarkably constant, as indicated in Table 5.5.

Table 5.5   Number of comprehensive schools and pupils attending them 1999–2004

Year	Number of comprehensive schools	Number of pupils
1999–2000	217	186,718
2000–2001	215	189,368
2001–2002	215	193,596
2002–2003	215	195,906
2003–2004	213	194,371

Source: Statistisches Landesamt

In discussion with the author (interview IIIa), Minister Wolff stressed that she did not wish to favour any particular school form (unlike the SPD, which she believed favoured comprehensive schools), and the key issue was the ability of the individual school to perform. This focus on outputs rather than structures was also emphasised by a senior civil servant in the ministry (Interview CC). Jochen Nagel, from the GEW, was more sceptical, and believed that comprehensive education was subject to gradual erosion in Hesse, through greater emphasis on the individual types of school (in particular with the changes to curricula mentioned above). However, he also felt that the CDU was constrained by the popularity of the existing comprehensives (Interview AA).

5.2.5 Timing of education

There was a significant early conflict over the hours of education in Hesse. Indeed, this was one of the main points of political disagreement during the passage of the first Law to secure the quality of Hesse's schools.

The previous government had introduced the concept of the 'Primary School with fixed opening times'. These schools – which were a pilot project – integrated formal lessons for all children from 7.30am to 1pm, with the rationale, firstly, to make it easier for parents who needed to work, fulfilling a childcare need, and secondly for educational reasons, spreading teaching out across the time at school, rather than having a concentration. These opening times were compulsory for all children. This model was attempted in 150 schools out of around 1,020 (FR, 14th September 1999).

The new government instead introduced a change towards the 'Primary School with reliable opening times'. The idea behind this change was that pupils should not be sent home early from primary school under any circumstances, in the core opening times (four hours per day for classes 1 and 2, five hours per day for classes 3 and 4). It also spread the funding available around all schools, rather than focusing it on a smaller number (Hessische Landesregierung 2002, p.13).

Such a move was inadequate for proponents of the previous model. First, it meant a move away from extended education. At best, schools would offer some sort of supervision or activity beyond the core lesson period. Frank-Peter Kaufmann, for the Greens, said that 'Your [the CDU/FDP] model even gives up the aspiration that parents with schoolchildren should be able to work for at least half a day. That affects women more than men, Herr Kartmann [CDU Fraktionsvorsitzender], you should get the women in your Fraktion to explain that to you' (Plenarprotokoll 1999, p.298). Secondly, it reduced the ability to integrate education and other activities.

There were disagreements on this issue within the coalition. There was an agreement to spread the funding for extended school opening across more schools; however, some, notably the conservative Secretary of State, Hartmut Müller-Kinet, were sceptical of extended opening, and had a more conservative view of the desirable family structure than the FDP and Minister Wolff (Interview EE).

There was a further disagreement over extended school hours in late 2002, when the federal government proposed to establish a fund (known as IZBB) for the capital costs for extended schools. At first, Hesse responded critically, regarding this as an attack on Land autonomy in education policy, and suggested it would spend the money instead on school libraries (SZ,

19th November 2002)! An agreement was subsequently reached, although Hesse achieved the compromise that the money could be spent on schools which had the offer of all-day education for those who wanted it (so *voluntary* all-day education), rather than just those which had compulsory all-day education for all children (FR, 13th May 2003).

Over the course of the 1999–2003 parliament, and particularly from 2003 onwards, pressure for the extension of education into the afternoon grew. Minister Wolff pointed out that, by 2006, the number of all-day schools in Hesse had more than doubled, and said that the balance had shifted within the CDU in favour of those supportive of all-day education (Interview IIIa). This was insufficient, in particular, for the GEW, who argued that this was achieved by offering supervision, rather than education, in the afternoon (Interview AA). The additional provision also required payment of fees, which attracted criticism from opposition politicians (FR, 30th January 2002). After 2003, some all-day schools with compulsory education, all day, were created, but even by 2007/8, they were in the minority (70), compared to the 365 schools which offered voluntary educational support in the afternoon (Hessisches Kultusministerium 2007b).

In summary, then, the CDU showed itself sceptical about the assumption that children should be required to attend school all day, and wanted to continue to provide the traditional model of half-day education alongside other forms; however, over time there was a shift towards children being in school longer. The expansion of this provision happened predominantly during the time of the second CDU-led government, not during the period under consideration here, although there was an increase in funding from four million Euros per year in 1999, to 7.1 million Euros per year for extended education under the CDU/FDP coalition (Hessische Landesregierung 2002, p.13).

5.2.6   Repetition of years

Hesse's government, through a decree issued in 2000 (Amtsblatt 2000, p.602) tightened the rules on repetition of years, so that if a child got a grade 5 (poor) in a major subject, it could only be 'cancelled out' by a grade 2 (good) in a major subject, or a grade 3 in two minor subjects. There was also no way of cancelling out a grade 6 (the lowest grade), under the new decree.

However, this did not appear to lead to an increase in the number of children repeating a year; for Hesse, the proportion was 3.2% in 2000–01, and this rose with the changed rule to 3.8% in 2001–02, but fell back again to 3.2% in 2004–05 (*Source*: Statistisches Bundesamt).

5.2.7   Religious studies

There were no legislative changes concerning Religious Studies from 1999 to 2003 in Hesse, with Religious Studies education continuing to take place other than for those who opted out, who received teaching in Ethics instead (Hessische Landesregierung 2002, p.29). The CDU/FDP government was content with the existing model.

There was one controversy in this area, when the CDU declined to give permission for an Islamic group to offer Religious Studies education in the same way as churches did (which was possible under Hesse's school law). Minister Wolff pointed out that the organisation of Islam was different to that of the Churches, making it difficult to allocate provision to one particular group. This did not appear to be a particularly polarised debate, with a prominent Turkish SPD politician, of the Muslim faith, taking the same view (FR, 16th June 2001).

5.2.8   Grading and testing regimes

As was suggested by the coalition treaty, the CDU/FDP coalition introduced a number of changes to grading and testing regimes, which accorded with a shift towards the Christian democratic paradigm of education.

Firstly, numerical grades were reintroduced by two decrees in August 2000 for children from the second half of the second year of primary school; either a verbal report, or grading, for work and social behaviour was also introduced (Hessische Landesregierung 2002, p.13). This was criticised by some educationalists, who felt it failed to encourage children who had made a real improvement, and it had the potential to demotivate them; in particular, it could badly affect children from less well-off or supportive families, who did not have books at home (FR, 19th October 1999).

Secondly, a range of new tests were introduced: school-leaving examinations were introduced for the Hauptschule and the Realschule (FR, 8th August 2002), and the law for the Abitur was changed so that a teacher could choose one of a number of centrally-set questions. The legal basis for this was created by the Second Law to Secure the Quality of Hesse's Schools (Hessische Landesregierung 2002, p.19). The FDP had successfully resisted the introduction of a fully centralised Abitur (Interview EE).

Thirdly, a competition for pupils in Maths was undertaken across the whole Land by pupils in year 8, and end of year tests were introduced for children in all core subjects in years 6, 8 and 10. The results for the Maths competition were published by region in 2002 (Hessische Landesregierung 2002, p.19).

The increase in the number of tests was criticised by the SPD and the Greens: Lothar Quanz, for the SPD, said that 'Examinations alone do not necessarily lead to an increase in quality', and he warned against 'greater selection, which will exclude children from education', while Priska Hinz called the change 'senseless' (FR, 8th August 2002), and the Chairman of Hesse's GEW referred to 'testitis' (Interview Y).

5.2.9   Pupil choice

The Christian democratic paradigm focuses on particular subjects, regarded as essential, and thus reduces pupil choice. Minister Wolff made proposals in October 2000 in this direction (specifically for pupils attending grammar schools), which would strengthen German, Mathematics and foreign languages, and reduce the degree of specialisation which pupils could undertake. This was criticised by the Land's Headteachers' Society (FR, 26th October 2000). A further proposal was to remove all the *Leistungskurse* (specialist subjects), but the Minister subsequently rowed back from this proposal, at the request of the FDP. The final agreement allowed for pupils to choose two Leistungskurse, one of which had to be Mathematics, a foreign language or a natural science, and teaching of Maths and German was extended to a minimum of four lessons per week for pupils in the final two years of grammar school (FR, 27th March 2001).

This did represent a shift towards the Christian democrat paradigm; in particular, in order to free up time for the additional Mathematics and German lessons, one optional subject (chosen by the pupil) would no longer be offered (FR, 27th March 2001).

5.2.10   Charges for school books

Hesse remained one of the Länder where no fee is charged for school books. Indeed, this is the case across both state and private schools in the Land (Hessisches Kultusministerium 2007c). The education ministry makes it clear that this applies to books, rather than, for instance, pocket calculators or writing materials. There was no reference in the literature or in interviews to any plans to depart from this situation – which is a deviation from the Christian democrat paradigm.

5.2.11   Relations with unions

Hesse was unusual in having a particularly strong GEW, which was organised amongst all types of teachers, including those with Beamte status. As discussed above, the relationship between the GEW and the previous, SPD/Green government had broken down. At the start of the new government, according to Jochen Nagel, who was senior functionary and subsequently Chair of the GEW in Hesse, relations at first were relatively cordial (Interview AA). In particular, and unsurprisingly, the GEW welcomed the employment of extra teachers and the additional investment in schools, although it was less content with some of the qualitative changes, such as the introduction of curricula specific to particular forms of school, and the extension of numerical grades (FR, 11th May 1999). However, this rapprochement did not last for long: by September 1999, the Chair at the time, Gonhild Gerecht, said that while 1,400 extra teaching jobs were well and good, 'the quality of teaching is being criminally neglected' (FR, 14th September 1999).

Both Jochen Nagel and Karin Wolff confirmed that, for most of the period in discussion, relations between the GEW and the government reverted to their normal acrimony (Interview AA, Interview IIIa). The GEW had also decided not to have any negotiations with the CDU's spokesperson on education, Hans-Jürgen Irmer, because of his 'anti-immigrant' views (Interview AA). Irmer was a highly conservative politician, who according to the SPD, had demanded freedom for Hitler's deputy Rudolf Hess in 1977, and who had written an article for the right-wing newspaper *Junge Freiheit* (Hessischer Rundfunk 2006). In fact, after the 2003 election, one meeting did take place between the GEW and Irmer, but without any particular progress being made (Interview AA). In the elections to the main representative body of Hesse's teachers, the GEW became more and successful, winning a clear majority of the seats; in return, according to the union side, little attention was paid by the government to this body (Interview AA).

The relative strength of the GEW compared to other unions in Hesse's schools – along with the clearly conservative trend of some of the education reforms – meant that cordial relations between the government and the unions were not to be expected, in line with the Christian democratic paradigm, and there were no surprises in this regard between late 1999 and 2003.

5.2.12   PISA

The results of the PISA study, both showing Germany in international comparison and by Land (with Hesse's results below the German average), were published during the period under consideration here. Reactions to PISA were, predictably, polarised, with each side in Hesse's long-standing education debate claiming vindication. For the CDU, Minister Wolff suggested that the failures of the previous SPD/Green government were responsible, and that Hesse needed to learn from Bavaria, amongst other Länder. The FDP also saw Hesse as having been let down by repeated 'experimentation' in schools under the red-green coalition (FR, 26th June 2002; FR, 27th June 2002).

By contrast, the SPD and Greens emphasised Germany's underperformance across the country, and proposed more individual support, longer learning before selection by age, and a shift towards all-day education (FR, 4th December 2001). The GEW said that the PISA results were not insightful, as they consisted of raw data, without consideration being given to the social background of children, and said the decision to publish such data was 'irresponsible' (FR, 18th June 2002).

In summary, the reaction of the CDU/FDP government in Hesse to the PISA study entirely fitted the Christian democratic paradigm; that of the opposition also entirely matched expectations.

5.2.13   The federal dimension

The federalism reform took place after the period in question – as did the failed Convention on Federalism Reform, chaired by Edmund Stoiber and Franz Müntefering (see Chapter 3), the latter collapsing in part because of the refusal of Roland Koch to compromise on the issue of Land competence in education policy (Spiegel, 20th December 2004). As was discussed above, even in relation to extra funding for all-day schools, the Land government was extremely sensitive to any suggestion of federal interference in its education policy.

Minister Wolff was extremely satisfied with the efforts of the KMK, especially between 1999 and 2003, and felt that good progress was made in responding to PISA. She felt that the agreement on expected, rather than minimum standards, was important and reflected Hesse's priorities (Interview IIIa).

5.2.14   Other developments

Five other developments are worth highlighting in relation to the CDU/FDP coalition's education policy.

First, as outlined in the coalition agreement, the government did indeed introduce the 'lesson guarantee', that the planned timetable would be delivered. It claimed that this was achieved, although these claims were disputed by the opposition (FR, 3rd May 2001). The Land created 2,900 extra teaching jobs, moved a further 1,200 posts into regular teaching duties, and created a further 1,600 trainee teacher positions (Hessische Landesregierung 2002). Private discussion with a ministry official suggested that the extent to which the guarantee was in fact fulfilled depended on interpretation: the jobs to deliver the timetable had indeed been created, but in some subjects, there was a shortage of teachers available to be recruited (Interview CC). Nonetheless, there was a significantly increased level of investment in staffing as a result of this aspiration.

Secondly, there was a significant emphasis placed, both between 1999 and 2003, and also from 2003 onwards, on 'quality assurance' – this is related to the increase in testing outlined above, as well as the commitment to the publication of test results. This point was confirmed in a number of interviews (Interviews Y, CC, EE). The Land government saw its role as moving away from detailed prescriptions of processes to be followed in schools, and had a stated intention to strengthen their autonomy.

Thirdly, the Land government introduced a pilot of 'Lesson Guarantee Plus' in 2001, which was rolled out across the Land in the second CDU-led term of office (FR, 3rd May 2001; Landesregierung Hessen 2003). This was intended to guarantee that lessons would not be cancelled because of staff sickness or other unscheduled absence. Schools were to be given funds to organise a pool of those who could step in to cover such circumstances. This proved intensely controversial: at first, the SPD and Green opposition claimed that this unfairly passed responsibility on to schools, and testified to the failure of the first 'lesson-guarantee'. However, controversy subsequently shifted to the possibility of non-teachers stepping in, which was bitterly opposed by the trade unions (Interview AA). They claimed this undermined educational standards. A civil servant in the Ministry took the view that the reason for resistance was less to do with non-teachers becoming involved in education – after all, there had never been any objection from the left about having 'all sorts of people' turn up in school, such as actors and musicians – and more to do with the change undermining wage agreements and reducing the status of teachers, as it was realised that non-teachers could do some of the work (Interview CC).

Fourth, again as spelt out in the coalition treaty, the government did indeed phase out compulsory provision of lessons in pupils' mother tongues other than German, and redeployed the staff previously engaged in this (Hessische Landesregierung 2002, pp.14–17). This was criticised by the GEW, which believed that the *quid pro quo*, pre-school lessons in German for those who otherwise wouldn't have sufficient knowledge, was inadequate and that in any event there should be a flexible introduction to school for all children, not learning at an identical tempo (FR, 31st January 2003). As noted in the introduction, some interviewees felt the emphasis on extra provision of German language teaching was a departure from the Christian democrat paradigm in education policy. The policy attracted further controversy in the subsequent parliamentary term when Minister Wolff arranged for a banner to be hung in the Education Ministry, stating 'Only those who can speak German enter the first year [of school]', attracting an incensed reaction from the GEW (FR, 4th October 2003).

Fifth, the government introduced a modest element of 'performance related pay' for teachers (FR, 31st March 2001), where headteachers were given the opportunity to reward exceptional performance with an additional payment.

5.1.15   Influencing and changing policy

The ensuing section gives a brief overview of those actors who, on this analysis, appeared to be influential in shaping education policy in Hesse between 1999 and 2003.

Role of the opposition: Given the quite exceptionally polarised nature of politics in Hesse in this period, and the history of polarisation in education policy in the Land, the opposition was not in a position to influence policy, and there were no informal channels for it to do so (Interview Ia, Interview AA, Interview IIIa).

Role of trade unions: As discussed above, trade unions (notably the powerful GEW but also the other unions) were marginalised in this period, with very little influence over the activities of the ministry. The GEW in Hesse (Interview AA) emphasised that it attempted to shape social discourse, rather than undertake detailed behind-the-scenes lobbying to achieve policy change, so the aspiration to build day-to-day relations with officials was limited.

Role of local and state parties: Both the CDU and FDP possessed formal and informal mechanisms with which to involve interested parliamentarians in policy-making, and those from outside – typically supporters who worked in the education sector, for instance as head teachers. Interviewees did not mention that these ever acted as a particular constraint upon policy-making, although they provided useful ideas and a sense of what was happening 'on the ground' (Interview EE).

Constraints upon government by the CDU Fraktion: Interviewees stated, first, that most impulses for policy change came from the government, and not from the CDU-Fraktion in the Landtag. However, there were regular meetings between the Minister and the Fraktion, and, although Minister Wolff confirmed that there were no disagreements, it was necessary for the Fraktion to be involved from the outset in significant policy changes, and for different parts of the Fraktion to 'come together' (Interview IIIa). As Norbert Kartmann, the CDU Fraktionsvorsitzender stated, 'Hesse's CDU is famous for its unity' (Interview W), and there was no reference to disagreement on any fundamental issue in education policy over this period.

Constraints upon the minister by the coalition partner: The FDP's education spokesperson, Dorothea Henzler, felt that the party had a significant impact upon education policy in this period (Interview EE). Certainly, as discussed above, the FDP did appear to have an influence on the CDU over the introduction of a centralised Abitur, and it was more positively disposed towards all-day education than the CDU. Minister Wolff also mentioned that she had to compromise with the FDP over transfer from years 4 to 5, and the method of choosing which type of school a child should attend (Interview IIIa). Dorothea Henzler believed the FDP was a counter-weight to a 'dirigiste' philosophy on the part of the CDU over the period, which was in evidence, in her view, from 2003 onwards. There was an impact at the margins, but both sides testified to the strength of the working relationship at the time, and the FDP did not appear to be a major constraint upon the CDU in its policy decisions in this field.

Blocking of change by the civil service: As discussed above, there are two reasons to feel that Manfred Schmidt's hypothesis that the civil service would resist policy change would apply particularly strongly to Hesse's education policy: it was an area of policy which was severely politicised, indeed polarised; and the SPD had been in government long enough previously to ensure that civil servants were loyal to it. In fact, the evidence for this proposition for the period 1999–2003 was more mixed. Minister Wolff felt that there was a consensus, across the board in the Education Ministry, that change was needed, and did not feel obstructed (Interview IIIa). This was supported by Dorothea Henzler of the FDP, who, although she cited a saying ('The leadership comes and goes, the Beamte stays', referring to changes of government), felt that there was a good deal of loyalty towards the leadership at the time. There was also very little room to undertake reappointments, and a number of key civil servants in the Ministry were approaching retirement age, so by waiting a short while a change could be achieved. Dorothea Henzler did feel, though, that beyond partisan obstruction, there was a 'mentality' which was focused on handing out resources rather than scrutinising the way they were spent. Wolff believed that teachers themselves were often the greatest obstacle to achieving change in the education system (Interview EE, Interview IIIa).

Relations with sub-Land level government units: Although, as outlined above, local government has a role as the *Schultrâger* – the body responsible for the fabric of each school and some staff – there were few references made to any conflict within the press at the time of the 1999–2003 government, nor was it alluded to in interviews with those active in this area of policy at the time. It is worth noting that most of the reforms in Hesse could be realised without local governments' cooperation, concerning issues such as curricula, testing, and the provision of lessons, whereas a programme of school closures, or a fundamental school reorganisation, would have involved local government to a greater extent (as was the case in Saxony-Anhalt, for instance). The role of the lower levels of the ministry, in the form of the SSÄ, was rather more contentious, with some frustration expressed that they had not adapted to the new role of scrutinising results, rather than processes (Interview CC), and some change in their role was felt necessary by the Minister (Interview IIIa).

Role of formal procedures: Formal procedures in the Landtag were marginalised in education policy-making in this period (Interview IIIa, Interview EE, Interview Ia, Interview W). Decisions were taken by the governing parties' Fraktionen, with regular consultation on important issues between relevant figures (and, in the case of the CDU, its Fraktion working group), and subsequently – especially in the case of major decisions – by the full group. As a result, political fault-lines were determined prior to the formal consideration of legislation. Hearings of interested parties took place on legislation, with each side inviting 'its own' experts, but apart from changing 'dots and commas' (Interview AA), these had no impact upon policies chosen.

5.2.16   Education policy: Conclusions

There was, as is summarised in Table 5.6, quite a clear shift towards the Christian democratic paradigm in a number of areas of education policy.

It might have been anticipated from the history of Hesse's education policy that there would have been a *volte face* in all areas of education policy, with, in particular, a quick shift towards greater selection, and a decisive move against the Förderstufe and especially comprehensive schools.

Instead, this did not occur, and the CDU/FDP government sought to realise significant elements of the Christian democratic education policy paradigm within a school structure which was more akin to a social democratic vision,

Table 5.6   Education policy in Hesse 1999–2003

Social democratic paradigm	Christian democratic paradigm	Change
Comprehensive education (or if unacceptable, late and flexible selection)	Early and rigid selection, with limited movement between types of school	Slightly greater rigidity in selection, with reforms to Förderstufe and curricula specific to school type, but comprehensive schools remained
Any selection based on parental choice	Selection based on tests/teacher assessment	Move towards selection based on teacher assessment as well as parental choice
High level of discretion for individual teachers over curriculum content and testing	Centralised tests and examinations	Two centralised school tests, and centralised curricula, introduced with little discretion
Abitur after 13 years	Abitur after 12 years	Possibility of Abitur after 12 years, with roll-out to follow
Extensive pupil choice of subject	Limiting of pupil choice	Pupil choice slightly restricted
Compulsory, integrated all-day education	Half-day education with possibility of extension	Some voluntary all-day education introduced, compulsory elements at primary level rolled back
Teachers provide education all day	Some supervision undertaken by volunteers/ unqualified helpers	Additions to 'core' teaching provided by non-teaching staff
Limited reliance on grading	High reliance on grading	Greater emphasis upon grading
Grading only in secondary school	Grading from year 1	Grading reintroduced from the second half of year 2
No grading of behaviour and teamwork	Grading of behaviour and teamwork	Verbal reports or grades on behaviour and teamwork
Limited repetition of years in event of poor performance	High level of repetition of year in event of poor performance	Stricter rules on repetition of years, but no increase
Free provision of school books	Parental contribution towards school books	Free provision of school books remained
No compulsory religious education (RE)	Compulsory RE	No change: RE or ethics compulsory

Table 5.6   Education Policy in Hesse 1999–2003 – *continued*

Social democratic paradigm	Christian democratic paradigm	Change
Non-Christian RE provided	No non-Christian RE provided	No change: ethics provided but not other RE
Opposition to Länder having exclusive control over policy	Support for Länder having exclusive control over policy	Support for Länder having exclusive control over policy
Partnership with trade unions	Limited involvement with unions	Relations with unions broke down under SPD/Green government 1995–1999. In the CDU period there was first a thawing of relations, then hostility.

by using its control over curricula, the widespread introduction of testing, and subsequently school inspections and 'quality control' mechanisms.

CDU and government interviewees were at pains to argue that the CDU had moved on from debates about school structure, although there was still a presumption that a system with clear differentiation by ability would perform better. This may indeed reflect a change in the Christian democratic paradigm, although responses by CDU-Länder to PISA do not support that view, drawing unflattering conclusions about the potential of non-selective education.

Instead, these findings testify to a certain path dependence in education policy, an extension of the 'territorial null hypothesis' outlined in Chapter 2: the history of education policy in Hesse, with the creation of a large number of comprehensive schools, acts as a constraint upon future governments, with a potentially very high political cost of change. As a result, the Christian democrat policy paradigm had to be adapted to cope with this.

This case study does not indicate the ability of civil servants and formal institutions to block policy change. The CDU/FDP government led by Roland Koch provided clear political leadership; the Landtag – and particularly the opposition – was marginal to policy consideration; and the government had little difficulty pushing through those policy changes it had undertaken to pursue.

5.3   Childcare and family policy in Hesse

As discussed above, the issues of childcare and family policy played almost no role in Hesse's election campaign in 1999, although related issues in education policy, notably policy towards the opening times of primary schools, and support for all-day schools, did play some role (albeit a subordinate one to more basic issues).

5.3.1 Background to childcare and family policy in Hesse

The legal entitlement to childcare in Hesse was – prior to 1999 and also subsequently – restricted to the statutory legal entitlement, with there having been a legal entitlement to a nursery place from 1996 onwards (see Chapter 4 above).

The red-green government from 1991 to 1999 attempted to expand provision of different forms of childcare. From 1991 to 1999, around 650 million Euro of funding from the Land government was invested in extending childcare, and the *Sofortprogramm Kinderbetreuung* (the 'Immediate childcare programme') was established to support parental groups setting up their own, non-state childcare institutions, although this was subject to budget cuts in the latter years of the second parliamentary term. This expansion was partly to meet the new legislative duty to provide sufficient nursery places for 3–6 year olds. The Land also met around 90% of the local running costs of nurseries through the block grant to local authorities (*Kommunaler Finanzausgleich* – KFA). Overall, the proportion of children in various types of childcare was lower than in the eastern Länder, but higher than some in the west. In 1999, the proportion of nursery places to children was 97%, the proportion of crèche provision for under-threes was 1.41%, and after-school nursery care (*Hort*) was provided for 4.83% of children in the affected age group (Jaich 2001).

5.3.2 Coalition agreement

The coalition agreement contained a relatively short section concerning childcare and family policy, in its section on social policy. The opening sentence would be uncontentious in conservative circles: 'The family is the first and most important foundation of society' (CDU/FDP Hessen 1999, p.48).

Its measures included (pp.48–9):

- A commitment to start a 'family political offensive' for Hesse;
- A commitment to extend the educational function of childcare institutions;
- A commitment to increase flexibility in childcare institutions (for instance in staffing, opening times and individual support), and to deregulation;
- Support for private childcare initiatives and an emphasis on the role of childminders.

There is a repeated commitment to the need for childcare to increase the compatibility of work and family life:

> A central job of family politics exists, now as before, to make possible the combination of family and professional life. Within that are measures

which give a genuine freedom of choice between profession and family for mothers and fathers. Family and employment are seen as of equal value.

This does indicate a departure from the most traditional conception of family politics of the CDU.

5.3.3   Developments in childcare policy 2002–2006

In 2001, the Land government introduced the 'Offensive for Childcare'. The aim of the programme was to increase the availability of childcare, in particular for children under the age of three (where there was a significant shortfall – in comparison to the provision of nurseries, where the number of places almost reflected the level of need). The role of childminders was expanded, and the government increased funding for these (from 743,322 Euro in the first year of the programme to 1,425,726 Euro in the third). Payments were also made available of up to 400 Euro per year to individual childminders, in particular as a pension contribution. These could be obtained by those who agreed to engage in continuing professional development and undertake a first aid course (Hessisches Sozialministerium 2005, pp.18–21).

The emphasis on childminders, as well as 'institutional' forms of provision, was highlighted in several interviews (Interview IIa, Interview V). It was felt to offer greater flexibility, and perhaps reflected a Christian democratic scepticism about 'institutionalised' childcare. As will be discussed in Saxony-Anhalt, this is a trend adopted in several Christian Democrat-governed Länder, and is often criticised by politicians of the left, such as the SPD social affairs spokesperson in Hesse, Petra Fuhrmann, who questioned whether childminders are financially accessible to all (Interview X).

A further part of the 'Offensive for Childcare' was to increase the availability of childcare into the early afternoon – the number of places available for early afternoon childcare rose by 8,000 in the first year of the programme to 88,174 (ibid., p.22).

Opposition politicians claimed the 'Offensive for Childcare' represented the continuation of their previous initiatives. For instance Karin Hartmann (SPD) declared: 'I consider it positive that you want substantively to continue the *Sofortprogramm Kinderbetreuung*, which was often criticised by you, under the new name "Offensive for Childcare"' (Plenarprotokoll 2001, p.5183).

Alongside the continued expansion of childcare, especially for children under the age of three and in non-institutional and afternoon provision, the government moved to deregulate the sector. As it highlighted in its summary of achievements, previous regulations, dating back to 1963, were regarded as onerous, for instance regulating the number of coat hooks in childcare institutions (Hessische Landesregierung 2002, p.163). In a new directive, the government increased the maximum nursery group size to 25 children present (the previous limit was 25, but referred to children *registered*, and normally around five would be absent through illness or for other reasons; a standard group size of 20 had also been stipulated previously). The government claimed that the shift towards regulating the number of children present rather than registered would give parents greater flexibility. It also reduced regulation of opening hours (FR, 8th March 2001a; FR, 15th March 2001). The CDU and FDP drew a distinction between 'minimum standards', which should be set by government, and the opposition's view, which was that it 'wanted everything regulated' (Silke Lautenschläger, Plenarprotokoll 2001, p.4856). Underlying this was pressure from local government, which was keen to see deregulation of the sector to reduce costs (FR, 8th March 2001a). Independent childcare providers (in particular the churches), who of course received public funds for the service they provided, were extremely critical of this move and claimed, in particular, that the legal duty to provide education in childcare institutions was incompatible with the increased group size following the changes in regulation (FR, 8th March 2001b).

The Land government's emphasis between 1999 and 2003 was on the quantitative expansion of childcare, rather than a strengthening of the provision of education within it. With the exception of the incentive given to childminders to gain formal qualifications, no initiatives were undertaken in this direction; the only exception was some development of German teaching for children for whom it was a second language (Hovestadt 2003, pp.24–5). Although it falls outside the period under consideration here, this lack of focus on the educational element of childcare changed shortly after the 2003 Land election, with the announcement that an education plan for children from the ages of 0 to 10 would be developed (ibid., pp.24–5).

The government moved all of the responsibility for the running costs of childcare institutions into the local government bloc grant (KFA) (Landtagsdrucksache 15/1543). This was supplemented by the various funding provisions made to support the programmes described above. Minister Mosiek-Urbahn justified the ending of separate money to support the construction of new childcare institutions, outside the KFA, with the argument that provision – in terms of buildings – for children aged 3–6 was now sufficient; the money involved had been shifted into the general bloc grant, and could be used to construct new institutions if needed (Plenarprotokoll 2000, p.3250).

It is most instructive to consider not just the initiatives the government introduced, but also their actual outputs, particularly in the light of the opposition's frequent criticism that the Koch government's childcare policies were minimal, all talk and no action. Karin Hartmann, for instance, said of the Offensive for Childcare: 'This offensive is just a flop and consists just of a beautiful façade, a beautiful brochure, and dozens of press releases' (Plenarprotokoll 2001, p.5183). The Statistisches Bundesamt published an extensive piece of research comparing the point reached by the Länder in 2004, giving data for the very end of 2002 – at the very end of the parliamentary term under consideration here. It found that there were places for 4% of children in crèches of the relevant age (3% in all-day crèches), compared to a western German average of 3% and 2% respectively. There were places for 93% of children in nurseries, including 29% in all-day institutions, compared to a western German average of 88% and 21% respectively. There were places in dedicated after-school centres for 7% of children of the affected age, including 6% offering all-day provision, compared to a federal average of 5% and 4% respectively. The level of public subsidy per place was also above the national average (Statistisches Bundesamt 2004). Compared to the situation in 1999, outlined at the start of this chapter, the number of nursery places compared to the number of children had fallen slightly, but there was a growth in the availability of crèche and after-school centres, as well as in support for childminders.

5.3.4   Changes in family support

In addition to its changes to childcare (and indeed before the launch of the Offensive for Childcare), the Land government launched a 'Family-political Offensive' (Hessisches Sozialministerium 2000). This received 20.14 million Euro from 2000 to 2002 (Hessische Landesregierung 2002, p.162). The document expressed concern that Hesse was 'going single' ('*Hessen versingelt*', Hessisches Sozialministerium 2000, p.8) and also about the falling birth-rate, and spelt out three aims: the strengthening of consciousness concerning families and their needs; improving the compatibility of family and professional life; and improving financial support for families.

To help achieve the first aim, it constructed a 'family atlas' – a compendium of programmes and services for families, both in hard copy and on the internet and CD ROM (ibid., p.16). Other measures which were carried out included a competition amongst local authorities to promote 'family friendliness' (Hessisches Sozialministerium 2005, p.39). There was an audit of universities to ensure that they were supportive of families (a point which Minister Lautenschläger felt particularly strongly about, according to interviewees; Interview V, Interview DD). There was also a programme of support for mothers' centres – voluntary centres for mothers to exchange ideas and mutually support each other (ibid., pp.46–8). The Land government also introduced a 'family audit' of its ministries, to promote flexible working (Hessisches Sozialministerium 2005). The response of the opposition to this – akin to the changes in childcare policy – was that, in spite of the publicity, the actual substance of the 'Family-political Offensive' was minimal: as Dr. Judith Pauly-Bender (SPD) put it in the

Landtag, 'One pretty brochure doesn't do it' (Plenarprotokoll 2001, p.5234). The Chairman of the DGB in Hesse, Stefan Körzell, was equally scathing, pointing out that working hours for public servants had increased – in a way which was anathema to family life (Interview U).

The government also invited Dr. Jürgen Borchert, a judge at Darmstadt Family Court, who had worked on prominent cases at the Federal Constitutional Court and was a strident advocate of more support for families, to work with it on a 'Wiesbaden Proposal' for family politics. Borchert was based in the Staatskanzlei for six months working on this proposal. A Congress took place in early 2002, and a programme was published in 2003 (Hessische Staatskanzlei 2003), with Roland Koch writing an introduction. In the programme, Borchert identifies the significant cost of raising children, and claims there is a fundamental disparity in the financing of the welfare state, which disadvantages families. Amongst other proposals, he suggests a 'family voting right', with more votes for those with children (p.25); the definition of a minimum sum of money needed to live (p.26); and increasing tax thresholds for those with children (p.26).

Borchert was subsequently scathing about the Hesse government's progress in this area, comparing his role in the Staatskanzlei to that of a 'Court jester', suggesting that other Land governments had utilised the proposals in the 'Wiesbaden Proposal', not that in Hesse, and in particular criticising the 'per capita' model of health insurance favoured by Hesse's Social Affairs Minister, Silke Lautenschläger, which he believed was extremely disadvantageous to families (FAZ, 1st February 2005). A civil servant close to the Minister claimed that Hesse had made efforts in the Bundesrat to promote family-friendly policies, but that the Land's influence was limited, not least because of disagreements amongst the CDU-led governments. Minister Lautenschläger had also managed to bring some of Borchert's ideas into the CDU's Herzog Commission on welfare reform (Interview DD).

5.3.5 Influencing and changing policy

Here, the influence of different actors upon childcare and family policy is briefly considered.

Role of the opposition: As has been clear throughout this chapter, political relations in Hesse were completely polarised, such that there was absolutely no inter-party collaboration on these issues – a point readily confirmed by an SPD representative (Interview X).

Role of trade unions: Again, as in the field of education policy, the relationship of the CDU/FDP government to the trade unions was not positive, in this sector or in any other. The GEW, by far the most significant union in this area, was particularly opposed to the new nursery directive, which achieved the deregulation highlighted above.

Role of Land parties: Interviewees did not refer to a particular role played by Land parties in shaping policy in this area. Instead, the reverse is true: several interviewees alluded to the role of Roland Koch and Silke Lautenschläger, in particular, in shaping opinions within the CDU. Koch 'massively supported' the childcare initiatives of the CDU, and '[they] cost a lot of effort', according to one close observer in the social affairs ministry (Interview V).

Role of CDU Fraktion: Within this area of policy, the executive appeared to be highly dominant – no interviewees mentioned any exogenous influence from the CDU Fraktion. As with the CDU Landesverband, the Fraktion needed to be led on the issue of family support, in particular by Roland Koch. Norbert Kartmann, the Fraktion Chair said, on the issue of family support:

> It's an interesting topic, because the development of today's policies happened before the development in the party – the practice moved ahead of the party. There weren't conferences, or discussions; it's not to be found in any party programmes. We did have an out of date version of family politics, and that was modernised, and supported by the Fraktion, although not without some complaints, saying it's a load of rubbish (Interview W).

Role of FDP Fraktion: Interviewees did not refer to the FDP having a major role, although some key FDP objectives, in particular around the deregulation of childcare and support for childminders, were realised.

Role of the civil service: In this area of policy, there was no suggestion of the civil service being obstructive of change or steering policy in a particular direction.

Role of the sub-Land level: Local authorities in Hesse faced significant financial challenges throughout this period. As a result, they were particularly keen on the deregulation of nurseries, and supportive of the increased group-sizes that were permitted. Local government was also supportive of more use of childminders, as well as of formal institutions for children under three, as childminders were significantly cheaper (Interview V). There is no evidence, however, that this led directly to the policy choices detailed above. A senior civil servant in this area (Interview IIa) noted a tendency amongst SPD-led local authorities to try to find fault with Land-level initiatives, even when they shared their aims.

Role of formal procedures: As in other areas of policy-making in Hesse, there was strong executive dominance – a point recognised on all sides (Interview V, Interview X). Debates in the Landtag were highly polarised, with repetition of well-worn mantras (the accusation that support for childcare and families was all talk and no action from the SPD and Greens, and robust defences of the government's progressive credentials, as well as complaints about the Land's contribution to the Länderfinanzausgleich, from the CDU and FDP).

5.3.6 Childcare and family policy: Conclusions

Developments in policy can be summarised in the table below:

Table 5.7 Family and childcare policy in Hesse 1999–2003

Social democratic paradigm	Christian democratic paradigm	Change
Provision free for all	Provision only available at cost	Still means-tested, no change
Subsidised provision starts at age 0	Subsidised provision starts at age 3	Modest extension of Land support for institutions for under-3s and for childminders
Subsidised provision extensively available	Subsidised provision available where demand exists	Subsidised provision after age 3 remains extensively available due to legal entitlement, very limited provision before that age
Provision in formal institutions	Flexible methods of provision	Switch towards greater flexibility, in particular enhancing role of childcare
Close regulation of childcare institutions	Light-touch regulation of childcare institutions	Switch towards lighter-touch regulation setting minimum standards through new Nursery Directive
No preference about types of family unit	Support for 'traditional' family	No stated preference about type of family unit

Hesse's CDU-led government enjoyed an extremely conservative reputation (in the light, in particular, of Roland Koch's predilection for polemicism, as discussed in the introduction to this chapter), and the CDU Landesverband is amongst the most conservative. Against that background, the expansion of support for childcare might come as a surprise. Three points are worth making here. Frequently, in interviews, there was reference to the changed social parameters facing the government. The CDU felt pressure to meet public demand for more provision, and this is an area where, even in Hesse, changed public expectations of what Land governments should do rendered a shift towards the Christian democrat paradigm untenable. Secondly, the model of childcare policy the CDU pursued – with significant deregulation of the nursery sector and support for childminders – represented a new and distinctive conservative version of childcare policy, or elements of a new Christian democrat paradigm, in response to the change in public expectations. Finally, the opposition was keen to argue that, in expanding childcare, it would have gone further, and faster, so, it claimed, the actual impact of the change of government was to drastically slow policy change which might otherwise have occurred. This cannot be judged scientifically, but as was outlined above, in spite of a challenging budgetary situation, provision of childcare expanded beyond the statutory requirement in this period, and in 2003 levels of provision in Hesse were greater than the west German average.

5.4   Labour market policy in Hesse 1999–2003

5.4.1   Introduction

As outlined in the introduction, Hesse was amongst the most prosperous Länder in 1999, at the time of the change of government. Unemployment was fairly low – as it had been throughout the 1990s – and the economy was performing well. As a result, Hesse, in common with other wealthier, southern German Länder, focused its labour market policies primarily on 'problem groups' such as the long-term and older unemployed, or those in receipt of social assistance, in a way comparable to that pursued by Bavaria and Baden Württemberg, although it did engage in active labour market policy to a greater level than those two Länder (Blancke and Schmid 1998, p.56). As discussed in Chapter 4, Länder can be placed into the three categories 'push', 'pull' and 'stay', depending on the extent to which they pursue an active labour market policy, and their degree of innovation. Studies (Blancke and Schmid 1998; Blancke 1999; Schmid et al. 2004) have tended to see Hesse as being – even under the SPD/Green government – a 'pull' Land, with limited levels of innovation and expenditure, or partially in the 'stay' category, as it had a slightly higher level of expenditure than Bavaria and Baden Württemberg. As a result, the legacy of the SPD/Green government in this area bore some resemblance to the Christian democratic paradigm in labour market policy, concerning the important question of the scope of active labour market policy (whether it focused on just problem groups, or more widely).

A particularly important instrument in labour market policy was the programme *Arbeit statt Sozialhilfe* – 'Work instead of social support' (Blancke and Schmid 1998, p.31). This was a Land-supported programme deploying the possibility in social assistance legislation of allowing the municipalities responsible (Landkreise and cities) to create subsidised job opportunities for those who would otherwise receive social assistance payments. These were funded by the social assistance which would have been paid, as well as a top-up from the Land government, and from payments from the beneficiaries of whatever work was done, and included pension and health insurance contributions. The stated aim was reintegration into the regular labour market. Measures were paid at the level of the relevant wage agreement (Rechnungshof Hessen 1995). This was a popular programme – and Hans Eichel, the Minister President, was defeated at a party conference when he attempted to reduce its budget. Municipalities had a further reason for supporting the programme:

they were concerned that the Federal Labour Office would declare too many people 'unfit to work' and pass them from their own responsibility – as recipients of unemployment assistance – to the municipality, who would then be obliged to pay them social assistance, with a consequent impact upon local authority budgets. By demonstrating an ability to work, the programme helped overcome this (Interview BB).

5.4.2   The election campaign and the coalition agreement

During the election campaign, as noted in the section above, the SPD-led government was more widely trusted on issues of economic and labour market policy than the CDU, and indeed these areas of policy were a key feature in its election campaign. By contrast, the CDU and FDP focused very strongly on other issues, notably education and immigration policy.

Labour market policy, like childcare policy, featured only to a limited degree in the coalition agreement (CDU/FDP Hessen 1999, pp.47–8), under the heading 'Social labour market policy'. The starting point was thus: 'In order to improve the effectiveness of labour market measures, these will be focused on the first labour market' (p.47). It promised greater flexibility in the Land's programmes to secure reintegration in the first labour market (such as *Arbeit statt Sozialhilfe*), active involvement in the Bundesrat in this policy area, and consideration of whether support for training and re-training programmes had been sufficiently adapted to extensive structural changes in the economy. There was a further full section of the agreement devoted to 'efficient use of resources', stating that the government would create incentives for municipalities responsible for social assistance to improve case management and support, reduce accommodation costs, and combat fraud.

As will be demonstrated, the government gave significant prominence to this area of policy, notably after Roland Koch's visit to Wisconsin – this was not reflected in the coalition agreement.

5.4.3   Active labour market policies

One of the first steps of the new government in this area was to reduce the amount of funding available for the programme *Arbeit statt Sozialhilfe*, making 21 million, rather than 28 million DM available. Per job, rather than 20,000 DM per year, only 16,700 DM would be made available, although there would be the possibility of payment below the level of the prevailing wage agreement (FR, 7th May 1999). This represented a shift towards the Christian democratic paradigm in labour market policy. Alongside this change, the government brought back funding for a programme 'Training instead of social assistance', which had been cancelled by the SPD/Green government.

In 2000, the government then introduced its own programme: HARA (*Hessisches Aktionsprogramm Regionale Arbeitsmarktpolitik* – Hesse Programme of Action Regional Labour Market Policy). Initially, there were six elements in this programme:

- Preparatory work for access to the labour market (such as training in making job applications);
- Individually tailored training;
- Training for employees to provide job support and placement for those in receipt of social assistance;
- The creation of a job placement agency, in cooperation between the local authority and the local labour office;
- 'Trampoline' – a programme which provided Land support of 700 Euro per month for job creation for unemployed people whom it was hard to place in jobs;
- Experiments – supporting innovative projects by the Landkreise and cities to help social assistance recipients get qualifications, job placements or work (Hessisches Sozialministerium 2006).

Local authorities could choose which of these streams to apply for, and *de facto* this meant that they had the option of continuing with measures similar to *Arbeit statt Sozialhilfe*, because the 'Trampoline' part of the programme was substantially the same, although it now ran under a different name (Interview BB).

In 2002, four new elements were added to the HARA:

- 'Close support': funding provided to local authorities at a level of 1,000 Euro per employee per month, to a maximum of three employees, to provide intensive support to recipients of social assistance to get them into work;
- Job Centre: funding for the creation of an agency to assist social assistance recipients and hard-to-place unemployed people, in combination with the local labour agency, in order to get them into work;
- Employer assignment: funding for work placements (with support and training in time off) for those in receipt of social assistance, received additional funding;
- *Kombilohn* (wage top-ups): Payments were introduced to localities who placed social assistance recipients into wage top-up programmes.

In fact, Hesse had pursued the idea of wage top-ups since 1999, using provisions in social assistance legislation (Spiegel, 30th July 1999). A pilot project, involving five cities and three Landkreise was established. Access was restricted to long-term recipients of social assistance, and was in some cases targeted at even more specific groups (Dann et al. 2002, p.7). A wage top-up was paid to the employee, at a (steadily declining) percentage over social assistance (ibid., pp.9–10) in order to create the possibility of employment.

Only 1,500 people were supported through this pilot programme, and, of those, around 6% found continuing employment (ibid., p.19). The project was not regarded as a success within the Ministry (Interview BB). Not surprisingly, the trade unions in Hesse were sceptical of this, and particularly concerned about substitution effects, where regular workers would be replaced by those on wage top-ups (FR, 3rd August 1999; Interview U).

In 2002, the Land government reached an agreement with the Land Labour Office and four Landkreise to create *Job-OFFENSIV* centres (the title relating to the OFFENSIV proposal put to the Bundesrat, discussed below). The idea was to bring together support, training and placement of unemployed people – both for those who were in receipt of social assistance and also unemployment benefit (Hessisches Sozialministerium 2006). Individual case management and placement was a priority (Hessische Landesregierung 2002, p.161).

Overall, between 2000 and 2004, HARA saw 11,365,451 Euro spent by the Land, 17,305,090 Euro spent by the European Social Fund, 1,444,783 Euro spent by the Labour Office/Agency, 63,304,849 Euro spent by local government, and 1,377,139 Euro spent from other sources (Landtagsdrucksache 16/183, p.5).

Two points stand out here: first, notwithstanding Roland Koch's polemical contributions to debate about workfare, the Land-level programmes were quite pragmatic, with significant effort being devoted to supporting the long-term unemployed through tailored training and placement. The Land also made strenuous efforts to involve both local government and the Federal Labour Office.

Secondly, there was a significant degree of continuity with the policies of the SPD/Green government. It, too, was mostly focused on the 'first' (or regular) labour market. In addition, the programme *Arbeit statt Sozialhilfe*, which in effect developed a second (subsidised) labour market, continued, slightly amended, under a new name.

5.4.4   Initiative in the Bundesrat

In August 2001, Roland Koch visited Hesse's partner state Wisconsin. He was particularly impressed by the 'Wisconsin Works' programme, which increased the conditionality of benefit payments. On the one hand, additional support was given to the unemployed in finding jobs (for instance in preparing applications, or in extra training), and job placements were sometimes arranged by private companies. On the other hand, unemployed people who failed to cooperate with the programme faced the loss of public funds. In some cases, the unemployed also had to carry out community service (FR, 7th August 2001). Upon his return (and undeterred – or perhaps encouraged – by the resignation of Minister Müller-Urbahn), Roland Koch announced his desire to establish the Wisconsin Model in Germany, using the Bundesrat to secure agreement. Koch particularly emphasised greater elements of compulsion to take work: 'We are too soft with pressure, and too bad in giving help'; those who were fit to work but chose not to 'should have a very modest life, with just accommodation' (FR, 6th August 2001). In response, Tarek Al-Wazir, the Greens' parliamentary leader, said that Koch was thinking 'not of help, but of ways and means of making life even harder for recipients of social assistance' (FR, 6th August 2001).

In 2002, Koch and Lautenschläger introduced the OFFENSIV Bill into the Bundesrat (Bundesrat Drucksache 52/02). OFFENSIV stood for *Gesetz zum Optimalen Fördern und Fordern durch engagierten Service in Vermuttlungsagenturen* ('A Law for optimal support and demand by engaged service in placement agencies'). Key elements were:

- Rolling together of responsibility for recipients of social assistance and other forms of unemployment benefit into 'job centres';
- The requirement that the Länder should be able to determine the nature of the relationship of these with the Federal Labour Office, with the Länder able to access the funds of the Federal Labour Office for active labour market measures;
- Rules on what job it is reasonable to expect an unemployed person to accept were tightened, with work below the level of unemployment benefit becoming acceptable;
- The possibility of 'work-fare', with community work being required in return for extra payment, but no social insurance contribution being paid for this work;
- Support for wage top-ups and paid employment placement became possible with the aim of expanding the availability of low-paid employment.

This was agreed by the Bundesrat on 31st May 2002 (Bundesrat Drucksache 433/02). Hesse got support from other CDU-led Länder, although as will be discussed in the case of Saxony-Anhalt, the eastern Länder were only supportive in the knowledge the law was unacceptable to the red-green Bundestag. Because its passage was interrupted by the federal election of 2002, the Bundesrat again agreed the law on 8th November 2002 (Bundesrat Drucksache 812/02); it was discussed, although finally rejected, by the Bundestag in 2003. Public debate on the OFFENSIV bill was polarised, although Koch found some support for his ideas from Social Democrats, such as Sigmar Gabriel, the Minister President of Lower Saxony (Die Zeit, 30th August 2001).

In all of its elements, from the extension of Land and local level responsibility for labour market policy to increased elements of compulsion, and support for a low-wage sector beneath the level of wage agreements, the OFFENSIV bill reflected a particularly strong version of the Christian democratic paradigm of labour market policy.

5.4.5   Hesse and the Hartz reforms

The Hartz commission reported in August 2002 (Spiegel, 16th August 2002). As a result, only the laws referred to as Hartz I and Hartz II were considered during the 1999–2003 parliament in Hesse. Hesse opposed both in the Bundesrat, supporting their referral to the Conciliation Committee (Protokoll 2002, pp.520–1), with Ruth Wagner speaking for the Land government. In particular, there was dissatisfaction with the structure of the proposed Personal Service Agencies. Koch declared himself satisfied with the outcome of the Conciliation Committee, saying that the resulting agreement 'clearly bore the handwriting of Hesse' (Koch 2008). Moreover, several other elements of Hesse's OFFENSIV Bill, such as the possibility of Landkreise taking full responsibility for placements, were taken up by the subsequent Hartz reforms.

The more contentious elements of the Hartz reform fell outside the period under consideration. It is worth noting as an aside, however, that the 'Option model', whereby full responsibility for job placement was transferred to a Landkreis or city, rather than being shared, was particularly favoured in Hesse. It was taken up by 12 Landkreise and by Wiesbaden city. It was suggested to the author that Hesse localities' previous experience in job placement and support for the unemployed, created by the *Arbeit statt Sozialhilfe* programme and subsequently the HARA, meant that they had a particular appetite to undertake this work (Interview BB).

5.4.6   Payment of apprenticeships and job creation schemes

Hesse did not undertake any initiatives to change the payment of apprenticeships during this period. However, as noted above, it did amend rules on payment of jobs created under the *Arbeit statt Sozialhilfe* and the HARA, so that these could be paid at a level below that of sectoral wage agreements. This was clearly a consequence of the change of government (Interview BB).

5.4.7   Partnership with trade unions

The CDU-led government in Hesse made no great effort to forge relations with the trade union sector, in contrast to the cases of the Saarland and Saxony-Anhalt which are discussed in Chapters 5 and 6. The government did claim that elements of HARA were developed in consultation with social partners (Landtagsdrucksache 16/183, p.2). Hesse did not – unlike almost every other Land – experiment with an 'Alliance for Jobs' at a Land level (Blancke 2004, p.173). Stefan Körzell, the Chair of the DGB in Hesse, felt that policy changes from 1999 onwards had been anathema to the trade unions at every step – from union involvement in public services to the commercialisation of education, and privatisation. Relations had clearly worsened as a result of the change of government in 1999 (Interview U).

In this respect, there was no deviation at all from the Christian democratic paradigm.

5.4.8   Influencing and changing policy

Role of the opposition: As with education and childcare reform, political positions were polarised, and there was no involvement of the opposition in the Landtag. When asked whether the government had ever tried to involve the opposition in any decisions in this area, Petra Fuhrmann, the SPD's social affairs spokesperson, responded 'absolutely not' (Interview X). The SPD had little or no informal contact with the ministry during this period (Interview X, Interview BB).

Role of trade unions: Although there was informal consultation over the implementation of 'top up' wages (Interview U), trade unions otherwise appeared to have no role in shaping policy in this area.

Land parties: None of the interviewees alluded at all to the role of the CDU or FDP Landesverbände in shaping policy at this level, nor were references made to their involvement in the contemporary media.

Role of the CDU Fraktion: There is no evidence of extensive involvement of the Fraktion in developing policy in this period. This may partly be explained by the limited role of the Landtag (see below).

Role of the FDP: The FDP Fraktion was not cited as having an influence on policy in this area. A civil servant significantly involved in these developments believed that, here, *Ressortskompetenz* – the authority of a minister to decide what happens in her own ministry – was paramount (Interview BB). FDP agreement on conduct within the Bundesrat was necessary, but measures like the OFFENSIV Bill were unlikely to be opposed – as they reflected the FDP's priorities in any case.

Role of the civil service: There was no particular feeling of civil service obstruction of policy in this period, and both civil servants and those on the political side were keen to emphasise the technical expertise needed to undertake labour market policy, and that this was respected by the Land government (Interview BB, Interview DD). In some cases, Social Democrats remained in senior positions in the Ministry – sometimes outlasting Christian Democrats drafted in by the new government (Interview BB, Interview DD).

Role of the sub-Land level: The strong involvement of local government in this area of policy-making in Hesse is striking. The Land government's active labour market policies, in HARA, allowed local authorities to choose which programmes to draw upon – allowing those interested to continue, for instance, with the new variant of the *Arbeit statt Sozialhilfe* Programme. Roland Koch's enthusiasm for allowing local authorities to take responsibility for job placement was particularly shared by Erich Pipa, the high-profile *Sozialdezernent* (Head of Social Affairs) of Main-Kinzig Kreis, although he was an SPD member (FAZ, 2nd July 2004). Pipa's support for increased local responsibility in this area was not shared by the SPD in the Landtag (Interview X).

Formal procedures: Policy in this area was largely in the domain of the executive, with decisions not requiring primary legislation. As a result, the involvement of the Landtag was very limited. This partly reflects the extent of 'interlocking policy-making' in labour market policy: the federal government, Land governments and local government are all involved (the latter particularly so in Hesse) – and it is invariably members of the executive, not the legislature, who negotiate with the other tiers of government (be it through the Bundesrat, or informally with local government).

5.4.9   Conclusion

Developments in Hesse's labour market policy are summarised in the table below:

Table 5.8   Labour market policy in Hesse 1999–2003

Social democratic paradigm	Christian democratic paradigm	Change
Willingness to contemplate long-term subsidised state jobs	Rejection of long-term subsidised state jobs	Continuation of subsidised, publicly created jobs for social assistance recipients
Reluctance to subsidise private sector	Willing to subsidise private sector	Introduction of work placements and limited wage top-ups within private sector
Active labour market measures appropriate for general labour market	Active measures only for special needs groups (e.g. disabled, long-term unemployed) for limited period	No change – active measures only for 'special groups'
Rejection of promotion of low-paid sector	Encouragement of low-paid sector, e.g. through 'Kombilohn' (wage subsidies)	Introduction of wage top-ups but on very limited scale. Wider promotion of low-wage sector through Bundesrat
Rejection of localisation/ decentralisation	Support for localisation/ decentralisation	Support for radical decentralisation
Rejection of deregulation	Support for deregulation	Support for deregulation (e.g. lifting restrictions on *Scheinselbstständigkeit* – false claims of self-employment)
Apprenticeships and jobs-creation schemes paid at Tarif (collectively agreed) level	Apprenticeships and job-creation schemes paid at lower level	No change on apprenticeships. Shift to paying subsidised publicly created jobs below Tarif level
Privileged partnership with unions	Parity of partnership with social partners, or limited partnership	No partnership with unions

In its outward-facing activities, through its OFFENSIV Bill, as well as Minister President Koch's contributions to public debate, Hesse saw a clear shift towards the Christian democrat paradigm. Koch's advocacy of the Wisconsin model – and associated, polemical public statements – attracted widespread coverage in the national media, and the Hesse government became associated in the public mind with demands for a rightward shift in labour market policy.

The picture inside Hesse is more nuanced, however. At the outset, at the end of the SPD/Green government, the Land's policies did not fit squarely within the social democratic paradigm, with the active labour market policies not enjoying particular prominence within the Land budget or displaying a high degree of innovation. In some areas, the policy switched clearly – most notably over payment of publicly created jobs at sub-Tarif level, and in relations with trade unions – from the social democratic to Christian democratic paradigm. However, the Land government did not back away from support for the second labour market completely, with changes occurring mainly at the level of presentation rather than substance (for instance, changing the name of the programme previously known as *Arbeit statt Sozialhilfe*). The government's promotion of 'job centres', and desire, alongside the Landkreise, to 'join up' job placement and associated support, rather than leaving it to the federal labour agency, were particularly innovative. On the one hand, this demonstrates support for federalisation – part of the Christian democratic paradigm. However, the degree of innovation in labour market policy undoubtedly rose during the period between 1999 and 2003.

5.5   Conclusion

As discussed in the introduction to this chapter, circumstances at the start of the Koch government appeared likely to see a significant shift towards the Christian democratic paradigm across all areas of policy. The CDU Landesverband was highly conservative, and politics in the state had long been polarised, so there was no expectation of involving the opposition in change. The election campaign was divisive, and Koch himself appeared to be a divisive figure, and certainly not one who looked to integrate those sceptical about his political direction, such as the trade unions. The party finance scandal, which came close to bringing down the government, had the effect of entrenching the government's position, leading to a particularly poisonous atmosphere in the Landtag, rather than restricting the government's room for manoeuvre.

Two counter-weights to this expectation of policy change were expressed: first, that the structures created by the SPD/Green government over a period of years might have attracted popular support and developed their own institutional anchor, in a path-dependent manner, such that it would be difficult to change them. Secondly, the factors leading to civil service resistance to policy change appeared to be strong: there had been an extended period of SPD incumbency in the Land, and there was extensive political polarisation in the Land (particularly in education policy).

These expectations were absolutely realised in the manner in which policy was developed in Hesse: the Landtag – marginal at best to decision-making on substantive policy – was utterly polarised and there were no efforts to involve the opposition in decisions, nor was any effort made to reach out to trade unions.

In substantive policies, however, in each of the three areas under consideration, there was a shift from social democratic towards Christian democratic policy paradigms, but in each case the shift was more nuanced than might have been expected. In the field of education policy, there remained a large number of comprehensive schools; in childcare and family policy, the CDU expanded childcare provision and appeared to have departed from a highly conservative view of the family; and in labour market policy, at a Land level, there were elements of continuity and also of innovation (including within SPD-led local authorities). Each of these points to the importance of *path-dependent constraints* upon a Land government's potential to effect policy change: it is difficult to undertake a school closure programme, and it will meet with resistance, so a Land government will face less opposition if it tries to realise some of its aims within existing structures. Where, as in this case, there is a public desire for and expectation of the expansion of childcare, retrenchment will be hard to achieve. Similarly, it is difficult and potentially politically unwise to end popular programmes which provide work to social assistance recipients.

By contrast, there is little evidence for civil service obstruction of policy change. This might partly be attributed to the clear policy leadership given by Hesse's Staatskanzlei, with it playing an active coordinating role and overseeing the delivery of pledges in the coalition agreement. The government did take some of the (few) opportunities that presented themselves to replace SPD with CDU sympathisers in key ministries, but it also left a number of SPD members in senior positions. If anything, bureaucratic lethargy rather than wilful political resistance was a more powerful obstacle to policy change, and the government was willing to accept that administrative competence could sometimes trump party sympathy in recruitment and retention decisions about senior civil servants.

The political hypothesis outlined in the introduction was partially realised in each of the three areas of policy discussed for the case of Hesse. Where it was not realised, a variation of the territorial counter-hypothesis was confirmed: the nature of existing policies of the Land might make it hard to secure policy change, or changing public expectations – as in the case of childcare – could prove too strong an obstacle to overcome, and could demand a 'rethink' of policies that might traditionally have been demanded.

6
The Saarland 1999–2004

6.1 Background

The Saarland was chosen as a case study for three reasons. First, like Hesse, it experienced a change of government in 1999, from an SPD-led to a CDU-led administration. However, two features distinguish it sharply from Hesse: it is one of the smallest Länder, and it had significant economic difficulties, even though it is in the west of Germany. It was a net recipient of transfers from the fiscal redistribution mechanism (*Länderfinanzausgleich*), receiving 294 million DM in 1999 (Statistisches Bundesamt). As hypothesised in the introduction, the Land's economic situation might be expected to affect the extent to which policy change could be effected, and also the nature of that change. Like Hesse, prior to 1999 the SPD had been in power for an extended period (although it had not enjoyed the hegemony it did in Hesse throughout the post-war period). As a result, civil service appointments would have reflected the preferences of successive SPD-led governments, which might hinder policy change.

The Saarland has a unique history. From 1945 to 1959, it was an autonomous region, independent from both Germany and France, with its own passports, its own currency (the Saar-Franc, linked to the French Franc) and its own national football team. In 1957, there was a referendum on the Saar-Statute, which would have enshrined its independent status, but this was defeated, and instead taken as a sign that the Saarland would join the Federal Republic of Germany, and adopt the German Mark, under the provisions of the Basic Law, Article 23. This was formally agreed by the Landtag and realised in 1959 (Linsmayer 2007).

6.1.1 Social structure/Religious affiliation

In 1945, the Saarland had a population of just over 745,000; this grew rapidly in the immediate post-war years, and then more slowly, reaching a high point of 1,132,127 in 1966. There then followed a period of modest decline, followed by slow population growth in the years 1987–1995. In 1999, the population was 1,071,501 (Statistisches Landesamt).

The Saarland's demographic structure gives policy-makers cause for concern. Like Saxony-Anhalt, discussed in Chapter 7, its population is forecast to decline sharply, reaching around 916,000 by 2030. It is anticipated that the proportion of those aged 20 and under in relation to the overall population will fall from 18.7% in 2006 to 15.1% in 2030, while the proportion of those aged 65 and over will rise from 21.5% to 30.5%, as the Land's birthrate is significantly below the German average (Statistisches Landesamt). Although less dramatic than in Saxony-Anhalt, this does have an impact upon the policies Land governments pursue, for instance in provision of schools and childcare institutions.

The proportion of non-Germans in the Saarland is relatively small: only 78,502 out of a population of 1,061,376 (7.4%) in 2003. Of those, 31,280 were from countries in the European Union (Italians being the largest single group), and 14,000 were from Turkey, with smaller African and Asian minorities.

The Saarland is predominantly Catholic – in 2004, 65% of the population were members of the Catholic Church, with a further 20% being members of the Protestant Church. The proportion of Catholics was therefore the highest of any of the Länder, as was the proportion of the population who were members of either church (in both cases comfortably exceeding even Bavaria). This might generate an expectation that governments (of either colour) would face pressure to pursue a more conservative course on social issues.

The Saarland's economy is becoming ever more reliant on the service sector. In particular, the number of workers in the mining sector fell (from 14,100 in 1997 to 6,500 in 2007); in the past, this had been a major component of the Saarland's economy, employing 48,000 workers in the immediate post-war period (FAZ, 25th February 2008). This reflected the painful industrial restructuring the Land had faced – and indeed was still undertaking.

6.1.2   Economy and fiscal position

The Saarland's economy, in part because of the decline of its industrial base, was in a weak position, falling between Hesse and Saxony-Anhalt in its level of prosperity. The average level of GDP per inhabitant was 24,610 Euro (Statistisches Bundesamt 2006, p.67), compared to a national average of 26,390 Euro, putting it in 7th place overall. Wage rates were consistently below the federal average between 1991 and 2004, although ahead of the eastern Länder (ibid., p.74).

The Saarland's unemployment was substantial (see Table 6.1), and close to the federal average, remaining above the west German average – in part because of the shift away from manufacturing which the Land's economy had been forced to make. This would obviously impact upon policy choices at the Land level. High levels of unemployment may make policy-makers resistant to moving in the direction of the Christian democrat paradigm.

Table 6.1   Unemployment in Saarland 1999–2004

Year	1999	2000	2001	2002	2003	2004
Unemployment in %	12.1	10.7	9.8	9.9	10.4	10.0
Federal unemployment in %	11.7	10.7	10.3	10.8	11.6	11.7

Source: Statistisches Bundesamt

Saarland's budget was in an extremely precarious position. Seitz' 2000 study (containing a comprehensive analysis of 1995 data) shows that the Saarland's per capita debt was 12,531 DM per person – far higher than any of the other western Länder; for comparison, the next highest was Schleswig-Holstein at 9,301 DM. In comparison, Hesse's was 5,955 DM (Seitz 2000, p.193). Per capita expenditure was the highest of the western Länder at 5,769 DM, well above the Land's income. The level of expenditure on debt servicing was very high: in 1999, when the new government came into office, it represented 13.6% of all expenditure (Saarland Ministerium der Finanzen 2005, p.26). The Land's income from tax also fell steadily from 1993 to 2004 (ibid., p.35), in contrast to the modest growth experienced by most other western Länder. The Land received payments from the fiscal redistribution mechanism throughout the period in question as well as significant federal supplementary transfers (Statistisches Bundesamt 2007, p.570).

Overall, Saarland's public finances would be expected to play a significant role in policy choices in two different ways: they might make the Land particularly keen to attract external funding for projects (even if these did not reflect the government's policy preferences); and they would be expected to colour policy choices, making budget cuts, rather than expansion, favourable to policy-makers.

6.1.3   Politics in the Saarland

As mentioned above, the Saarland only acceded to Germany in 1959, with its first Landtag election as part of Germany taking place in 1960. The party system prior to accession was strongly influenced by the Catholic character of the Land – with the CVP (Catholic People's Party – which later merged into the CDU, although a breakaway continued until 1970) winning an overall majority of the vote in 1947 and 1952. Only in 1959 did the CVP merge with the CDU. Initially, the DSP (a social democratic party based in the Saarland) had also been separate from the SPD, although they also merged in 1955 (Rütters 2004, pp.361–5). A further feature of the post-war party system was the presence of the DPS (Democratic Party of the Saar), which was of a Christian-social nature, with a strong German nationalist view on the Saarland's future; for federal political reasons, it was connected to the FDP, and, following the accession, lost its distinctive profile.

Table 6.2   Landtag election results (%) in the Saarland 1960–2004

	CDU	SPD	DDU[1]	SVP/ SVP-CVP	Greens	FDP[2]- DPS	Others
1960	36.6	30.0	5.0	11.4	–	13.8	3.2
1965	42.7	40.7	3.1	5.2	–	8.3	–
1970	47.8	40.8	–	0.9	–	4.4	6.1
1975	49.1	41.8	–	–	–	7.4	1.7
1980	44.0	45.4	–	–	2.9	6.9	0.3
1985	37.3	49.2	–	–	2.5	10.0	1.0
1990	33.4	54.4	–	–	2.6	5.6	4.0
1994	38.6	49.4	–	–	5.5	2.1	4.4
1999	45.5	44.4	–	–	3.2	2.6	4.3
2004	47.5	30.8	–	–	5.6	5.2	10.9

Source: Landesregierung Saarland

Table 6.3   Land governments in the Saarland 1959–2007

Year	Parties in Government	Minister President
1959–1961	CDU/SPD	Franz Josef Röder (CDU)
1961–1965	CDU/DPS	Franz Josef Röder (CDU)
1965–1970	CDU/FDP-DPS	Franz Josef Röder (CDU)
1970–1974	CDU	Franz Josef Röder (CDU)
1974–1977	CDU	Franz Josef Röder (CDU)
1977–1979	CDU/FDP	Franz Josef Röder (CDU)
1979–1980	CDU/FDP	Werner Zeyer (CDU)
1980–1984	CDU/FDP	Werner Zeyer (CDU)
1984–1985	CDU/FDP	Werner Zeyer (CDU
1985–1990	SPD	Oskar Lafontaine (SPD)
1990–1994	SPD	Oskar Lafontaine (SPD)
1994–1998	SPD	Oskar Lafontaine (SPD)
1998–1999	SPD	Reinhard Klimmt (SPD)
1999–2004	CDU	Peter Müller (CDU)
2004–	CDU	Peter Müller (CDU)

Source: Landesregierung Saarland

---

[1]Deutsche Demokratische Union – a left-wing party formed as part of the German Freedom Union, formed to unite left-wing forces following the banning of the KPD; cf. Spiegel, 11th January 1961.

[2]To this day, the FDP in the Saarland is named FDP/DPS (Democratic Party of the Saar), although the DPS name is no longer commonly used.

By the late 1960s, the party system had 'normalised'. Two particular features are worth flagging for the purposes of this study: first, the CDU initially enjoyed strong support amongst the working-class population, owing to the rural, village-based population structure and the strength of Catholic trade unions. At the same time, this meant that the CDU Landesverband was significantly more moderate than several of its counterparts, notably that in Hesse, discussed in Chapter 5 (ibid., p.362). Secondly, with the diminishing links between Catholicism and social and political organisation in the 1960s and 1970s, the SPD gradually gained ground amongst Catholic workers, assisting it towards government. As can be seen in Table 6.2, both the Greens and the FDP have been relatively weak, with the Saarland having a predominantly two-party system.

Until the change of government, the Saarland was led by two dynamic, left-wing social democrats, Oskar Lafontaine and subsequently Reinhard Klimmt. The Saar-SPD retained a strong commitment to the retention of some mining in the Saarland (Klimmt 2003), earning the criticism from some other Länder that they were paying, through the fiscal redistribution mechanism, for the Saarland's failure to reform (Berliner Zeitung, 27th November 1997).

6.1.4   Political structures in the Saarland

It is worth outlining in brief the small number of variations in the political system in the Saarland, compared to other Länder.

Landesverfassung

In common with other Länder, the Saarland has its own constitution or Landesverfassung, dating back to 1947. This was subject to significant revision in 1952, when one of its most distinctive features, the five-year term of office for the Landtag (Article 67), was adopted. As in other Landesverfassungen, alongside provisions on the political structure of the Land, there are a number of statements regarding social rights, such as the right of mothers to the protection and support of the state (Article 23) and the right of children born out of wedlock to receive the same treatment as others (Article 24). In order to be amended, a two-thirds majority is needed in the Landtag (Article 101).

The Landesverfassung makes provision for direct democracy (Articles 99 and 100): those seeking a referendum must first put forward a potentially valid law, with justifications, supported by 5,000 citizens. It cannot affect financial matters and may only affect issues within the Land's competence, and it cannot propose a constitutional change. If one-fifth of all eligible voters declare their support for the proposal, the Landtag must either adopt the law, or hold a referendum. In order for the proposal in the referendum to pass, it requires the support of the majority of all eligible voters. In 1979, these provisions replaced a previous requirement that a referendum proposal needed the support of a third of the Landtag (Rütters 2004, p.383). In fact, no referendum has been held since 1979 under these provisions: two of the proposed laws were agreed by the Landtag, and one was rejected as it related to financial matters (ibid., p.384).

One element of the Landesverfassung of immediate relevance to this study is that certain different types of school – primary schools, schools for the disabled, extended secondary schools (*erweiterte Realschule*), grammar schools, comprehensive schools and vocational colleges (*Berufsschule*) are guaranteed in the Landesverfassung (Article 27). This provision was a constitutional amendment agreed between SPD and CDU in 1996 (Amtsblatt 1996, p.422), and was part of a bipartisan agreement to allow the abolition of the Hauptschule, which was previously also anchored in the Landesverfassung (SBZ, 8th February 1996; Interview JJ). This then places an obvious constraint upon any future government seeking to introduce a fundamental reform of school structures: it would require a two-thirds majority in order to be achieved, as will be discussed further below.

The electoral system

The electoral system is established by the Landesverfassung and the Land election law (Landeswahlgesetz). The Landtag consists of 41 members elected by three district lists, and a further ten are added from Land lists. Each voter has only one vote, for a party's district list; the D'Hondt formula is used to ensure that the overall distribution of seats reflects the number of votes cast for each party. There is no specific rule concerning 'overhanging mandates', but given the presence of just three, multi-member constituencies, there is little chance of a disproportional outcome.

Civil service and local government

From 1974 onwards, the Land's local administration contained the level of the Landkreise (counties) and the 'City Association' of Saarbrücken, which fulfilled the same functions as the Landkreise, including school planning, youth affairs, social assistance administration, and the legal supervision of local government below the district level (Das Parlament, 3rd July 2006). There are 52 towns and villages below this level. The Land adopted the South German Council model, so that mayors and heads of districts are directly elected. Localities work within the legal framework provided by the KSVG (Kommunalselbstverwaltungsgesetz – Local self-administration law).

It is striking that, although it is smaller than Berlin and Hamburg, the Saarland devolves more power to local government. Whereas in the city-states of Berlin, Hamburg and Bremen, the 'Land'-level actually fulfils some of the roles played by the Landkreise (such as, until the Hartz reforms, administering social assistance), in the Saarland the Landkreise jealously guard their powers (Das Parlament, 3rd July 2006). Local government could, therefore, be a source of obstruction towards Land-level policy-makers.

6.1.5   The Saarland's election campaign of 1999

The election campaign in the Saarland was unusual: Reinhard Klimmt, who had become a popular Minister President, sought to defend the SPD's overall majority with a campaign focused against the unpopular SPD/Green coalition at a federal level (Winkler 2000, p.31). Although Klimmt was personally popular, the Land's SPD was particularly affected by the sudden resignation of the former Minister President, Oskar Lafontaine, as SPD Chair and Federal Finance Minister. Klimmt launched strong attacks on the SPD-led government in Berlin, particularly on the issue of pensions, including concerning the ending of the link between pension increases and increases in earnings.

Peter Müller, the CDU's candidate for Minister President, was keen to present a centrist image of the CDU, with a 'competence team' including figures such as August Wilhelm Scheer, a well-regarded businessman, and Regina Görner, a trade unionist. Perhaps inspired by the CDU's petition against dual nationality in Hesse, Müller launched his own petition, this time against the federal government's pensions proposals. Müller was clearly on the moderate wing of the CDU. The party's election programme included cutting fees for nursery schools, reducing class sizes in primary schools, and the introduction of a hundred new teaching posts (CDU Saar 1999, p.32). Müller also propagated a planned ending of the coal industry in the Saarland (Berliner Zeitung, 17th May 1999). The main issues in the campaign, apart from the unpopularity of the federal government, were the state of the Saarland's fragile economy, and dealing with unemployment. Neither the Greens (who had had significant internal difficulties having gained representation in the Landtag for the first time in 1994), nor the FDP, appeared to be in a strong position (Winkler 2000, pp.29–30).

The result was a narrow win for the CDU, with just 6,500 votes separating the CDU and the SPD, and other parties falling well below the 5% hurdle. This gave the CDU an overall majority of one seat in the Landtag. Turnout fell by 14.8% to 68.7%, suggesting the SPD did not manage to sufficiently mobilise its voters (ibid., p.35). As in previous elections, the CDU did better amongst rural voters and Catholics, while the SPD did better amongst urban voters and Protestants (Forschungsgruppe Wahlen 1999a).

To great surprise, Reinhard Klimmt was, immediately after the election, appointed Federal Transport Minister by Chancellor Schröder, and Heiko Maas, the youthful Environment minister under Klimmt, became the SPD's parliamentary leader.

In the absence of coalition negotiations, the formation of the government occurred quickly. Peter Hans, a teacher by background, became the CDU's parliamentary leader (although he became ill and Annegret Kramp-Karrenbauer looked after the Fraktion for some time in his absence). Key ministerial appointments for the purposes of this study included Regina Görner as Minister for Women, Labour, Health and Social Affairs, and Jürgen

Schreier as Minister for Education and Culture. Görner was, until that time, a full-time member of the DGB's Federal Executive and the most senior CDU politician in the trade union movement. Schreier had been a teacher, and then a headteacher, before entering politics.

6.1.6   Politics in the Saarland 1999–2004

The government did not publish a formal programme of government (which is often the coalition treaty – not applicable in this case). Instead, the guidelines of policies to be pursued were set out by Peter Müller in his statement to the Landtag (*Regierungserklärung*) of 27th October 1999.

The period of government between 1999 and 2004 was not marked by great controversy, in contrast, in particular, to the situation in Hesse. There was only one change in the cabinet during this period: Interior Minister Klaus Meiser resigned in 2000, after the Landtag lifted his immunity from prosecution. Along with Reinhard Klimmt (who resigned from the federal cabinet, and was subsequently convicted), Meiser was alleged to have facilitated an illegal sponsorship agreement by a charitable organisation of the football club 1. FC Saarbrücken (Spiegel, 22nd November 2000a). He was replaced by Annegret Kramp-Karrenbauer (Spiegel, 22nd November 2000b). Otherwise, a significant part of the government's effort was focused on boosting the Saarland's economy – it had the highest economic growth of any Land in 2003, and had the greatest 'economic dynamism' of any Land between 2000 and 2002, according to a study by the Institute for the German Economy in Cologne and the Institute for the New Market Economy. This Institute designated Peter Müller 'Minister President of the Year' (Spiegel, 29th July 2003), which became a regular feature of CDU press releases over the coming year.

Peter Müller's popularity over the four years previous to 2004 had grown significantly, such that he was favoured by a clear majority of voters to continue in office as Minister President (Winkler 2005a, p.19). At the 2004 election, the SPD suffered both from the unpopularity of the SPD/Green government on a federal level, notably over the Hartz reforms, and also, again, the divisive role of Oskar Lafontaine (Spiegel, 17th August 2004). Having initially sought to involve Lafontaine in a similar election campaign as 1999, criticising the federal government from the left, Maas had to distance himself from Lafontaine's growing polemicism (Winkler 2005a, pp.24–5). The economy and unemployment, as well as, this time, education policy and responses to the PISA study were major issues in the campaign (ibid., p.23). In the end, Müller led the CDU to an entirely expected election victory: the CDU won an overall majority, increasing its vote share by 2%, while SPD support collapsed, falling by over 13%. The Greens and the FDP narrowly entered the Landtag again, beating the 5% hurdle (Forschungsgruppe Wahlen 2004). One further point worth noting is that Regina Görner was no longer included in the cabinet.

6.2   Education

The hypothesis was put forward in the introduction that parties were likely to make the biggest difference to policies pursued at a Land level in areas where the Land enjoyed sole policy-making competence, such as education. However, there are two reasons why this might be doubted in the Saarland. First, one of the biggest issues – that around school structure – appears to have been restricted by the Landesverfassung, and requires a two-thirds majority to be amended. Secondly, the CDU Landesverband is more centrist in orientation (and the CDU's electorate traditionally more working class) than in many other Länder, so it might be that the policy aims of the Saar-CDU depart from the Christian democratic paradigm.

6.2.1   Background to education in the Saarland

Until 1996, the Saarland's school system was classically divided: after Primary School, a decision was taken by parents, on the basis of a recommendation by the school, to send their children to one of four sorts of school: the Hauptschule, the Realschule, the Gymnasium (grammar school), or the Gesamtschule (comprehensive school). There was, however, a consensus that the Hauptschule wasn't working – it had, by the 1990s, become a 'Restschule' ('Scrap-heap school'), to adopt the word used by several interviewees (Interview KK, Interview LL), often for those who had dropped out of the comprehensive school. Children were very unlikely to find employment after having been to the Gesamtschule, and parents lost respect for it (Interview KK). However, the different types of school were anchored in the Land's constitution, meaning it was impossible to abolish the Gesamtschule.

As a result, the 'School compromise' came about under Oskar Lafontaine's SPD-led government: this involved the merger of the Realschule and the Hauptschule into the *erweiterte Realschule* (extended Realschule); these would offer a pathway both to the Hauptschule leaving qualification (*Hauptschulabschluß*) and the Realschule leaving qualification (*Realschulabschluß*). Each of the four types of school was written into the Land's constitution. Any fundamental change to school structure in the Land would therefore require a two-thirds majority in the Landtag (the majority for constitutional amendment required in the Saarland). The Saarland had, for the entirety of the post-war period, had a centralised Abitur examination; parents were also required to pay for school books, unless they were on a low income. One education reform which was undertaken by the SPD-led government was a reduction in the number of lessons in the primary schools, down to 89 lessons per week over the first four years, in 1985, in a move which was criticised by the CDU (SBZ, 8th August 2002).

It is worth noting that successive SPD-led governments under Oskar Lafontaine only managed to achieve one school structural reform, namely the abolition of the Hauptschule, and the school system otherwise bore many of the hallmarks of the Christian democrat paradigm. This suggests an element of path-dependent constraint applied to the SPD-led governments between 1985 and 1999.

In the election campaign of 1999, education did not play a particularly major role, although the CDU pledged to employ extra teachers, ensure that the full timetable was delivered, and in particular to extend the number of lessons delivered in primary school, as discussed above.

6.2.2   The Regierungserklärung (statement of government) by Minister President Müller, 27th October 1999

In place of a coalition treaty, the Statement of Government delivered by Minister President Müller in October 1999 stated some of the government's aims, which were similar to those mentioned in the manifesto for the Landtag election (Plenarprotokoll 1999, pp.19–20). Müller started his section on schools stating that 'In schools … the recognition of performance has to move more strongly into the foreground'. This emphasis on 'performance' (*'Leistung'*) is a common feature of statements from CDU politicians on educational issues and draws an implicit contrast with alleged social demo-cratic indifference about standards and lack of rigour. Key features were then:

- Reliable opening times in schools;
- Changes to rules around transfer from primary to secondary schools, with more weight being given to the primary school's recommendation [compared to parental choice];
- A centralised examination to be introduced as part of school leaving cer-tificates undertaken at the extended Realschule (the *Hauptschulabschluß* and *Mittlerer Bildungsabchluß*);
- Grades to be awarded for behaviour, engagement in the school and the overall 'personality' of a pupil, at the end of year 9 and 10;
- Working with other Länder to develop the *Oberstufe* (final two years of grammar school), which Müller said was 'too specialised, too free in the choice of subject, and divides the year-group too much';
- Employ extra teachers (to reduce class sizes and lesson cancellation and the average age of teaching staff);
- Be the first Land to introduce Abitur after eight years of secondary school at all grammar schools (interestingly, this did not feature in the election manifesto, which only contained a desire to shorten the time to 12.5 years – CDU Saar 1999, p.24);
- Continued involvement of parents and pupils in decision-making at schools.

Other issues not mentioned, but which were in the CDU's election mani-festo, included numerical grades being introduced from grade 2 onwards and an aspiration to reverse the reduction in the number of lessons taught in primary school introduced in 1985 (ibid., p.23).

Several of the proposals here – notably the emphasis on testing, grading for behaviour, and strengthening the importance of school choice, are familiar from the Christian democratic paradigm.

6.2.3   Abitur: From 13 years to 12

Minister Schreier immediately set to work to introduce the Abitur for pupils after 12 years of school, rather than 13, for those attending Gymnasium (it would still be after 13 years for those undertaking it from comprehensive schools). It was agreed by the Landtag on 22nd November 2000 (Plenarprotokoll 2000, p.815). Minister Schreier emphasised the potential advantage to children by entering the world of work a year earlier, which would make the Saarland's school-leavers more competitive: 'The overly long education period of our young people is a competitive disadvantage, particularly in the border region here in the Saarland' (ibid., p.809).

One point mentioned in support of this by a CDU politician involved was that, sooner or later, it was felt that all Länder would move in the direction of a shorter Abitur, giving them, for one year, two year-groups converging on a university at once. By bringing forward the change in the Saarland, it would ensure that the 'double year group' from larger Länder had not yet reached universities, and give the pupils a comparative advantage (Interview LL).

The SPD was unsupportive of the change, initially citing four reasons: in other countries with a 12-year school leaving exam, even more lessons are delivered than in Germany with 13 years, and the change might necessitate the introduction of pre-university courses. Secondly, it might reduce the possibility of pupils from the Realschule switching to do Abitur, as they would be too far behind. Thirdly, the declining number of lessons taught might lead to the introduction of university entrance exams, whereas the Abitur should demonstrate suitability for university. Fourth, the KMK (Conference of Education Ministers) required at least 265 weekly hours of teaching to be delivered prior to Abitur; if these weren't delivered in eight years, then the Abitur might be de-recognised; if they were, it could put pupils under excessive pressure (cf. Plenarprotokoll 1999, p.53).

The Minister, in implementing the shorter period up to Abitur, did respond to concerns from parents in the consultation period by reducing the number of lessons per week in the 8th grade from 34 to 32 (Plenarprotokoll 1999, p.809).

6.2.4   Changes to selection

As discussed in Chapter 4 and in the introduction to this section, the education system in the Saarland was partially in accordance with the traditional wishes of the Christian Democrats, with selection between the extended Realschule and grammar school taking place at the end of grade 4, and without a *Förderstufe* (so that in the Saarland, children of different abilities were taught together in years 5 and 6). However, it might have been expected that the continuing existence of comprehensive schools would be anathema to Christian Democrats.

In fact, there were no reforms to educational structure undertaken in the 1999–2004 period. The network of comprehensive schools remained intact, as is demonstrated by Table 6.4.

Table 6.4   Number of schools and pupils by school type (selected 2000–2005)[3]

Year	Extended Realschule		Grammar School		Comprehensive school	
	Schools	Pupils	Schools	Pupils	Schools	Pupils
2000–01	50	21,229	37	29,387	15	10,557
2001–02	50	26,870	37	29,904	15	10,498
2002–03	50	29,334	37	30,463	15	10,616
2003–04	52	28,661	37	30,341	15	10,716
2004–05	51	27,625	35	30,435	15	10,993

Source: Statistisches Landesamt

There were also no reforms made to the school structure, other than to grading, in contrast with the situation in Hesse, where there was an increase in differentiation by ability in comprehensive schools. The GEW had a suspicion that comprehensive schools were subtly undermined by not benefiting from extra teaching staff, unlike other forms of school, but this was on the basis of hearsay from members, rather than exact numbers (Interview PP).

There was a change in the way pupils could be nominated for grammar school. Previously this had been a matter for parental choice, on the basis of a recommendation by the school. As in Hesse and Saxony-Anhalt, the school's recommendation was given greater weight – it became binding, but with the possibility, if parents disagreed, for the child to sit a test, and to attend grammar school if he or she passed. The GEW and the SPD were critical of this move, which does accord with the Christian democratic paradigm.

---

[3]For the sake of simplicity, this table excludes the remaining 'secondary schools' which were being wound down as a result of the school reform of 1996, evening schools, evening grammar schools, independent schools, and special schools. The sudden jump in numbers at extended Realschulen is explained by the closure of the final 'secondary schools' and the completion of the 1996 reform.

The question of why the CDU, contrary to expectations, had not eroded the extent of comprehensive education in the Saarland was raised in several interviews. The most obvious explanation is that the Landesverfassung would have required amendment, in order to undertake a fundamental school reform, which would have required a two-thirds majority, with support unlikely to be forthcoming from the SPD (Interview JJ). However, a prominent representative of the CDU on education policy stated that a reform would not have been undertaken even in the absence of this obstacle:

> I think comprehensive schools have their justification, and we want choice for parents so that they can have the school that they think is right for their child. We want a variety of offers, so that everyone can have the right school (Interview LL).

This point was put even more strongly by a senior civil servant in the education ministry, who was close to the Minister and a CDU member:

> The SPD, which now propagates an *Einheitsschule*, [would want a reform] although I'm not sure whether they'd do it, because funnily enough most of their politicians send their children to the grammar school and not the comprehensive; as I say, if the SPD wants a change, it needs our [*sic.*] agreement. We want no change. We think this whole question of school structure is nonsense. What's important is what is actually done at school, the engagement of those in the school, the teachers, the parents, and the pupils, and that is independent from the school type. We have neutralised the debate about school type. What is important is that we have transparency, and we don't need another structural reform (Interview KK).

Einheitsschule is a derogatory term (translatable as 'one size fits all' school) sometimes used by Christian Democrats to characterise the SPD's vision. Two points are worth highlighting here: first, the constitutional change of 1996 went a long way towards neutralising debate on school structure in the Saarland, by requiring a *de facto* grand coalition, between the CDU and the SPD, for any change. Secondly, as in Hesse, the CDU claims to have undertaken a paradigm shift, away from an assumption that comprehensive education is a bad thing, towards greater openness.

6.2.5   Timing of education

The government pursued the extension of the 'open all-day school' model in the Saarland between 1999 and 2004, the key features of which were that afternoon activities were voluntary, and provided by a mixture of qualified teachers and other staff; that fees were payable for afternoon activities; and that the government went for a wide spread of all-day schools, with a large number of schools having some sort of extended offer, rather than concentrating on a few. This latter point was the subject of criticism by the GEW, which felt that in some cases only a tiny amount of additional provision was being provided, in order to boost the number of schools able to call themselves 'all-day schools' (SBZ, 15th September 2004).

The SPD was critical of this in two respects. First, it argued that what was being provided was supervision, rather than education, in the absence of qualified teachers (SBZ, 15th September 2004). Secondly, it claimed that the government had failed to prioritise the extension of all-day education (Interview JJ), though this inevitably drew the criticism that the SPD itself had provided relatively little when in government, even at the end of an extended period of SPD incumbency (Interview LL).

6.2.6   Repetition of years

The government tightened the grading requirement in order for pupils to progress to the next year (SBZ, 28th August 2003). The proportion of children repeating a year in 2004–2005 was 3.2%, compared to a German average of 2.8%. This represented a modest increase of 0.1% compared to 2001–2002 (before the new rules came into effect), whereas the German average was 3.3% in this year (Statistisches Bundesamt).

This accords with the Christian democratic paradigm, which sees a continuing necessity for children to repeat years. The new rules were criticised by the opposition and the GEW (SBZ, 1st August 2001).

The rules were amended for the school year 2003–2004, with pupils being given the chance to cancel out a bad grade by undertaking a test at the start of the next school year (Saarland Ministerium für Bildung 2005, p.4).

6.2.7   Religious studies

Religious studies remained on the curriculum in the Saarland between 1999, without change: it was compulsory, though with the possibility of an opt out. This was enshrined in the Landesverfassung (Article 29), and as a result could not be amended without the consent of the opposition.

There were two related points of contention. The first was that, in spite of requests, the government did not give its consent for Islamic religious studies teaching to be offered, with Jürgen Schereier saying it hindered integration (SBZ, 19th January 1999; SBZ, 8th October 2001).

Second, the government and the SPD opposition agreed a variation to the School Law in the light of the decision of the Federal Constitutional Court in 2003 that bans on wearing headscarves were compatible with the constitution. The legislative proposal – which was agreed unanimously (Plenarprotokoll 2004, p.3686) – stated that:

> The school educates children, with appropriate consideration for pupils who think differently, on the basis of Christian educational and cultural

values. The educational mission is to be fulfilled in a way which by the representation of religious, or political values or other external manifestations, neither the neutrality of the Land vis-à-vis parents and pupils nor the political, religious or ethical peace in schools can be endangered or damaged (Landtagsdrucksache 12/1072).

In the official rationale for this proposal, explicit mention is made of the headscarf. One SPD parliamentarian, Ikbal Berber, made a personal statement criticising the law, even though she voted in favour, stating that its explicit support for Christian values as the basis of education, did not do justice to a society of several religions (Die Welt, 24th June 2004).

6.2.8   Grading and testing regimes

The Land government undertook several variations to testing and grading regimes, as was promised in the CDU's election manifesto and Peter Müller's statement of government. A written test was introduced for the *Hauptschulabschluss* and the *Mittlere Reife* (middle-level school qualification) (Saarland Ministerium für Bildung 2005, p.4). Moreover, for the school-year 2004–2005, comparative tests would be carried out in German (grade 7), Mathematics (grade 8) and a major foreign language (year 9) in all secondary schools. The Saarland had a centralised Abitur for the entire post-war period and this continued. In primary schools, 'orientation tests' were introduced at the end of the third year, for all children, in Mathematics and German. These were evaluated in 2003 by a university-based team (ibid., pp.3–6).

In addition, numerical grades were reintroduced from the half-year point of the second year at primary school (SBZ, 8th February 2000). The government also introduced grades for behaviour at school in years 9 and 10 (SBZ, 6th June 2000).

None of these measures attracted the support of the SPD – or the GEW trade union – as exponents of a different educational paradigm. They both accused the government of 'Testitis' (Interview JJ). For example, Reiner Braun, the SPD's education spokesperson in the Landtag, stated that 'All educational experts say that comparative output controls make no immediate contribution to the improvement of quality. A pig does not become fat if you weigh it' (Plenarprotokoll 1999, p.51). Iqbal Berber, in a later debate on the subject, attacked the CDU's support for school-leaving tests: 'Fear is the only thing you want to create. You call it quality ... You define quality by scaring children and fostering fear ... What do people say? Get the stick, and if the children don't comply, they'll feel it' (Plenarprotokoll 2000, p.528).

Throughout the debates on this aspect of education, it was clear that the differences between CDU and SPD were fundamental.

6.2.9   Subject choice

There were some changes to the school curriculum over the period of this parliament. For the school year 2004–2005, core curricula relating to binding educational standards were introduced in German, Mathematics, and the first foreign language (Saarland Ministerium für Bildung 2005, p.4). In addition, the extension of tests and comparative assignments reduced the extent to which teachers could determine the curriculum.

Beyond this, pupil choice was not affected; the reduction in pupil choice was an element of the planned reform to the Oberstufe, which was planned by the government in 2006, and thus falls outside the scope of this study.

6.2.10   Charges for school books

The Saarland continued to charge for school books, as it had done prior to 1999; a subsidy was provided for children from families on a low income. This is governed by Saarland's *Schülerförderungsgesetz* (Pupil Support Law) of 1984 (Amtsblatt 1984, p.661). This policy was unaffected by the change of government, save for amendments, in line with inflation, to the income levels at which there is an entitlement to subsidy.

6.2.11   Relations with unions

In the Saarland, decisions about appointments of teachers are taken at a Land level, and involve *Personalräte* (Personnel committees), according to the *Saarländisches Personalvertretungsgesetz* (Saarland Personnel Representation Law). In most cases, the relevant personnel committees, which are seated in the education ministry, are chaired by a leading official of a relevant trade union. For instance, Klaus Kessler, the Chair of the GEW in the Saarland, chaired the Land-level personnel committee for comprehensive schools (Interview KK). Moreover, although most teachers were Beamte, and thus were unaffected (until the federalism reform of 2006, which falls outside the scope of this study), there are some who are state employees (*Angestellte*), and who were therefore represented by trade unions in negotiations about wage rates. Even in the case of Beamte, decisions over precise working requirements (for instance, the number of hours to be worked) was a matter for determination at the Land level, and again the trade unions were involved in negotiation on this (Interview PP, Interview KK).

Throughout the period, the GEW, and to a lesser extent the other trade unions, were critical of the government's education policies, regularly putting out hostile press releases (cf. SBZ, 28th November 2003), and making critical representations to public hearings in the Landtag. At the same time, the day-to-day business of union involvement in personnel issues, including teacher appointments, continued throughout the period, although Klaus Kessler believed less importance was attached to it by the government (Interview PP). Relations did dip when there was a strike (illegal for Beamte) in comprehensive schools, and Minister Schreier introduced disciplinary proceedings against Kessler (who is a Beamte on secondment to the trade union), resulting in a DM 20,000 fine for the latter (FR, 8th September 2001).

6.2.12 PISA

In common with other CDU-led Länder, the Saarland's government felt its views were confirmed by the results of the Pisa study, in which the Land did not fare well. It said that the failure was due to a lack of educational rigour, as well as cuts to the primary school timetable, and so the study confirmed the course of the Land government. The opposition, unsurprisingly, did not share this analysis, instead highlighting the disparities in educational attainment depending on a child's background, and called for less selection in schools (SBZ, 17th June 2002a; SBZ, 17th June 2002b).

One variation in Saarland's response compared to other Länder was the strong emphasis on German courses for children without German as a first language (Saarland Ministerium für Bildung 2005, p.1). It offered free, voluntary language courses for children who do not have sufficient German language skills for ten hours per week, prior to starting school. This was felt to be a particular priority for the CDU Fraktion, and was supported by the SPD (Interview LL).

Finally, one other reaction from the CDU government – criticised by the opposition – involved pupils being required to undertake practice tests (SBZ, 30th December 2002).

6.2.13 The federal dimension

Along with other CDU-led Länder, the Saarland supported complete responsibility for school-level education being given to the Land level, although it did see some role for the federal government in university provision (SBZ, 6th February 2002). A slight variation was that the Land did – supported by the SPD opposition – call for a national curriculum (SBZ, 19th April 2002).

One other piece of involvement from the Saarland's CDU leadership in national-level policy-making was its unsuccessful, and rather surprising attempt to shelve the proposed reform of German spelling (Spiegel, 27th July 2004). This did not find support from other Länder.

6.2.14 Other developments

Apart from the roll-out of Abitur after eight years of secondary school, the greatest coverage of Saarland in the national media concerned the introduction of 'behaviour lessons'. This was criticised by the opposition (SBZ, 30th August 2003).

Part of the extension of hours to primary schools gave them the opportunity to have a daily session of *Förderunterricht* (often translated as 'remedial teaching' but better conceived of as 'individually tailored, additional teaching') in the first two years of primary school (Saarland Ministerium für

Bildung 2005, p.3). The Land also introduced 'schools for parents', which involved collaboration between adult education institutions, parents' representatives and primary schools, in order to help parents support their children and promote effective learning (ibid., p.3). Interviewees supportive of the government felt these constituted important evidence of innovation on the part of the Land government (Interview KK, Interview LL).

6.2.15 Influencing and changing policy

Role of the opposition: According to the SPD, the government did not attempt to undertake any joint initiatives in education policy during this period, although as was noted above, the law banning headscarves in schools was proposed by both the CDU and SPD Fraktionen. Although Reiner Braun, the SPD's education spokesperson, did feel that the party managed to persuade Minister Schreier of the merits of its case in one area (payment of teachers at vocational colleagues), this falls outside the area under consideration (Interview JJ). As in all the other case studies, in education policy the opposition did not have a great deal of impact.

Role of trade unions: As discussed above, trade unions continued to have formal input into personnel discussions, as well as negotiations about wage rates. There were also extensive informal contacts with the Land government. On the one hand, there was not a breakdown in the relationship even between the GEW and the government, as happened in Hesse and Saxony-Anhalt. Klaus Kessler, the GEW Chair, stated that he had no difficulty securing appointments with the minister, and said 'The Minister and I still go for a beer together' (Interview PP). This would be quite unthinkable in either of the other two cases discussed. This is not to say, though, that informal access meant a great deal of influence: the government's education policies were often anathema to the GEW, and it was not in a position to change them. Notwithstanding the possibility of access to the Minister, Kessler felt that such access would often not achieve anything. The GEW sometimes secured changes in the detail of proposed policies (for instance on working time of teachers in the Oberstufe), but this was through public pressure, not informal lobbying: 'In detail we did manage to get changes, but only when we did big demonstrations, not through persuasion; [we succeeded] only when putting them under pressure, and not when we tried to persuade them' (Interview PP). The GEW also mentioned that it used its relationship with opposition parties to extract information from the government, through prompting the opposition to table parliamentary questions.

Representatives of trade unions would attend meetings of the Fraktionen in the Landtag, notably around budget time, to put their point of view, although according to a CDU politician involved in education policy, it was not always possible to respond positively (Interview LL).

The slightly less acrimonious relationship between the government and the GEW, notwithstanding the obvious differences in educational policy preferences, is partly attributable to the size of the Saarland – something emphasised by several interviewees (Interview LL, Interview KK, Interview PP). People knew each other through a variety of contexts. For instance, three of the people interviewed – not just in the education policy field – had links to a particular comprehensive school, and many involved in policy-making in the Land attended the same events about education policy, and this regular contact was believed on all sides to have prevented a break-down in the relationship.

Role of local and state parties: Interviewees did not refer to any con-straints being imposed or influence being exerted by the local or Land-level CDU.

Constraints upon government by the CDU Fraktion: In interviews, two occasions were mentioned when the CDU Fraktion had an influence, independently of the government. The first (mentioned independently by a civil servant and a CDU politician) concerned budget setting: at times, the budget proposed by the Finance Ministry required amendment after its presentation to the Landtag, but such an amendment needed to come from the government Fraktion, as the proposal was formally, at that stage, in the hands of the legislature and the executive had no further role. The Fraktion did sometimes take this opportunity to make minor adjustments to the budget, and gave these late changes additional scrutiny (Interview KK, Interview LL).

Secondly, immediately after the 2004 election, the government intro-duced a very large programme of primary school closures. This was the subject of significant debate in the Landtag, and one proposed legal pro-vision – which would have given the education ministry additional dis-cretion to close schools – was rejected by the Fraktion (Interview LL). However, this falls outside the scope of this study, as it did not happen in the first term of office, and in any event, as in the other Länder, there is a clear picture of executive dominance, with the Fraktion only making changes to the detail rather than the substance of policy.

Blockage of change by the civil service: Upon taking office, the CDU took the opportunity to make extensive personnel changes at senior levels in the education ministry. In some cases, this could be done because of the age of the occupants, but in other cases, senior officials were dispatched to other ministries, into less significant positions. All the new officials were close to, or members of, the CDU; at least one was an old friend of the Minister's who had been a CDU office-holder in local government (Interview JJ, Interview KK, Interview LL, Interview PP). As a result, obstruc-tion by the civil service was overcome.

Relations with sub-Land level government units: No reference was made in interviews to difficulties with sub-Land level local government units in this area of policy. In any event, because of the nature of the reforms pursued (which concerned what happened in schools, rather than changes to their fabric – with the modest exception of the installation of some bistro areas to facilitate all-day education), these fell exclusively within the control of the Land government, rather than local authorities (who would have had a role if, for example, there was to be a reform of school structure).

Role of formal procedures: As noted above, there was clear executive dominance in this area of policy. Legislative proposals were discussed thoroughly within the government, and with the CDU Fraktion, before entering the formal legislative process, so by then the fault-lines were clear, and changes would only happen at the margins. Klaus Kessler of the GEW said that hearings held by committees would sometimes have the character of a 'farce', with the opposition asking lots of questions to tease out problems in what was being proposed, and the parliamentarians of the CDU remaining silent, before agreeing to the law in the Landtag.

There remains a *Landesschulkonferenz* (Land school conference), consisting of representatives of parents, pupils and teachers (in equal proportion), along with certain other invited representatives, elected by three regional variants of the same body, themselves elected by those from each school. It is consulted on all changes to policy, although there was no suggestion that it wielded great influence over government policy. A senior civil servant said of the body: 'Sometimes we have to decide against [it]. But we have no interest in bringing all sorts of people and groups against us' (Interview KK).

6.2.16   Education policy: Conclusions

Changes in education policy in the Saarland over this period are summarised in Table 6.5.

As can be seen, on most dimensions the Saarland successfully effected education reforms taking it away from the social democratic, and towards the Christian democratic paradigm in education policy. In particular, the greater emphasis on testing and associated centralisation of the curriculum and the greater emphasis on grading demonstrate a clear shift in a conservative direction.

However – as was the case with Hesse, discussed in Chapter 5 – there were variations. Some innovative projects were pursued, which might not have been expected of a CDU-led government (such as the introduction of Förderunterricht, additional tuition, for all first and second-year pupils), and, more significantly school structures were almost untouched by the government (unlike in Hesse, there was no attempt to strengthen differentiation within schools either).

As in Hesse, this does point to the importance of a Land's history, its institutional legacy, in shaping the constraints under which present-day policy-makers act. In the Saarland, this became a legal constraint as well as

Table 6.5 Education policy change in the Saarland 1999–2004

Social democratic paradigm	Christian democratic paradigm	Change
Comprehensive education (or if unacceptable, late and flexible selection)	Early and rigid selection, with limited movement between types of school	No change to school system; some increased rigidity feared as a result of switch to twelve-year Abitur
Any selection based on parental choice	Selection based on tests/teacher assessment	Move away from parental choice towards selection based on school assessment, supported by a test in the event of disagreement
High level of individual teacher discretion over curriculum content and testing	Centralised tests and examinations	Two centralised school tests introduced
Abitur after 13 years	Abitur after 12 years	Introduction of Abitur after 12 years across the Land
Extensive pupil choice of subject	Limiting of pupil choice	No change (followed in subsequent legislative period)
Compulsory, integrated all-day education	Half-day education with possibility of extension	Some voluntary all-day education introduced
Teachers provide education all day	Some supervision undertaken by volunteers/unqualified helpers	Additions to 'core' teaching provided by non-teaching staff
Limited reliance on grading	High reliance on grading	Greater emphasis upon grading
Grading only in secondary school	Grading from year 1	Grading reintroduced from the second half of year 2

Table 6.5 Education policy change in the Saarland 1999–2004 – *continued*

Social democratic paradigm	Christian democratic paradigm	Change
No grading of behaviour and teamwork	Grading of behaviour and teamwork	Introduction of grades for behaviour in classes 9 and 10
Limited repetition of years in event of poor performance	High level of repetition of year in event of poor performance	Stricter rules on repetition of years, with a slight increase in the number of pupils repeating
Free provision of school books	Parental contribution towards school books	Continued parental contribution
No compulsory RE	Compulsory RE	No change: RE or ethics compulsory, Christian ethos of school reaffirmed in legislation
Non-Christian RE provided	No non-Christian RE provided	No change: ethics provided but not other RE
Opposition to Länder having exclusive control over policy	Support for Länder having complete control over policy	Support for Länder having complete control over policy
Partnership with trade unions	Limited involvement with unions	Continuing involvement of unions in personnel issues, and continued informal discussion though significant substantive disagreement

a political one, through the anchoring of the existing forms of school in the Landesverfassung.

The particular nature of the Saarland – a small Land, with quite a strong tradition of Catholic trade unionism within the CDU – is also reflected in the relations with the GEW being less disastrous than in the other cases, and perhaps also in the willingness of the SPD opposition to join the CDU in banning headscarves in schools. However, this collegial approach was not reflected in other areas of education policy, where the opposition was not involved in policy-making, and clear executive dominance was demonstrated.

6.3   Childcare and family policy in the Saarland 1999–2004

As mentioned in the introduction to this chapter, the issue of childcare was raised in the election campaign by the CDU, when it demanded an end to fees being charged for nursery school. This stance does not fit the Christian democratic paradigm, with its scepticism of institutional childcare, and is perhaps all the more surprising in a Land with a highly Catholic population.

6.3.1   Background to childcare and family policy in the Saarland

Following the introduction of a legal entitlement to nursery provision from age three, the Saarland was amongst the first Länder to meet this obligation. There was also a more limited network of after-school provision, and provision for under-threes in crèches. Over 70% of provision was through independent providers (such as the welfare associations of the churches) rather than the government (SBZ, 8th June 2000). The cost of nursery education was met by a formula whereby parents paid 25% of the cost, the Land bore 25% of the cost, the municipality with the *Jugendamt* bore 35%, and the provider (such as the Protestant Church) itself bore 15% (Landtagsdrucksache 12/115, p.5). Nurseries are governed by the *Gesetz zur Förderung der vorschulischen Erziehung* (Law on support of pre-school education).

In the election manifesto, as noted above, the CDU pledged gradually to end fees for nurseries, on the grounds that they were pre-school educational establishments, and education should be free (CDU Saar 1999, p.21). The CDU also had an extensive section on the family:

Today the family appears in the most varied forms, overwhelmingly as a partnership of married parents with the natural, adopted or foster children, lone parents with children, 'patchwork families', and a growing number of unmarried couples with children. All forms share the fact that there are at least two generations who live together and that the parents, or a parent, takes responsibility for their children. The CDU wants to support and strengthen this core of the family, regardless of the chosen form of the family (CDU Saar 1999, p.56).

There followed some specific measures (pp.56–9):

- Reducing the cost of pre-school education for families;
- Introducing supplementary child benefit, depending on how much money was available in the Land budget;
- Support for the family-friendly policies in the Bundesrat;
- Extending the network of childcare outside the family, with childcare institutions throughout the Land;
- Pledging to create rules so that day-carers can receive education in looking after children of all ages;
- Extending childcare for schoolchildren with the aim of offering sufficient provision to meet need across the Land;
- Extra support for parents who need it, for example in advice provision and homework support;
- Make possible and promote flexible working time models, and improve the conditions for part-time working;
- Starting a competition for family-friendly companies.

6.3.2   The Regierungserklärung (statement of government) by Minister President Müller, 27th October 1999

By contrast with the quite extensive section on the family in the election manifesto, there were few concrete pledges in the first statement of government by Minister President Müller. He reiterated, however, the desire of the Land government to support families where possible, and in particular to gradually reduce parental payments for nursery schools to zero (Plenar-protokoll 1999, p.22). Ministerial responsibility for pre-school education switched into the education ministry, from the social affairs ministry, and so Jürgen Schreier took responsibility.

6.3.3   Developments in childcare policy 1999–2004

The most prominent development in childcare policy in the Saarland came early in the legislative period, when a decision was taken to make the final year of nursery school free of charge prior to school starting. There had been discussion within the CDU about which year to make free – it would have been possible to make the first year free, for instance (Interview LL), but in the end this was not proposed. The Land proposed to invest 13.4 million DM into the project; the municipalities would no longer have to pay the fees, through the youth service, for those on a lower income. Instead this money was clawed back, and given to the providers, in order to raise the quality of provision. It was also specified that free childcare was for an entitlement of six hours per day, with parents needing to pay extra if they wanted to extend the hours (Landtagsdrucksache 12/115, p.2).

During the course of the legislation, some minor amendments were made – most notably the provision that, if a child started school early (there is some discretion over the exact age) and had not had a full year's free nursery, fees could be repaid to the parents so that all benefited from a free 12 months. The final version was agreed on 7th June 2000; the SPD opposed the change (rather awkwardly), stating that the institutions would get worse, some were in danger of closing, and that it would be better to continue to levy a charge upon parents who could afford it, and reinvest the money saved by declining numbers of children overall, and therefore a declining demand for nursery places, in improving quality (Plenarprotokoll 2000, p.352).

The change did get attention across Germany – in particular from Länder who contributed to the fiscal redistribution mechanism. Karl-Heinz Weimar, the Finance Minister of Hesse, commented: 'Obviously I'm annoyed. People in Hesse are paying for it. They should give me a billion DM of the 5.4 billion [that they receive] back, then I can make nursery school free too' (FR, 9th August 2000).

The government was not in a position to extend free nursery provision further, and there were no further amendments to the Law on support for pre-school education in the 1999–2004 parliamentary term.

Overall, the number of children in childcare institutions did grow in the Saarland over this period, as can be seen from Table 6.6. In a written answer, the government claimed that all the need was met, in all three forms of childcare, because there were vacancies (Landtagsdrucksache 12/1121, p.56), but it was accepted by a CDU politician that this was not the case, and there was significant unmet demand for crèches and after-school provision which was not being met (Interview LL).

There were no changes in the regulatory framework for childcare in this period, nor was there any expansion of the role of day-carers, in contrast to the situation in Saxony-Anhalt and Hesse. There was an expansion of the number of all-day places in Kindergarten from 3,048 in 1999 to 5,021 for children aged between three and six (Saarland Ministerium für Bildung 2004).

The other development in childcare policy was the introduction, in mid-2004, of a draft educational programme for pre-school institutions, which was finally agreed by all the providers in 2006 (Saarland Ministerium für Bildung 2006). It was supported by an expert institute in Berlin, and emphasises the common responsibility for parents, nursery teachers, providers and the Land for early learning. It contains basic elements of Mathematics, scientific, and technical learning, and health, social and cultural, value, religious, speech-related, and artistic and musical elements of education which are to be covered in the early years (Saarland Ministerium für Bildung 2005, p.2).

Table 6.6 Provision of institutional childcare 1980–2005

Type of provision	Nursery school		After-school provision		Creches	
	No. of institutions	No. of children	No. of institutions	No. of children	No. of institutions	No. of children
1980	401	26,932	20	618	N/A	N/A
1990	418	29,479	18	606	12	183
1995	452	32,840	32	868	37	506
1998	467	34,719	62	1,448	50	599
1999	466	33,696	65	1,503	56	621
2000	467	33,445	80	1,723	62	707
2001	467	32,984	85	1,909	68	705
2002	467	32,795	101	2,196	73	761
2003	461	32,193	107	2,458	83	841
2004	461	31,160	120	2,585	101	903
2005	460	30,569	116	2,667	120	1,023

Source: Statistisches Landesamt

6.3.4 Other developments in policy towards families 1999–2004

There were several other developments worth highlighting in the area of policy towards families in the Saarland.

Probably the most significant was the introduction of the overall family political framework in 2004 (cf. Stabel-Franz 2004). This meant that every measure undertaken by the Land government had to undertake a 'family sustainability assessment', to consider the impact upon families. This measure was demanded by the CDU Fraktion, in a motion agreed on 27th November 2002 (Landtagsdrucksache 12/771). According to Minister Görner, the Minister responsible, this did sometimes have an impact, for instance on policies towards payment of civil servants (Interview Z). The government also introduced, in its own ministries, an initiative to promote more part-time jobs (SBZ, 16th February 2002). The Land introduced, in 2004, a Family Guidebook, giving details of services available to families (Saarland Ministerium für Frauen, Gesundheit, Arbeit und Soziales 2004). The SPD was supportive of this initiative, and indeed claimed it as its own (Interview JJ). Regine Görner stated, however, both in parliamentary debates, and in an interview with the author, that there are clear limits to what a Land government can do, certainly in financial terms, in this area (Interview Z).

There were several parliamentary debates about family policy in the Saarland (cf. Plenarprotokoll 2001, pp.1386–98; Plenarprotokoll 2002, pp.2311–33), which did not – for the most part – demonstrate great differences in substance between the views of the parties on family-related issues. On the one hand, the CDU defended its record, notably on the extension of free childcare, congratulated the SPD on having discovered the family now it was in opposition, and sometimes claimed that the SPD did not want women to have the choice whether to work or stay at home. For its part, the SPD claimed that the government was inactive – at least for the first few years of its term of office – in supporting families, with the exception of its one, high-profile initiative.

6.3.5 Influencing and changing policy

Role of the opposition: On issues relating to the family, there did not appear to be any great influence exercised by the opposition, apart from its suggestion of the 'family guidebook'. Minister Görner did emphasise, however, that she attempted to get the SPD's support on more important issues of social policy, sometimes with success – for instance on the reform of medical emergency provision (Interview Z). Given its obvious popularity, the CDU had no incentive to allow the SPD to get close to its initiative to make the last year of nursery school free.

Role of trade unions: The trade unions did not appear to play any role in this area of policy-making.

Role of Land parties: Minister Görner stated that she did seek to involve the local units of the Land party (the *Kreisverbände*) in her decisions, although in more significant areas of her ministerial portfolio, rather than particularly in this one, which was a source of unity. She felt that the CDU was fully supportive of the agenda on childcare – unlike during the time when Rita Süssmuth was Federal Family Minister and Dr. Görner was her assistant (Interview Z).

Role of CDU Fraktion: The CDU Fraktion did not, according to any of the interviewees, have any internal divisions or disagreements on this issue (Interview Z, Interview LL). Again, Dr. Görner mentioned that there were times when she could not get all her proposals through the Fraktion, but not in this area of policy.

Role of the civil service: The civil service was, apparently, fully supportive of the changes to childcare, in particular making the final year free of charge, so there was no hindrance to policy change in this area. More generally, Minister Dr. Görner noticed two things which could be an obstacle: first, civil servants at the time of a change of government were unfamiliar with the new leadership, and were sometimes rather anxious about change. She found that draft speeches were presented to her which were inspired by the federal CDU's website and contained things that, as a trade unionist, she wouldn't dream of saying. Secondly, this uncertainty on the part of civil servants meant that they might misunderstand instructions that filtered down the ministry, and would not challenge things that were not sensible. It took some time for a culture of discussion to establish itself (Interview Z).

Role of the sub-Land level: Since the only formal reform on childcare policy took the form of a law on fees, which had little impact upon local government, and the initiatives in family policy were of a relatively minor nature, local government did not have a great deal of involvement. More generally, Minister Dr. Görner met regularly with figures from local government ('You can't avoid it … they all come and want something'); it made little difference in dealing with local government whether the politicians were from the CDU or the SPD – she maintained that one always had to get used to hard negotiations with them (Interview Z).

Role of formal procedures: The formal procedures of the Landtag did have an impact upon childcare policy, as mentioned above, inasmuch as some amendments were made to the proposal to make childcare free, in line with suggestions made at the Committee hearing on the issue (see above). On other issues of family policy, the Landtag played no substantive role.

6.3.6   Childcare and family policy: Conclusions

Developments in childcare and family policy in the Saarland in this period are summarised in Table 6.7.

Table 6.7 Family and childcare policy in the Saarland 1999–2004

Social democratic paradigm	Christian democratic paradigm	Change
Provision free for all	Provision only available at cost	Free provision available for children in the final year of nursery school
Subsidised provision starts at age 0	Subsidised provision starts at age three	Very modest extension of support for crèches
Subsidised provision extensively available	Subsidised provision available where demand exists	Provision of support for under-threes and schoolchildren increased but still very limited; comprehensive provision of nursery schools
Provision in formal institutions	Flexible methods of provision	No change – emphasis still on provision in institutions
Close regulation of childcare institutions	Light-touch regulation of childcare institutions	No change in regulation
No preference about types of family unit	Support for 'traditional' family	Explicit statement that all types of family will be supported

As has been discussed, on the one hand childcare policy in the Saarland gained significant prominence on a federal level for its extremely popular decision to make the final year of nursery school free of charge. This was an interesting step for several reasons: it showed that a high-profile initiative with a significant, recurring cost was not impossible for a Land under significant budgetary pressure to achieve. It was also a change that might not have been anticipated from a CDU-led government, confirming the sense that the CDU's paradigm on childcare policy has evolved in recent years, and one which thoroughly wrong-footed the opposition.

On the other hand, other changes in childcare and family policy were modest or non-existent, although initiatives on educational provision in childcare institutions were launched as the parliamentary term was drawing to a close, and continued after the government's re-election. This does imply that the Saarland's capacity to effect policy change was more restricted than that of the larger and more prosperous Länder.

6.4 Labour market policy in the Saarland 1999–2004

6.4.1 Introduction

As discussed in the introduction, the Saarland faced significant economic challenges, caused by the decline in its industrial base, from both the steel industry and mining, leading to higher than average unemployment for western Germany, and also the need to achieve structural change. This level of unemployment might be expected to prompt politicians – notably those from the Saar-CDU, with its traditionally strong labour wing, to deviate from the Christian democrat paradigm of labour market policy.

There was some history of cooperation between the different sides of industry, and the government, in the Land. There was for example the *Saar-Gemeinschaftsinitiative* (SGI – Saar Community Initiative), which brought together representatives of both sides of industry, the Land government, and local government, created in 1993 (cf. Blancke 2004, pp.168–73).

Blancke and Schmid (1998) saw the Saarland in the 'stay' category of labour market policy, in their categorisation (discussed in Chapter 4): there was a significant level of expenditure on active labour market policies by the Land government, but a relatively low level of innovation, with the Land government tending to co-finance federal programmes. They found that support for training and qualification was a significant part of programmes in the Saarland.

6.4.2   The election campaign, the CDU manifesto and the statement of government

The fragile state of the Saarland's labour market played a role in the Land's election campaign. Attracting particular attention was the pledge of the CDU to end the coal industry in the Saarland, in a section of the manifesto entitled 'Socially acceptable solutions in mining' (CDU-Saar 1999, pp.15–16). Although this might have seemed politically suicidal, as outlined in the introduction to this chapter the number of workers in mining had fallen significantly, and according to the Saarland's DGB Chairman, Eugen Roth, it allowed Peter Müller to give the impression of modernity, and a willingness to change course (Interview HH). Other measures in the manifesto included:

- Support for small and medium-sized industry rather than a 'fixation' on old, large industries (ibid., p.6);
- The creation of 60,000 new jobs by 2010 (p.6);
- Reducing the number of public holidays and reducing special holiday rules down to the federal average (p.8);
- The establishment of a 'deregulation commission' to reduce the level of regulation in the Land (p.8);
- A variety of market-support measures to create jobs, such as bonuses for start-up companies (p.11);
- Inclusion of political parties in the Saar-GSI (p.17);
- Supporting the creation of an 'Alliance for Jobs' at a Land level (p.17);

- 'Developing special offers for the long-term unemployed and those with limited qualifications to open the route to the first labour market for them' (p.17).

Although there is no statement in this that existing programmes supporting the second labour market would be wound down, several other features do fit the Christian democrat paradigm of labour market policy.

Similar priorities were reflected in the statement of government by Peter Müller in October 1999, though with a greater emphasis on active labour policies:

> Alongside economic and structural policies, an active labour market policy is indispensable: the aim is to finance work rather than unemployment and facilitate transfer into the first labour market. The new Land government will introduce a model project to create jobs for those with limited qualifications [referring to the CAST programme discussed below]. Career opportunities must be created particularly for these people. It is not acceptable that they are continually excluded from the modernisation processes as losers of modernisation. ... We want to improve the quality of labour market programmes. ... The Land government will reduce the number of programmes, coordinate their contents better and make them more targeted. The fundamental rule applies: 'Whatever creates jobs is the caring thing to do'. (Plenarprotokoll 1999, p.17)

6.4.3   Active labour market policies

At the very start of the parliamentary term, the Land government inherited a commitment to participate in the CAST programme (*Chancen und Anreize zur Aufnahme sozialversicherungspflichter Tätigkeiten* – 'Opportunities and Incentives to take on activities paying social insurance contributions'); a federal government pilot which had been supported by the SGI. The CAST programme also supported the better-known Mainz model of wage top-up. This model (known as the SGI model) is a particular type of top-up wage, or *Kombilohn*. Key elements were:

- A subsidy of up to 10 DM per hour towards social insurance payments made by the employer;
- A requirement for the employer to demonstrate that the job created is additional, and not a replacement for other jobs or programmes – the SGI model payments could not be combined with other programmes;
- No payment was received by the worker, but instead s/he received support for qualification measures, to match the level of subsidy received by the employer;

- Because of the focus on social insurance payments, very low-paid jobs, falling below the threshold for such payments, were excluded (Forschungs-verbund 2000, pp.10–11).

Behind the scenes, this programme was the subject of hard negotiation between employers' representatives, the two relevant ministers (Dr. Hans-Peter Georgi, the Economics Minister who had previously been head of the employers' association of the Land, and Dr. Görner, who had ministerial responsibility for labour market policy), trade unions (as part of the SGI), and relevant civil servants. In fact, employers and the Economics ministry wanted to allow the programme to be combined with other programmes, and for subsidies to be able to continue for several years, whereas the trade unions – and the Federal Chancellor's Office, who were involved because of the federal funding – felt this would lead to excessive subsidies for employers, and substitution effects, where places on the SGI scheme would replace other jobs (SBZ, 18th August 2001; Interview GG; Interview HH). Nobody was surprised when the programme was an abject failure, with just 77 workers being supported including only five in the capital, Saarbrücken (Forschungsverbund 2001, p.56). The Economics ministry felt the project was 'mutilated' by the social affairs politicians (Interview GG), while unions and Dr. Görner were sceptical about the model in any case (Interview HH; Interview Z).

There were no further Land-specific Kombilohn programmes in this period; there were some relatively small active labour market programmes ('Work and Environment', 'Work and Culture', and 'Qualification in Work – instead of Social Assistance' focused at particular groups (Schmid et al. 2004, pp.125–6)) which involved support for jobs in the second labour market, for a limited period, alongside qualification measures, for hard-to-place groups.

There were two clear priorities for policy-makers in this period in the Saarland: first, active labour market policy required a strong element of support for education and training, in order to secure reintegration into the first labour market at the earliest possible opportunity. Secondly, there was a strong emphasis on the 'quality control' of measures. This was accompanied by significant reduction in funding for active labour market measures in the Land budget over the period (Schmid et al. 2004; Interview HH; Interview Z; Interview OO).

Overall, the starting point in the Saarland was not classically social democratic, with a relatively low degree of innovation in labour market policy. There was, under the CDU, a shift from the 'stay' model (high spending, low innovation) towards the 'pull' model, with the second labour market being focused on a few hard-to-place groups, and instruments being designed to make available labour more useful to the market, through helping the unemployed to obtain qualifications – measures associated with the Christian democratic paradigm. However, contrary to the expectations of the Christian democratic paradigm, the SGI model of wage top-ups was not pursued.

6.4.4 Initiatives in the Bundesrat

The Saarland did not have a high profile in policy-making in the Bundesrat in this period. It did support Hesse's OFFENSIV law, discussed in Chapter 5, but with reservations, notably about the localisation of responsibility for unemployment placement (Interview Z; Interview OO). This support was attributed to the ongoing election campaign at the time.

One proposal the Saarland did support in the Bundesrat was the reduction in tax paid by private households taking on domestic help, with Minister Dr. Görner setting up a press conference to suggest this would be a far better use of federal money than questionable wage top-ups. This was not accepted by the federal government or SPD-led Länder (SBZ, 2nd February 2002).

6.4.5 The Saarland and the Hartz reforms

In the vote on the first two Hartz reforms in the Bundesrat, the Saarland supported their referral to the conciliation committee, along with the other CDU-led Länder, where compromises were subsequently reached (Bundesrat 2002). Although the Saarland did not deviate in its voting from the line taken by other west German, CDU-led Länder in the Bundesrat (Spiegel, 9th July 2004), it did deviate from other CDU-led Länder in the role it played in one aspect of the reforms: arrangements regarding the proposed localisation of unemployment benefit payment and facilitation. In common with the eastern Länder (cf. Chapter 6 for a discussion regarding Saxony-Anhalt), the Land government was very anxious that, because of the high proportion of long-term unemployed in receipt of unemployment benefit (met by the Federal Labour Organisation) rather than social assistance payments, the cost to the Saarland of the reform would be substantial, and experts from the ministerial side were drafted in to confirm this. Secretary of State Josef Hecken represented the Land, and held the line that localisation had to be optional, receiving significant criticism from other CDU-led colleagues (Interview OO). Reflecting this scepticism about decentralisation, only one locality in the Saarland, St. Wendel, decided to take up the opportunity to have full responsibility for labour placement, as offered by the Hartz reforms (Deutscher Landkreistag 2005). This was a clear case of the Land's territorial interests trumping the party interest – and the expectation of what a CDU-led Land might favour in policy terms – in the Bundesrat.

In a speech to the Landtag on 28th August 2002, Minister Dr. Görner made a remarkable speech attacking the Hartz reforms from a perspective which clearly reflected her trade union background, and which was hard to reconcile with the Christian democrat paradigm in labour market policy (or, for that matter, the government's subsequent support for the reforms):

> And what is in Hartz' bag of miracles? Let's ask whose interests these proposals serve, which are being presented to us with nice sounding names like 'Me-Inc.', 'Masterplan' and 'Job floater'. Do they serve the interests of the unemployed? Or the interests of those who have a job? Or perhaps the interests of the trade unions? Or the interests of the small and medium-size companies, who the experts expect to bring the real increase in jobs? Not at all … what Hartz proposes with his commission serves above all the interests of large companies who now get all their wishes fulfilled, which previously have been refused by the trade unions of big industries and the works councils. … For instance – the rules on what jobs can be deemed acceptable [for unemployed people]. First there was talk of making them tougher generally. Then family fathers aged over 50 were taken out. An act of particular social responsibility? Not at all! Why would big companies want older, less mobile, perhaps less healthy workers? They have been 'releasing them' for years, as it's cynically called. No, big industry wants to solve its shortage of workers with the young, mobile, well-qualified, and they want to get them at a cheaper rate across the country! (Bundesratsprotokoll 2002, pp.2125–6).

In an interview with the author, Dr. Görner made reference to making life difficult for the opposition by overtaking them from the left (Interview Z). Although it did not appear to affect the Land government's actual stance in the Bunderat on the Hartz reforms, the approach stated here, by Dr. Görner, marks an obvious and radical departure from the policies that might be expected from a minister in a CDU-led government.

6.4.6   Payment of apprenticeships and job-creation schemes

Unlike the SGI's 'top-up' wage model, which, as explained above, *de facto* set a minimum level for payment of jobs, there was no such restriction for the other initiatives in the level of remuneration they could offer. No initiatives on payment of apprenticeships were undertaken by the Land government.

6.4.7   Partnership with trade unions

In contrast to the situation in Hesse discussed in Chapter 5, relations with the trade unions in the Saarland remained reasonably cordial. The SGI continued, although, in line with the election pledge, representatives of political parties were brought into it, which according to the DGB Chairman did not add to its effectiveness. The SGI's meetings also become sporadic (Interview HH). The DGB Chairman appreciated the presence of Dr. Görner within the government, and felt she was helpful 'behind closed doors', and regretted the decision not to include her in the cabinet after the 2004 elections.

The greatest example of cooperation between the DGB and the Minister President concerned a new law on the agreement of building contracts (the *Gesetz über die Vergabe von Bau-Aufträgen im Saarland*, Landtagsdrucksache 12/150), otherwise known as the *Tariftreuegesetz* ('Adherence to wage agreement law'). The law regulated all building contracts given by public bodies in the Land, and insisted that both contractors and sub-contractors adhered to sector-level wage agreements (*Tarif*). The background to this was the Labour Day demonstration in May 2000, when the DGB demanded that this regulation, similar to that existing in Bavaria, be introduced. Privately and then publicly, Minister President Müller agreed, providing such a law did actually exist in Bavaria (which it did).[4] Saarland's law in fact went further than the Bavarian equivalent, applying to all works, including road construction, as well as the construction of public buildings (Interview OO).

6.4.8   Influencing and changing policy

Role of the Opposition: In this area of policy, there were moments of agreement (such as the law on building contracts alluded to above). However, there was no need for the opposition to be brought into discussions on labour market policy, and there is no evidence that they had a great impact.

Role of trade unions: As noted above, the trade unions did retain links to the government, in particular through the SGI and also informally, and this occasionally bore fruit. However, the general direction of – and reduced expenditure upon – active labour market policies was not something over which they could exert a great deal of influence. The DGB felt its influence was severely counteracted by strong influence exerted by the employers' organisations on the CDU (Interview HH).

Land parties: No interviewees alluded to a major role being played by Land parties in this area, nor is there any evidence of strong involvement.

Role of the CDU Fraktion: In most aspects of labour market policy – whether relating to active labour market projects, communication between the land and social partners, or the actions of the Land in the Bundesrat, it was the executive, and not the legislature, which was represented. Interviews with senior civil servants confirmed that, apart from committee hearings, the influence of parliamentarians was very limited (Interview GG; Interview OO).

---

[4]In fact, his first reaction to this demand behind the scenes, according to Eugen Roth, the DGB Chairman, was 'You can't even rely on the Bavarians'! Müller and Roth were on first-name terms and appeared to enjoy a cordial relationship.

Role of the civil service: As discussed in the section concerning child-care and family policy in the Saarland, there were some 'teething problems' between Minister Dr. Görner and her civil servants, although these could not be construed as ideologically or politically motivated obstruction (Interview Z). There were sometimes disagreements between the Economics and Social Affairs Ministries, however (Interview GG; Interview Z; Interview HH). Some tensions were to be expected given that the Economics ministry was headed up by the former head of an employers' association, and the Social Affairs ministry was headed up by a trade unionist. This was changed after the 2004 election, with Dr. Görner not being reappointed to the Cabinet, and labour market policy being moved into the Economics ministry.

Role of the sub-Land level: As discussed in the section relating to child-care, Dr. Görner met regularly with representatives of the sub-Land level, and of course they had to be involved in the delivery of labour market pro-grammes, especially those relating to social assistance recipients. No interview participant mentioned this as an obstacle to policy change, however.

Formal procedures: The Landtag – and the formal legislative process – did not feature strongly in determining policy in this area, and as a consequence non-statutory networks – both informal, and through the SGI, were more important in shaping action.

6.4.9   Conclusion

Developments in the Saarland's labour market policy are summarised in Table 6.8 below.

Table 6.8   Labour market policy in the Saarland 1999–2004

Social democratic paradigm	Christian democratic paradigm	Change
Willingness to contemplate long-term subsidised state jobs	Rejection of long-term subsidised state jobs	Land-level subsidies only as a method of securing reintegration into first labour market, greater emphasis on education within them, and limited Land-level programmes. Reduction in programmes compared to previous policy
Reluctance to subsidise private sector	Willing to subsidise private sector	Mixed views on wage 'top-ups' to private sector, only minor programme introduced and then phased out. No change to previous policy

Table 6.8 Labour market policy in the Saarland 1999–2004 – *continued*

Social democratic paradigm	Christian democratic paradigm	Change
Active labour market measures appropriate for general labour market	Active measures only for special needs groups (e.g. disabled, long-term unemployed) for limited period	No change – active measures only for 'special groups'
Rejection of promotion of low-paid sector	Encouragement of low-paid sector, e.g. through 'Kombilohn' (wage subsidies)	Introduction of wage top-ups but on very limited scale, only at start of period
Rejection of localisation/ decentralisation	Support for localisation/ decentralisation	Support for only very limited decentralisation
Rejection of deregulation	Support for deregulation	Support for deregulation expressed on a federal level, only limited changes on Land level
Apprenticeships and jobs-creation schemes paid at Tarif (collectively agreed) level	Apprenticeships and job-creation schemes paid at lower level	No change on apprenticeships. Kombilohn initiative paid at Tarif level; extension of Tarif requirement for building sector on public contracts; other initiatives not paid at Tarif level
Privileged partnership with unions	Parity of partnership with social partners, or limited partnership	Continued partnership with unions alongside employers' representatives

Three broad conclusions can be drawn regarding policy change in the Saarland in this area. First, there *was a shift* in labour market policy, moving towards instruments that were supportive of the market working, rather than a direct intervention, and with only very limited Land-level support for publicly funded job-creation schemes. The Land shifted away from the 'stay' model of labour market policy, towards the 'pull' model, as would be expected of a CDU-led Land.

This draws attention to an important point: although the Saarland, as a small and relatively poor Land, is not in a position to pursue its own autonomous labour market policy, this very fact *may drive policy change towards the Christian democratic paradigm*. Certainly, this change in policy was promoted by conscious choices of political actors; the point is that being small, and poor, is not an obstacle to all change: it would be an obstacle to an

SPD-led government trying to pursue expansive and expensive active labour market policies, but it was not to the CDU.

At the same time, there were other areas where the Saarland did not shift towards the Christian democratic paradigm in the way that might have been expected. These can be linked to the nature of the Land: in its relations with the trade unions, several interviewees (Interview Z; Interview HH) mentioned the importance of the tradition of the Catholic trade union movement, this in turn shaping the moderate nature of the CDU in the Land. A complete breakdown in relations – as was seen in Hesse – was unlikely. The Land also retained a scepticism about wage top-ups, in spite of enthusiasm from the Economics minister, Dr. Georgi, and the Economics ministry. And the Land, again driven by factors directly relating to its particular situation, rejected the line of other CDU-led Länder on the localisation of job-placement activities.

The tone – and in some cases the substance – of labour market policy was also affected by the trade union background of the minister responsible, Dr. Görner. Her inclusion in the cabinet, in turn, reflected the nature of the CDU in the Saarland, and Peter Müller's desire to see all parts of it represented in his cabinet. A rightward shift, after she was not reappointed to the cabinet after the 2004 election, might have been expected.

6.5   Conclusion

As in Hesse (and, as will be shown, Saxony-Anhalt), the extent to which the change in the party leading government led to policy change varied across the three different policy areas considered. As in both the other cases, change was most pronounced in the area of education policy, and some change was also visible in labour market policy. The paradigm of childcare policy appeared to have shifted in the CDU, taking change in a different direction to that which was anticipated.

Certain particular features of the Saarland had a significant impact, both on the substance of policies pursued (for instance, in labour market policy) and also in the way in which politics was carried out over the legislative term. As was the case in Hesse, the history of previous educational institutions presented a path-dependent constraint (which in the Saarland had also become a constitutional constraint) preventing major change to the structure of the education system. The history of a working-class, Catholic element in the Land's CDU was reflected in the appointment of Dr. Regine Görner, as a trade unionist, to the Cabinet (itself then impacting upon labour market policies), and also helped shape the Land government's links with the trade unions.

Even in the polarised field of education policy, relations between the Land government and the most critical trade union, the GEW, did not break down, as they did in Hesse and Saxony-Anhalt. Several interviewees referred to the Saarland by its sometime slogan, the 'Land of short paths', and pointed out that people were very likely to meet each other in all sorts of different contexts, and so there was a greater sense of collegiality than would be felt in a larger Land.

Within ministries (which were naturally smaller than in the other cases), the size of the Land meant that there was more direct contact between ministers and officials (Interview Z; Interview KK); it would be harder for officials to resist ministerial pressure than in a large Land. One further point Dr. Görner raised as an outsider was that she found attempts to recruit personnel from outside the Saarland could be resented, and viewed as an insult (Interview Z).

In comparison with Hesse, the *Staatskanzlei* (Minister President's Office) did not appear to play anything like as active a role in steering policy, and Minister President Müller was accepting of policy differences, allowing cabinet members to make it plain that they were representing different parts of the CDU's coalition of support (such as Dr. Görner and the trade union movement) at the expense of presenting a united picture, in a way which would have been unthinkable in Hesse. There were elements within the election programme put forward by the CDU which were obviously not realised, with several examples coming from the areas of policy examined here (such as a reduction in public holidays, ending charges for all years of nursery school, and the idea of a Land-based child benefit top-up). This might have suggested a less rigid degree of policy coordination than in Hesse – a point also confirmed by the absence of a published 'programme of government', instead relying on the Minister President's statement of government to the Landtag. It also suggests that the CDU might not have expected to win the election, and therefore did not construct the programme with a view to having to implement it (a point which accords with informal comments made in interviews). In addition, in contrast to the situation in both Hesse and Saxony-Anhalt, there was no opportunity to revise the programme after the election, at the time of coalition negotiations, and remove any commitments which did not seem deliverable. Several, though not all, of these unfulfilled commitments involved spending money which, in its desperate budgetary situation, the Land simply did not have.

Although there were some instances of collaboration between the CDU and the SPD opposition in the Landtag (for instance over the ban on head-scarves, and also the agreement on the Law on wage levels during building contracts), the Landtag, and formal procedures within it, such as committee hearings, played at most a peripheral role in each of the policy areas under consideration. Policy choices were driven by the election manifesto (chosen by the Land party, but with members of the Landtag Fraktion playing a significant role within it, on account of the Land's size), the Minister President, and the government, with no evidence being found of the Landtag exerting an exogenous influence, other than at the margins.

Overall, as with Hesse, we see a partial confirmation of the political hypothesis. The party composition of the government in the Saarland had a major impact upon education policy (although it did not lead to anything approaching a complete transformation of the school system), a limited impact on labour market policy, and an impact – albeit a different one to that anticipated – on childcare policy. We also see confirmation – especially in labour market policy but also in education – of the territorial hypothesis, both in relation to the specific features of the Land (for instance, the high level of long-term unemployed people making it resistant to localisation of job-placement activities) and on account of 'path dependence' (with the history of the school system creating barriers to reform). Finally, the nature of the Land's CDU appeared to have an exogenous impact upon policy aims and choices, and in particular on relations with the trade unions.

7
Saxony-Anhalt 2002–2006

7.1 Background

As noted in the introduction, the case of Saxony-Anhalt was chosen primarily because it was the only eastern Land which experienced a direct switch from a government without CDU participation, to a government without SPD participation, within the time frame under consideration. There are, however, a number of other factors which make Saxony-Anhalt a useful case study, which will be discussed below. Policy-makers in Saxony-Anhalt might be expected to be highly constrained in the choices which they can pursue: as alluded to in the introduction, the budgetary position of the Land is extremely precarious, with a high level of indebtedness – 7,857 Euro per inhabitant at the Land level, as at 31st December 2006 (Statistisches Bundesamt). Additionally, the position of the Land in the east might be expected to have a profound impact upon the shape of public opinion, for instance in the view of public expenditure, gender equality and organised religion. The Land has also been subject to challenging demographic trends, which have the effect of reducing the tax base and affecting federal subsidy arrangements, as well as shaping infrastructure requirements, such as for schools.

Although the current state of Saxony-Anhalt has its origins in the Prussian state of Saxony, and had a brief forerunner in 1947, the GDR's Länder were converted into smaller *Bezirke* (Districts) in 1952, and so Saxony-Anhalt was divided into the Districts of Magdeburg and Halle (Dobner 2004, pp.418–19). As a consequence, unlike the other two case studies discussed here, Saxony-Anhalt did not have a long-standing political history.

With minor amendments, the Districts of Halle and Magdeburg were merged to form the new Land on 14th October 1990, which was also the day of the first elections (ibid., p.420).

7.1.1 Social structure/Religious affiliation

Within the state of Saxony-Anhalt, the proportion of Church members is relatively low: some 16% are members of the Protestant Church, and a further 4% are members of the Catholic Church (Statistisches Landesamt). For the purposes of this study, we might expect that the influence of the Church (and, for that matter, of the confessional welfare organisations) would be less on Land-level politics than in the other case studies, and also that there would be a structural preference for secular politics. As was discussed in Chapter 4, this could lead to a softening of the CDU's policy paradigm on issues such as religious education and childcare.

Only 1.9% of the Land's 2006 population were 'foreigners' (non-German nationals), representing the lowest proportion of any Land, with the largest group amongst these being those from Vietnam (Statistisches Landesamt). However, this does not mean that policy towards foreigners is remote from Land-level political debate. Saxony-Anhalt has a significant problem with right-wing extremism in comparison with other Länder. For instance, the probability of being the victim of a right-wing extremist attack is 12 times as high as in Hesse (Spiegel, 13th October 2006).

7.1.2   Demographic changes

Saxony-Anhalt has been subject to two negative developments: a dramatically ageing population, caused by a falling birth-rate as well as growing life-expectancy, and also the movement of people away from the Land in order to find work, a reflection of the Land's high level of unemployment. Indeed, Saxony-Anhalt had the highest level of outward migration from 1991 to 2002 amongst the east German Länder (Rosenfeld 2006, p.203).

There has been a pronounced downward trend in the Land's population as is illustrated by Table 7.1 below:

Table 7.1   Population development in Saxony-Anhalt (actual or projected, as at 1st January 2007)

Date	Population
31st December 1985	3,021,008
31st December 1989	2,964,971
31st December 1990	2,873,957
31st December 1995	2,738,928
31st December 2000	2,615,375
31st December 2005	2,469,716
31st December 2010 (projected)	2,350,427
31st December 2015 (projected)	2,238,286
31st December 2020 (projected)	2,155,271
31st December 2025 (projected)	1,976,237

Source: Statistisches Landesamt

The problematic age-profile is shown below:

Table 7.2   Age breakdown of population in Saxony-Anhalt

Age-group	Population as at 31st December 2006
Under 6	102,729
6–15	141,452
15–25	306,436
25–45	635,494
45–65	705,263
65–75	330,247
Over 75	220,166

Source: Statistisches Landesamt

7.1.3   Economy and fiscal position

As has been outlined, one reason for the choice of Saxony-Anhalt as a case study is that it is important to assess the potential for political action in times of economic difficulty. Even well over a decade after reunification, Saxony-Anhalt's GDP per citizen, at 18,250 Euro per inhabitant, lagged well behind the national average of 26,390 (Statistisches Bundesamt 2006, p.67). Productivity was 21% below the federal average, although this reflected a significant improvement compared to the 1991 position, when the Land's productivity was 52% below average (ibid., p.68). Wage rates were also comparatively low. In 2004, wages in the Land were only 74% of the national average, and given that the comparative statistic for 1995 was 75, they have worsened in relative terms over time (ibid., p.74).

Unemployment is also extremely high in Saxony-Anhalt. Although during the period of study it was surpassed by Mecklenburg Lower Pomerania at the bottom of the league, unemployment figures for the period under discussion were as follows:

Table 7.3   Unemployment in Saxony-Anhalt

Year	2002	2003	2004	2005	2006
Unemployment in %	20.9	21.8	21.7	21.7	19.9
Federal unemployment in %	10.8	11.6	11.7	13.0	12.0

Source: Statistisches Landesamt/Statistisches Bundesamt

As might be expected, unemployment was viewed as an extremely significant challenge for Land-level policy-makers, notwithstanding their constrained ability to address it, and was a significant electoral issue.

For the purposes of this discussion, we are not only interested in the structural problems which policy-makers need to address at a Land level, and the backdrop to them, but also the tool-kit which they enjoy, so it is worth discussing briefly the budgetary position of the Land government, as well as the political apparatus in place in the *Land*.

Wolfgang Renzsch, an expert on fiscal federalism and more specifically on Saxony-Anhalt, summarises the budgetary position of the Land as follows:

> The budgetary position of the Land of Saxony-Anhalt can hardly be described in any way other than as 'almost hopelessly indebted'. In the fifteen years of its existence the Land ran up more debt per citizen than every other [non-city state] Land of the Federal Republic of Germany in their, generally far longer, histories. ... This terrible situation is not the consequence of too limited income, but far more of expenditure being too high. Looking back one will have to accuse the state government, especially the first two state governments, of acting without discipline on budgetary matters. In the third and fourth election periods attempts were made to turn things round, but the results left much to be desired (Renzsch 2006, p.107).

In his analysis of the 2003 budgetary position, Renzsch (ibid., pp.108–10) unearths some important statistics: the per capita expenditure of the Land and its local governments is 4,987 Euro per inhabitant, compared with an average of 4,725 Euro for eastern non-city Länder and 4,188 Euro for western non-city Länder. By contrast, per capita government income for Saxony-Anhalt is 4,358 Euro; this is some 1% above the east German average and 16% above the west German average.

Of the Land's income, around 57% came from non-tax income, including the fiscal redistribution mechanism, which compares with a west German average of 31%; moreover, quite a lot of Saxony-Anhalt's tax income was generated outside the Land. Renzsch further finds that the Land's personnel, or staffing, costs (for those still at work – a quirk of accounting makes this the most useful measurement) are extremely high: some 1,054 Euros per inhabitant, the second highest of the 13 non-city Länder; 4% above the east German average and some 23% above the west German average, in spite of lower public sector pay-rates (ibid., p.111). This is in part due to its weaker intermediary associations compared with the west, with more public services being delivered directly by local authorities in the east (Goetz 1999, p.105). Given this background, one might expect Land-level policy-makers to endeavour to reduce the public sector payroll, with its associated political consequences, including campaigns by trade unions and the threat, amongst some employees, of industrial action.

The indebtedness of Saxony-Anhalt presents a significant constraint upon policy-makers' choices. Initially, and under the terms of the first solidarity pact, eastern Land level politicians ran up high levels of debt, with the encouragement of western politicians. At this stage, obtaining credit was the clearest way for Land level governments to raise income autonomously (ibid., pp.105–7). This led, in 2003, to annual debt servicing payments of 414 Euro per person, compared with an eastern average of 308 Euro per person, and 278 Euro per person in the west. Saxony-Anhalt's debt servicing payments are the second highest overall, with only the Saarland's being higher (ibid., p.113). The level of debt in 2003 at the Land level was 6,570 Euro per head.

An improvement in this situation is unlikely to come from exogenous sources. In fact, a declining position should be anticipated: while a higher level of tax income would of course be beneficial, because of the demographic factors alluded to above, there is likely to be a significant drop in income from the fiscal redistribution mechanism, as this is based on the overall population, which, as has been shown above, is in sharp decline (ibid., p.118).

7.1.4 Politics in Saxony-Anhalt

As can be seen with reference to Table 7.4, the electorate in Saxony-Anhalt displays, in common with other eastern Länder, quite high electoral volatility. No party has been able to establish anything approaching hegemonic support (or indeed, break the 40% mark). One oddity, compared to other eastern Länder, is that the FDP has entered the Landtag on three separate occasions, and indeed gained over 10% of the vote on two occasions. In 1990, this was attributed to the prominence of the then Foreign Minister Hans-Dietrich Genscher, who originally came from Halle (Schnapp 2006, p.157).

The early years of Land-level politics were turbulent: between the first and second elections to the Landtag after reunification, the Land had three Minister Presidents. Gerd Gies (CDU) was the Chair of the eastern CDU in Stendal prior to reunification, and then took over the role of the Land's CDU Chair after 1990. Gies topped the Land's electoral list, but such was the success of the CDU in the district contests (winning 48 out of 49), this did not give him a seat in the Landtag. He instead allegedly pressurised a number of MPs to resign because of alleged *Stasi* (collaboration), and indeed it was claimed that that he used a security advisor, Klaus Matschke, to spy on his colleagues and persuade them to resign. However, this pressure was apparently applied not only to some collaborators, but also some *Stasi* victims, and this led to the withdrawal of the support of his Fraktion, leading to his resignation as Minister President in July 2001. Gies' successor, Werner Münch (the Finance Minister and a western politician), was in office for a little longer. However, he also resigned in 1993 as a result of the 'salary affair', where he was alleged to have taken illegal payments for working in the east, along with his other western colleagues (Dobner 2004, p.437; Schnapp 2006, p.158). The turbulent picture was complemented by the resignation of one CDU MP in protest, and the subsequent formation of a rebel Fraktion in the Landtag. The third Minister President, Christoph Bergner, enjoyed an equally problematic reception, with the SPD and parts of the FDP coalition partner calling for new elections, in the end without success (Dobner 2004, p.438).

Table 7.4   Election results in Saxony-Anhalt 1990–present (results of list votes)

Year	1990		1994		1998		2002		2006	
Party	%	Seats	%	Seats	%	Seats	%	Seats	%	Seats
CDU	39.0	48	34.4	37	22.0	28	37.3	48	36.2	40
SPD	26.0	27	34.0	36	35.9	47	20.0	25	21.4	24
PDS	12.0	12	19.9	21	19.6	25	20.4	25	24.1*	26
FDP	13.5	14	3.6	–	4.2	–	13.3	17	6.7	7
B90/Green	5.3	5	5.1	5	3.2	–	2.0	–	3.6	–
REP	0.6	–	1.4	–	0.7	–	–	–	0.5	–
DVU	–	–	–	–	12.9	16	–	–	3.0	–
Schill	–	–	–	–	1.5	–	4.5	–	–	–
Others	4.3	–	1.8	–	1.5	–	2.6	–	4.7	–
Turnout	65.6		54.9		71.7		56.6		44.4	

*Stood as *Linke*
Source: Landeswahlleiter Sachsen-Anhalt

The period from 1994 to 2002 saw SPD-led Land governments under Reinhard Höppner, a mathematician and senior Church figure in east Germany (Schnapp 2006, p.156), with a coalition known as the 'Magdeburg model'. Under this model, from 1994 to 1998, an SPD/Green coalition was 'tolerated' by the PDS. In 1998, once the Greens had left the Landtag, failing to reach the 5% hurdle, government was taken over by an SPD minority administration, again tolerated by the PDS. As the first example of cooperation with the PDS at a Land level, this generated a predictably hostile response from political opponents, as well as from some within the SPD. The CDU then undertook a high-profile campaign against cooperation with the 'red socks' (the PDS) for some years (Tagesspiegel, 19th September 2006).

One notable feature of the 1998 election campaign was the relative success of the right-wing extremist DVU, coming from nowhere to get 12.9% of the vote. The DVU enjoyed particularly strong support amongst young voters (getting 32% of votes amongst young voters, ahead of the SPD and CDU). A lively debate ensued amongst political scientists as to the motivation of DVU voters, with some, such as Walter, arguing that this reflected a protest vote, while others, such as Schumann, saw ideological attachment to the far right as a more significant factor (for a summary see Schnapp 2006, pp.162–3). In common with other far right parties, the DVU had next to no influence in the Landtag, suffering various splits, as well as the prosecution of one of its MPs for animal cruelty (Tagesspiegel, 23rd March 2006). Nonetheless, there was a danger that the DVU could return, and its influence upon Land governments was twofold. First, the DVU's emphasis on unemployment (and ability to mobilise young, unemployed voters) added extra pressure on policy-makers in this area; and secondly, given the wider problem of right-wing extremism, the DVU's success added urgency to the need for all mainstream Land parties to seek solutions to the far right problem.

7.1.5   Political structures in Saxony-Anhalt

In addition to the structures common to all the Länder and discussed in Chapter 3, in common with other cases it is worth briefly outlining the distinctive features of the political system in Saxony-Anhalt.

Landesverfassung

The Landesverfassung was agreed in 1992 by the necessary two-thirds majority, and without a referendum (Dobner and Schüttemeyer 2006, p.20). Amongst the distinctive provisions, alongside numerous aspirations around housing (Art. 40), work (Art. 39), protection of families and children (Art. 24), and support for human rights (Art. 2 and 4), are:

- Rights for opposition groups in the Landtag (Art. 48 and 53), in the form of individual MdLs being able to table questions, a quarter of a committee's members being able to request information and access to files before a committee, and also in stating that the 'Opposition factions have the right to equality of opportunity in Parliament and in public, and the right to the necessary resources to fulfil their particular roles';
- The right to self-dissolution (Art. 60);
- Direct democratic components (see below).

Direct democracy in the Landesverfassung

Under Article 80, a minimum of 30,000 citizens can persuade the Landtag to consider a subject, or indeed draft a piece of legislation. More significantly, under Article 81, a petition for a referendum can be launched, provided a draft law, with reasons, is presented (budgetary laws are not permitted); this petition must be supported by 11% of those eligible to vote.

The Landtag must then either accept the law, or a referendum must take place. The referendum vote either takes place on the new law, or between that proposed by the petitioners and one proposed by the state government. In order for the petitioners' law (in the absence of an alternative) to pass, it needs a majority in the referendum, but also the support of at least a quarter of the electorate as a whole. If the petition changes the Landesverfassung, a higher hurdle applies: it needs a two-thirds majority and the support of at least half the population. As will be discussed, these provisions became important in the 2002–2006 period in the CDU/FDP government's attempt to change the law regarding childcare.

Electoral system

The electoral system in Saxony-Anhalt is common to most of the Länder, and indeed the federal level (with regards to both systems' personalised proportional representation system). There is a 5% hurdle for representation, with citizens casting two votes, one for a district MdL, and the other for a party list. One peculiarity concerns the provisions for 'overhanging mandates'. If a party wins so many constituency seats in the direct vote that the number of seats across the Land that it has will be higher than its percentage of the party list vote, then the number of seats in the Landtag increases overall, and the other parties receive extra list seats to make up for this. So, for instance, after the 2002 elections, the Landtag increased in size from its normal 99 seats to 115 seats, owing to the CDU winning 48 of the 49 direct contests (Schnapp 2006, pp.152–4). This provision removes a potential source of a slightly more 'majoritarian' outcome to Land-level elections.

Civil service

Following reunification, the civil service in the Land had to be radically recast, in order to bring it under the rule of law (for a full discussion, see Goetz 1999, pp.87–9). The Unification Treaty established the principles for this. Article 20/2 required the creation of a professional civil service, and Article 15/2 said that the new Länder were to receive assistance from the Federation and the western Länder (ibid., p.90). Significant subsidies were provided, in particular from the federal government, in order to facilitate the employment of officials recruited from the west (ibid., p.92). Saxony-Anhalt was twinned with the western Land of Lower Saxony, and significant numbers of civil servants from Lower Saxony played, and continued to play, a significant part in the reconstruction (Wollmann 2002). This twinning primarily affected the more senior levels; staff at the subordinate levels of the Civil Service were recruited locally. The practice of recruitment was obviously affected by the rules on the recruitment of former employees of the GDR state, in particular in relation to former *Stasi* collaborators (Goetz 1999, p.100).

For the purposes of this study, the extent to which this might shape parties' ability at a Land level to affect policy is important. Here, Goetz (1999, pp.102–8) discusses three consequences (he considers the eastern Länder generally, rather than the specific case of Saxony-Anhalt). First, as discussed above, the size of the 'establishment', i.e. the number of public servants, is significantly higher than in the west (and is particularly high in Saxony-Anhalt). While this might provide additional options for service delivery, given the fiscal position it will also throw up some budgetary challenges (as were experienced by the 2002–2006 CDU/FDP administration). By contrast, the number of Beamte is far lower than in the west, as there was no parallel status in the GDR, partly due to a lack of suitable personnel, but also as a result of conscious political choice (ibid., p.103). Secondly, attitudinal differences are highlighted: according to a study by Reichard and Schröter, those in eastern administrations 'tend to be more attached to 'old' materialist values; put more emphasis on a stable and powerful executive operating above individual interests; are more averse to politics and have a more technocratic understanding of public administration' (cited in Goetz 1999, p.103). Thirdly, the structure is different, and in particular organised interests such as the trade union confederation, are weaker (Goetz 1999).

Although these factors could appear to constrain rather than unburden policy-making at the Land level, the relatively recent appointment of civil servants there (as well as the regular changes of government) would be expected to inhibit somewhat the extent to which any party would be able to establish hegemonic control of particular ministries (see Chapter 2 above).

Local government

Saxony-Anhalt's local government structures were in need of reformation after the demise of the GDR in 1990 (Kregel 2006, p.127). Over the period between 1990 and 2005, the workforce at a local level had shrunk to around a quarter of its previous level. As everywhere in Germany, local government enjoys the right to 'local self-administration' (*kommunale Selbstverwaltung*). In Saxony-Anhalt, local government has been in flux since 1990. In 1990, there were 1,367 districts (*Gemeinden*); these were gradually grouped together into different models of 'administrative communities' (*Verwaltungsgemeinschaften*), which preserved the structures of the individual locality but pooled administrative functions. The next level of local government 'up' is the county (*Landkreis*), of which there are 21 (with populations ranging from 64,000 to 153,000). In three cases (Magdeburg, Halle and Dessau), there is instead a City-District (*Kreisfreie Stadt*), which combines a district with a county (ibid., pp.132–7). Political leadership of the *Gemeinde* combines a directly-elected mayor with a council. Political leadership of the *Landkreis* combines, again, a directly-elected *Landrat* (a status similar to a mayor) and a council, known as a *Kreistag*. These structures have been the subject of significant debate, and, in fact, as will be discussed below, local government reform proved one of the thorniest issues for the 2002–2006 CDU/FDP coalition.

The functions of each level are divided into statutory functions, which they are required to perform for the federal or Land government, and discretionary functions. Nonetheless, as Kregel (ibid., p.130) notes, amongst the latter are some services of local significance which cannot easily be cut, such as the provision of libraries, theatres and sporting facilities. The Land's constitution enshrines the 'connexity principle' (*Konnexitätsprinzip*), which decrees that, if the local government units are required to take on extra tasks, they need to receive adequate financial compensation (Art. 83.3). This applies, for instance, to childcare, which local government is required to carry out, but for which the Land level is responsible (ibid., p.130). The division of responsibility between the two levels of local government is not straightforward: the presumption of subsidiarity applies, so that the *Gemeinde* level is, as a default, responsible for local functions. *Landkreise* take on functions where they are of importance beyond the local area, or if financial administrative necessities so demand, or if a law specifically states their responsibility (ibid., p.130).

Unsurprisingly, the financial position of local government units in the Land is desperately bleak. In 2006, almost all the *Landkreise* and 90% of districts could not set a balanced budget, and there were tensions between the level of the localities and the districts, as the latter required increasing funds from the former. There are high levels of indebtedness at a local level, and permission for new borrowing is rarely given (ibid., p.141).

One important point referred to by several interviewees, including Jürgen Scharf, the CDU Parliamentary Leader in the Landtag (Interview A), and Bernd Kregel, the Business Leader of the City and Locality Association of Saxony-Anhalt (Interview L), is that many Land-level parliamentarians have dual mandates, also holding responsibility at a local level, and more (indeed most) have local government experience. While this may facilitate cooperation, it is at least as likely to force the Land government to take on board local government interests. Parties, of course, also provide an important tool of communication between the different levels (and can be a means by which local decision-makers raise issues with Land-level parliamentarians). There are also informal cooperation mechanisms across the different levels of government (which were confirmed, for instance, by the interview with Jürgen Scharf (Interview A)).

This situation, then, would appear to impose significant constraints upon Land-level policy-makers. Local government enjoys legally-enshrined autonomy; it cannot be required to undertake tasks without being given the necessary financial support, and in addition the local government 'lobby' enjoys a significant presence in all parliamentary groups, and strong informal access rights. Moreover, the precarious fiscal situation means local government will not be in a position to do the Land government any favours.

7.1.6 Saxony-Anhalt's election campaign 2002

The election campaign of 2002, leading to the change of government, was focused on the record of the SPD-led minority administration, tolerated by the PDS, as well as the Land's high level of unemployment and poor economic performance (Holtmann 2003). Across a range of indicators, the public's assessment of the Land's development was negative, and this applied particularly to its economic performance. On a scale of 1 to 6, with 1 being the best and 6 being the worst, the Land's economic development was graded 4.0 in a January 2002 survey, while the labour market's development was rated 4.7 (ibid., p.45). This became a focus of the CDU's campaign, under the slogan 'The red lamp has to go' (ibid., p.44), referring to the red lamp of a train's last carriage (Saxony-Anhalt, at the time, was bottom of the national rankings in levels of unemployment). By April 2002, the CDU was perceived to be more able to solve the Land's problems in a range of areas, including fiscal policy, bringing new employers into the Land, reducing unemployment, tackling crime, guaranteeing equality of opportunity in education, and representing the Land at a federal level (ibid., pp.47–8). The SPD, in the April 2002 survey, led the CDU only in the perception of guaranteeing social justice (and even then was behind the PDS).

The FDP, meanwhile, pictured its leading candidate Cornelia Pieper under the slogan: 'Höppner geht, die Arbeit kommt' (Höppner's going, jobs are coming) (Das Parlament, 20th February 2006). Its campaign was highly focused on Pieper. According to Holtmann, it emphasised the FDP's 'freshness' (not being represented in the Landtag) and focused on its interest in economic and education policy. It also explicitly aimed to present Pieper as a possible Minister President, in a model adopted subsequently by the FDP's national leader, Guido Westerwelle (ibid., pp.51–2).

A further difficulty was caused for the SPD by its apparent desire to continue in government with PDS support (Volksstimme, 17th April 2002). This desire was not universally shared in the SPD, with criticism coming from senior figures only days before the election. In particular, the popular Interior Minister, Manfred Püchel, was known to be sceptical (Volksstimme, 18th April 2002). The situation was further complicated by the possibility that the PDS would in fact get more votes than the SPD. For this situation, the PDS demanded the right to lead the government, prompting further internal debate in the SPD (Volksstimme, 8th April 2002).

In the event, this dilemma resolved itself, with, as discussed above, the results showing a convincing win for the CDU and gains for the FDP, with those two parties winning sufficient seats to form an overall majority, and the SPD actually falling behind the PDS and experiencing, with a 15.9% decline in its vote, its worst losses in any state election since 1950 (ibid., p.53). Public scepticism about the ability of parties at a Land level to make a difference, visible in opinion surveys before the election, was doubtless also reflected in the sharply reduced turnout (which fell some 15% to 56.5%).

7.1.7   Coalition negotiations and formation

The coalition negotiations began on 24th April (Volksstimme, 24th April 2002), and finished on 13th May (Volksstimme, 14th May 2002). There were relatively few disagreements, and public and media discussion focused at least as much on the distribution of ministries between the parties and the personalities chosen to fill them, as on the policies themselves (ibid., p.58). For the first few days after the coalition negotiations, Cornelia Pieper demanded the role of Minister President for herself, only to have to publicly climb down (Volksstimme, 25th April 2002). The FDP demanded the key ministries of Education and Economics, while also supporting a reduction in the number of ministries from eight to seven (Volksstimme, 6th May 2002). It demanded three ministries for itself, while the CDU was, initially, only willing to concede two. The greatest conflict in the negotiations was focused, predictably, on interior policy, with agreement reached quickly in, for example, the field of education (Volksstimme, 27th April 2002).

Wolfgang Böhmer was confirmed as Minister President on 14th May 2002, and the full cabinet was agreed; indeed, Böhmer actually got three votes from opposition MPs in his election, conducted by secret ballot, to the office (Volksstimme, 17th May 2002). Cornelia Pieper did not, in the end, take on a ministerial position, but instead agreed to lead the FDP Fraktion, and gave up her seat in the Bundestag (Volksstimme, 13th May 2002). For the purposes of this study, key ministerial appointments included Prof. Jan-Hendrik Olbertz to Minister for Education (Kultusminister). Olbertz was not a member of a political party and had previously been an education studies academic at the University of Halle, although he was appointed on the CDU ticket and identified strongly with the party. His 'deputy', in the office of Secretary of State in the Ministry, was the CDU member Winfried Willems. The newly created role of Minister for Economics and Labour was Dr. Horst Rehberger (FDP), a businessman who had previously held a ministerial role in the Saarland. Rehberger was assisted by Dr. Reiner Haseloff (CDU), who was previously head of the Labour Office in the city of Wittenberg, and enjoyed significant respect across party boundaries (This was emphasised, in interview E, by Ude Gebhardt, the Chair of the DGB in Saxony-Anhalt and an SPD member). The new Minister for Health and Social Affairs (including childcare) was Gerry Kley (FDP), a biologist.

7.1.8   Politics in Saxony-Anhalt 2002–2006

Obviously the precise changes to policy in the three specific areas of policy under scrutiny will be outlined in subsequent sections. However, some description of the substance and style of government in the Land from 2002 to 2006 will be helpful in setting the scene.

Clearly, and in particular in comparison with his counterpart Roland Koch in Hesse, Wolfgang Böhmer was a more centrist figure, who attached some importance to dialogue beyond his party coalition (as will be discussed in the case of childcare below). Böhmer was also willing to question the federal CDU's stance when it suited his – or the Land's – purposes. For instance, Böhmer frequently pursued a different agenda on labour market policy to his western counterparts (Berliner Morgenpost, 13th July 2004), as is discussed below, and he also broke from the 'party line' on the Law on Stasi Documents (Spiegel, 9th December 2002).

There were few reports of coalition conflict, and numerous interviews with participants appeared to confirm cabinet unity broadly prevailed. However, several CDU politicians alluded to problems in the relationship with Gerry Kley, the Social Affairs minister. In particular, one interviewee (speaking confidentially), revealed that Kley planned to reorganise his ministry, and shift certain, senior civil servants – who were members of the CDU – into peripheral roles. Wolfgang Böhmer took the unusual step of vetoing this change in Cabinet (Interview D). Another early conflict with Kley came when he gave an assurance to the media that childcare would not face budgetary cuts. This brought an irritated reaction from Böhmer, and a *volte face* (Volksstimme, 19th September 2002).

Although the CDU was generally united, the issue of local government reform was particularly sensitive and led to tensions throughout the four years (Mitteldeutsche Zeitung, 13th March 2005). As noted above, the fact that CDU members of the Landtag often held local mandates as well added to the difficulties (Interview A). At the instigation of the CDU, the quite radical plans of the previous government for unitary local government (*Einheitsgemeinden*) were abandoned, and far more limited plans were pursued.

The most significant personnel conflict in the administration occurred with the resignation of Thomas Leimbach, the CDU's Vice-Chair at Land level and leader of the Land Administrative Office (*Landesverwaltungsamt*). Leimbach resigned from the Coalition Committee after reading deprecatory comments that had been made about him in the newspaper. He apparently – some years previously – had suggested Böhmer was too old for the office of Minister President, and, according to insiders, Böhmer had 'the memory of an elephant' and had not forgotten the insult (Volksstimme, 3rd May 2005).

On substantive issues, other than those which will be subject to detailed consideration, the most significant changes brought about by the government concerned attempts to consolidate the Land's precarious financial state, and introduce cuts to the size of the public sector. Although it did not achieve all its targets in reducing the size of the public sector workforce, around 10,500 jobs were cut between 2002 and 2006, leading to a saving of around 500 million Euros (Elbe-Report, 12th March 2006).

The next Land election took place on 26th March 2006, following an election campaign significantly less polarised than the previous one (SZ, 16th March 2006). The CDU led the parties on issues around economic competence, but results were more balanced in education policy, family policy and social affairs (Forschungsgruppe Wahlen 2006, pp.31–3). Böhmer was strongly favoured to continue as Minister President, with some 45% saying they would opt for him if the post were directly elected, compared to 22% for the SPD's candidate for the office, Jens Bullerjahn, and 10% for the PDS candidate, Wulf Gallert (ibid., p.10).

In the end, the CDU and SPD's results were little different to those in 2002: the CDU was down 1.1%, the SPD up 1.4%. Bigger switches were experienced by the PDS (standing as the *Linke*), which gained 3.7%, and by the FDP, which fell dramatically from 13.3% to 6.7%. This result for the FDP made the formation of a grand coalition – explicitly favoured by the SPD in its election campaign – a certainty (Volksstimme, 22nd March 2006 and 27th March 2006). Indeed, Wolfgang Böhmer appeared to distance himself from the FDP during the election campaign, owing to its oppositional stance at the federal level (ibid., p.16).

7.2   Education policy in Saxony-Anhalt 2002–2006

As discussed in the introduction, given the high level of autonomy enjoyed by education policy-makers at the Land level, it is to be expected that significant policy change would occur in this area. However, in contrast to the situation in Hesse, education policy was not a major feature of the Land's election campaign, there was no enormous public impulse for change, and the pressures felt in this area of policy were at least as significantly related to the fiscal and demographic issues discussed above as to political pressure.

7.2.1   Background to education in Saxony-Anhalt

Saxony-Anhalt in 2002 had (and retained throughout the legislative period) a relatively unusual education system; rather than the 'classical' three-band school system, there was instead a two-band system, consisting of the *Gymnasium* ('Grammar school') and the *Sekundarschule* ('Secondary modern'). The SPD had weakened the existence of streaming within the latter – in the initial years after the demise of the GDR, in most *Sekundarschulen* there were two streams, reflecting the *Hauptschule* and the *Realschule* in other Länder. However, even prior to then, the possibility of having combined classes within the two streams in the *Sekundarschule* existed, specifically for rural regions where otherwise the school might not have been sustainable (Interview R). At the time the CDU/FDP government took over, selection took place at the end of the 6th year of school; years 5 and 6 were a *Förderstufe* ('orientation phase') without selection, which was an initiative of the SPD-led government, opposed by the CDU and FDP. This reflected the fact that selection took place later in the school system in the GDR, as discussed in Chapter 4. Saxony-Anhalt also retained a number of comprehensive schools, though with only around 5,000 pupils in total – including some which were internally differentiated rather than 'integrated' – these will not be the focus of discussion in this chapter (Land Sachsen-Anhalt 2007).

One other relatively unusual feature of the Land's education system was the high proportion of children going on to grammar school. In 1991/2, 38.5% of children of secondary age were at a grammar school (excluding those at a comprehensive), in 1995/6 this figure had risen to 40.7%; and when the CDU/FDP took over government, it was 38.2% (Land Sachsen-Anhalt 2007). A leading CDU politician with a keen interest in education attributed this in part to the fact that, in GDR days, relatively few got the opportunity to go to the equivalent of a grammar school, and access was sometimes restricted for political reasons, strengthening the aspiration to attend such a school today (Interview R).

The previous governing coalition introduced two particularly significant innovations which were contentious, and which were criticised by the CDU in the election campaign. The first was the switch to the *Grundschule mit festen Öffnungszeiten* ('Primary school with fixed opening times'). It required primary schools to have fixed opening times of 5.5 hours (for classes 1 to 4), where children were required to be present (according to the Law to Introduce the Primary School with Fixed Opening Times). This was subject to unsuccessful legal action, first before the Land's Constitutional Court, and subsequently before the Federal Constitutional Court. It was criticised by the participants in the legal action (as well as the CDU) as removing parental choice, supporting state intrusion into family life, removing differentiation, and constituting a covert attempt to reduce unemployment amongst childcare workers (BVerfG, 1 BvR 279/02).

Secondly, in the face of strong opposition from the CDU and FDP, as well as teaching unions other than the left-leaning GEW, the SPD-led government increased the length of time needed to reach Abitur from 12 years to 13 (Traeger 2005, pp.53–148). This was, in part, dictated by the need to reach the minimum required number of hours of lessons in order to achieve a federally recognised Abitur, and also by spare capacity in the school system (caused by demographic changes, and a previous school reform). The CDU supported a different way of getting the required number of lessons to Abitur: there should be earlier selection – prior to the orientation phase – which would then meet the requirement, and would also remove the spare capacity which supported the move (ibid., p.84). This view was shared by business representatives. It was clear that, in the event of a CDU victory, these policies faced reversal.

7.2.2   The coalition agreement

As noted above, negotiations on the coalition agreement reached a swift conclusion, and no interviewees noted any great dissent between the CDU and FDP. Amongst the highlights (Land Sachsen-Anhalt 2002) were:

- An increase in the quality of teaching with a general expression of conservative values ('The learning function of the school has to be moved to the forefront more than before … the more individual responsibility individual schools get … the more important is the securing of teaching quality' (ibid., p.27));
- The introduction of binding performance standards for schools and regular comparisons of performance between schools (p.27);
- A move to set relations between pupils, teachers and parents on a more clearly defined footing, at the level of the individual school (p.27);
- An end to the primary school with fixed opening times, and its conversion into a primary school with 'reliable but voluntary care outside teaching hours' (p.28);
- An emphasis on teachers' recommendations to advise parents on choice of further schools for their offspring (p.28);
- The switch from a comprehensive orientation phase to a selective one specifically related to the type of school (p.28);
- Clear differentiation throughout the secondary modern school, leading to the nationally recognised *Hauptschulabschluss* or *Realschulabschluss*;
- Reintroduction of Abitur after 12 years 'as soon as possible' (p.29);
- A switch to a centrally-set Abitur with centralised questions and examination (p.29);
- The decision on whether to send children to a special school 'has to be taken in the interests of the children objectively according to individual need and not according to ideological perspectives' (p.29);
- Some – relatively vague – commitment to increasing schools' autonomy (p.30);
- Strengthening of parental choice (p.30);
- The introduction of grades for behaviour and attitude to work ('behaviour, hard work, teamwork, order' (p.30));
- The extension of religious studies and ethics across the Land as soon as possible, to be delivered by qualified teachers (pp.30–1);

- An examination of whether a switch to Beamte status is appropriate for teachers (pp.30–1).

Many of these aspects will be familiar from the discussion in Chapter 4, and indeed from previous case studies: the aspirations in this document represent a clear and unmistakable shift in a conservative direction.

7.2.3 Abitur: From 13 years to 12

It was no surprise that an early priority for the government was to switch back to Abitur after 12 years, given the bitterness with which the change in the opposite direction had been fought, and the commitment in the coalition agreement. It was announced – to take place from 2005/6 school year – by Minister Olbertz in 2002 (Volksstimme, 13th June 2002). This was a top priority of the 2003 School Law (Volksstimme, 2nd October 2002). Perhaps having realised its previous position was unpopular, the SPD chose at first to criticise the change around the margins, for instance, the fact it would not apply to comprehensive schools, placing them at a comparative disadvantage to grammar schools (Volksstimme, 7th October 2002). The timetable for the change subsequently slipped to 2007, but Minister Olbertz did not rule it out for comprehensives, as previously, and the SPD and PDS did not oppose the change at the law's first reading (Volksstimme, 12th October 2002). After the enormous battle to extend the school period, it was perhaps surprising that the opposition allowed such a swift reversal, reflecting strong social pressures in favour of the change.

7.2.4 Changes to selection

The 2003 School Law extended selection in two ways. First, it amended the 'orientation phase' in years 5 and 6, so as to make it selective, rather than comprehensive; as noted above, this was in part necessary in order to meet the KMK's minimum requirements. Secondly, the Law reintroduced two separate streams in the *Sekundarschule*, with pupils being divided into two streams (akin to the Hauptschule and the Realschule in other Länder). Debate over this change was significantly more polarised than that over the number of years taken to reach Abitur (Volksstimme, 5th December 2002). Thomas Lippmann, for the GEW, provoked particularly strong reactions when he talked of *Notverordnungen* ('emergency powers') – referring to the speed of change – and *Selektion* ('selection'), both phrases which were associated with the Nazi era. This provoked a strongly critical reaction from the CDU (Volksstimme, 6th December 2002a).

Later in the legislative period, the SPD tried, with no great public resonance, to counter-attack. Rita Mittendorf, the party's education spokesperson, launched a paper in April 2005 arguing for a return to the GDR's *Allgemein bildende Oberschulen* ('comprehensive upper schools'), until the end of the 8th class. Predictably, the PDS and the GEW were supportive, while the FDP and the government remained critical, arguing it would mean weak students were too stretched, and stronger students would be pushed back. Minister Olbertz argued it would 'upset once again the internal reform process of the schools, which is just beginning to bear fruit' (Mitteldeutsche Zeitung, 27th April 2005a). Eva Feussner, speaking in the Landtag for the CDU, said the opposition didn't need to use so many words to explain what it wanted: 'You can say in one sentence what you actually want: the old GDR school' (Volksstimme, 26th January 2006).

A further change to selection occurred as part of the 9th School Law, passed in 2005. The government identified a problem with too many children ending up at the grammar school but being unable to cope, and noted an increasing number of children entering without a teacher's recommendation (Mitteldeutsche Zeitung, 4th January 2005). Here, the government's final proposal – which made its way into legislation – was to insist on a certain level of grades in order to gain a recommendation for the grammar school, but, if this was not met, there was the possibility of taking part in a centrally organised examination, at the request of parents. Interviews suggest, in fact, that there was a division between Minister Olbertz and the CDU on this point (hinted at by a comment made, after the first round of the new procedure, by Eva Feussner, the CDU's education spokesperson, when she warned of 'undermining the procedure to determine suitability through lax grading' (Mitteldeutsche Zeitung, 24th February 2006)). It would appear that the CDU had some sympathy for a fully centralised test, removing parental discretion, whereas Minister Olbertz was reluctant to go this far, and instead the compromise was agreed.

7.2.5   Timing of education

As noted above, the change of government also heralded a change in approach towards the concept of all-day education. The previous 'primary school with fixed opening times' was replaced – by Ministerial decree – by the 'primary school with reliable opening times', with the start and end of the school day being voluntary (GVBl LSA 2002, p.392). Minister Olbertz justified the change by arguing that 'parents and not the state should decide if their children should stay in school or go home after the end of lessons' (Volksstimme, 31st May 2002). The GEW argued that the change was a disgrace, highlighting the lack of consultation (Volksstimme, 21st June 2002).

The other major development in this area (aside from pre-school provision, which will be the subject of a separate discussion) concerns the implementation of all-day education as part of the federal government's programme. Initial reactions to this were polarised, with the SPD welcoming the change (Volksstimme, 8th March 2003), while arguing it had not been a priority for the Land government, and the FDP grumbling about the federal government's control and lack of revenue funding (and indeed demand for a 10% local contribution to capital costs – Volksstimme, 10th March 2003). Eva Feussner, for the CDU, went further, arguing that 'We should ask ourselves if we support our children, in ever growing measure, being subjected to state supervision rather than being brought up by their parents' (Volksstimme, 14th March 2003).

However, notwithstanding these initial, rather polarised, reactions, the implementation of the federal government's programme appeared rather less contentious politically. For instance, Rita Mittendorf stated during an interview that she had privately lobbied the federal minister for funds for Saxony-Anhalt, and while the Land had been relatively slow in dispensing funds, this reflected a sensible need to get priorities right (Interview H).

7.2.6   Repetition of years

Although detailed data on the repetition of years is not available, there was a tightening of the grade requirements needed to progress from one school year to the next in Saxony-Anhalt (Volksstimme, 26th January 2006). An interviewee, Thomas Lippmann, Chairman of the GEW in the Land, also pointed to an impression that more pupils were repeating years (Interview K).

7.2.7   Religious studies and ethics

The coalition partners agreed to strengthen this area, but in practice this appeared not to be a priority, and was not mentioned as an area of significant shift by any interviewees. Indeed, even in mid-2005, a third of all children received no teaching in RE or Ethics (Mitteldeutsche Zeitung, 14th April 2005). However, at that time, on the basis of a legal opinion from the University of Halle, Ethics, unlike RE, could be considered a compulsory subject, and the Land launched an initiative to get more church employees to teach RE. Previously, pupils only had to choose one subject if both Ethics, and both Catholic and Protestant forms of RE were available. Owing to a shortage of teachers, this was rarely the case, resulting in a situation summarised by Secretary of State Willems as 'the choice between going for an ice-cream and having an ethics lesson' (Volksstimme, 7th April 2005).

7.2.8   Grading and testing regimes

Several switches from the social democratic to the Christian democratic paradigm on grading can also be observed.

Early in the legislative period, the CDU/FDP coalition announced that grades would be awarded from the first year onwards, although Minister Olbertz indicated that he expected this to be pursued with a degree of flexibility by teachers. This was agreed as part of the 2003 School Law (Volksstimme, 27th June 2002).

As part of the 2003 education law, centralised Land-level tests were introduced. From 2003 onwards, they were carried out in Mathematics and

German in years 3, 4 and 8, with further tests being introduced for year 6 in 2005. Furthermore, the Land government moved towards a centralised Abitur in its 2005 School Law, with grading by a teacher based at a different school reintroduced from 2007/8 (GVBl LSA 2006, p.46).

In early 2003, Minister Olbertz also announced that behavioural grades would be introduced for the first time, with a grade for social behaviour and one grade for 'order' (Volksstimme, 8th January 2003). This move was criticised by the GEW, whose Chair, Thomas Lippmann, felt it was a negative step which would punish bad behaviour, rather than reward good behaviour, and that the time should be spent more usefully. He also argued it was wrong to introduce them at the time of savings being made to school social work (Volksstimme, 9th January 2003).

7.2.9   Pupil choice

The amount of flexibility enjoyed by pupils in grammar schools in choosing their Abitur subjects was reduced by the 2003 School Law. The previous provision of main and subsidiary subjects was abolished, and replaced by a system of core subjects, including Maths and German, with variations only permitted at the margins (Volksstimme, 10th July 2002). A senior CDU politician with an interest in education suggested public support for this measure could be traced to the broad curriculum which operated in GDR times; the politician also regretted a failure to persuade colleagues to include a second natural science amongst the core subjects (Interview R).

7.2.10   Charges for school books

In 2003, charges for school books were introduced (as had been planned by the SPD-led government in 1997, until a furore forced a climbdown). Parents would either have to pay for the books, or pay a fee to borrow them (Volksstimme, 29th January 2003). Minister Olbertz justified the change by arguing that it was fundamental that the money could be reinvested by schools, and that it was right to have a fundamental discussion over whether parents should be expected to contribute (something he also emphasised to the author privately – Interview N). Perhaps surprisingly, this idea was not rejected out of hand by the SPD either, as Rita Mittendorf conceded it made it clear that education cost money (Volksstimme, 29th January 2003). Although the PDS at the time was opposed to the change, its spokesperson subsequently conceded the change was probably sensible (Interview P). Hence, although this did represent a shift in the paradigm of education policy towards the Christian Democratic end of the spectrum, it commanded some cross-party support, perhaps because of the obvious fiscal pressures. Minister Olbertz subsequently expressed some pride in the model's adoption elsewhere, and felt there were educational reasons for it, as well as generating a saving (Interview N).

7.2.11   Relations with trade unions

Given the sharp demographic changes in the Land, as well as the fiscal pressures, pay negotiations were always going to be fraught. However, both sides had something to lose from a failure of the negotiations, which were begun shortly after the new government was formed. For the government, if a voluntary agreement on short-time working could not be reached, it would be liable for the full eastern tariff (Deutscher Beamtenbund 2003). On the other hand, this would almost certainly necessitate job losses, which were feared by unions.

The compromise which was eventually reached – and was scheduled to run until 2009/10 – included moving around 2,000 teachers to the status of Beamte (which brought a saving in pensions and health insurance costs, but also helped tie them to the Land), and a continuation of the short-time working agreement (Volksstimme, 6th December 2002b). Notwithstanding the obviously tough negotiations, the atmosphere in these discussions was significantly less poisonous between the GEW and the government than in discussions over educational principles (Interview K). A leading CDU politician with an interest in education noted that the issue of making teachers Beamte was contentious in all political groups. The argument in favour was particularly strong in shortage subjects, and it could bring a saving to the Land. On the other hand, there was disquiet at creating two classes of teacher in the classrooms – those with Beamte status, and those who remained *Angestellte* (Interview R).

7.2.12   PISA

Political analysis of the Länder ranking within the PISA study in 2000 was predictably polarised. Minister Olbertz argued that it showed the positive side of federalism, although in a 2002 interview he was more critical, saying that 'Parties and ideological boundaries were hindering the exchange of concepts and experience' (Volksstimme, 26th June 2002). Rita Mittendorf (SPD) argued that the children tested in 2000 had experienced neither the non-selective orientation phase (introduced in 1997) nor the new secondary modern-school, which ended differentiation between the Realschul- and Hauptschul paths (introduced in 1999 (Volksstimme, 13th December 2002)). This perspective was shared by the GEW (Volksstimme, 21st February 2003). Reaction to the 2003 PISA study – in which Saxony-Anhalt rose from 13th to 5th place out of the 16 Länder – was similarly polarised, with the CDU seeing a confirmation of its policies, while Mittendorf argued that in fact the children tested in 2003 were those who had undertaken the non-selective orientation phase (Volksstimme, 26th January 2006). The PDS considered as equally superficial the government's attempts to make the PISA success its own (Interview P).

7.2.13　The federal dimension

Although the Land, in common with the rest of the CDU, did not endorse a transfer of power over education policy to the federal government, there was support for common standards in education and leaving exams. A further suggestion from the FDP, to have a centralised Abitur for the Länder of Thuringia, Saxony and Saxony-Anhalt, was welcomed by Minister Olbertz, as a potential step on the way to national standards (*Mitteldeutsche Zeitung*, 10th January 2005). Private discussions suggested that all sides were unhappy with the outcome of the 2006 federalism reform, and that eastern interests were insufficiently reflected in the outcome (Interviews H, N, P).

Minister Olbertz, for instance, felt that the opportunities of federalism were not being fully realised:

> I am very much for federalism, but it has to be modern federalism where commonalities can be articulated, and there have to be platforms where common ground can be articulated, and I'm missing that at the moment. The KMK could be such a platform, and we are practicing this with the national educational standards, which reflect the idea of constructing more common goals but more diverse means, that you can learn from the most successful ways and conflicts. But we are a long way off that (Interview N).

Minister Olbertz also emphasised that some jobs – such as provision of university infrastructure – had to be recognised as a challenge for the whole country, not just for one Land, otherwise there was a risk of 'Mezzogiorno relations' – referring to the impoverishment of the Mezzogiorno region of Italy.

The Minister emphasised that his first meeting of the KMK had been particularly frustrating, but things had improved since. He also noted that it was rare for a Land to be 'defeated' as such at the KMK, because by its nature only issues the KMK was likely to be able to solve were brought before it. He had hoped to bring further flexibility to the number of teaching hours required for the Abitur to be recognised across Germany, but had not been successful in this (Interview N).

7.2.14　Other developments

As was outlined in the coalition agreement, Minister Olbertz launched a contract between teachers and parents. Under the contract, parents promised their children that they would ensure homework was completed and school materials were in order, as well as promising to listen to children. In return, schools promised to deliver certain learning outcomes, such as basic reading skills. In an interview, Olbertz suggested it would make it easier for schools to remind parents of their responsibilities, and said he wanted 'to strengthen the consciousness of parents and teachers of their responsibility' (SZ, 2nd September 2003).

One further, thorny issue confronted by the Land's government, in response to the enormous demographic challenge (discussed above) faced by the government, concerned school closures. The Education Ministry's chosen method was to set a minimum number of pupils for introductory year groups, particularly at the level of secondary schools (Volksstimme, 19th February 2003). There was discussion over whether school choice would lead to school closures, but the enshrinement of catchment areas in legislation was said to prevent this (Volksstimme, 11th October 2002). The SPD and PDS opposed these changes, arguing for a reduction in the minimum number per school as enshrined in the 2003 School Law, while still accepting some closures (Volksstimme, 18th October 2003).

City and district councils had to present plans, and, in the end, some 59 secondary schools (out of a total of 265) had to close by 2009, with a further 33 to follow later that year. Minister Olbertz announced in 2005 that, at that stage, the school network would become too thinly spread to bear further closures, and so he would allow some exceptions if an introductory year group at a school fell below 40 in number (Mitteldeutsche Zeitung, 27th April 2005b). It is worth noting that representatives of all parties identified this as an internally difficult issue. Rita Mittendorf highlighted the role of SPD local politicians in working with her own Fraktion to win exceptions, but suggested backbench CDU MPs were also responsible (Interview H). This was supported by the resignation of a CDU mayor over a local closure (Volksstimme, 10th May 2003). The CDU in the Landtag, almost as soon as the change was announced, demanded exceptions for some rural areas (Volksstimme, 24th February 2003). For the PDS, Rosemarie Hein noted that it could lead to tensions between urban and rural members of the Fraktion (Interview P). Some in the CDU wanted to go further, removing catchment areas and the centralised school planning procedures, and instead letting the market decide which schools became unviable. For the advocates of this approach, the effects of competition would have been positive. Such an approach was not adopted, however, and this was partly attributed to the civil service (Interview R).

Apart from the areas related explicitly to the policy paradigms set out here, three further features of the 2005 School Law are worth mentioning. First, it established a new framework for quality assurance in schools, concerning internal and external inspection, learning from other schools, and more in-service training for teachers. Second, it improved the environment for private schools, and allowed for an organisation which already ran one recognised private school to get funding for another after one year's operation. Third, it also wanted to put local authorities in a position to get rid of catchment areas wholly or in part by March 2006 (Wochenspiegel, 29th December 2004). A further step in this direction was announced by

Minister Olbertz in March 2006, when he stated that Land-wide league tables for schools would be introduced from 2008. This had been impossible before because of the number of school closures (Mitteldeutsche Zeitung, 22nd March 2006).

7.2.15   Influencing and changing policy

As has been illustrated, a clear shift in education policy towards the Christian democratic paradigm was clear, in spite of the fiscal and demographic changes which might have been expected to shape policy change. However, this assessment is subject to two caveats. First, fiscal pressures might actually promote some policy change in a conservative direction (such as, for instance, with the introduction of charges for school books). In addition, demographic change, while identified by Minister Olbertz in an interview as being the single biggest constraint upon education policy formation, did not necessarily impact upon the ability to implement the specific reforms as part of the shift from the Christian democratic to the social democratic paradigm (Interview N).

In interviews, several points became clear about the way in which education policy was agreed in Saxony-Anhalt.

Role of the opposition: Although the PDS and the SPD both testified to the genial personality of Minister Olbertz, and accepted his willingness to undertake changes at the margins, they were not able to influence the general thrust of his policy. Although – on the SPD side – there continued to be contacts with the operational side of the education ministry, these had to be carefully pursued, and did not shape policy (Interviews H and P).

Role of trade unions: Discussions with the VBE trade union suggested a great thawing of relations compared to the time of the SPD-led government (Interview C). However, the relationship with the GEW was, with the exception of a brief 'thawing' following agreement on the pay deal in 2002 (which, according to GEW Chair Lippmann, lasted 'about five minutes' – Interview K), extremely acrimonious. This view was also expressed by Minister Olbertz (Interview N). Contacts between the GEW and the operational level of the education ministry were discouraged, and could lead, in the view of Lippman, to professional consequences for the civil servants concerned. For his part, Minister Olbertz felt he had tried to set down ground rules for dealings with GEW, but this had not been fruitful (Interview N). A leading CDU politician with an interest in education was rather more positive about relations with the GEW, and felt that regular dialogue was important, and its attendance sometimes led attendees of the education working group to at least reconsider their views (Interview R). Nonetheless, there is no doubt the GEW's influence and relations with government declined steeply compared with the 1994–1998 period (Traeger 2005).

Role of the local and state parties: All parties testified to the need to involve local government actors in policy formulation, and it was clear that, in particular in the area of school closures, players in the CDU below the Land level had an impact (although given the high number of closures, their ability to 'swim against the tide' should not be over-stated). All parties had working groups (discussed at some length in Traeger 2005), consisting of interested members with professional expertise in education policy, which worked closely with the education working groups in the Landtag party groups.

Constraints upon the government by the CDU Fraktion: In confidential interviews, some CDU members did express a frustration that Minister Olbertz was not 'one of them', and could be hard to influence (Interview R). In particular, on the issue of mechanisms to determine choice of school, he was perceived not to have been robust enough, and to have given parents too much influence. Also, the CDU would have preferred the promotion of greater parental choice and the introduction of market mechanisms to determine which schools closed, and which ones stayed open, rather than the formal mechanism chosen by the Minister. Minister Olbertz did not allude to either issue in his interview.

Constraints upon the minister by the coalition partner: The FDP was never mentioned as a constraint upon policy in this area, and education did not appear to be a particular area of expertise for the FDP group. This also reflects the high level of autonomy individual ministers enjoy in the German system, under the principle of *Ressortskompetenz*, as well as the small size of, and thus obvious time constraint on, the FDP group. Minister Olbertz noted that he met with the FDP group once or twice a year. He said there was hardly any potential conflict in education policy, and that it was perhaps 'not a classical domain of the FDP' (Interview N).

Blocking of change by the Land civil service: Actors on the governmental side were questioned about the validity of Manfred Schmidt's hypothesis, outlined in the introduction, which suggested that civil servants, appointed by the previous administration, would be hostile to reforms (with many even being members of the previous governing party). Minister Olbertz did not see this as a problem, and was at pains to emphasise that he was willing to work with any civil servants, and it became clear who was most capable. He noted that he still had those who he knew were SPD members in senior posts in the Ministry, and that, for instance, his press officer had held the same position under the previous government (Interview N). However, other interviewees on the CDU side disputed this view, noting the particularly polarised nature of education policy and suggesting SPD members at senior levels in the Ministry were definitely obstructive (Interviews A and P). One interviewee felt that – although not irrelevant – the party political dimension of the blocking of change was secondary, and the main issue was insufficient turnover, with a dusty, inflexible bureaucracy with too few new ideas. This bureaucracy was very good at finding reasons not to be able to do things and was felt to be a real obstacle to change (Interview P).

Minister Olbertz noted that he could still appoint his closest officials personally (the Head of his private office, and the Secretaries of State), and that, over time, it became clear who was loyal, and willing to work, and who was not:

> Well, I'm not a professional politician, perhaps there are good reasons to radically change the personnel in a ministry, but in order to do this you have to have a 'mistrustful hypothesis' as a starting point, and I freely admit that I did not have this experience, I was used to approaching people and winning them over, and I tried that, and I didn't have any problems worth mentioning, and I didn't have this thought that I needed to change all the personnel (Interview N).

He did, however, need to make some changes at the periphery, and also made sure that new appointments reflected the current political situation. He was aware of at least one *Abteilungsleiter* who was an SPD member, and had no problem with it, though of course some were CDU members too. He also noted the difficulty of making changes, and the potential risks:

> You mustn't forget that according to Beamte law in Germany your hands are very much tied and you can't do much; demoting people, and demotivating them, and then in the end believing that they would do good work for you is also illusory (Interview N).

Finally, Minister Olbertz felt that the relatively new democracy and bureaucracy in the east, compared to the west, could have an impact on this; he was not aware of significant shifts in personnel in other ministries either.

Relations with sub-Land level governmental units: In education policy, some areas of implementation lie with the cities and *Landkreise*, particularly concerning 'school development planning' – planning which schools would remain open, and in which locations. The executive side of these units – typically a *Landrat* – would be party political, and directly elected. However, Minister Olbertz did not see any obstruction caused by these, although he conceded that dealing with CDU members might be slightly more straightforward. Nonetheless, he saw the relationship as 'collegial and reasonable' (Interview N).

Role of formal procedures: All interviewees agreed that formal procedures – committees and public hearings in the Landtag, as well as the 'corporatist', formal body, where all stakeholders in education policy were represented (*Landesschulbeirat*), were only able to agree changes at the margins, for instance on the development of curricula. Minister Olbertz also stated the great value he attached to these bodies, although informal, unstructured meetings were also important (Interview N). However, in no way could they constrain major changes to be pursued by the government. There did not appear to be any rebellions on issues of education policy in the Landtag, reflecting the high level of party cohesion there.

7.2.16   Education policy: Conclusions

In summary, in education policy in Saxony-Anhalt there was an extremely clear shift, across almost all dimensions, towards the Christian democratic paradigm, as summarised in the Table 7.5.

On the key dimensions around selection, in particular, the CDU/FDP government's line was uncompromisingly conservative. Arguably, on two elements, the Land's eastern status made a difference. The continuing high proportion of pupils studying Ethics, rather than religious studies, reflected the largely secular population; and there was stronger support for giving the federal government influence over education policy than might have been expected. This no doubt reflects the Land's fiscal situation, as discussed in the introduction. However, the expectation discussed in Chapter 4 that an eastern Land might have a propensity to promote the value of 'equality' in the education system was in no way realised.

The case of education in Saxony-Anhalt, then, appears strongly to confirm our 'political' hypothesis, and indeed suggests that, in this area of policy at least, reunification – and the consequent greater inequality between the Länder – has not constrained the ability of a government to effect policy change.

7.3   Childcare and family policy in Saxony-Anhalt

Having a history of generous provision, which had been unchallenged by the SPD-led governments from 1994–2002, and having played almost no role in the state election campaign, it is perhaps surprising that this area of policy became extremely prominent in the 2002–2006 parliament. It led to significant political polarisation, split the SPD, and culminated in a referendum on reform. Nonetheless, as will be discussed, change in this area probably stemmed more from the Land's fiscal situation than from a desire on the CDU's part to achieve a paradigm shift.

7.3.1   Background to childcare policy in Saxony-Anhalt

Childcare and family policy appeared to play even less of a role in the Land election campaign than did education. Saxony-Anhalt had, as will be discussed below, a legacy of extremely generous childcare provision, which had been maintained by the SPD-led governments, and had not been fundamentally challenged by the CDU or the FDP in the election campaign, although one interviewee, Markus Kurze (CDU), felt that the whole concept of *Familienpolitik* had got lost before the CDU got back into office, and needed to be reintroduced (Interview I).

Table 7.5   Education policy in Saxony-Anhalt

Social democratic paradigm	Christian democratic paradigm	Changes
Comprehensive education (or if unacceptable, late and flexible selection)	Early and rigid selection, with limited movement between types of school	More selection, brought forward two years
Any selection based on parental choice	Selection based on tests/teacher assessment	Switch to selection based on teacher assessment, with appeals mechanism
High level of individual teacher discretion over curriculum content and testing	Centralised tests and examinations	Introduction of two centralised tests, and switch to centralised Abitur
Abitur after 13 years	Abitur after 12 years	Switch (back) to Abitur after 12 years
Extensive pupil choice of subject	Limiting of pupil choice	Restriction on pupil choice of subjects
Compulsory, integrated all-day education	Half-day education with possibility of extension	Extension of all-day schools, on voluntary basis; reduced compulsory hours at primary level
Teachers provide education all day	Some supervision undertaken by volunteers/unqualified helpers	Most education still provided by teachers
Grading only in secondary school	Grading from year 1	Grading reintroduced from year 1
No grading of behaviour and teamwork	Grading of behaviour and teamwork	Grades for behaviour and teamwork reintroduced
Limited repetition of years in event of poor performance	High level of repetition of year in event of poor performance	Anecdotal evidence of more repetition of years, tightening of rules for non-repetition

Table 7.5 Education policy in Saxony-Anhalt – *continued*

Social democratic paradigm	Christian democratic paradigm	Changes
Free provision of school books	Parental contribution towards school books	Parental contributions introduced
No compulsory RE	Compulsory RE	Strengthening of RE but with Ethics element
Non-Christian RE provided	No non-Christian RE provided	No change
Opposition to Länder having exclusive control over policy	Support for Länder having exclusive control over policy	Some support for federal standards, positively disposed towards some federal involvement in education
Partnership with trade unions	Limited involvement with unions	Good relations with conservative unions, breakdown of relations with GEW

In May 1991, the CDU/FDP state government proposed the *Kindertages-stättengesetz* (Children's Centre Law, abbreviated to KitaG), which was passed by the Landtag in June 1991. It gave all children a legal entitlement to a subsidised childcare place, and the Land was responsible for all 'applicable costs', notably salaries, with the rest being paid for by local government, providers and parents. Notwithstanding the dramatic fall in the Land's birth-rate, the cost of childcare provision in the Land's budget barely fell. The SPD-led government in 1995 put forward a new *Kinderbetreuungsgesetz* (childcare law, abbreviated KibeG), which was agreed in May 1996, following extensive negotiations with the PDS. This law, rather than setting a percentage level for Land subsidy of childcare, instead set levels of subsidy per child, depending on the type of childcare institution, thereby giving a greater incentive to local authorities and providers to deliver savings. The CDU argued, unsuccessfully, for some of the high standards (such as the requirement for one worker for every nine children) to be reduced, in order to deliver a saving, and was pessimistic about whether the new law would in fact save money (Volksstimme, 11ᵗʰ January 2005).

In 1996, the SPD-led government, for fiscal reasons, needed to row back from this commitment. Höppner's cabinet proposed in October 1998 to reduce the Land's subsidies for childcare by around 35%, and reduce the minimum staffing level in childcare institutions to one worker for every 12 children. The PDS predictably expressed its opposition to this, and indeed the issue had the potential to bring down the SPD's minority government (Volksstimme, 11ᵗʰ January 2005), if, as it threatened, the PDS did not agree to support the budget in the Landtag (Volksstimme, 12ᵗʰ January 2005). In the end, stepped reductions of around a third to all the subsidies were agreed. In opposition to the new law, an initiative was formed (the *Bündnis für ein kinderfreundliches Sachsen-Anhalt*, the 'Alliance for a Saxony-Anhalt which is friendly to children'). It comfortably gathered sufficient signatures to force the Landtag to reconsider the issue, although following a legal hearing, it was not able to force a vote on its own proposed law (Volksstimme, 12ᵗʰ January 2005). Amongst the reasons the government gave for being unable to revert to more generous provision was that, in fact, Saxony-Anhalt already had the most extensive legal entitlement to childcare in Germany, and that it was negotiating on the Solidarity Pact (subsidy for the eastern Länder from the federal government). As Minister President Höppner put it:

We would endanger this discussion, if we created the impression that we would spend this money on consumption spending, rather than in closing the gaps in economic and infrastructural provision. The western Länder would obviously say that we were taking money for things that they couldn't afford themselves (Quoted in Volksstimme, 12th January 2005).

In fact, this argument was used repeatedly to justify reductions in childcare spending over the coming years. It implies a further informal constraint on the policy choices of Länder dependent on subsidies (either from the Solidarity Pact or elsewhere).

7.3.2   Coalition agreement

Unlike the section on education policy, the discussion of family and child-care policy runs to less than a page of the entire agreement (Landes-regierung Sachsen-Anhalt 2002). Two features are notable. First, there is a clear commitment to 'the family', as might be expected from a CDU-led government:

> The family as a life and educational community is the heart of our society. It secures the course progression of generations and offers the found-ation for responsibility, achievement, solidaristic behaviour and thus the preconditions for our ability to face the future. Family is particularly important where parents take responsibility for their children, and children for parents (ibid., p.39).

This quite general model of what a family is reflects the FDP's more liberal approach compared with that of the CDU. At least two inter-viewees noted this throughout the parliamentary term (Interview D and Interview I).

Secondly, there is a clear commitment to enabling women to work, to the extension of state support to non-institutional forms of childcare, such as childminders, and importantly a commitment to retaining the legal entitlement to childcare:

> A central aim of family policy continues to be making compatible jobs and family life. The coalition partners will work to see that there is genuine freedom to choose between family life and a career, for mothers and fathers. Family work and jobs in the economy are seen as of equal value. Against the background of difficult financial circumstances, the coalition partners attach a great importance to the development of childcare. The legal entitlement to childcare should be secured and the Childcare Law should be opened for alternative forms of care, such as childminders (ibid., p.39).

The only other commitment in this section was to extend the educa-tional function of the Kindergarten, in conjunction with the Education Ministry.

7.3.3   Developments in Childcare Policy 2002–2006

In an early interview, Minister Kley explained that he did not expect any budget cuts in childcare: 'That is definitively not anticipated' (Volksstimme, 1ˢᵗ June 2002). He emphasised that the cost-effectiveness of childcare in different municipalities varied, and he hoped to promote positive knowledge transfer. He also argued that childminders could be a useful alternative to large childcare institutions in rural areas.[1]

This cheerful prognosis was shot down by Minister President Böhmer, who gave an interview explicitly criticising Kley, and arguing that no areas of expenditure were taboo (Volksstimme, 19ᵗʰ September 2002), including childcare. The first rumour to emerge was that the subsidy for childcare would be reduced (Volksstimme, 28ᵗʰ September 2002), and then that a reduction to the legal entitlement was being considered (Volksstimme, 30ᵗʰ September 2002). This was the subject of some criticism from within the CDU, as well as more predictable opposition from the PDS, the SPD, the GEW and interest groups (Volksstimme, 8ᵗʰ October 2002). Although the savings target of 40 million Euros had been confirmed, the government had to postpone publication of its proposals, in spite of a confusing leak from the Social Affairs Ministry (Volksstimme, 23ʳᵈ October 2002). One suggestion put forward was that regulation of local authorities should be reduced (specifically, the number of staff per assistant), along with the reduction in subsidy. The possibility of a reduction in the legal requirement was welcomed by local government representatives (Volksstimme, 25ᵗʰ October 2002). A further proposal, again initially rejected by the opposition, was to allow unqualified assistants to work in childcare institutions in support of qualified staff (Volksstimme, 9ᵗʰ November 2002).

The government finally announced its proposals on 12ᵗʰ November 2002 (Volksstimme, 13ᵗʰ November 2002). It proposed to remove the legal entitlement to childcare for children under the age of three, unless both parents were in work or there was another pressing social need. Minister Kley also proposed to relax minimum staffing levels (with a complete opt-out possible under some circumstances) and to the legal requirement to childcare to be fulfilled by childminders, as well as crèches, for the first time. Norbert Bischoff (SPD) criticised the plan as being motivated by a desire to send women 'back to the kitchen sink'. Ominously for the government, the Alliance for a child-friendly Saxony-Anhalt announced its intention to start collecting signatures against the new law, to force a re-examination of the issue in the Landtag and a possible referendum (Volksstimme, 19ᵗʰ November 2002).

---

[1] As an aside, Kley was also asked if he felt comfortable, as a man, with his role as Minister for Women. He said he did, and that 'Since a man is responsible for the Ministry, I hope that the topic will be taken more seriously in public'! It is not surprising others in the Land felt this Minister had a propensity for *faux pas*!

Demonstrations and continued opposition in the press followed. However, the SPD then made the highly unusual move, on 13th January 2003, of offering the CDU a compromise deal (Volksstimme, 18th January 2003), in spite of the absence of an obvious political incentive to do so. The core of this deal was that the legal entitlement to childcare should remain for all children, but it should be reduced to five hours per day in the case of children where at least one parent was not in work. Initially, the CDU rejected this offer, arguing that the children of the unemployed should have no legal entitlement to childcare in the early years; the PDS, and the Alliance for a child-friendly Saxony-Anhalt were vehemently critical.

The new Kinderförderungsgesetz (Child Support Law) was agreed on 7th February 2003, with the CDU, FDP and SPD voting in favour (although four SPD MdLs abstained, and more were known to have reservations (Interview B and Interview O)). Norbert Bischoff, speaking for the SPD, argued that:

> Obviously one can say that we want the existing law and nothing else besides. But taking into account the parliamentary majority, which exists because of democratic elections, such a stance is, in our view, not constructive. Whether there will be a referendum is firstly uncertain and secondly its outcome is open. In the meantime a new situation will be created, which could only be reversed with great difficulty. In our view, the government's proposals would have led to the cold liquidation of the [0–2 year olds] crèche network ... So we say, in the interests of our children ... we have reached an outcome which is acceptable ... we couldn't have got any more (Plenarprotokoll 4/14, p.989).

Bischoff also emphasised that there had been other changes at the margins agreed by the government, including an increase to ten hours for all-day childcare, a reduction in the previously proposed role of unqualified childcare assistants, some paid non-contact time for heads of childcare institutions, and priority for the integration of disabled children (Plenarprotokoll 4/14, p.989). The PDS opposed the law, in particular focusing on the fact that the children of unemployed parents would be singled out, and, in effect, sent home early. Eva von Angern, speaking for the PDS Fraktion, argued thus:

> I'm curious to hear what recommendation you will make to childcare workers who have to explain to the children why one has to go home after an afternoon nap, while others stay. The privilege of being picked up at lunchtime will become a badge of shame (Plenarprotokoll 4/14, p.992).

Norbert Bischoff, both in the parliamentary debate and also in an interview with the author, felt that the compromise was justified as, if the legal entitlement to crèches for 0–2 year olds had been removed, in practice the network would have collapsed, as there would have been insufficient children to support it. He also emphasised that the educational functions could take place in the five hours of core childcare, provided for all children. He attributed the decision of the CDU to engage in the compromise to the fact it could deliver a larger saving than the government's initial proposal; something he could not be sure of at the time (Interview B).

However, this did not prove to be the end of the story. The Alliance for a child-friendly Saxony-Anhalt continued its campaign, gathering sufficient signatures for the Landtag to be forced to reconsider the law, which it did on 8th July and 15th October 2004, and then for a referendum. This was agreed for 23rd January 2005, even though, in fact, the Land's government would probably have been able to refuse to consider the referendum, as it affected the Land's budget. However, Markus Kurze, the CDU's childcare spokesperson, emphasised that the government was keen to win the argument and have the referendum (as well as being confident of winning it (Interview I)). The Landtag debates were ill-tempered, with the heckling of the spokesperson for the Alliance for a child-friendly Saxony-Anhalt by CDU MdLs, as well as the absence (apparently owing to a clash of appointments) of Minister President Böhmer, generating a certain ill-will (Volksstimme, 13th January 2005a). In the referendum campaign itself, the CDU and FDP urged opposition, while being careful to point out to voters that non-participation was an equally good way of registering content with the new law: Minister Kley said the best thing for people to do on election day was to 'make children', as on other days as well, in order to address the problem of the Land's low birth rate! (Wochenspiegel, 19th January 2005). The SPD was 'neutral' and left the decision to individual members, while the PDS was involved in organising the 'Yes' campaign (Volksstimme, 8th January 2005). The CDU and FDP also made it clear that, if the referendum succeeded in changing the law, the cost would have to come from the Social Affairs Ministry budget. As Minister Kley said in an interview (Volksstimme, 4th January 2005), 'If our Ministry has to find 40 Million Euros, almost everything which is provided voluntarily will be condemned to death. Support for young people, women's refuges, Land support for sport, all that would be greatly in jeopardy'.

In the end, the referendum failed to change the law: although 331,913 voters voted in favour of the alternative law, with 216,621 voting against, the proportion voting in favour represented well below the necessary 25% of the electorate (which would have been 521,258) needed for change. Minister President Böhmer declared he was 'relieved' at the result, and surprised at its scale, while Katrin Esche, the SPD-member and childcare worker who had run the 'yes' campaign, expressed disappointment, in particular at the fact too few young parents went to vote (Volksstimme, 25th January 2005).

Notwithstanding the SPD's moderating influence, the law steered childcare towards the Christian democratic paradigm in several ways. First and foremost, it reduced the Land's expenditure on the service, and restricted access to it. The weakening of regulation also accorded with the Christian democratic paradigm.

A consequence of the law, which was not entirely expected, was that it led to a wave of privatisations, as local authorities looked harder for savings in the area, and were in any case prompted to rationalise provision. In particular, the greater labour flexibility in the not-for-profit sector, as well as the fact it was not bound into local government wage agreements, reduced the cost of provision; state employees' terms and conditions were only protected for one year after transfer into the private sector (Interview D). Indeed, the *Arbeiterwohlfahrt* (AWO, 'Workers' Welfare Association') reported that, even though they had campaigned against the reduction in the legal entitlement, the new law had been good for business (Interview F).

The law's decision to bring childminders (*Tagesmütter*) into the statutory childcare framework was greeted with criticism, most notably in Magdeburg, where the local authority was accused of blocking their registration, and laying bureaucratic obstacles (such as planning consent) in order to hinder the law's implementation (Volksstimme, 13th January 2005b). Armin Jahns, of the Children's Daycare Centre Society (*Kita-Gesellschaft*) in Magdeburg indicated a number of reasons to be concerned about the change (Volksstimme, 14th January 2005). He argued that while childminders were shown to be inferior to qualified institutional provision by the PISA study and by experience in the western Länder, they were being favoured in the east. He also argued that, for every childminder who received a license to work, a qualified worker in a child daycare centre would lose her job. The parents who are in work and who pay for a full day effectively cross-subsidise those who only pay for a half-day; if the former group of parents opt out, and go to a childminder, the poorer parents will suffer. Jahns also suggested that 'The competitive advantages of childminders cannot be overcome by any children's centre provider', because childminders were less subjected to regulation (for instance, on salaries, qualification, and health and safety). This confirms, then, that this aspect of the Child Support Law should be seen not just as increasing the diversity of provision, but also as a conscious attempt to promote deregulation and competition, in line with the Christian democratic paradigm.

7.3.4 Changes in family support: The Familienfördergesetz (Family Support Law)

Although far less significant than the Child Support Law, one further piece of legislation is of relevance: the Family Support Law, or *Familienfördergesetz* of 2005. It contained five main provisions: first, a 'family impact assessment' should take place in the Land administration before issuing decrees and regulations, and the Land should set a good example for the wider economy. Secondly, the Land would do without the share of income it would regularly expect to receive from absent fathers, instead passing this to local government for family projects. Thirdly, a 'family passport' should be created, giving families a range of promotional offers. Fourthly, the private purchase of family housing should be supported, with families potentially getting a discount if they buy local authority land. Finally, better information about services for families should be provided, and a 'family handbook' would be created by the Land government (GVBl LSA 2005, p.760).

The Landtag debate on this law revolved less around issues of principle, and more around whether the law actually achieved anything. For instance, Peter Oleikiewitz (SPD) argued that those who addressed the parliamentary committees believed 'that few duties are incorporated in the law and in fact only those things are covered which are already customary, are regulated already, or are already in other laws' (Plenarprotokoll 4/67, p.4802). Minister Kley disagreed, arguing that previous customs would now have legislative status, and there were also many new initiatives, such as the passing of Land maintenance funds to local government, and also the family passport. One of the CDU's speakers attempted to emphasise the importance of the law, as it was the first family support law: 'We've got a law, we've got the first law, so we have got the best family law in all of Germany, because there's no other such law' (Plenarprotokoll 4/57, p.4804).

In the final vote, on most issues the SPD abstained or supported the government, while the PDS abstained or voted against the law (Plenarprotokoll 4/67, pp.4807–8).

As will be discussed below, this seemingly uncontroversial piece of legislation, while illustrating the relatively limited room for manoeuvre of a Land government in this field, also showed the relative weakness of the FDP within the coalition.

7.3.5   Influencing and changing policy

Role of the Opposition: As discussed above, the SPD opposition in the Landtag appeared to exercise some influence on government childcare policy, trading a higher saving on childcare for the ability to shape the policy in a direction it felt to be desirable (it also achieved some minor changes to the Family Support Law). One point emphasised by several interviewees was the possibility of a grand coalition at some point in the future: Markus Kurze (CDU), for instance, stated that they wanted a childcare law for more than one legislative period, and so getting the SPD on board brought stability (Interview I). Although the influence was exercised at a parliamentary level, Norbert Bischoff, the architect of the compromise on the SPD side, was convinced that the character of Minister President Böhmer played a role:

At the start, when I had the idea right at the outset, I spoke to him, and he supported it, independently of the minister, and Böhmer is someone who said that, if we found a way [to agree], he'd support it. Without him it would have been difficult for the [CDU] Fraktion to speak to us (Interview D).

In formulating the agreement with the SPD, it was striking that the FDP appeared not to be involved in the negotiations, even though they concerned a core issue of an FDP-led ministry. Two explanations were posited for this: first, one interviewee suggested that, as Minister Kley came from the environmental arena, this was not his greatest area of expertise, and the FDP's spokesperson in the Landtag was also relatively weak (Interview I). Norbert Bischoff thought that Minister Kley felt that, having been on the receiving end of a lot of criticism for the initial proposal, he'd brought it to the Landtag and he'd done his job, and it was now the task of the Landtag to see it through. Still, this level of involvement of the opposition – through the parliamentary process – did appear to undermine the minor coalition partner.

All of the discussions in this area occurred between the CDU and the SPD. The PDS opposition – other than in assisting with the organisation of the petition and subsequent referendum campaigns – was not involved in shaping policy and did not find any way of influencing it (Interview J).

Role of trade unions: As noted above, the compromise on childcare was agreed in an informal arena by members of the Landtag, and as such there was little room for unions to get involved. No interviewee on the government side alluded to the unions forming any constraint on policy in this area. The DGB and GEW consistently opposed the change to the Child Support Law.

Land parties: In this area, there were two potential 'flashpoints' where Land parties might have been a constraint. First, the CDU's membership could have resisted the changes in childcare policy (or the concept of compromise with the SPD); but apart from one reference in a newspaper (Volksstimme, 8th October 2002), when a CDU MdL said the proposed change to the childcare law made her feel 'queasy', there was no evidence of this. A greater risk was that the SPD's *Landesverband* would fail to go along with the change. Norbert Bischoff explained that it was 'split down the middle', and thus left the decision on what to do to each individual member (Interview B).

Constraints by CDU Fraktion: Again, there is no evidence of any constraint upon the government by the CDU Fraktion in this period.

Role of FDP: As demonstrated by the above discussion, even though the FDP held the social affairs ministry, its room for manoeuvre was significantly constrained by the CDU. One particular issue revolved around the concept of 'family'. Initially, Minister Kley held a more 'liberal' view of the family, and was brought into line by Böhmer:

One area which was also difficult [in coalition relations] was policy towards families. There were personal conversations with the Minister

President, because at first Herr Kley, from his very liberal position, tried to relativise the position of the family, but perhaps through internal conversations in the coalition and with the [Minister President], he had to change sides completely, and then put himself at the forefront of family policy. The argument became that it was better for the family to look after children, rather than delegating it to the state, whereas previously he [Kley] supported the singularisation in individual lives, the equal value of being single or in a couple, that was the issue at the start (Interview D).

This difficulty resurfaced towards the end of the legislative period, when the proposed Family Support Law was passed back from the Cabinet to the Ministry, for further modifications, on three occasions (Interview D). Several interviewees also noted that Minister Kley appeared to enjoy a particularly acrimonious relationship with Böhmer and the CDU, which did not aid the liberal influence (Interview D; Interview I). The Volksstimme, in an apparently well-briefed article (which led to the resignation of Thomas Leimbach), stated that 'Most liberals know that Kley is at the foot of Böhmer's scale [of popularity]. It's got around that Böhmer has cut Kley off speaking in cabinet meetings, telling him to "stop his unqualified chatter"' (Volksstimme, 20th April 2005).

Civil service: Although Minister Kley did not respond to requests for interview, it is clear that there were occasions when he found the civil service frustrating. As mentioned in the introduction, Kley initially tried to restructure his ministry, promoting FDP members and demoting CDU members (who were well represented in the upper echelons of the social affairs ministry at the time). One interviewee compared it to 'the persecution of Christians' (Interview D). However, Kley had reckoned without the opposition of Minister President Böhmer, who blocked the changes in cabinet, and instead sent the new FDP appointees to the periphery: 'It was a real coalition power struggle which was reflected in the personnel area.'

On another occasion, in dealing with a particular issue in this policy area, Minister President Böhmer made direct contact with a senior official at the Ministry, asking him to produce a policy paper, which he then took to the CDU Fraktion apparently without the involvement of Kley; this in turn surfaced later, in legislation (Interview D).

Sub-Land level: The sub-Land level political units had a keen interest in this area of policy. As outlined above, they were directly involved in its delivery (either as a commissioner or as a provider), as well as being responsible for a hefty proportion of the cost. In drawing up proposals, their involvement – through the representative organisation – was necessary, in order to assess the likely take-up of subsidised childcare under the reformed law, and therefore its likely cost (Interview B). According to Norbert Bischoff of the SPD, local government was keen to see a reform of the Child Support law:

> The local [government] people, whatever party, were happy with [the compromise]; they'd have supported the original proposal as well, because they noticed that the biggest saving was to local government. Local government (the *Landkreise*) had to pay 40% of costs, and they had big debts, and so they had a saving, and the content wasn't really an issue for them because there was still childcare for those who wanted it, and so there wasn't resistance.

Other interviewees confirmed that the party composition of local government did not affect the extent or ease with which the changes were implemented (Interview D; Interview J).

As discussed above, local authorities did, at times, and to the frustration of the Ministry, attempt to block competition between childminders and their own (or their favoured) childcare centres, and this is an example of local obstruction of a Land government's goals (Volksstimme, 13th January 2005b).

Formal procedures: Although significant changes to the Child Support Law were agreed during the committee stage, which encompassed formal hearings with relevant actors, interviewees did not feel they made a significant difference to the outcome. Each Fraktion could invite 'its own' experts, and Markus Kurze, the CDU's spokesperson in this area, commented that you noticed who invited whom. However, he also stated that the process was not without value:

> You heard the same arguments that you were already familiar with. However, you shouldn't dismiss it too much, it was interesting to hear from those who were directly involved in this area. There were small problems in the implementation, and it is helpful to hear those affected by those areas [of policy], regardless how they see it politically. They did present objectively what would have to be done, and what consequences it would have. It wasn't unimportant, but obviously some people brought supporters, and others brought complete opponents (Interview I).

As with the committee process on education policy, it was clear that if an issue is polarised, the Landtag committees will reflect the wider plenary, and will not be a constraint upon the government.

At an operational level, regular meetings are held with representatives of local government and of the welfare organisations, but these do not steer policy (Interview D; Interview F).

7.3.6   Childcare policy: Conclusions

In summary, in this area there was a shift from the social democratic to the Christian democratic paradigm, as is illustrated below:

Table 7.6   Childcare policy in Saxony-Anhalt

Social democratic paradigm	Christian democratic paradigm	Change
Provision free for all	Provision only available at cost	Still means-tested, no change
Subsidised provision starts at age 0	Subsidised provision starts at age three	Retention of subsidised provision for all ages, but reduction to half a day where one or both parents were unemployed
Subsidised provision extensively available	Subsidised provision available where demand exists	Subsidised provision remains extensively available due to legal entitlement
Provision in formal institutions	Flexible methods of provision	Switch towards greater flexibility
Close regulation of childcare institutions	Light-touch regulation of childcare institutions	Switch towards lighter-touch regulation
No preference about types of family unit	Support for 'traditional' family	Modest stated support for 'traditional' family, not greatly reflected in legislation

However, it should also be remembered that this shift – while it might have been expected – was achieved with the cooperation of the SPD opposition in the Landtag, against a backdrop of significant fiscal constraints upon Land-level decision-makers. As noted above, the eager gaze of those paying the Land's transfer payments, and the view that this money should not be used to subsidise ongoing, discretionary revenue spending, sustaining a service at a higher level of provision than in the west, was explicitly given as a reason for change (at least as often as a more traditional emphasis on parental responsibility). Above all, it is worth noting that Saxony-Anhalt retains amongst the most generous provision of childcare in the Federal Republic, in spite of its precarious fiscal position (OECD 2004).

Four general conclusions can be drawn in relation to this area of policy. First, the *political hypothesis* is to some extent confirmed, but to a lesser degree than with education policy. Secondly, as in the other Länder examined here, the CDU's position is not so far removed from the SPD's. Thirdly, the CDU/FDP government's desire for change was constrained by public opinion which it could not take for granted in support of the change. Fourthly, the *territorial counter-hypothesis* also finds some confirmation, as the policies pursued in the Land are still more 'social democratic' than in many SPD-governed Länder, as a result, in particular, of the legacy of the GDR's institutions and the social expectations these have conditioned.

7.4 Labour market policy in Saxony-Anhalt 2002–2006

7.4.1 Introduction

As discussed at the start of this chapter, Saxony-Anhalt's economy, and with it its labour market, has faced enormous challenges since reunification. The swift privatisation of former state enterprises – or their collapse – led to significant numbers of workers being laid off (Carlin 1998, pp.18–19), subsequently manifesting itself in long-term unemployment, as well as a significant exodus of skilled workers to the west. Indeed, from 1991 to 2002, Saxony-Anhalt had the highest level of outward migration of any east German Land (Rosenfeld 2006, p.203). The over-valuation of the East German Mark at the time of reunification (seriously diminishing east Germany's export base), the addition of reunification costs to the payroll-financed social insurance system, and the restructuring of Saxony-Anhalt's chemical industry also contributed to its enduring economic difficulties (Haddow et al. 2006, p.332). One response of the Land and federal governments was to turn to job-creation schemes (ABMs – *Arbeitsbeschaffungsmassnhahmen* – and SAMs – *Strukturanpassungsmassnahmen*), as instruments of an active labour market policy: these represented 12% of Saxony-Anhalt's GDP in 1992 (ibid., p.330). However, it is worth noting that most of the Land's expenditure in this area went on co-funding federal programmes (through the Federal Labour Organisation) or those of the European Union (ibid., p.331).

In truth, the shape of Saxony-Anhalt's labour market stemmed far more from the legacy of the GDR's moribund economy, and slow growth in the German economy more generally, than through decisions by policy-makers on a Land level. Indeed, as Carlin notes (1998, p.25), east German economic growth was stronger than that in the western Länder. As is also clear from examination of the Hartz reforms, supply-side changes could have only a limited impact on the Land's precarious position. Moreover, as discussed in Chapter 4, the potential for autonomous action by a Land government on labour market policy is limited, with co-development and funding of programmes with the Federal Labour Agency or the EU, and action through the Bundesrat, being the major instruments available. In spite of the state of Saxony-Anhalt's labour market being the greatest concern to the public, and the greatest challenge to politicians, it is an area where Land-level policy-makers are very significantly constrained.

7.4.2   The election campaign and the coalition agreement

Notwithstanding the above, as discussed earlier in this chapter the labour market was a significant theme in the 2002 election campaign: the FDP's placard stating 'Höppner geht, die Arbeit kommt!' ('Höppner's going, jobs are coming') was a typical theme. By the time of the election, only 17% of electors felt the SPD in Saxony-Anhalt was best placed to reduce unemployment, compared to 36% for the CDU, and a further 7% for the FDP – although 19% of electors trusted no party to do this (Holtmann 2003, p.47). Of the three areas of policy examined here, the lack of progress in revitalising the labour market (alongside the related economic woes in the Land) doubtless made the greatest contribution to the election result (ibid., p.44). Notwithstanding the rhetoric, party election programmes were relatively thin on actual proposals in labour market policy. For instance, the FDP devoted one paragraph of its 31-page election manifesto to this, calling for an increase in the level of earnings before tax and national insurance liabilities were incurred (a change which would need the support of the federal government), more private sector involvement in job placement, and more support for part-time working (FDP Land Sachsen-Anhalt 2002, p.9).

Initially, the CDU appeared to have some interest in getting a high-profile minister to look after labour market and economic policy, and Johannes Ludewig (CDU), a former Chairman of the German Railways, was touted in the media, although in the end he declined to take on a formal role, instead offering to advise the government (Volksstimme, 26th April 2002). Responsibility for labour market policy instead fell to Horst Rehberger (FDP), with Dr. Reiner Haseloff (CDU) as deputy. The move of the labour market policy division from the Social Affairs into the Economics ministry was particularly welcomed by business representatives (Volksstimme, 10th May 2002). Interestingly, one interviewee suggested that the merger of the ministries did not reflect the FDP Minister's wishes, and was a CDU priority – Dr. Rehberger would rather have had responsibility for transport policy (Interview M).

Like the party manifestos, the coalition agreement was relatively thin on specific pledges concerning labour market policy, although the general statements made were unmistakably those of a right-of-centre Land government:

> The coalition will pursue a unified and cross-cutting economic and labour market policy, which will create more jobs in Saxony-Anhalt. Economic and labour market policy will therefore be brought together in one ministry. The creation of a flexible labour market, which supports individual initiative and willingness to perform, is the aim of this policy. The first labour market enjoys absolute priority. ... The coalition will represent the interests of Saxony-Anhalt more strongly at a federal level.

… The labour market should become more modern and flexible, so that economic growth brings more jobs. The coalition will press in the Bundesrat for rules on low-paid employment which are more supportive of employees and employers (Land Sachsen-Anhalt 2002, p.7).

There was, however, still a recognition of the role of social partners – both sides of industry – in the document, and there was no discussion of expanding the role of the private sector in job facilitation.

7.4.3   Policy change from 2002–2006: Job creation schemes

On the basis of the Christian democratic paradigm of labour market policy (let alone the FDP's more neoliberal view), and in particular the commitment to private-sector, rather than public-sector job creation, as stated in the coalition agreement, one might have expected the Land government to withdraw from co-funded job creation schemes, and to be resistant to long-term, publicly-funded job creation schemes.

In the end, Saxony-Anhalt remained committed to some ABM and SAM (job creation) measures, however, as well as retaining a high-profile third labour market programme (Interview M). The number of participants in ABM and SAM programmes fell dramatically (from 30,971 in 2002 to 6,073 in 2006), but this represented the continuation of a trend which pre-dated the CDU/FDP administration – in 1998, 56,019 workers were in these programmes. However, as will be discussed below, this had relatively little to do with decisions at a Land level, and instead reflected the new focus of the Federal Labour Organisation (as well as changes which came about as a result of the Hartz reforms). Over the same period in Mecklenburg Lower Pomerania, which was governed by an SPD/PDS coalition, the number of those in ABM programmes fell from 12,571 in 2002 to 3,664 in 2006 (Böckler-Stiftung 2003 and Böckler-Stiftung 2007). Following the Hartz reforms, so-called 'One Euro Jobs', agreed locally along similar principles to the ABM programmes (that is, short-term work for the long-term unemployed, which serves the community and is in the public sector) were introduced, and their take-up was similar to that of ABM and SAM: in 2006, there were 23,800 people in One-Euro-Jobs in Saxony-Anhalt, up 46% from 2005 (Böckler-Stiftung 2006).

To emphasise the point further, when the Federal Labour Organisation proposed to reduce the number of ABM places in Saxony-Anhalt, Reiner Haseloff objected noisily in the media, claiming that the cuts would lead to an increase of 20,000 in unemployment, as well as leading to increased administrative costs for the Land government (Volksstimme, 11th December 2002).

The 'third labour market' is particularly anathema to centre-right policy-makers: unlike the 'second labour market', where time-limited placements can claim to have reintegration into the regular labour market as a plausible aim, the 'third labour market', with its long-term focus, at least implies an accept-ance that employment in the first labour market is unlikely. As a result, the discontinuation of the programme *'Aktiv zur Rente'* ('Active until retirement'), which began under the SPD-led government in 2001, might have been expected. The idea behind the programme was that older, long-term unemployed people, rather than simply going onto unemployment benefit, should con-tinue to work until retirement in state-funded positions of benefit to the com-munity, in return for a modest wage, co-funded by the Land government and the Federal Labour Organisation (Bundesagentur für Arbeit 2006, pp.9–10).

However, in early 2006, the Federal Labour Agency decided to end this programme prematurely. CDU politicians, including Detlef Gürth, the labour market spokesperson of the CDU Landtagsfraktion, were extremely critical (Volksstimme, 2nd February 2006). The Land government subsequently agreed to continue the programme, using its own resources, funding from the European Social Fund, and by converting a number of the affected jobs into 'One-Euro-Jobs' (Mitteldeutsche Zeitung, 18th February 2005).

Discussions with politicians and civil servants in Saxony-Anhalt (inter-views A, E, G, M, Q) confirmed this view. Indeed one civil servant inter-viewed went further, describing the government's approach as the 'politics of the forked tongue'. He argued that, while publicly stating its commit-ment to the first labour market, the CDU/FDP administration would gladly embrace any initiatives bringing extra jobs. In front of a business audience, they would express scepticism, and talk about measures to avoid sub-stitution effects (whereby jobs – such as the painting of public buildings – which would normally be performed by the private sector are replaced by those on job creation schemes), but would in fact actively embrace such proposals. This was felt to be a result of the high level of unemployment, and the Land's specific situation.

7.4.4   'Kombilohn' – public 'top up' to wages

As discussed in Chapter 4, 'Kombilohn' has been a favoured tool – notably but not exclusively of centre-right politicians – to promote employment. Saxony-Anhalt's CDU/FDP administration was keen to take advantage of the possibility, given in Paragraph 29 of the revised Social Code, to intro-duce an *'Einstiegsgeld'* ('introductory payment'). This would subsidise the private sector to create jobs which would not be worthwhile if they were paid at normal rates. A senior civil servant in the Land, Ulrich Cramer, spelt out how three sides could benefit from this instrument:

> The unemployed, because they are introduced to the first labour market and their financial situation improves (through the introductory payment) and the allowances (according to paragraph 30 [of the Social Code]) are more than would be the case with a One-Euro-Job; the employer, because they can pay for the labour they employ at a level reflecting its produc-

tivity; and the state, because it – all in all – saves money. Einstiegsgeld is always less than the saving with passive support (Cramer 2007, p.1).

Cramer also points out that policy-makers hope this top-up to wages will prove genuinely introductory, as employers discover the capability of their new employees, and wish to employ them without the additional support.

In this area of labour market policy as in others, the Land government's role was to steer this process. This was challenging because of the need to get support from the ARGEN (joint placement organisations of local government and the labour agency) and local government (in those areas taking full responsibility). As Cramer put it, 'You have to persuade, you can make recommendations, but you cannot command' (ibid., p.2). In particular, the Land ran competitions to reward those who created the most jobs.

The introduction of this measure proved politically contentious. The IG Bau trade union (from the building trade) rejected the measure out of hand, claiming it was part of a political battle with the red-green federal government (Volksstimme, 17th February 2005). The PDS spoke out against the plans, stating that 'With small actions like this, the problems of the five million officially registered unemployed people cannot be solved' (Altmark-Zeitung, 18th February 2006). The Head of the DGB in Saxony-Anhalt was more measured, but expressed particular concern at the suggestion that the two-year legal limit on these subsidies might be lifted, as this would then mean employers would take the subsidy for regular jobs they would have created anyway (Mitteldeutsche Zeitung, 4th January 2006), possibly dismissing long-standing employees to make way for those attracting subsidy (Interview E). Another 'blip' in the introduction was Minister Rehberger's initial suggestion that 85,000 jobs might be created this way, although this was apparently a mistake (Interview E).

From January 2005 until mid-2007, Saxony-Anhalt was responsible for 23% of all cases of the application of Einstiegsgeld across Germany – 7,200 out 31,500. Notwithstanding the limited room for manoeuvre of the Land government, this demonstrates a significant commitment, fitting the Christian democrat paradigm of labour market policy.

7.4.5 Deregulation: Saxony-Anhalt's Arbeitsrechtliches Öffnungsgesetz

Saxony-Anhalt also attempted to make use of its ability to influence labour market policy through the Bundesrat, bringing in its *Arbeitsrechtliches Öffnungsgesetz* (Labour market opening law). The proposal was to allow Länder with unemployment at 50% or more above the national average to deregulate their labour markets in the following ways:

• Raising the size of companies where protection from dismissal applies from five to 20 employees;

- Reducing restrictions on compulsory redundancy;
- Increasing from two to four years the maximum length of temporary employment contracts;
- Lowering the age at which employment contracts could be time-limited without other cause;
- Allowing company-level wage agreements (Bundesrat Drucksache 308/03).

This proposal fitted with the Christian democratic paradigm, albeit with an eastern flavour: deregulation being permitted only in those Länder with higher unemployment would give them a comparative advantage.

It was entirely clear that this law stood no chance of passing, as it required the agreement of the Red-Green federal government. There is also reason to feel that it was intended to be a symbolic gesture (a point confirmed by interviews, such as interview M), and reinforced by the fact it was tabled by Saxony-Anhalt alone.

7.4.6   Hesse's OFFENSIV-Gesetz

An early forerunner to the Hartz reforms was Hesse's *OFFENSIV-Gesetz*, proposed to the Bundesrat in 2002, and discussed above. Saxony-Anhalt supported this law, which perhaps was surprising for an eastern Land. Punitive measures focused at activating the long-term unemployed were developed on the assumption that the problem was a lack of incentive to 'become activated', rather than the lack of work – a point made by Wolfgang Böhmer himself in the Volksstimme, 9th July 2002. Furthermore, localisation of responsibility for unemployment benefit could have brought detrimental consequences for all Länder with high long-term unemployment, including Saxony-Anhalt. However, interviews suggested that this was supported in the knowledge that the law stood no chance – in the face of the red-green Bundestag – of becoming law. Solidarity with Hesse's CDU could be proclaimed without any political cost, as the law was not covered by local newspapers at all (Interview M).

7.4.7   Saxony-Anhalt and the Hartz reforms

Altogether more serious was Saxony-Anhalt's engagement with the Hartz reforms (discussed in Chapter 4). Three particular elements are of greatest significance here, namely the reduction of benefits for the long-term unemployed, the merger of social assistance and unemployment assistance, and the localisation of responsibility for job facilitation. Reducing payments for the long-term unemployed, while fitting with the Christian Democrat policy paradigm, was a potentially dangerous business in eastern Länder: firstly, they were far more numerous than in the west, and secondly the lack of jobs was felt to be the problem, not the lack of incentives to take them. Merging unemployment and social assistance was also a perilous endeavour for eastern politicians: the east, with its high unemployment, had far more people taking unemployment assistance than social assistance, so extra costs would result. Finally, localising responsibility for employment facilitation transferred a significant risk, and area of work, to local authorities in areas of high unemployment.

Saxony-Anhalt, in the decisive vote in the Bundesrat, voted against the so-called *Optionsgesetz* which brought about the merger of social and unemployment assistance, and changes to unemployment facilitation.[2] Moreover, two interviews suggested that Dr. Reiner Haselloff, representing the Land, had been a challenging member of the Bundesrat working group on Hartz issues, and had to be brought back into line by Minister President Böhmer (interviews E and M).

This stance represented a deviation from the Christian Democratic paradigm, which would have predicted support for the Hartz IV reforms (and which was demonstrated by Hesse, and to a lesser extent the Saarland). It represents a confirmation of the territorial hypothesis: that a Land's socio-economic make-up can, on occasions, 'trump' the partisan colour of the government. Minister President Böhmer, in various public pronouncements, tended not to oppose the principal reducing benefits for the long-term unemployed, and merging social and unemployment assistance, but instead argued that eastern Germany needed more jobs before this could be viable: Böhmer stated: 'We can take away the money from people in our area, but we can't offer them any jobs ... we are not the puppets of other Länder' (Spiegel, 6th July 2004), and again 'We fundamentally voted in favour of the merger of unemployment and social assistance in December [2003]. We think this is justified. At the second vote [in July 2004 on the detail of the Hartz IV reforms] ... we didn't vote in favour, because in our opinion the particular situation of the east was not sufficiently considered. ... There are insufficient opportunities for more jobs. Federal Economics Minister Clement wants to increase the number of employment facilitators. That is well intended, but so long as they have got nothing to place people into, it doesn't take us any further forward' (Volksstimme, 27th August 2004).

Böhmer spelt out the Land's position before the Bundesrat in the sitting before the vote (Bundesrat Sitzungsprotokoll 2004, pp.332–3), accepting that some reductions in tax-financed transfers were unavoidable, but these should be coupled with a job offer of some sort. He noted that the federal government had intended that some of the reduced costs to local government could be put back into giving unemployed workers the opportunity to earn the money that they had lost in benefits. However, this proved impossible under the thresholds whereby, Böhmer argued, 85% of additional earnings of up to 400 Euro per month were clawed back.

---

[2]Unfortunately, except in the case of roll-call votes, the votes of each Land are not recorded in the Bundesrat, only the overall outcome. Nonetheless, this decision was well-documented in the media (for instance, FAZ, 9th July 2004b).

The suggestion of publicly-funded, low-wage jobs to top up benefits for the long-term unemployed is obviously an extension of the second, or third, labour market, representing a further departure from the Christian Democratic paradigm. Böhmer defended this: when asked 'Wouldn't then a second, inflated job creation market arise which would fizzle out like all such attempts the decade before in the east?', Böhmer replied: 'We certainly don't want to repeat that. But: a measure in the second labour market is obviously better than none at all. ... We simply have specific problems in the east' (Spiegel, 13th July 2004b).

In the debate, Böhmer also alluded, more briefly, to the potential loss to Saxony-Anhalt's local government (in common with the rest of the eastern Länder, as they had fewer recipients of social assistance, paid for by local government, compared to the west), or at least the lower gains than western Länder. This anxiety was also shared in the senior echelons of the civil service (Interview M) – losses of 100 million Euro to the Land were predicted (compared with the Bund's prognoses of a profit of 80 million Euro).

On the issue of the Hartz IV (by contrast with Hesse's OFFENSIV-Gesetz) the way in which the Land conducted itself in the Bundesrat serves as a confirmation of the territorial counter-hypothesis, rather than the political hypothesis, as discussed in Chapter 2. A caveat is necessary, however: it was clear beforehand that the reforms would pass, with the votes of the western Länder. As a result, the vote against was of symbolic importance – a politically-expedient gesture against the policy, without substantive consequences. Views differed on whether Saxony-Anhalt would have conducted itself differently if its vote could have brought down the reforms – Detlef Gürth, the labour market spokesperson of the CDU Fraktion, was convinced it wouldn't have done (interview Q), whereas others (such as a senior civil servant, interview M) were sceptical. Of course, the federal government could, in such a position, have offered more resources to the east, as partially happened following the Bundesrat decision (Spiegel, 13th July 2004a), so it is impossible to draw firm conclusions on this counter-factual.

Following the decision on Hartz IV, Böhmer obtained brief prominence in the national media when he broke ranks with the CDU nationally and backed a suggestion from Sigmar Gabriel (the SPD leader in the Landtag of Lower Saxony), to cancel the planned reduction in the top rate of income tax, which coincided with the implementation of the Hartz IV reforms (Spiegel, 15th August 2004). The suggestion was not pursued.

7.4.8   Payment of apprenticeships and job creation schemes

Another initiative of Saxony-Anhalt's government in the Bundesrat concerned payment for apprenticeships (Bundesrat Drucksache 15/4112).

The proposal – which was very much in line with the Christian Democratic paradigm of labour market policy – set a minimum level of remuneration for apprentices (related to social insurance thresholds), which, at the time, was at

152.50 Euro in the eastern Länder and 180.25 Euro in the west (ibid.). This compared to the prevailing requirement, which was that apprentices' wages should not be set at a level less than 20% below the agreed sectoral wage (*Tarif*) in those companies where it applied. The average wage was around 500 Euros per month in the east, and 600 per month in the west (Berliner Zeitung, 29th March 2004). The context for this proposal was a strong disagreement between the red-green coalition federal government and the CDU-led Länder over the right way to fund training, and in particular the possibility of an *Ausbildungsplatzabgabe* ('Training place levy'), which the Bund threatened to introduce if firms did not provide sufficient training places (ibid.).

Unsurprisingly, although it passed the Bundesrat on 24th September 2004, the Bundestag rejected the proposal (Das Parlament, 31st January 2005), although other changes to the training regime were agreed.

7.4.9   Partnership with unions

As outlined above, there remained a commitment to tripartite discussions – between government, unions and employers – and the government moved quickly to establish this, replacing the existing, Land-level *Bündnis für Arbeit* ('Alliance for Jobs') with a new body, the *Forum für Wirtschaft und Arbeit* ('Forum for Economy and Labour'). This was agreed between representatives of business, the DGB and the Land government in November 2002. Amongst other things, the Forum would consider improvements to infrastructure, attracting investment, and training for young people. It met once to twice a year. Employers' representatives wanted to include discussions about pay levels within the group's remit, but this was not agreed by the trade unions (Volksstimme, 27th November 2002). Udo Gebhardt (interview E), the Chair of the DGB in Saxony-Anhalt, felt this organisation proved useful, notably in its agreement on the training places, and this enduring commitment to corporatist discussions, above and beyond wage negotiations, contrasts with the case of Hesse, discussed in Chapter 4.

7.4.10   Influencing and changing policy

Role of the opposition: None of the interviewees in this area of policy mentioned that the opposition played any role in developing labour market policies. Indeed, Udo Gebhardt from the DBG went further, saying 'I can't achieve anything with the SPD when they are in opposition' (interview E).

Role of trade unions: As noted above, even though during the period from 2002 to 2006 there were a number of issues (the Hartz reforms, payment of apprenticeships, and wage top-ups) where tension would have been anticipated, relations between the government and the trade unions remained surprisingly cordial. Much of this appeared to hinge on Reiner Haseloff, in particular. Gebhardt stated that 'He [Haseloff] took our representation more seriously than ever before' (interview E), and Gebhardt and Haseloff enjoyed extensive informal contact on a range of issues, including the Land's role in the Bundesrat.

Land parties: None of the interviewees alluded to the role of the CDU or FDP Landesverbände at all in shaping policy at this level, nor were there references to their involvement in the contemporary media.

Role of the CDU Fraktion: On matters falling within the Land's sphere of decision-making, the Minister and Secretary of State enjoyed a good deal of policy-making autonomy, and of course Minister President Böhmer steered the Land's stance in the Bundesrat. One reason for this is that, as discussed above, much of what the Land government can do in this area of policy is dependent upon other actors (such as the Federal Labour Organisation, local government, or the European Union) and it is the executive, rather than the legislature, which deals with these issues. The Land's proposals to the Bundesrat, and the extensive use of introductory payment (Einstiegsgeld), for instance, required no involvement of the Landtag. There are also significant differences of opinion on labour market policies within the CDU group: several interviewees (interview E; interview B) referred to the fact that Jürgen Scharf, the CDU Landtagsfraktion Chair, had publicly supported legal minimum wages (and was also Chair of the Land's CDA – the workers' wing of the CDU), whereas Detlef Gürth, the Fraktion's Business leader and Chair of the Land CDU's *Mittelstandsvereinigung*, business wing, said that 'National minimum wages are poison for the Economy' (Mittelstandsvereinigung Sachsen-Anhalt 2007).

Role of the FDP: It might appear surprising that, in several areas of policy, Saxony-Anhalt deviated quite sharply from a market liberal paradigm, where a Ministry with an FDP Minister might have been expected to go even more strongly in a market-oriented direction. Several reasons for this might appear: firstly, although the Ministry was led by the FDP, Secretary of State Haseloff enjoyed significant autonomy (Interview M); Haseloff was a moderate figure unlikely to take policy in a sharply neoliberal direction; moreover, economic development policy, rather than labour market policy, was the Minister's real passion. Secondly, the Land's engagement in the Bundesrat was led by the Minister President, and he included Dr. Haseloff in the working group on the Hartz reforms (Land Sachsen-Anhalt 2003, p.8). However, it was also emphasised that Minister Rehberger had a personal passion for Einstiegsgeld, and applied significant political pressure for its extension (Interview M). No reference was made to the FDP's parliamentary group exercising particular influence in the contemporary media or in interviews with the author.

Role of the civil service: Unlike the more polarised area of education policy, as has been discussed above, Saxony-Anhalt's labour market policies owed as much to the Land's situation as to the political composition of the government. One of the senior civil servants responsible for delivering labour market policy was an SPD member, who was actually promoted under the CDU-led government (private information from interview M). It was argued that Saxony-Anhalt has always had a 'subject driven', rather than politically motivated, labour market policy (interview M). However, Detlef Gürth, the Chair of the CDU Landtagsfraktion, did note that, in individual cases, civil service blockage of policy change was possible, and felt a certain attraction to the 'American model', whereby ministers had a greater capacity to assemble their own team (Interview Q).

Role of the sub-Land level: Local government in Saxony-Anhalt has an important role of play in the delivery of labour market policy, and within that there are elements of discretion (for instance, on the extent to which Einstiegsgeld is used); this applies both to the four *Optierende Kommunen* ('Option authorities'), where the local authority takes full responsibility for placement of unemployment for recipients of unemployment benefit (ALG2), and those where the local authority is in a partnership (ARGE) with the local branch of the Federal Labour Agency. The Minister and Secretary of State at times expressed frustration at different levels of achievement in job facilitation, or at different levels of use of Einstiegsgeld (for instance, Mitteldeutsche Zeitung, 1st February 2006). There was no suggestion in any of the interviews that the partisan composition of the relevant local administration made any difference to approaches to labour market policy and the relationship with the government.

Formal procedures: Again, because of the limited role of the Landtag, formal procedures, such as committee hearings, played a very limited role in policy development in this area, and were not highlighted by interviewees as being influential in shaping policy.

7.4.11 Conclusion

Throughout this chapter, it has been demonstrated that, although the CDU-led government did pursue some measures which shifted the Land from a social democratic towards a Christian democratic paradigm, in significant areas of policy, the Land actually resisted a decisive shift to the right, due to its particular situation as an eastern Land. This is demonstrated in particular by the Land's abstention on the Hartz reforms, and its enduring commitment to the second labour market.

In relation to this study's research questions, this provides a partial refutation of the political hypothesis, instead confirming the territorial null-hypothesis: that policies chosen reflect the particular situation of the Land, rather than the party composition of the government. The trends here are particularly pronounced, suggesting that, as an eastern Land, Saxony-Anhalt's policy-makers' room for manoeuvre is particularly constrained. Indeed, the thought that reliance on external funding (coming with stipulations as to its use) has a particular impact on an eastern Land is confirmed: the Land actively sought federally-funded ABMs and SAMs, in spite of its apparent support for the first labour market.

Table 7.7 Labour market policy in Saxony-Anhalt

Social democratic paradigm	Christian democratic paradigm	Change
Willingness to contemplate long-term subsidised state jobs	Rejection of long-term subsidised state jobs	Continuation of ABMs and SAMs where funding is available (in spite of rhetoric)
Reluctance to subsidise private sector	Willing to subsidise private sector	Slightly greater willingness to subsidise private sector through Einstiegsgeld
Active labour market measures appropriate for general labour market	Active measures only for special needs groups (e.g. disabled, long-term unemployed) for limited period	No obvious change – active measures only for 'special groups', including the high number of long-term unemployed
Rejection of promotion of low-paid sector	Encouragement of low-paid sector, e.g. through 'Kombilohn' (wage subsidies)	Introduction of *Einstiegsgeld*, a form of wage subsidy, relatively wide usage
Rejection of decentralisation/localisation	Support for decentralisation/localisation	Support for decentralisation but only in knowledge it would not pass. Sceptical about complete switch to local facilitation
Rejection of deregulation	Support for deregulation	Support for deregulation
Apprenticeships and jobs-creation schemes paid at Tarif (collectively agreed) level	Apprenticeships and job-creation schemes paid at lower level	Attempted to reduce pay to below Tarif level for apprenticeships; job creation schemes paid at low level
Privileged partnership with unions	Parity of partnership with social partners, or limited partnership	Relations with unions have remained extremely positive

No doubt the collegial labour relations, and in particular the strong links between the Land government and the DGB, are partially attributable to the government's policy choices often being amenable to trade unions, but they also stem from a commitment to tripartite discussion, strong representation of the CDA amongst senior CDU politicians (most notably Jürgen Scharf) and the collegial relationship Reiner Haseloff enjoyed with the trade unions.

7.5   Conclusion

As with the other two case studies, but to an even greater extent, the degree to which the party hypothesis can be confirmed varies significantly depending on the area of policy in question. In the field of education policy, this hypothesis is unequivocally confirmed, with a clear shift towards the Christian democratic paradigm. In the cases of childcare, and in particular labour market policy, although some shift is recognisable, the Land government neither set out to achieve, nor achieved, full convergence upon the Christian democratic paradigms. The more generous level of childcare, and support for the second labour market, both instead appear to confirm the territorial null-hypothesis, whereby policies pursued owe more to the Land's situation than to the party composition of its government.

There are also some differences in the way politics is conducted in Saxony-Anhalt compared to the other Länder considered (and standing in particularly sharp contrast to Hesse). In some areas (most obviously childcare policy) real efforts were made to form a super-majority to agree change with the SPD opposition, and there was a strong commitment to good relations with the trade unions. In part this reflects a willingness to compromise on the SPD side, and indeed a strong commitment to realistic opposition. Jens Bullerjahn, once elected Chair of the SPD Landtagsfraktion in 2004, pursued a moderate agenda during the period in question, in particular publishing a series of booklets in the series *Sachsen-Anhalt 2020*, which considered the challenges posed by the Land's demographics and economic position (SPD Sachsen-Anhalt 2006). Norbert Bischoff quoted Böhmer as having remarked that he wished his own Fraktion worked in the way the SPD Fraktion did (Interview B). This stance, of course, also reflected the possibility of a grand coalition after the 2006 elections.

An important issue raised by this case study is whether these characteristics of Saxony-Anhalt, both in the substance of the policies it pursues (with a more limited room for manoeuvre for politicians, and a greater impact of the Land's territorial features) and the more consensual style of policy-making in some areas, is generalisable across eastern Länder, or whether it is specific to Saxony-Anhalt at the time in question. The consideration of childcare and labour market policy both demonstrate that the Land's eastern history and socio-economic position (in particular, the level of unemployment), are generalisable across the eastern Länder: they have a record of more generous childcare provision (Dienel 2002), and higher unemployment, than in the west, although as outlined earlier in this chapter, Saxony-Anhalt is at the most extreme end in both cases.

The moderate character of the Land's CDU, as well as the course of the SPD, also contributed to the lack of polarisation in two of the three areas of policy. The author's discussions with Detlef Gürth (interview Q) and Jürgen Scharf (interview A), both senior CDU politicians in the Land, indicated that this was common across the eastern CDU Landesverbände, with the partial exception of Saxony. In turn, this reflects the nature of the Land (a neoliberal CDU ditching active labour market measures and slashing benefits would struggle electorally), but the strength of the CDA (workers') wing appears to be an exogenous feature. At the same time, Minister President Böhmer provided particularly moderate leadership, a point recognised by Norbert Bischoff, the Business Leader of the SPD's Landtagsfraktion, who recalled Böhmer stating that, if the social democrats had been at his house ten minutes sooner, he'd have joined them (interview B). Throughout the case studies of childcare and the labour market policy, Böhmer presented a moderate face of the CDU, willing to deviate from traditional CDU policy paradigms and achieve compromise with the opposition.

An introduction to Germany's political institutions by Manfred G. Schmidt was entitled 'The Grand Coalition State' (Schmidt 2002). This, of course, referred to the institutional as well as societal pressures to achieve informal grand coalitions. In Saxony-Anhalt, deviation from the Christian Democratic policy paradigm in two of the three areas under consideration – leading to significant areas of overlap between the Volksparteien, if not an informal 'grand coalition' – was driven not by such institutional pressures, but the characteristics of the Land pushing the CDU-led government in particular directions, as well as the moderate character of the Land's CDU and its leadership.

8
Conclusion

8.1 Do parties really matter in the German Länder? An assessment

The key question posed at the start of this study is whether the 'political hypothesis' can be confirmed: whether a change of government at a Land level would make a difference to the policies pursued. The short answer, based on these nine case studies, is that it does: *parties do matter at a Land level*.

However, there are significant variations in the extent to which parties matter, with differences between Länder and between areas of policy. In some cases, change of government is a good predictor of policies pursued. In others, the socio-economic context of the Land, the history of policies pursued, the character of the CDU Landesverband, and to a more limited degree the presence or absence of a coalition partner, and the institutional architecture at a Land level, temper the impact of a change of government.

Of the three areas of policy discussed, in each of the Länder the greatest shift, prompted by the change of government, was in education policy. The Christian and social democratic policy paradigms continue to diverge in education policy, and in all cases Christian Democratic politicians successfully changed policy in a number of areas (for instance, placing a strong emphasis on testing and examination). These changes were often vehemently opposed by SPD politicians, suggesting that they were a result of the change of government, rather than 'going with the flow' of external pressures. Christian Democratic governments also demonstrated a commitment to differentiation by ability. However, they were constrained, in a path-dependent way, from undertaking wholesale reforms to school structure in the cases of the Saarland and Hesse, and ended up leaving a network of comprehensive schools in place, and strengthening differentiation within school forms. Christian Democratic politicians sought to realise their policy paradigm within a school structure which was not of their choosing.

It was suggested, in Chapter 4, that the history in the GDR of education was not being differentiated by ability until a later stage than in West Germany could give the population a greater attachment to non-selective education, and provide a path-dependent barrier to policy change. This was not confirmed. In contrast to the obstacles that the presence of comprehensive schools in Hesse and the Saarland created, the Christian democratic policy paradigm was probably most fully realised in Saxony-Anhalt (this in spite of the Land's eastern position, as well as the position of Education minister being taken by a non-CDU member).

Although there were different accents set by the CDU in each of the Länder, for instance in Hesse on quality assurance and promotion of German teaching prior to school entrance, there does appear to be a common vision of education policy amongst CDU politicians, at least in the three cases examined here. Schmid (1990a) found some variations, but within the three Länder examined here, these do not appear particularly significant.

In contrast to Schmidt's 1980 study, this research examined qualitative changes in education policy, rather than the overall level of expenditure on schools. This decision was vindicated, inasmuch as, first, some of the most important changes did not have a budgetary impact, and secondly, in the Saarland and particularly in Hesse, the CDU was not adverse to investing extra money in schools. Indeed, this matches the findings of Wolf (2006, p.265), who found school expenditure to be higher under CDU governments than under the SPD.

The nature of relations with education trade unions, and particularly the GEW, differed somewhat in the Saarland to that in the other two Länder discussed. This appears to relate to the nature of the Saarland – informal links between trade union, civil service and party political actors existed, both by virtue of the Land's size and also the statutory involvement of teachers' representatives in day-to-day personnel issues – and that appears to have prevented the full breakdown of relations that ensued in Hesse and Saxony-Anhalt. This matches Eilfort's prognosis (2006, p.220) that relations between parties are likely to be slightly more cordial in smaller Länder, with familiarity taking some of the heat out of political arguments.

However, education policy remains polarised between CDU and SPD politicians on a Land level. Apart from the different normative starting-points, two (complementary) explanations for this arise from this study, and both stem from the fact that in party groups in the Landtag, there is a high degree of delegation to a particular member, or groups of members, in responsibility for policy (and this is mirrored by the organisation of different groups developing policy on different subjects in the Land party). First, these education spokespeople almost always have a background in the education sector, which differs between the two parties. Hence, the Christian Democrats responsible tend to come from selective education, while the Social Democrats often hail from comprehensive schools, professional schools, or adult education institutions.

This trend is sometimes exacerbated when civil service appointments are made by the CDU, as those with a background in selective education are frequently appointed. Secondly, education policy spokespeople in the SPD groups are frequently on the left of the party, which again fosters polarisation.

In childcare and family policy, it is clear from each of these case studies that the paradigm of the CDU has shifted. Although it still emphasises the need to facilitate a 'real choice' for women between staying at home and looking after children, and continuing to work, there is a far greater acceptance of the need for institutional childcare (and indeed its extension) than was anticipated by the paradigm of Christian democrat childcare policy specified in Chapter 4. This view is supported in a study of CDU policies at the federal level (Seeleib-Kaiser et al. 2005). In Hesse and the Saarland, childcare provision was extended rather than retrenched during the period in question. In Saxony-Anhalt, although there was retrenchment (from a very high starting point), the CDU made strenuous efforts to secure the agreement of the SPD opposition in the Landtag, even though its agreement was superfluous in order to secure the policy change. Other (arguably less central) elements of the paradigm remain distinct, such as the commitment to deregulation and to more flexible provision, and these were realised in two of the three cases discussed here. In the cases when childcare provision expanded, the SPD opposition suggested that, had it been in government, it would have gone further and faster in promoting expansion, and the effect of having a CDU government has been to slow the shift towards the social democratic paradigm. This is a counter-factual which cannot be proven (there is no telling what an SPD government would have done in the Saarland between 1999 and 2004, say, because there wasn't one, and the exact conditions in which one would have existed can never be replicated). In any case, such claims should be treated with caution: in Hesse and the Saarland the CDU expanded childcare beyond the extent to which it existed under the previous SPD-led government, and the level of childcare provision in each Land, or the amount of investment in it, does not appear solely determined by the party composition of its government alone. For instance, in 2002, the proportion of children aged below three in the Saarland and Hesse (CDU-led) exceeded that in North-Rhine Westphalia and Rheinland-Palatine, led by the SPD (OECD 2004, p.65).

In contrast with the other two areas of policy, Land-level labour market policy appears to be affected significantly less by the change of government: the shape of the policy, and such changes that do take place, are often prompted instead by the particular characteristics of the Land in question, and its labour market. Senior civil servants in this area (who, even under these CDU-led governments, were sometimes SPD members) regularly suggested that continuity predominated in Land-level programmes, with change being only at the level of the language used to discuss them. Indeed, one interviewee suggested that an expert reading details of Land-level labour market programmes would struggle to guess which party was in government (Interview OO). This is not to say that there was no shift towards the Christian democratic ideal type. In each of the Länder, some limited change took place (for instance, on support for deregulation of payment of apprentices, for a low-paid sector, or in the stance taken by the Land towards decentralisation), but the picture of a shift from one paradigm to another is by no means as consistent as in the case of education policy.

In the case of the relationship between trade unions and the Land government, where variety between the Lander was clearly observed (partnership and informal contacts being surprisingly strong in the Saarland and Saxony-Anhalt, and near to non-existent in Hesse), the relative strength of the CDA (trade union wing) in the CDU at a Land level appeared to restrict shifts towards the Christian democratic paradigm. In the cases of both the Saarland and Saxony-Anhalt, pre-existing informal links between key actors in the trade union sector and the government were also important.

This is an area of policy where the availability of external funding, from the federal government and the EU, gives these external actors the ability to shape what happens on a Land level, thus diminishing the autonomy of Land-level politicians and dampening the impact of a change of government. The impact of this factor is asymmetrical – funds are offered to poorer Länder more than to their wealthier counterparts, and concomitantly, poorer Land budgets are more constrained, increasing their reliance on external funding. However, as can be seen with the case of Hesse, even in a Land with a more buoyant labour market and a slightly less precarious (although still highly constrained) budgetary situation, there was no desire to turn away external funding in order to make a political point.

The actions of the Länder in the Bundesrat in labour market policy were sometimes explicitly political (as with Hesse's OFFENSIV-Gesetz, and Saxony-Anhalt's push for deregulation for weaker Länder) and conformed to the Christian democratic paradigm. However, civil servants in those Länder regarded these as political 'stunts', and questioned the extent to which deregulation, for example, would have an impact upon the economy of the Land in question. The economy of all the Länder, to a greater or lesser degree, is based upon high skill levels and relatively high wages, and scope for the development of a low-wage sector, and a significant boost to the number of jobs through deregulation, was felt to be low (Interview OO, Interview BB).

A recent study (Malik 2008) focuses on spending on active labour market measures, in two of the three of the Länder discussed here (albeit within a different time frame; that following the Hartz reforms). The conclusion here is confirmed: in Hesse, there is an increase in active labour market measures, with continuity being shown in the Saarland. In Hesse, this is sufficient to justify a shift in the classification of the Land from being a 'pull' to a 'push' Land (cf. Chapter 4) in its labour market policies.

Having discussed each area of policy in turn, the question is whether any more general conclusions can be drawn. The first, and most obvious conclusion, is that parties make more of a difference in areas of policy where they have sole competence (notably education) than where they are reliant on other actors (labour market). They make less of a difference, too, when other actors become involved in steering policy through the provision of funds. In particular in the case of education policy, there may be a desire to introduce change precisely because it is an area where a clear shift, in an ideologically polarised area of policy, can be demonstrated to a government's supporters, making up for less progress elsewhere. Schmidt (1980, p.132), in his earlier study, does indeed note the importance of 'securing the loyalty of [a party's] own voters'.

Von Blumenthal, in her discussion of parties' action in the Bundesrat, hypothesised that:

> Land-level political interests will be dominant when [decisions] concern the institutional and financial interests of the Land. In other socio-political questions federal party competition dominates. The raising of the Land's specific profile only happens in isolated instances on account of particular clientelistic interests or the traditional profile of a state party (2008, p.101).

This hypothesis is confirmed here. In discussions about concrete measures in labour market policy (such as the localisation of responsibility for benefits), CDU-led Länder were robust in pursuing putting their Land before their party. By contrast, on symbolic questions in the same area of policy, party interests came to the fore. Developing this point, if Land-level politicians put their territory first *when it really matters*, and if we expect, in a context of greater disparity between Länder, territorial interests do matter ever more, party cohesion in the Bundesrat on major decisions will weaken (even if this is masked by symbolic shows of party unity).

In the two cases examined where the FDP was a coalition partner with the CDU, its ability to act as a constraint, and to affect the character of policy change, appeared limited. In Hesse, it did resist a shift towards a centralised Abitur, and perhaps assisted in promoting all-day schools; in Saxony-Anhalt, the FDP minister's enthusiasm for wage top-ups was reflected in policies pursued (although this accorded with the Christian democratic paradigm specified here in any event). In ministries not held by the FDP, the principle of *Ressortkompetenz* (autonomy for the individual minister) precluded extensive involvement. In the ministries it did hold, in Saxony-Anhalt, the presence of a strong CDU Secretary of State (as the minister's effective deputy) in the Labour and Economics Ministry ensured the CDU was able to retain some control; in the case of the Social Affairs ministry, there were direct interventions by the Minister President in policy and personnel matters to ensure that policies did not deviate from the CDU's wishes. From these case studies at least, minor coalition partners' influence on policies pursued at a Land level appears limited. In order to test this conclusion more fully, it would be necessary to consider policy areas where the views of the CDU and the FDP diverge more fundamentally – for instance, where issues of civil liberties are at stake.

Budgetary constraints, of course, shape the policies a Land government pursues. In the cases examined here, however, service expansion is not, for the most part, foreseen by the Christian democratic paradigm, and so it is hard to draw firm conclusions about the extent to which budgetary constraints played a role. It is worth noting, also, that they can be a double-edged sword: budgetary constraints may promote a shift towards the Christian democratic paradigm, if such a change offers the opportunity to reduce spending (the retrenchment of childcare in Saxony-Anhalt is an example of this). The general conclusion can be drawn, though, that the poorer a Land, the more its range of policy options will be constrained, and the more reliant it will be on funding from other sources, reducing its autonomy.

The specific character of a CDU's Landesverband has been shown to have an exogenous impact upon policy choices in some areas – most obviously in labour market policy, and in the nature of relationships with trade unions. The character of each Landesverband is partly, but not completely, related to the Land's socio-economic position. For instance, the lack of convergence upon the Christian democratic paradigm in labour market policy in Saxony-Anhalt was in part attributable to the relative strength of the CDA (the trade union wing) in Saxony-Anhalt's CDU. In the Saarland, the historical ties between Catholic trade unions and the CDU, which were important in shaping the nature of the Landesverband there, had an enduring influence on the relations between the Land's government and the trade unions, which were significantly more positive than in Hesse. The moderate nature of the CDU's Landesverband also made possible the appointment of a Labour and Social Affairs Minister with strong links to the trade union movement, and she, in turn, led to the rejection by the Land government of major elements of the Christian democratic paradigm of labour market policy. Notwithstanding the difficulty of isolating the character of a Landesverband from the environment in which it operates, Detterbeck and Jeffery appear to be confirmed in their view that: 'Since the 1990s a tendency can be observed to a stronger political autonomy of the Landesverbände of the parties in their electoral strategies [and] their policy orientations' (2004, p.52).

Hough and Koß (2006), in a recent study, considered the different Landesverbände of the PDS, finding significantly different motivations and policy preferences amongst the actors in them, and such a study could usefully be replicated for the CDU. Schmid (1990b) wrote the last such study, but given the increasing divergence between the Länder, as well as greater 'territorialism', with a growing willingness to put the Land's needs ahead of partisan interest in taking decisions in the Bundesrat (Jeffery 2005), there is a strong case for revisiting this topic.

One clear conclusion which can be drawn from this study concerns the balance of power at a Land level, affecting the extent to which Land-level institutions, especially the Landtag, can be a constraint upon a Land government. In each of the policy areas considered – most obviously in the case of labour market policy – the Landtag plays a marginal role in developing the substance of policies pursued, and there is a clear picture of executive dominance. Interviewees were universally dismissive of committee hearings as a method of influencing policy, and it became clear that, where the legislature had a formal role because primary legislation was necessary, agreement between the Minister and the CDU Fraktion before the start of the legislative process arose from informal consultation. With the exception of the compromise over the reform of childcare in Saxony-Anhalt, and some more minor initiatives in the Saarland, the opposition in each of the Landtage were not involved in decision-making, nor did the government undertake great efforts to achieve consensus with opposition Landtag members. This confirms scepticism in other recent studies (e.g. Patzelt 2006) about the influence of Landtage.

The ability of other specific, Land-level institutions to influence policy was also quite limited. There are two examples of this: the anchoring of the nature of the school system in the Saarland's constitution puts a constraint upon actors in education policy at its Land level; and the threat of a referendum on childcare in Saxony-Anhalt provided the CDU with an extra incentive to attempt to get the SPD on board, and secure a compromise. However, referendums, and constitutional courts, did not otherwise appear to place a constraint upon the Land governments during the period in question.

One difference in the political institutions at a Land level in the cases examined here is the difference in the power of the Staatskanzlei. In particular in Hesse, Roland Koch expanded the Staatskanzlei, and it coordinated the work of individual ministries and steered progress delivering the pledges in the coalition treaty. Its influence was less pronounced – although still demonstrable – in Saxony-Anhalt, and it appeared to be a weaker institution in the Saarland, with less emphasis being placed on coordination and the presentation of a unified picture of government by the Minister President, Peter Müller. The powers of the Staatskanzlei are not constitutionally anchored, and therefore could be enhanced, or diminished, by a new Land government, so the nature of a Staatskanzlei will not have an enduring influence upon the ability of a Land government to effect policy change, in contrast to, for instance, the Land's constitution, or the power of its constitutional court. Nonetheless, a powerful Staatskanzlei appears to be a powerful instrument for a determined Minister President to overcome bureaucratic inertia.

Two other potential blockages to policy change, and therefore restrictions on partisan influence on policy, were noted in Chapter 2. The first was the nature of local government, and in particular the extent to which achieving cooperation from local politicians (including those from a different party) was a necessary precondition for achieving change. In each of the Länder examined here, two conclusions can be drawn. First, because of local government's subordinate legal position to the Land government, which is responsible for 'supervising' it, its ability to refuse to implement Land-level decisions is highly restricted. Secondly, local politicians of both the SPD and the CDU were widely considered to be pragmatic, and highly focused on the needs of their municipality. This meant, on the one hand, that unconditional support could not be expected from CDU local politicians, and that some cooperation might well be possible with Social Democrats (the most obvious example of this was in the cooperation between the CDU-led government in Hesse, and Main-Kinzig county on job placement).

A second potential restriction was blockage resulting from civil servants, appointed by, and perhaps sympathetic to, the previous government. There were variations in the extent to which this was experienced by different actors, in different Länder, in different areas of policy, and it is difficult to draw general conclusions, beyond the fact that it can be an obstacle to policy change, but not an insurmountable one. Two trends are evident, however: the first is that it is significantly more likely to be a factor in the more ideologically polarised areas of policy, such as education, than in those perceived to be more technical, and determined by a Land's structural features, like labour market policy. There was far higher turnover of personnel, following the change of government, in each case in education policy than in labour market policy (with responsibility for childcare falling in between). Secondly, a new Minister does enjoy some room for manoeuvre, appointing the head of her or his office, and having some say over the new Secretary of State (who conventionally has responsibility for the internal workings of the ministry).[1] There are also limited possibilities to reshuffle personnel and redraw the boundaries of departments to promote supportive civil servants and marginalise others, as well as regular opportunities to replace those who retire on grounds of age. However, interviewees stressed the limits of these opportunities: reshuffling personnel brought with it a cost which could not always be met, given budgetary constraints. The picture which emerges of the senior civil service at a Land level in Germany is one of significant party penetration: senior appointments are almost invariably made taking

---

[1] As an aside, the degree of influence exercised by these Secretaries of State varied widely, with in particular Reiner Haseloff (in Saxony-Anhalt's Economics Ministry) and Josef Hecken (in the Saarland's Social Affairs Ministry) playing a leadership role, while some others were felt to be extremely weak, and lacking in influence.

into account the party affiliation of appointees, which are usually known to their peers. Nonetheless, several interviewees suggested that frustrations with civil servants owed more to a general resistance to change, and reluctance to try out new ideas, rather than being rooted in politically motivated resistance to proposed policies.

Schmidt (1980, p.131) suggests that partisan impact upon policies pursued is strongest when one party is able to establish a hegemony over an extended period. This study suggests that, even in the first term of government, after a prolonged period in opposition, a new government can make a difference: the problem of unsupportive civil servants is a barrier to change, but not an insurmountable one (after all, the area where it is said to apply most strongly, education, is the area which saw the greatest level of change). More challenging are path-dependent obstacles: institutional or social barriers to change which mean that the political cost of changing course is high. In the face of such obstacles, change is, sometimes, still achieved (as it was in Saxony-Anhalt's childcare policies, where the history of generous provision and expectation of its continuation certainly added to the political cost of change and reduced its scope). Where change is not achieved, even an extended period of government might not allow obstacles to be overcome: there is no reason to think that abolishing popular comprehensive schools, for example, would get any easier after several terms of CDU-led government.

8.2   The partisan hypothesis in federal states: Moving beyond the German case

These conclusions raise a number of significant issues, of wider relevance in political science.

First and foremost, the conclusion that the partisan composition of a government has an exogenous influence upon policies that are pursued – even set against the inauspicious backdrop of German federalism, where interlocking policy-making constrains the extent to which policy-makers at the Land level can act autonomously – suggests that accounts of public policy development which neglect partisan influence (e.g. Streeck and Thelen 2005; Genschel and Zangl 2007) risk failing to capture an important point. This conclusion is heartening: overly deterministic accounts of public policy, which suggest that electors, in their choice of government, cannot really shape the policies they then live under, should be rejected. There are different, competing visions of what policies should be pursued, and voters – and the politicians they elect – are in a position to shape their destinies, rather than being passive in the face of pressures for convergence.

This points to two, related effects which federalism can have upon public policy. First, and most obviously, it confirms the view that federalism can enable diversity in policy choices, with federal systems allowing variations in policy responsive to either local opinion about priorities (with, say, the particular attachment to institutional childcare provision in Saxony-Anhalt leading to far more generous provision than elsewhere), or the particular needs of specific areas (with, for instance, a Land's labour market policies being affected by the nature of the local labour market). This confirms a claim sometimes advanced in the literature on federalism – that the variation it allows can lead to a better fit of policy to local circumstances than in a unitary system (Kincaid 2001).

Secondly, different histories of policy development in sub-national units, such as Länder, can combine with the existence of sub-national political institutions to 'lock in' sub-national variation in policy, and lead to resistance to pressures for convergence. As was noted above, amongst the most powerful obstacles to change – where the CDU-led governments under consideration did not converge upon the Christian democratic ideal type in the policy area in question – were path-dependent barriers. For instance, the willingness of CDU-led governments in Hesse and the Saarland to allow comprehensive schools to continue, contradicting the clear expectations generated by the Christian democratic paradigm of education policy, can be traced to the 'locking in' of policy. Once comprehensive schools are in place, parents, teachers, trade unions and other interested actors could be expected to resist their abolition, meaning that the political costs of change are higher than the costs of sticking with the policy of allowing the schools to stay, even if their existence sits at odds with the policy preferences of the government. In the Saarland, we have seen how Land-level political institutions – specifically, the enshrining of the existence of different types of school, including comprehensives, in the Land's constitution, reinforce this trend. Alongside the ability to respond to local circumstances and public opinion, this is a more subtle reason for federalism to lead to and entrench policy variation, and could usefully be incorporated into accounts of the impact of federalism upon public policy.

This study provides reason to be sceptical of claims that federalism will inevitably lead to a 'race to the bottom' in terms of regulation or public spending. Childcare policy in each of the Länder provides a strong counter-example here. In the case of Saxony-Anhalt, both the expectation of generous provision in the population, and the formation of strong interest groups in support of it, placed a brake upon retrenchment, through path dependence at the regional level. In the cases of Hesse and the Saarland, increases in childcare provision suggest a dynamic of public expectations at work: the governments in both cases were at pains to stress they were at the forefront of improving provision compared to other Länder – an incidence of a 'race to the top' as a result of public pressure. We should, then, treat with caution accounts of the impact of federalism that neglect any role for political parties. Moreover, in none of the areas of policy examined (with the partial exception of labour market policy, and then only at the margins) do we find a quest for global competitiveness really affecting Land-level politics.

As was discussed in the introduction, this study deliberately focused on qualitative changes in policy, rather than focusing primarily on levels of expenditure. It was questionable whether statistically significant conclusions could be generated based upon a study of 16 Länder, and there was a significant danger of spending patterns being affected by changes in the dependent population, rather than political choices. This approach has been vindicated in two respects. First, in generating the ideal types for each of these areas of policy, it became clear that there were very important qualitative differences between the preferences of Christian and Social Democrats (for instance, in decisions about selection, curricula and grading in schools) which were completely unrelated to levels of state expenditure. Esping-Anderson's view that differences in programme design (or, more broadly, policy design) can be as important as levels of spending is certainly confirmed (Esping-Andersen 1990). On a related point, the study has also demonstrated that parties can matter in the German Länder in spite of their limited ability to raise funds (as was discussed in Chapter 3). This limited revenue-raising ability restricts partisan influence upon policy, but by no means eliminates it.

This study looked at the ability of sub-national parties to shape policy, and saw the role of the national government as a potential constraint upon their ability to do so. Yet the substantial difference that those sub-national governments can make to public policy should lead us to turn this claim on its head. In a federal state, such as Germany, where significant policy competences are reserved for sub-national territories, policy can be significantly shaped by sub-national governments, and this constitutes a constraint upon the power of the centre. Critics of the partisan hypothesis at a national level might well be right to point to the forces of globalisation as a constraint upon national politicians, but the less frequently highlighted constraint of sub-national government appears also to be significant.

Parties continue to matter at a Land level. Their policy paradigms are still distinct – there is some convergence, for sure, though this is by no means universal – and even in a system of interlocking policy-making, with growing asymmetries, decisions taken by voters in Land-level elections still make a difference to the policies they see pursued. There are variations: parties matter more in some areas of policy than others, and the policy options at their disposal are shaped, to differing degrees, by the scale of the financial resources they enjoy (or, differently put, by the budgetary pressures they face). Different territorial, institutional and historical factors also shape Land-level policy outcomes. However, the bleak picture of party democracy at a Land level being an irrelevant sideshow, with competing providers of patronage scrapping for control of 'Länder [which are] little more than administrative provinces, in spite of all the decoration and symbolism' (Schneider 1997, p.424), has been refuted by this study.

Appendix 1   Bibliography

Official and public documents

Bundesagentur für Arbeit (2006): *Rahmenvereinbarung zwischen dem Rahmenverein-barung zwischen dem Ministerium für Wirtschaft und Arbeit des Landes Sachsen-Anhalt (Ministerium) und der Regionaldirektion Sachsen-Anhalt-Thüringen der Bundesagentur für Arbeit (Regionaldirektion) über die kooperative Förderung arbeitsmarktpolitischer Maßnahmen in Sachsen-Anhalt* (Halle: Bundesagentur, Regionaldirektion Sachsen-Anhalt and Thüringen).

CDU (1993): *Erziehung und Ausbildung in unserem freiheitlichen und demokratischen Bildungssystem* (Bonn: CDU).

CDU (1994): *Grundsatzprogramm der CDU Deutschlands: Freiheit in Verantwortung* (Bonn: CDU).

CDU Hessen (1999): *Programm zur Landtagswahl 1999* (Wiesbaden: CDU Landesverband).

CDU and FDP Hessen (1999): *Hessen Handelt: Chancen nutzen – Zukunft gewinnen: Koalitionsvereinbarung zwischen CDU und FDP für die 15. Wahlperiode des Hessischen Landtags 1999–2003* (Wirtschafts- und Sozialpolitik Verlag: Wiesbaden).

CDU Saar (1999): *Zukunftsprojekt Saar: Programm der CDU Saar zur Landtagswahl 1999* (Saarbrücken: CDU Landesverband).

FDP Land Sachsen Anhalt (2002): *Wahlprogramm* (Wiesbaden: FDP Landesverband).

Hessisches Sozialministerium (2000): *Familienpolitische Offensive der Hessischen Landesregierung* (Wiesbaden: Hessisches Sozialministerium).

Hessisches Sozialministerium (2001): *Hessen schafft Arbeit: Das integrierte Arbeitsmarkt-programm und andere Fördermaßnahmen der Landesregierung* (Wiesbaden: Hessisches Sozialministerium).

Hessisches Sozialministerium (2005): *Vierter Hessischer Familienbericht* (Wiesbaden: Hessisches Sozialmiisterium).

Hessisches Sozialministerium (2006): *Arbeitsmarktpolitik*; Unpublished paper summarising labour market policy (Wiesbaden: Hessisches Sozialministerium).

Land Sachsen-Anhalt (2002): *Koalitionsvereinbarung zwischen der Christlich-Demokratischen-Union Deutschlands Landesverband Sachsen-Anhalt und der Freien Demokratischen Partei Landesverband Sachsen-Anhalt über die Bildung einer Regierungskoalition für die 4. Legislaturperiode des Landes Sachsen-Anhalt* (Magdeburg: Landesregierung).

Landesregierung Hessen (2003): *Verantwortung für heute – Visionen für morgen: Unser Versprechen für Hessen: Regierungsprogramm 2003–2008* (Wiesbaden: Staatskanzlei Hessen).

Landesregierung Hessen (2007): *Haushaltsplan*, http://starweb.hessen.de/cac47he/haushalt/haushaltsplan/HHPlan2007StatistischerAnhang.pdf, accessed 18th October 2007.

Saarland Ministerium für Bildung, Kultur und Wissenschaft (2004): Press release: 'Kultus-minister Jürgen Schreier zur Bildungsstudie: Ja, es gibt viel zu tun! Aber Zahlen sagen nicht alles', 25th November 2004.

Saarland Ministerium für Bildung, Kultur und Wissenschaft (2005): *Qualitätssteigernde Maßnahmen an saarländischen Schulen: Ausgewählte Maßnahmen* (Saarbrücken: Ministerium für Bildung, Kultur und Wissenschaft, unpublished paper).

Saarland Ministerium für Bildung, Kultur und Wissenschaft (2006): *Bildungsprogramm für Saarländische Kindergärten* (Weimar: verlag das netz).

Saarland Ministerium der Finanzen (2005): *Bericht des Saarlandes zur Sanierung des Landeshaushaltes* (Saarbrücken: Ministerium der Finanzen).

Saarland Ministerium für Frauen, Gesundheit, Arbeit und Soziales (2004): *Familienratgeber* (Saarbrücken: Ministerium für Frauen, Gesundheit, Arbeit und Soziales).

SPD (1989): *Grundsatzprogramm der Sozialdemokratischen Partei Deutschlands* (Bonn: SPD).

SPD (1997): 'Bildung für die Zukunft: Bildung in einer lernfähigen und lernenden Gesellschaft', Beschluß I, 283, Ordentlicher Parteitag Hannover, 2nd–4th December 1997, accessed at http://dezember1997.spd-parteitag.de/inno_283.html, 15th June 2008.

SPD-BW (2008): 'SPD: Sitzenbleiben ist pädagogisch überholt und teuer', Undated Press Release, accessed at http://www.spd.landtag-bw.de/index.php?docid=2677& pdf=default, 15th June 2008.

Statistisches Bundesamt (2004): *Kindertagesbetreuung in Deutschland: Einrichtungen, Plätze, Personal und Kosten 1990 bis 2002* (Wiesbaden: Statistisches Bundesamt).

Statistisches Bundesamt (2006): *Die Bundesländer: Strukturen und Entwicklungen – Ausgabe 2005* (Wiesbaden: Statistisches Bundesamt).

Statistisches Bundesamt (2007): *Statistisches Jahrbuch* (Wiesbaden: Statistisches Bundesamt).

Unpublished papers

Hessisches Sozialministerium (2006): *Broschüre 'Arbeit'.*

Other sources

Adelberger, Karen (2001): 'Federalism and its discontents: Fiscal and legislative power-sharing in Germany, 1948–99', *Regional & Federal Studies*, Vol. 11/2, pp.43–68.

Allan, J.P. and Scruggs, L. (2004): 'Political partisanship and welfare state reform in advanced industrial societies', *American Journal of Political Science*, Vol. 48/3, pp.496–52.

Allmendinger, Jutta and Leibfried, Stephan (2005): 'Bildungsarmut: Zum Zusammenhang von Sozialpolitik und Bildung', in Opielka, Michael (ed.) *Bildungsreform als Sozialreform: Zum Zusammenhang von Bildungs- und Sozialpolitik* (Wiesbaden: VS Verlag), pp.45–60.

Alvarez, R. Michael, Garrett, Geoffrey and Lange, Peter (1991): 'Government partisanship, labor organization and macroeconomic performance', *American Political Science Review*, Vol. 85/2, pp.539–56.

Annesley, Claire (2002): 'Reconfiguring women's social citizenship in Germany: The right to Sozialhilfe; the responsibility to work', *German Politics*, Vol. 11/1, pp.81–96.

Armingeon, Klaus (1989): 'Trade unions under changing conditions', *European Sociological Review*, Vol. 5/1, pp.1–23.

Arndt, Nina and Nickel, Rainer (2003): 'Federalism revisited: Constitutional court strikes down new immigration act for formal reasons', *German Law Journal*, Vol. 4/2.

Arthur, W. Brian (1989): 'Competing, technologies, increasing returns, and lock-in by historical events', *Economic Journal*, Vol. 99 (March 1989), pp.116–31.

Arthur, W. Brian (1990): 'Positive feedbacks in the economy', *Scientific American*, Vol. 262, pp.92–9.

Barenberg, Mark (2000): 'Labor federalism in the United States: Lessons for international labor rights', *Journal of International Economic Law*, Vol. 3/2, pp.303–29.

Baum, Annerose, Baumgarten, Britta and Lahusen, Christian (2004): 'National template: Unemployment and social security in Germany', *The Contentious Politics of Unemployment in Europe*, part of a series of national studies (Bamberg: University of Bamberg).

Bebchuck, Lucian Ayre and Roe, Mark J. (1999): 'A theory of path dependence in corporate governance and ownership', *Stanford Law Review*, Vol. 52/1, pp.127–70.

Benz, Arthur (1999): 'From unitary to asymmetric federalism in Germany: Taking stock after 50 years', *Publius: The Journal of Federalism*, Vol. 29/4, pp.55–78.

Benz, Arthur (2003): 'Reformpromotoren oder Reformblockierer? Die Rolle der Parteien im Bundesstaat', *Aus Politik und Zeitgeschichte*, 1999/29–30, pp.32–8.

Benz, Arthur (2005): 'Kein Ausweg aus der Politikverflechtung? Warum die Bundesstaats-Kommission scheiterte, aber nicht scheitern musste', *Politische Vierteljahresschrift*, Vol. 46/2, pp.207–17.

Bercham, Sascha von (2005): *Reform der Arbeitslosenversicherung und Sozialhilfe – Markt, Staat und Föderalismus* (Hamburg: Dr. Kovač).

Bertelsmann Stiftung (ed.) (2007): *Die Bundesländer im Fokus 2007: Aktive Arbeitsmarkt- und Beschäftigungspolitik* (Gütersloh: Bertelsmann).

Beyme, Klaus von (2003): 'Dis Asymmetrisierung des postmodernen Föderalismus', in Mayntz, Renate and Streeck, Wolfgang (eds) *Die Reformierbarkeit der Demokratie: Innovationen und Blockaden* (Frankfurt and New York: Campus), pp.239–58.

Birsl, Ursula (2006): 'Pfadwechsel: Vom deutschen Föderalismus zum transnationalen Neoregionalismus', *Zeitschrift für Parlamentsfragen*, Vol. 37/2, pp.384–401.

Blais, Andre, Blake, Donald and Dione, Stephane (1993): 'Do parties make a difference? Parties and the size of government in liberal democracies', *American Journal of Political Science*, Vol. 37/1, pp.40–62.

Blancke, Susanne and Schmid, Josef (1998): *Die aktive Areitsmarktpolitik der Bundesländer im Vergleich*, EZFF Occasional Paper No. 18 (Tübingen: Europäischen Zentrum für Föderalismus-Forschung).

Blancke, Susanne (1999): 'Push, Pull und Stay: Strategien gegen Arbeitslosigkeit: Bericht aus dem Forschungsprojekt 'Aktive Arbeitsmarktpolitik der Bundesländer', in Blancke, Susanne and Schmid, Josef, *Die aktive Areitsmarktpolitik der Bundesländer – Dokumentation des Workshops 'Push, Pull und Stay – Strategien gegen Arbeitslosigkeit in Deutschland* (WiP Occasional Paper 6, 1999: Tübingen: Institut für Politikwissenschaft), pp.28–36.

Blancke, Susanne (2003): 'Die Diffusion von Innovationen im deutschen Föderalismus', in Europäischen Zentrum für Föderalismus-Forschung Tübingen, *Jahrbuch des Föderalismus 2003: Föderalismus, Subsidiarität und Regionen in Europe* (Baden-Baden: Nomos), pp.31–48.

Blancke, Susanne (2004): *Politiknnovationen im Schatten des Bundes: Policy-Innovationen und – Diffusionen im Föderalismus und die Arbeitsmarktpolitik der Bundesländer* (Wiesbaden: VS Verlag).

Blumenthal, Julia von (2008): 'Zwischen Unitarisierung und föderaler Vilfalt: Parteienwettbewerb im Bundesstaat seit der deutschen Einheit', in Jesse, Eckhard and Sandschneider, Eberhard (eds) *Neues Deutschland: Eine Bilanz der deutschen Wiedervereinigung* (Baden Baden: Nomos), pp.83–105.

Blumenthal, Julia von (2009): *Das Kopftuch in der Landesgesetzgebung: Governance im Bundesstaat zwischen Unitarisierung und Föderalisierung* (Baden Baden: Nomos).

Böckler-Stiftung (2003): *Datenkarte 2003: Mecklenburg-Vorpommern*, http://www.boeckler. de/pdf/pub_datenkarte_mecklenburg_vorpommern_2003.pdf, accessed 10th October 2007.

Böckler-Stiftung (2006): *Datenkarte 2006: Sachsen-Anhalt*, http://www.boeckler.de/pdf/ pub_datenkarte_meck_vorpommern_2007.pdf, accessed 10th October 2007.

Böckler-Stiftung (2007): *Datenkarte 2007: Mecklenburg-Vorpommern*, http://www.boeckler.de/pdf/pub_datenkarte_sachsen_anhalt_2006.pdf, accessed 10th October 2007.

Boix, Carles (1998): *Political Parties, Growth and Equality: Conservative and Social Democratic Economic Strategies in the World Economy* (Cambridge: Cambridge University Press).

Boll, Bernhard (1994): 'Interest, organisation and intermediation in the new Länder', *German Politics*, Vol. 3/1, pp.114–28.

Borchert, Jürgen (2003): 'Der "Wiesbadener Entwurf" einer famlienpolitischen Strukturreform des Sozialstaats', in Hessische Staatskanzlei (ed.) *Die Familienpolitik muss neue Wege gehen! Der 'Wiesbadener Entwurf' zur Familienpolitik. Referate und Diskussionsbeiträge* (Wiesbaden: Westdeutscher Verlag), pp.19–152.

Brueckner, Jan K. (2000): 'Welfare reform and the race to the bottom: Theory and evidence', *Southern Economic Journal*, Vol. 66/3, pp.505–25.

Brunner, Wolfram and Walz, Dieter (1998): 'Die Hamburger Bürgerschaftswahl vom 21. September 1997', *Zeitschrift für Parlamentsfragen*, Vol. 29/2, pp.275–89.

Bunce, Valerie (1999): *Subversive Institutions: The Design and the Destruction of Socialism and the State* (New York: Cambridge University Press).

Bundesministerium der Finanzen (2003): *Schuldenstatistik* (14th February 2003).

Bundesrat (2002): 'Hartz-Gesetze im Vermittlungsausschuss', Press Release, 29th February 2002, http://www.bundesrat.de/nn_15524/DE/presse/pm/2002/243-2002.html, accessed 1st August 2008.

Burgess, Michael and Greß, Frank (2004): 'The representation of distinctiveness: Regional parties in Canada and Germany', in Hrbek, Rudolf (ed.) *Political Parties and Federalism: An International Comparison* (Schrifenreihe des Europäischen Zentrums für Föderalismusforchung, Band 22: Baden-Baden: Nomos), pp.114–30.

Burgess, Michael (2006): *Comparative Federalism: Theory and Practice* (London: Routledge).

Burkhart, Simone (2007): 'Der Einfluss der Bundespolitik auf Landtagswahlen', in Schmid, Josef and Zolleis, Udo (eds) *Wahlkampf im Südwesten: Parteien, Kampagnen und Landtagswahlen 2006 in Baden-Württemberg und Rheinland-Pfalz* (Münster: LIT), pp.191–207.

Busch, Andreas (2008): 'Warum ist Reformpolitik in der Bundesrepublik so schwierig? Die Interaktion von Föderalismus, Parteiensystem und Semisouveränität', in Jesse, Eckhard and Sandschneider, Eberhard (eds) *Neues Deutschland: Eine Bilanz der deutschen Wiedervereinigung* (Baden Baden: Nomos), pp.107–24.

Cameron, David R. (1978): 'The expansion of the public economy: A comparative analysis', *American Political Science Review*, Vol. 72/4, pp.1243–61.

Carlin, Wendy (1998): 'The new east German economy: Problems of transition, unification and institutional mismatch', *German Politics*, Vol. 7/3, pp.14–22.

Castles, Francis G. (ed.) (1982): *The Impact of Parties: Politics and Policies in Democratic Capitalist States* (Beverly Hills: Sage).

Castles, Francis G. and McKinlay, R.D. (1979): 'Public welfare provision, Scandinavia, and the sheer futility of the sociological approach to politics', *British Journal of Political Science*, Vol. 9/2, pp.157–71.

Clayton Richard and Pontusson, Jonas (1998): 'Welfare-state retrenchment revisited: Entitlement cuts, public sector restructuring and inegalitarian trends in advanced capitalist societies', *World Politics*, Vol. 51/1, pp.67–98.

Corina, J., Van Arnhem, M. and Schotsma, Guert J. (1982): 'Do parties affect the distribution of incomes? The case of advanced capitalist democracies', in Castles, Francis G. (ed.) *The Impact of Parties: Politics and Policies in Democratic Capitalist States* (Michigan: Sage), pp.283–364.

Cramer, Ulrich (2007): 'Fordern und Fördern mit Einstiegsgeld', paper to the SGB-II Bundeskongress, Munich, 1st October 2007 (reproduced at http://www.bundeskongress-sgb2.de/foren-doku-content/forum_a3/downloads/A3_6b_Cramer %20(Text).pdf, accessed 10th August 2008).

Dann, Sabine, Kirchmann, Andrew, Speerman, Alexander and Volkmann, Jürgen (2002): *Modellversuch 'Hessischer Kombilohn': Wissenschaftliche Begleitung des Hessischen Modellversuchs – Kurzfassung* (Tübingen: IAW, reproduced at http://www.iaw.edu/pdf/hk_ kurzfass.pdf, accessed 5th March 2008).

David, Paul A. (1985): 'Clio and the economics of QWERTY', *American Economic Review* Vol. 75/2, pp.332–7.

Debus, Marc (2008): 'Parteieinwettbewerb und Koalitionsbildung in den deutschen Bundesländern', in Jun, Uwe, Haas, Melanie and Niedermayer, Oskar (eds) *Parteien und Parteiensysteme in den deutschen Ländern* (Wiesbaden: VS Verlag), pp.57–78.

Detterbeck, Klaus and Renzsch, Wolfgang (2003): 'Multi-level electoral competition: The German case', *European Urban and Regional Studies*, Vol. 10/3, pp.257–69.

Detterbeck, Klaus and Renzsch, Wolfgang (2004): 'Regionalisierung der politischen Willensbildung: Parteien und Parteiensysteme in föderalen oder regionallisierten Staaten', in Europäischen Zentrum für Föderalismus-Forschung Tübingen, *Jahrbuch des Föderalismus 2004: Föderalismus, Subsidiarität und Regionen in Europe* (Baden-Baden: Nomos), pp.88–106.

Detterbeck, Klaus and Jeffery, Charlie (2008): 'Rediscovering the region: Territorial politics and party organizations in Germany', in Swenden, Wilfried and Maddens, Bart, *Territorial Party Politics in Western Europe* (Basingstoke: Palgrave Macmillan), pp.63–85.

Detterbeck, Klaus and Renzsch, Wolfgang (2008): 'Symmetrien und Asymmetrien im bundesstaatlichen Parteienwettbewerb', in Jun, Uwe, Haas, Melanie and Niedermayer, Oskar (eds) *Parteien und Parteiensysteme in den deutschen Ländern* (Wiesbaden: VS Verlag), pp.39–55.

Deutscher Beamtenbund (2003): Untitled Press Release, http://www.sachsen-anhalt. dbb.de/meldungen/archiv_2003/030203_1142.htm, accessed 10th November 2007.

Deutscher Bundestag (2006): http://www.bundestag.de/dasparlament/2006/08-09/ Inland/003.html, accessed 1st October 2007.

Deutscher Landkreistag (2005): 'Liste der Optionskommenen', http://www.kreise. de/landkreistag/special/optionskommunen/liste-optionskommunen.htm, accessed 1st August 2008.

Dienel, Christiane (2002): *Familienpolitik: Eine praxisorientierte Gesamtdarstellung der Handlungsfelder und Probleme* (Weinheim und München: Juventa).

Döbert, Hans (1997): 'Schulentwicklung in den neuen Ländern zwischen vorgegebenem Wegen und Eigengestaltung', *Bildung im Vereinten Deutschland: Perspektiven und Bilanz einer Entwicklung*, Dokumentation der 17. Deutsche Gesellschaft für Bildungsverwaltung-Jahrestagung, 24–26 October 1996, Leipzig (Frankfurt: DGBV), pp.27–38.

Dobner, Petra (2004): 'Der Landtag von Sachsen-Anhalt', in Mielke, Siegfried and Reutter, Werner, *Länderparlamentarismus in Deutschland* (Opladen: Leske und Budrich), pp.417–46.

Dobner, Petra and Schüttemeyer, Suzanne S. (2006): 'Der Landtag als Institution und politischer Akteur', in Holtmann, Everhard (ed.) *Landespolitik in Sachsen-Anhalt: Ein Handbuch* (Magdeburg: Sachsen Anhalt Landeszentrale für politische Bildung), pp.17–43.

Downs, Anthony (1957): *An Economic Theory of Democracy* (New York: Harper and Row).

Downs, William M. (1998): *Coalition Government Subnational Style: Multiparty Politics in Europe's Regional Parliaments* (Colombus: Ohio State University Press).

Eichhorst, Werner (2006): 'Kombilöhne: Erfahrungen und Lehren für Deutschland', *Neue Gesellschaft and Frankfurter Hefte*, Vol. 6/3, pp.54–7.

Eilfort, Michael (2006): 'Landes-Parteien: Anders, nicht verschieden', in Schneider, Herbert and Wehling, Hans-Georg (eds) *Landespolitik in Deutschland: Grundlagen, Strukturen, Arbeitsfelder* (Wiesbaden: VS Verlag), pp.207–24.

Eisele, Hansjörg (2006): *Landesparlamente – (k)ein Auslaufmodell? Eine Untersuchung zum deutschen Landesparlamentarismus am Beispiel des Landtags von Baden-Württemberg* (Baden-Baden: Nomos).

Ellwein, Thomas (1998): 'Die deutsche Gesellschaft und ihr Bildungswesen. Interessenartikulation und Bildungsdiskussion', in Führ, Christoph and Furck, Carl-Ludwig: *Handbuch der deutschen Bildungsgeschichte: Band VI – 1945 bis zur Gegenwart, Erster Teilband: Bundesrepublik Deutschland* (München: C.H. Beck), pp.87–109.

Erikson, Robert S., Wright, Gerald C. Jr. and McIvor, John C. (1989): 'Political parties, public opinion and state policy in the United States', *American Political Science Review*, Vol. 83/3, pp.729–50.

Esping-Andersen, Gosta (1990): *The Three Worlds of Welfare Capitalism* (Cambridge: Polity Press).

Europäisches Zentrum für Föderalismus-Foschung Tübingen (2005): *Jahrbuch des Föderalismus: Föderalismus, Subsidiarität und Regionen in Europa*, Band 6 (Baden-Baden: Nomos).

Evers, Adalbert, Lewis, Jane and Riedel, Birgit (2005): 'Developing child-care provision in England and Germany: Problems of governance', *Journal of European Social Policy*, Vol. 15/3, pp.195–209.

FES (2003): *Gering Qualifizierte – Verlierer am Arbeitsmarkt?! Konzept und Erfahrungen aus der Praxis* (Bonn: Friedrich-Ebert-Stiftung).

Fischer, Thomas (2005): 'Reformziel Aufgabenentflechtung – Die Beratungen der Föderalismuskommission zur Neuordnung der Gesetzgebungskompetenzen', in Europäischen Zentrum für Föderalismus-Forschung Tübingen, *Jahrbuch des Föderalismus 2005: Föderalismus, Subsidiarität und Regionen in Europe* (Baden-Baden: Nomos), pp.100–17.

Fischer, Thomas and Hüttmann, Martin Große (2001): 'Aktuelle Diskussionsbeiträge zur Reform des deutschen Föderalismus – Modelle, Leitbilder und die Chancen ihrer Übertragbarkeit', in Europäischen Zentrum für Föderalismus-Forschung Tübingen, *Jahrbuch des Föderalismus 2001: Föderalismus, Subsidiarität und Regionen in Europe* (Baden-Baden: Nomos), pp.128–42.

Forschungsgruppe Wahlen (1999a): 'Wahl in Hessen: Eine Analyse der Wahl vom 7. Februar 1999', *Berichte der Fergungsgruppe Wahlen e.V.*, Nr. 93, 10th February 1999 (Mannheim: Forschungsgruppe Wahlen).

Forschungsgruppe Wahlen (1999b): 'Wahl im Saarland: Eine Analyse der Landtagswahl vom 5. September 1999', *Berichte der Fergungsgruppe Wahlen e.V.*, Nr. 96, 8th September 1999 (Mannheim: Forschungsgruppe Wahlen).

Forschungsgruppe Wahlen (2002): 'Wahl in Sachsen-Anhalt: Eine Analyse der Landtagswahl vom 21. April 2002', *Berichte der Fergungsgruppe Wahlen e.V.*, Nr. 107, April 2002 (Mannheim: Forschungsgruppe Wahlen).

Forschungsgruppe Wahlen (2003): 'Wahl in Hessen: Eine Analyse der Wahl vom 2. Februar 2003', *Berichte der Fergungsgruppe Wahlen e.V.*, Nr. 111, February 2003 (Mannheim: Forschungsgruppe Wahlen).

Forschungsgruppe Wahlen (2004): 'Wahl im Saarland: Eine Analyse der Landtagswahl vom 5. September 2004', *Berichte der Fergungsgruppe Wahlen e.V.*, Nr. 117, September 2004 (Mannheim: Forschungsgruppe Wahlen).

Forschungsgruppe Wahlen (2006): 'Wahl in Sachsen-Anhalt: Eine Analyse der Land-tagswahl vom 26. März 2006', *Berichte der Fergungsgruppe Wahlen e.V.*, Nr. 125, March 2006 (Mannheim: Forschungsgruppe Wahlen).

Forschungsverbund IAB, IAT and Dr. Kaltenborn (2000): *Evaluierung des arbeitsmarkt-politischen Sonderprogramms CAST* (Bonn: Projektkoordination Evaluierung CAST).

Forschungsverbund IAB, IAT and Dr. Kaltenborn (2001): *Ein Jahr Erfahrungen mit dem arbeitsmarktpolitischen Sonderprogramm CAST* (Bonn: Projektkoordination Evaluierung CAST).

Freitag, Markus and Vatter, Adrian (eds) (2008): *Die Demokratien der deutschen Bundes-länder: Politische Institutionen im Vergleich* (Opladen: Barbara Budrich).

Führ, Christoph (1998): 'Zur Koordination der Bildungspolitik durch Bund und Länder', in Führ, Christoph and Furck, Carl-Ludwig: *Handbuch der deutschen Bildungsgeschichte: Band VI – 1945 bis zur Gegenwart, Erster Teilband: Bundesrepublik Deutschland* (München: C.H. Beck), pp.68–86.

Führ, Christoph and Furck, Carl-Ludwig (1998): *Handbuch der deutschen Bildungs-geschichte: Band VI – 1945 bis zur Gegenwart, Erster Teilband: Bundesrepublik Deutschland* (München: C.H. Beck).

Furck, Carl-Ludwig (1998): 'Grund- und Rahmenbedingungen', in Führ, Christoph and Furck, Carl-Ludwig: *Handbuch der deutschen Bildungsgeschichte: Band VI – 1945 bis zur Gegenwart, Erster Teilband: Bundesrepublik Deutschland* (München: C.H. Beck), pp.27–34.

Garrett, Geoffrey (1998): *Partisan Politics in the Global Economy* (Cambridge: Cambridge University Press).

Garrett, Geoffrey and Lange, Philip (1986): 'Performance in a hostile world: Economic growth in capitalist democracies 1974–1980', *World Politics*, Vol. 38, pp.517–45.

Garrett, Geoffrey and Lange, Philip (1991): 'Political responses to interdependence: What's "left" for the left?', *International Organization*, Vol. 45/4, pp.539–64.

Genschel, Philipp and Zangl, Bernhard (2007): 'Die Zerfasung von Staatlichkeit und die Zentralität des Staates', *TranState Working Papers*, No. 62 (Bremen).

Gerlach, Irene (2004): *Familienpolitik* (Wiesbaden: VS Verlag).

Gerlach, Irene (2006): 'Familienpolitik: Kampf der Kinderlosigkeit?', in Sturm, Roland and Pehle, Heinrich (eds) *Wege aus der Krise? Die Agenda der zweiten Großen Koalition* (Opladen: Barbara Budrich), pp.77–94.

GEW (2008): 'Lernmittelfreiheit', Briefing Note, http://www.gew.de/Binaries/Binary-29229/Lernmittelfreiheit_Bundesländerübersicht.pdf (accessed 10th August 2008).

Goetz, Klaus H. (1999): 'Administrative reconstruction in the New Länder: The federal dimension', in Jeffery, Charlie (ed.) *Recasting German Federalism* (London: Pinter), pp.85–115.

Green, David A. and Harrison, Kathryn (2006): 'Races to the bottom versus races to the middle: Minimum wage setting in Canada', in Harrison, Kathryn (ed.) *Racing to the Bottom? Provincial Interdependence in the Canadian Federation* (Vancouver: UBC Press), pp.193–228.

Greer, Scott L. (ed.) (2009): *Devolution and Social Citizenship in the UK* (Bristol: Policy Press).

Grube, Norbert (2004): 'Unverzichtbares Korrektiv oder ineffective Reformbremse? Wahrnehmungen föderaler Strukturen und Institutionen in Deutschland', in Euro-päischen Zentrum für Föderalismus-Forschung Tübingen, *Jahrbuch des Föderalismus 2004: Föderalismus, Subsidiarität und Regionen in Europe* (Baden-Baden: Nomos), pp.163–75.

Gunlicks, Arthur B. (2003): *The Länder and German Federalism* (Manchester: Manchester University Press).

Gunlicks, Arthur B. (2004): 'The *Land* parliament deputies in Germany', in Hrbek, Rudolf (ed.) *Political Parties and Federalism: An International Comparison* (Schrifenreihe des Europäischen Zentrums für Föderalismusforchung, Band 22: Baden-Baden: Nomos), pp.97–113.

Haas, Melanie, Jun, Uwe and Niedermayer, Oskar (2008): 'Die Parteien und Parteiensysteme der Bundesländer: Eine Einführung', in Jun, Uwe, Haas, Melanie and Niedermayer, Oskar (eds) *Parteiein und Parteiensysteme in den deutschen Ländern* (Wiesbaden: VS Verlag), pp.9–38.

Haddow, Rodney, Schneider, Steffen G. and Klassen, Thomas R. (2006): 'Can decentralization alleviate labour market dysfunctions in marginal jurisdictions? Active labour market policies in Nova Scotia and Saxony-Anhalt', *Canadian Public Policy – Analyse de Politiques*, Vol. 32/3, pp.317–37.

Hagemann, Karen (2006): 'Between ideology and economy: The "time politics" of child care and public education in the two Germanys', *Social Politics*, Vol. 13/2, pp.217–60.

Hakim, Catherine (2000): *Research Design: Successful Designs for Social and Economic Research* (London: Routledge).

Harlen, Christine (2002): 'Schröder's economic reforms: The end of Reformstau?', *German Politics*, Vol. 11/1, pp.61–80.

Harrison, Kathryn (ed.) (2006a): *Racing to the Bottom? Provincial Interdependence in the Canadian Federation* (Vancouver: UBC Press).

Harrison, Kathryn (2006b): 'Are Canadian provinces engaged in a race to the bottom? Evidence and implications', in Harrison, Kathryn (2006) (ed.) *Racing to the Bottom? Provincial Interdependence in the Canadian Federation* (Vancouver: UBC Press), pp.257–70.

Hartwich, Hans-Hermann (1999): 'Konkurrenz-Föderalismus versus kooperativer Föderalismus', *Gegenwartskunde* 1999, pp.329–36.

Hartwich, Hans-Hermann (2006): '"Arbeitsmarktreformen" in der Agenda der neuen Bundesregierung', in Sturm, Roland and Pehle, Heinrich (eds) *Wege aus der Krise? Die Agenda der zweiten Großen Koalition* (Opladen: Barbara Budrich), pp.23–39.

Heinrich, Gudrun (2002): *Kleine Koalitionspartner in Landesregierung: Zwischen Konkurrenz und Kooperation* (Opladen: Leske und Budrich).

Hennis, Wilhelm (1968): *Politik als Praktische Wissenschaft: Aufsätze zur politischen Theorie und Regierungslehre* (München: Piper).

Hepp, Gerd F. (2006): 'Bildungspolitik als Länderpolitik', in Schneider, Herbert and Wehling, Hans-Georg (eds) *Landespolitik in Deutschland: Grundlagen, Strukturen, Arbeitsfelder* (Wiesbaden: VS Verlag), pp.240–69.

Hepp, Gerd F. and Weinacht, Paul-Ludwig (2003): *WievielSelbständigkeit brauchen Schulen? Schulpolitische Kontroversen und Entscheidungen in Hessen (1991–2000)* (München: Luchterhand).

Hesse, Konrad (1962): *Der Unitarische Bundesstaat* (Karlsruhe: C.F. Miller).

Hessischer Rundfunk (2006): Untitled report, http://www.hr-online.de/website/rubriken/nachrichten/index.jsp?rubrik=5710&key=standard_document_4926524, accessed 10th August 2006.

Hessisches Kultusministerium (2007a): 'Vorbild für andere Bundesländer – Hessen bei Ausländerintegration vorn', http://www.hessisches-kultusministerium.de/irj/HKM_Internet?cid=f2fd9845270981331a9685a4756782ec, accessed 10th October 2007.

Hessisches Kultusministerium (2007b): 'Ausbau von Ganztagsschulen', http://www.kultusministerium.hessen.de/irj/HKM_Internet?cid=54f479017cbf9dc1397bdef32b2922a5, accessed 10th October 2007.

Hessisches Kultusministerium (2007c): 'Lernmittelfreiheit', http://www.kultus-ministerium.hessen.de/irj/HKM_Internet?cid=1e2e6d977c6a19464b2197522981ff45, accessed 14th October 2007.

Hessisches Sozialministerium (2005): 'Hessische Familienpolitik: Eine erste Bilanz 2005', http://www.hessen.de/irj/hessen_Internet?uid=1fb10430-1dc1-8601-33e2-dc44e9169fcc, accessed 14th October 2007.

Hessische Landesregierung (2002): *Versprochen – Gehalten!* (Wiesbaden: Hessische Staatskanzlei).

Hessische Landesregierung (ed.) (2006): *Das HessenInfoBuch: Zahlen, Daten, Fakten. Und Service* (Wiesbaden: Hessische Staatskanzlei).

Hessische Staatskanzlei (ed.) (2003): *Die Familienpolitik muss neue Wege gehen! Der 'Wiesbadener Entwurf' zur Familienpolitik. Referate und Diskussionsbeiträge* (Wiesbaden: Westdeutscher Verlag).

Hibbs, D.A. (1977): 'Political parties and macroeconomic policy', *American Political Science Review*, Vol. 71, pp.1467–87.

Hicks, Alexander M. and Swank, Duane (1992): 'Politics, institutions, and welfare spending in industrialized democracies, 1960–82', *American Political Science Review*, Vol. 86/3, pp.658–74.

Hildebrandt, Achim and Wolf, Frieder (2008a) (eds): *Die Politik der Bundesländer: Staatstätigkeit im Vergleich* (Wiesbaden: VS Verlag)

Hildebrandt, Achim and Wolf, Frieder (2008b): 'Die Potenziale des Bundesländer-vergleichs', in Hildebrandt, Achim and Wolf, Frieder (eds) *Die Politik der Bundes-länder: Staatstätigkeit im Vergleich* (Wiesbaden: VS Verlag), pp.11–20.

Holtmann, Everhard (1998): 'Funktionen regionaler Parteien und Parteiensysteme – Überlegungen für ein analytisches Konzept', in Benz, Arthur and Holtmann, Everhard (eds) *Gestaltung regionaler Politik: Empirische Befunde, Erklärungsansätze und Praxistransfer* (Opladen: Leske und Budrich), pp.65–76.

Holtmann, Everhard (2003): 'Die sachsen-anhaltische Lantagswahl von 21. April 2002: Bürgervotum gegen das Tolerierungsbündnis von SPD und PDS', *Zeitschrift für Parlamentsfragen*, Vol. 34/1, pp.41–60.

Hough, Dan and Koß, Michael (2006): 'Landesparteien in vergleichender Perspektive: Die Linkspartei.PDS zwischen Regierungsverantwortung und Opposition', *Zeitschrift für Parlamentsfragen*, Vol. 37/2, pp.312–32.

Hough, Dan and Sloam, James (2007): 'Different road maps, similar paths? Social democratic politics in Britain and Germany', *German Politics*, Vol. 16/1, pp.26–38.

Hovestadt, Gertrud (2003): *Wie setzen die Bundesländer den Bildungsauftrag der Kinder-tageseinrichtungen um? Vom Gesetz zur Praxis. Eine Studie im Auftrag der Max-Traeger-Stiftung* (EDUCON: Rheine).

Hrbek, Rudolf (ed.) (2004a): *Political Parties and Federalism: An International Comparison* (Schrifenreihe des Europäischen Zentrums für Föderalismus-Forschung Tübingen, Band 22: Baden-Baden: Nomos).

Hrbek, Rolf (2004b): 'Auf dem Weg zur Föderalismus-Reform: Die Kommission zur Modernisierung der bundesstaatlichen Ordnung', in Europäischen Zentrum für Föderalismus-Forschung Tübingen, *Jahrbuch des Föderalismus 2004: Föderalismus, Subsidiarität und Regionen in Europe* (Baden-Baden: Nomos), pp.147–62.

Hrbek, Rolf (2007): 'The reform of German federalism: Part I', *European Constitutional Law Review*, Vol. 3, pp.225–43.

Huber, Evelyne, Ragin, Charles and Stephens, John D. (1993): 'Social democracy, Christian democracy, constitutional structure, and the welfare state', *American Journal of Sociology*, Vol. 99/3, pp.711–49.

Jaich, Roman (2001): *Finanzierung der Kindertagesbeetreuung in Deutschland: Gutachten im Rahmen des Projektes 'Familienunterstützende Kinderbetreuungsangebote' des DJI* (DJI: München).

Jeffery, Charlie (ed.) (1999): *Recasting German Federalism: The Legacies of Unification* (London: Pinter).

Jeffery, Charlie and Hough, Dan (2001): 'The electoral cycle and multi-level voting in Germany', *German Politics*, Vol. 10/2, pp.73–98.

Jeffery, Charlie (2002): 'Uniformity and diversity in policy provision: Insights from the US, Germany and Canada', in Adams, John and Robinson, Peter (eds) *Devolution in Practice* (London: ippr), pp.176–97.

Jeffery, Charlie (2005): 'Federalism: The new territorialism', in Green, Simon and Paterson, William E. (eds) *The Semi-Sovereign State Revisited* (Cambridge: Cambridge University Press), pp.78–93.

Jun, Uwe (1994): *Koalitionsbildung in den deutschen Bundesländern: Theoretische Betrachtungen, Dokumentation und Analyse der Koalitionsbildungen in den deutschen Bundesländern 1949 bis 2002* (Opladen: Leske & Budrich).

Keating, Michael (2010), 2nd edition: *The Government of Scotland: Public Policy Making after Devolution* (Edinburgh: Edinburgh University Press).

Kemmerling, Achim and Bruttel, Oliver (2006): '"New politics" in German labour market policy? The implications of the recent Hartz reforms for the German welfare state', *West European Politics*, Vol.29/1, pp.90–112.

Keohane, Robert O. and Nye, Joseph S. (1989), 2nd edition: *Power and Interdependence* (New York: HarperCollins).

Kersbergen, Kees van (1995): *Social Capitalism: A Study of Christian Democracy and the Welfare State* (London: Routledge).

Kilian, Michael (2006): 'Die Landesverfassungsgerichtsbarkeit in Sachsen-Anhalt', in Holtmann, Everhard (ed.) *Landespolitik in Sachsen-Anhalt: Ein Handbuch* (Magdeburg: Sachsen Anhalt Landeszentrale für politische Bildung), pp.44–76.

Kincaid, John (2001): 'Economic policy-making: Advantages and disadvantages of the federal model', *International Social Science Journal*, Vol. 53/167, pp.85–92.

Kitschelt, Herbert (1994): *The Transformation of European Social Democracy* (Cambridge: Cambridge University Press).

Kittel, Bernhard and Obinger, Herbert (2003): 'Political parties, institutions, and the dynamics of public expenditure in times of austerity', *Journal of European Public Policy*, Vol. 10/1, pp.20–45.

Klatt, Hartmut (1999): 'Centralizing trends in West German federalism, 1949–89', in Jeffery, Charlie (ed.) *Recasting German Federalism: The Legacies of Unification* (London: Pinter), pp.40–57.

Klemmer, Iris (2005): 'Arbeit und Ergebnisse der Föderalismuskommission im Bereich der Finanzbeziehungen zwischen Bund und Ländern', in Europäischen Zentrum für Föderalismus-Forschung Tübingen, *Jahrbuch des Föderalismus 2005: Föderalismus, Subsidiarität und Regionen in Europa* (Baden-Baden: Nomos), pp.118–34.

Klimmt, Reinhard (2003): *Auf dieser Grenze lebe ich* (Blieskastel: Gollstein).

Koch, Roland (2003): 'Vorwort zur Dikumentation: "Muss die Familienpolitik neue Wege gehen? – Der Wiesbadener Entwurf"', in Hessische Staatskanzlei (ed.) *Die Familienpolitik muss neue Wege gehen! Der 'Wiesbadener Entwurf' zur Familienpolitik. Referate und Diskussionsbeiträge* (Wiesbaden: Westdeutscher Verlag), pp.5–7.

Koch, Roland (2008): 'Hartz Kompromiss trägt klare hessische Handschrift', http://www.roland-koch.de/Hartz-Kompromiss-traegt-klare-hessische-Handschrift/1040249280.html, accessed 17th July 2008.

Koß, Michael and Hough, Dan (2006): 'Landesparteien in vergleichender Perspektive: Dis Linkspartei.PDS zwischen Regierungsverantwortung und Opposition', *Zeitschrift für Parlamentsfragen*, Vol. 37/2, pp.312–34.

Kregel, Bernd (2006): 'Kommunen zwischen Eigenverantwortung und Staatsauftrag', in Holtmann, Everhard (ed.) *Landespolitik in Sachsen-Anhalt: Ein Handbuch* (Magdeburg: Sachsen Anhalt Landeszentrale für Politische Bildung), pp.126–46.

Kropp, Sabine (2001): *Regieren in Koalitionen* (Wiesbaden: Westdeutscher Verlag).

Kropp, Sabine (2010): *Kooperativer Föderalismus und Politikverflechtung* (Wiesbaden: VS Verlag).

Land Sachsen-Anhalt (2003): Internal newsletter, http://www.sachsen-anhalt.de/LPSA/fileadmin/Files/Newsletter_7_03.pdf, accessed 10th August 2008.

Land Sachsen-Anhalt (2007): Untitled website giving educational statistics, http://www.sachsen-anhalt.de/LPSA/index.php?id=18522, accessed 15th November 2007.

Lautenschläger, Silke (2003): 'Vorwort', in Hessische Staatskanzlei (ed.) *Die Familienpolitik muss neue Wege gehen! Der 'Wiesbadener Entwurf' zur Familienpolitik. Referate und Diskussionsbeiträge* (Wiesbaden: Westdeutscher Verlag), pp.155–6.

Lees, Charles (2000): The *Red-Green Coalition in Germany: Politics, Personalities and Power* (Manchester: Manchester University Press).

Lehmbruch, Gerhard (1998): *Parteienwettbewerb im Bundesstaat* (Opladen: Westdeutscher Verlag) – second edition.

Lehmbruch, Gerhard (2000): *Parteienwettbewerb im Bundesstaat* (Opladen: Westdeutscher Verlag) – third edition.

Lehmbruch, Gerhard (2004): 'Das deutsche Verbändesystem zwischen Unitarismus und Föderalismus', in Mayntz, Renate and Streeck, Wolfgang (eds) *Die Reformierbarkeit der Demokratie: Innovationen und Blockaden* (Frankfurt and New York: Campus), pp.259–88.

Leibfried, Stephan, Castles, Francis G. and Obinger, Herbert (2005): '"Old" and "new" politics in federal welfare states', in Obinger, Herbert, Leibfried, Stefan and Castles, Francis G. (eds) *Federalism and the Welfare State: New World and European Experiences* (Cambridge: CUP), pp.307–55.

Leonardy, Uwe (2004): 'Federalism and parties in Germany: Organizational hinges between constitutional and political structures', in Hrbek, Rudolf (ed.) *Political Parties and Federalism: An International Comparison* (Schrifenreihe des Europäischen Zentrums für Föderalismus-Forschung Tübingen, Band 22: Baden-Baden: Nomos), pp.183–202.

Lijphart, Arendt (1971): 'Comparative politics and the comparative method', *American Political Science Review*, Vol. 65/3, pp.682–93.

Lijphart, Arendt (1994): *Electoral Systems and Party Systems: A Study of Twenty-Seven Democracies, 1945–1990* (Oxford: Oxford University Press).

Lijphart, Arendt (1999): *Patterns of Democracy: Government Forms and Performance in Thirty-Six Countries* (New Haven: Yale University Press).

Linsmayer, Ludwig (2007): *Die Geburt des Saarlandes* (Saarbrücken: Landesarchiv Saarbrücken).

Lhotta, Roland (2004): 'Verwaltung und Entflechtung im deutschen Bundesstaat. Der Widerstreit zwischen Einheitsdenken und Strukturflexibilisierung', in Decker, Frank (ed.) *Föderalismus an der Wegscheide: Optionen und Perspektiven einer Reform der bundesstaatlichen Ordnung* (Wiesbaden: VS Verlag), pp.149–67.

Lofland, John (1971): *Analyzing Social Settings: A Guide to Qualitative Observation and Analysis* (Belmont: Wadsworth).

Luthardt, Wolfgang (1999): 'Abschied vom deutschen Konsens-Modell? Zur Reform des Föderalismus', *Aus Politik und Zeitgeschichte*, Vol. 1999/13, pp.12–23.

Mackenstein, Hans and Jeffery, Charlie (1999): 'Financial equalization in the 1990s: On the road back to Karlsruhe', in Jeffery, Charlie (ed.) *Recasting German Federalism: The Legacies of Unification* (London: Pinter), pp.155–76.

MacIntyre, Alasdair (1984) 'Is a science of comparative politics possible?', in *Against the Self-Images of the Age* (South Bend: Notre Dame), pp.260–9.

Mair, Peter (2008): 'The challenge to party government', *West European Politics*, Vol. 31/1, pp.211–34.

Malik, Corinna (2008): 'Die Arbeitsmarktpolitik der Bundesländer nach den Hartz-Reformen', *WZB Discussion Paper*, January 2008 (Berlin: WZB).

Manow, Philip (2005): 'Germany: Co-operative federalism and the over-grazing of the fiscal commons', in Obinger, Herbert, Leibfried, Stefan and Castles, Francis G. (eds) *Federalism and the Welfare State: New World and European Experiences* (Cambridge: Cambridge University Press), pp.222–62.

März, Peter (2006): 'Ministerpräsidenten', in Schneider, Herbert and Wehling, Hans-Georg (eds) *Landespolitik in Deutschland: Grundlagen, Strukturen, Arbeitsfelder* (Wiesbaden: VS Verlag), pp.148–84.

Matthias, Jörg (2003): 'Farewell – Welfare state, hello, welfare regions? Chances and constraints of welfare management in the German federal system', *German Politics*, Vol. 12/3, pp.25–65.

McEwen, Nicola and Moreno, Luis (eds) (2005): *The Territorial Politics of Welfare* (London: Routledge).

McLean, Iain (2001): *Rational Choice & British Politics: An Analysis of Rhetoric and Manipulation from Peel to Blair* (Oxford: Oxford University Press).

Mielke, Siegfried and Reutter, Werner (2004): *Länderparlamentarismus in Deutschland: Geschichte – Struktur – Funktionen* (Opladen: VS Verlag).

Mill, John Stuart (1950): *Philosophy of Scientific Method* (New York: Hafner).

Mittelstandsvereinigung Sachsen-Anhalt (2007): Press Release (19th December 2007): 'Gürth: Flächendeckende Mindestlöhne sind Gift für die Wirtschaft', http://www.mit-sachsen-anhalt.de/news/text.php?lf_nr=134, accessed 17th August 2008.

Mokyr, Joel (1991): 'Evolutionary biology, technological change and economic history', *Bulletin of Economic Research*, Vol. 43/2, pp.127–49.

Münch, Ursula (1998): 'Entflechtungsmöglichkeiten im Bereich der Sozialpolitik', in Männle, Ursula (ed.) *Tagungs- und Materialienband zur Fortentwicklung des deutschen Föderalismus* (Baden-Baden: Nomos), pp.73–8.

Münch, Ursula (1999): 'Entwicklung und Perspektiven des deutschen Föderalismus', *Aus Politik und Zeitgeschichte*, Vol. 1999/13, pp.3–11.

Münch, Ursula (2001): 'Konkurrenzföderalismus für die Bundesrepublik: Eine Reform-debatte zwischen Wunschdenken und politischer Machbarkeit', in Europäischen Zentrum für Föderalismus-Forschung Tübingen, *Jahrbuch des Föderalismus 2001: Föderalismus, Subsidiarität und Regionen in Europe* (Baden-Baden: Nomos), pp.115–27.

Münch, Ursula (2005): 'Bildungspolitik als föderativer Streitpunkt: Die Auseinander-setzung um die Verteilung bildungspolitischer Zuständigkeiten in der Bundesstaats-kommission', in Europäischen Zentrum für Föderalismus-Forschung Tübingen, *Jahrbuch des Föderalismus 2005: Föderalismus, Subsidiarität und Regionen in Europe* (Baden-Baden: Nomos), pp.150–62.

Neumann, Arijana and Schmid, Josef (2008): 'Die Hessen-CDU: Kampfverband und Regierungspartei', in Schröder, Wolfgang (ed.) *Parteien und Parteiensystem in Hessen* (Wiesbaden: VS Verlag), pp.107–41.

Nullmeier, Frank, Pritzlaff, Tanja and Wiesener, Achim (2003): *Mikro-Policy-Analyse: Ethnographische Politikforschung am Beispiel Hochschulpolitik* (Frankfurt: Campus).

Oates, Wallace E. (1999): 'An essay on fiscal federalism', *Journal of Economic Literature*, Vol. 37/3, pp.1120–49.
Obinger, Herbert, Leibfried, Stefan and Castles, Francis G. (eds) (2005a): *Federalism and the Welfare State: New World and European Experiences* (Cambridge: Cambridge University Press).
Obinger, Herbert, Castles, Francis G. and Leibfried Stefan (2005b): 'Introduction: Federalism and the welfare state', in Obinger, Herbert, Leibfried, Stefan and Castles, Francis G. (eds) *Federalism and the Welfare State: New World and European Experiences* (Cambridge: Cambridge University Press), pp.1–48.
OECD (2004): *OECD Early Childhood Policy Review: 2002–2004 Background Report Germany* (München: Deutsches Jugendinstitut e.V.).
Opielka, Michael (2004): *Sozialpolitik: Grundlagen und Vergleichende Perspektiven* (Hamburg: Rowohlt).
Opielka, Michael (ed.) (2005a): *Bildungsreform als Sozialreform: Zum Zusammenhang von Bildungs- und Sozialpolitik* (Wiesbaden: VS Verlag).
Opielka, Michael (2005b): 'Bildungsreform und Sozialreform: Der Zusammenhang von Bildungs- und Sozialpolitik', in Opielka, Michael (ed.) *Bildungsreform als Sozialreform: Zum Zusammenhang von Bildungs- und Sozialpolitik* (Wiesbaden: VS Verlag), pp.127–55.
Patzelt, Werner J. (1998): 'Die vergelichende Untersuchung von Landesparteien', in Benz, Arthur and Holtmann, Everhard (eds) *Gestaltung regoionaler Politik: Empirische Befunde, Erklärungsansätze und Praxistransfer* (Opladen: Leske und Budrich), pp.77–88.
Patzelt, Werner J. (2006): 'Länderparlamentarismus', in Schneider, Herbert and Wehling, Hans-Georg (eds) *Landespolitik in Deutschland: Grundlagen, Strukturen, Arbeitsfelder* (Wiesbaden: VS Verlag), pp.108–29.
Payk, Bernhard (2005): 'Nach PISA 2000, Schulpolitikreformen der deutschen Bundesländer im Vergleich', paper presented to the Tagund des Forums Junge Staats- und Verwaltungwissenschaft in der Sektion politische Verwaltung und Staatslehre der DVPW, Hamburg, 7.7.2005–9.7.2005 (downloaded from http://www.uni-konstanz. de/bogumil/payk/downloads/schulpolitik_payk_24-06-05.pdf, 10th August 2006).
Payk, Bernhard (2009): *Deutsche Schulpolitik nach dem PISA-Schock: Wie die Bundesländer auf die Legitimationskrise des Schulsystems Reagieren* (Hamburg: Dr. Kovač).
Peterson, Paul E. (1995): *The Price of Federalism* (Washington: Brookings Institution).
Phillips, David (1995): 'Transitions and traditions: Educational developments in the New Germany in their historical context', *Education in Germany: Tradition and Reform in Historical Context* (London: Routledge), pp.243–58.
Pierson, Paul (1995): 'Fragmented welfare states: Federal institutions and the development of social policy', *Governance*, Vol. 8/4, pp.449–78.
Pierson, Paul (1996): 'The new politics of the welfare state', *World Politics*, Vol. 48/2, pp.143–79.
Pierson, Paul (2000): 'Increasing returns, path dependence, and the study of politics', *American Political Science Review*, Vol. 94/2, pp.251–67.
Przworski, Adam and Teune, Henry (1970): *The Logic of Comparative Social Enquiry* (New York: Wiley).
Putz, Sebastian (2006): 'Die Landesregierung als Zentrum politischer Steuerung', in Holtmann, Everhard (ed.) *Landespolitik in Sachsen-Anhalt: Ein Handbuch* (Magdeburg: Sachsen Anhalt Landeszentrale für politische Bildung), pp.80–104.
Quanz, Lothar (2003): 'Quanz: 12 Jahre zum Abitur – Landesregierung betreibt Bildungsabbau statt Qualitätsverbesserung', Press release, http://www.lothar-quanz.de/presse/pressemeldung/2003/pm20030120.htm, accessed 10th October 2007.

Rabe-Kleberg, Ursula (2005): 'Von Generation zu Genration? Kleine Kinder und soziale Ungleichheit in Deutschland', in Opielka, Michael (ed.) *Bildungsreform als Sozialreform: Zum Zusammenhang von Bildungs- und Sozialpolitik* (Wiesbaden: VS Verlag), pp.77–88.

Rechnungshof Hessen (1995): 'Zweiter Zusammenfassender Bericht', http://www.rechnungshof-hessen.de/index.php?seite=inhalt5.php&year=1993&K1=4&K2=13&K3=0&S1, accessed 4th January 2007.

Reinhardt, Sibylle (1999): 'Bildung und Bildungspolitik – nur Durcheinander oder auch Strukturen?', *Gegenwartskunde*, Vol. 1999/1, pp.19–30.

Reissert, Bernd (1994): 'Zur Verantwortung der Bundesländer bei der Bekämpfung der Arbeitslosigkeit – 10 Thesen', in Forschungsinstitut der Friedrich-Ebert-Stiftung, Abt. Arbeits- und Sozialforschung, Gesprächskreis Arbeit und Soziales, No. 38: *Der Berliner Arbeitsmarkt im Umbruch*, eine Tagung der Friedrich-Ebert-Stiftung und der BBJ Consult am 22. und 23. April 1994 in Berlin (Bonn: Friedrich-Ebert-Stiftung).

Reiter-Mayer, Petra (2005): 'Die Ständige Konferenz der Kultusminister im föderalen System: Zur Rollenfindung und Reformfähigkeit', in Europäischen Zentrum für Föderalismus-Forschung Tübingen, *Jahrbuch des Föderalismus 2005: Föderalismus, Subsidiarität und Regionen in Europe* (Baden-Baden: Nomos), pp.163–73.

Renzsch, Wolfgang (2005): 'Bundesstaatsreform – nach dem Scheitern der KOMBO?', in Europäischen Zentrum für Föderalismus-Forschung Tübingen, *Jahrbuch des Föderalismus 2005: Föderalismus, Subsidiarität und Regionen in Europe* (Baden-Baden: Nomos), pp.91–9.

Renzsch, Wolfgang (2006): 'Der Haushalt des Landes Sachsen-Anhalt', in Holtmann, Everhard et al. (ed.) *Landespolitik in Sachsen-Anhalt: Ein Handbuch* (Magdeburg: Sachsen Anhalt Landeszentrale für politische Bildung), pp.105–25.

Reuter, Lutz R. (1998a): 'Rechtliche Grundlagen und Rahmenbedingungen', in Führ, Christoph and Furck, Carl-Ludwig: *Handbuch der deutschen Bildungsgeschichte: Band VI – 1945 bis zur Gegenwart, Erster Teilband: Bundesrepublik Deutschland* (München: C.H. Beck), pp.35–57.

Reuter, Lutz R. (1998b): 'Administrative Grundlagen und Rahmenbedingungen', in Führ, Christoph and Furck, Carl-Ludwig: *Handbuch der deutschen Bildungsgeschichte: Band VI – 1945 bis zur Gegenwart, Erster Teilband: Bundesrepublik Deutschland* (München: C.H. Beck), pp.58–67.

Reutter, Werner (2005): 'Berlin's republic: Parliamentary government in a German land', *German Politics*, Vol. 14/4, pp.438–54.

Reutter, Werner (2006): 'The transfer of power hypothesis and the German *Länder*: In need of modification', *Publius: The Journal of Federalism*, Vol. 36/2, pp.277–301.

Reutter, Werner (2008): *Föderalismus, Parlamentarismus und Demokratie* (Opladen: Barbara Budrich).

Richter, Ingo (2003): 'Nationale Bildungsstandards im föderalen Staat Bildungsrepublik Deutschland?', in Europäischen Zentrum für Föderalismus-Forschung Tübingen, *Jahrbuch des Föderalismus 2003: Föderalismus, Subsidiarität und Regionen in Europe* (Baden-Baden: Nomos), pp.131–7.

Riker, William H. (1975): 'Federalism', in Greenstein, Fred I. and Polsby, Nelson W. (eds) *Handbook of Political Science: Governmental Institutions and Processes*, Vol. 5 (Reading MA: Addison-Wesley), pp.93–172.

Rodden, Jonathan A. (2003a): 'Reviving Leviathan: Fiscal federalism and the growth of government', *International Organization*, Vol. 57/4, pp.695–729.

Rodden, Jonathan A. (2003b): 'Soft budget constraints and German federalism', in Rodden, Jonathan A., Eskeland, Gunnar S. and Litvack, Jennie (eds) *Fiscal*

Decentralisation and the Challenge of Hard Budget Constraints (Massachusetts: MIT Press), pp.161–87.

Rom, Mark Carl (2006): 'Policy races in the American states', in Harrison, Kathryn (2006) (ed.) *Racing to the Bottom? Provincial Interdependence in the Canadian Federation* (Vancouver: UBC Press), pp.229–56.

Rose, Richard (1980): *Do Parties Make a Difference?* (London: Macmillan).

Rose, Richard and McAllister, Ian (1986): *Voters Begin to Choose: From Closed Class to Open Elections in Britain:* (London: Sage).

Rose-Ackerman, Susan (1981): 'Does federalism matter? Political choice in a Federal Republic', *The Journal of Political Economy*, Vol. 89/1, pp.152–65.

Rosenfeld, Martin T.W. (2006): 'Wirtschaftspolitik in Sachsen-Anhalt: Anforderungen und aktuelle Praxis', in Holtmann, Everhard (ed.) *Landespolitik in Sachsen-Anhalt: Ein Handbuch* (Magdeburg: Sachsen Anhalt Landeszentrale für politische Bildung), pp.202–20.

Roth, Reinhold (2004): 'Die Bremer Bürgerschaftswahl vom 23. Mai 2003', *Zeitschrift für Parlamentsfragen*, Vol. 35/2, pp.241–52.

Rudloff, Wilfried (2008): 'Schulpolitik und Schulkämpfe in Hessen', in Schröder, Wolfgang (ed.) *Parteien und Parteiensystem in Hessen* (Wiesbaden: VS Verlag), pp.332–60.

Rudzio, Wolfgang (2003): *Das politische System der Bundesrepublik Deutschland*, 6th edition (Opladen: Leske and Budrich).

Rütters, Peter (2004): 'Landesparlamentarismus – Saarland', in Mielke, Siegfried and Reutter, Werner, *Länderparlamentarismus in Deutschland: Geschichte – Struktur – Funktionen* (Opladen: VS Verlag), pp.359–88.

Scharpf, Fritz W. (1988): 'The joint decision trap: Lessons from German federalism and European integration', *Public Administration*, Vol. 66/3, pp.239–78.

Scharpf, Fritz W. (1994): *Optionen des Föderalismus in Deutschland und Europa* (Frankfurt and New York: Campus).

Scharpf, Fritz W. (2005): 'No exit from the joint decision trap? Can German federalism reform itself?', Max Planck Institute for the Study of Societies Working Paper 8/05 (September 2005).

Scheller, Henrik (2005): 'Der Finanzausgleich zwischen Bund und Ländern als föderatives Sozialversicherungssystem', in Europäischen Zentrum für Föderalismus-Forschung Tübingen, *Jahrbuch des Föderalismus 2005: Föderalismus, Subsidiarität und Regionen in Europe* (Baden-Baden: Nomos), pp.253–69.

Schiller, Theo (2004): 'Der Hessische Landtag', in Mielke, Siegfried and Reutter, Werner, *Länderparlamentarismus in Deutschland: Geschichte – Struktur – Funktionen* (Opladen: VS Verlag), pp.225–50.

Schmid, Josef (1990a): 'Bildungspolitik der CDU. Eine Fallstudie zu innerparteilicher Willensbildung im Föderalismus', *Gegenwartskunde*, Vol. 39/3, pp.303–13.

Schmid, Josef (1990b): *Die CDU. Organisationsstrukturen, Politiken und Funktionsweisen einer Partei im Föderalismus* (Opladen: Leske and Budrich).

Schmid, Josef and Blancke, Susanna (2001): *Arbeitsmarktpolitik der Bundesländer: Chancen und Restriktionen einer aktiven Arbeitsmarkt- und Strukturpolitik im Föderalismus* (Berlin: Sigma).

Schmid, Josef and Blancke, Susanne (2006): 'Arbeits- und Sozialpolitik in den Bundesländern', in Schneider, Herbert and Wehling, Hans-Georg (eds) *Landespolitik in Deutschland: Grundlagen, Strukturen, Arbeitsfelder* (Wiesbaden: VS Verlag), pp.295–315.

Schmid, Josef, Hörmann, Ute, Maier, Dirk and Steffen, Christian (2004): *Wer macht was in der Arbeitsmarktpolitik? Maßnahmen und Mitteleinsatz in den westdeutschen Bundesländern: Eine integrierte und vergleichende Analyse* (Münster: Lit Verlag).

Schmidt, Manfred G. (1980): *CDU und SPD an der Regierung: Ein Vergleich ihrer Politik in den Ländern* (Frankfurt: Campus).

Schmidt, Manfred G. (1987): 'Einleitung – Politikwissenschaftliche Arbeitsmarktforschung', in Abromeit, Heidrun, Blanke and Bernhard, 'Arbeitsmarkt, Arbeitsbeziehungen und Politik in den 80er Jahren', *Leviathan: Zeitschrift für Sozialwissenschaften*, Sonderheft 8/1987 (Opladen: Westdeutscher Verlag), pp.12–19.

Schmidt, Manfred G. (1990): 'Staatsfinanzen', in Beyme, Klaus von and Schmidt, Manfred G. (eds) *Politik in der Bundesrepublik Deutschland* (Opladen: Westdeutscher Verlag), pp.36–73.

Schmidt, Manfred G. (1995): 'The do-parties-matter hypothesis and the case of the Federal Republic of Germany', *German Politics*, Vol. 4/3, pp.1–21.

Schmidt, Manfred G. (1996): 'When parties matter: A review of the possibilities and limits of partisan influence on public policy', *European Journal of Political Research*, Vol. 30/2, pp.155–83.

Schmidt, Manfred G. (2002): 'Germany: The grand coalition state', in Colomer, Josep M. (ed.) *Political Institutions in Europe* (London: Routledge), pp.55–93.

Schmidt, Manfred G. (2003): *Political Institutions in the Federal Republic of Germany* (Oxford: Oxford University Press).

Schmidt, Manfred G. (2005): *Sozialpolitik in Deutschland: Historische Entwicklung und Internationaler Vergleich*: 3rd edition (Wiesbaden: VS Verlag).

Schmitt-Beck, Rüdiger (2000): 'Die hessische Landtagswahl vom 7. Februar 1999: Der Wechsel nach dem Wechsel', *Zeitschrift für Parlamentsfragen*, Vol. 30/1, pp.3–17.

Schmitt-Beck, Rüdiger and Weins, Cornelia (2003): 'Die hessische Landtagswahl vom 2. Februar 2003: Erstmals Wiederwahl einer CDU-Regierung', *Zeitschrift für Parlamentsfragen*, Vol. 34/4, pp.671–88.

Schmitz, Gerd (1997): 'Neue Wege der Schulentwicklung in den alten Ländern', *Bildung im Vereinten Deutschland: Perspektiven und Bilanz einer Entwicklung*, Dokumentation der 17. Deutsche Gesellschaft für Bildungsverwaltung-Jahrestagung, 24–26 October 1996, Leipzig (Frankfurt: DGBV), pp.39–44.

Schnapp, Kai-Uwe (2006): 'Wahlen, Abstimmungen und Wählerverhalten in Sachsen-Anhalt', in Holtmann, Everhard (ed.) *Landespolitik in Sachsen-Anhalt: Ein Handbuch* (Magdeburg: Sachsen Anhalt Landeszentrale für politische Bildung), pp.147–78.

Schnapp, Kai-Uwe and Burchardt, Susann (2006): 'Politische Parteien in Sachsen-Anhalt', in Holtmann, Everhard (ed.) *Landespolitik in Sachsen-Anhalt: Ein Handbuch* (Magdeburg: Sachsen Anhalt Landeszentrale für politische Bildung), pp.179–201.

Schneider, Hans-Peter (2005): *Strukturn und Organisation des Bildungswesens in Bundesstaaten: Ein internationaler Vergleich* (Gütersloh: Bertelsmann Stiftung).

Schneider, Herbert (1997): 'Parteien in der Landespolitik', in Gabriel, Oscar W., Niedermayer, Oskar and Stöss, Richard (eds) *Parteiendemokratie in Deutschland* (Bonn: Bundeszentrale für politische Bildung), pp.407–26.

Schram, Sanford F. and Soss, Joe (1998): 'Making something out of nothing: Welfare reform and a new race to the bottom', *Publius*, Vol. 28/3, pp.67–88.

Schröder, Wolfgang (2008): 'Der hessiche SPD zwischen Regierung und Opposition', in Schröder, Wolfgang (ed.) *Parteien und Parteiensystem in Hessen* (Wiesbaden: VS Verlag), pp.77–106.

Schumacher, Hajo (2004): *Roland Koch: Verehrt und Verachtet*, 2nd edition (Frankfurt: Fischer).

Seeleib-Kaiser, Martin (2008): *Welfare State Transformations: Comparative Perspectives* (Basingstoke: Palgrave Macmillan).

Seeleib-Kaiser, Martin, van Dyk, Silke and Roggenkamp, Martin (2005): 'What do parties want? An analysis of programmatic social policy aims in Austria,

Germany, and the Netherlands', *ZeS-Arbeitspapier*, 01/2005 (Zentrum für Sozialpolitik, Bremen).

Seitz, Helmut (2000): 'Fiscal politics, deficits and the politics of sub-national governments', *Public Choice*, Vol. 102, pp.183–218.

Skocpol, Theda (1979): *States and Social Revolutions: A Comparative Analysis of France, Russian and China* (Cambridge: Cambridge University Press).

SPD Sachsen-Anhalt (2006): *Sachsen-Anhalt 2020: Die Zukunftsdebatte*, http://www.spd-sachsen-anhalt.de/index.php?option=com_content&view=article&id=48&Itemid=51, accessed 17th August 2008.

Stabel-Franz, Martina (2004): 'Saarland: Vorreiter in der Familienpolitik', *Soziale Ordnung*, Vol. 6.4, pp.24–5.

Stanat, Petra (ed.) (2002): *PISA-2000: Die Studie im Überblick* (Berlin: Max-Planck-Institut für Bildungsforschung).

Stepan, Alfred (1999): 'Federalism and democracy: Beyond the US model', *Journal of Democracy*, Vol. 10/4, pp.19–34.

Stern, Jutta (2000): *Programme versus Pragmatik* (Frankfurt: Peter Lang).

Streeck, Wolfgang and Thelen, Kathleen (eds) (2005): *Beyond Continuity: Institutional Change in Advanced Political Economies* (Oxford: Oxford University Press).

Sturm, Roland (2005): 'Economic reform at the *Länder* level: New life for regional interventionism', *German Politics*, Vol. 14.2, pp.208–23.

Sturm, Roland (2006): 'Die Föderalismusreform: Gelingt der große Wurf?', in Sturm, Roland and Pehle, Heinrich (eds) *Wege aus der Krise? Die Agenda der zweiten Großen Koalition* (Opladen: Barbara Budrich), pp.113–32.

Sturm, Roland and Zimmermann-Steinhart, Petra (2005): *Föderalismus: Eine Einführung* (Baden-Baden: Nomos).

Sturm, Roland and Pehle, Heinrich (eds) (2006): *Wege aus der Krise? Die Agenda der zweiten Großen Koalition* (Opladen: Barbara Budrich).

Swank, Duane (1988): 'The political economy of government domestic expenditure in the affluent democracies, 1960–1980', *American Journal of Political Science*, Vol. 32/4, pp.1120–50.

Swank, Duane (2003): 'Withering welfare? Globalisation, political economic institutions and contemporary welfare states', in Weiss, Linda (ed.) *States in the Global Economy: Bringing Domestic Institutions Back In* (Cambridge: Cambridge University Press), pp.58–82.

Taylor-Gooby, Peter, Kananen, Johannes and Larson, Trine (2004): 'Paradigm shifts and labour market reform', paper presented at WRAMSOC conference Berlin, 23rd–24th April 2004.

Thaysen, Uwe (2004): 'Die Konventsbewegung zur Föderalismusreform in Deutschland: Ein letztes Hurra der Landesparlamente zu Beginn des 21. Jahrhunderts?', in Europäischen Zentrum für Föderalismus-Forschung Tübingen, *Jahrbuch des Föderalismus 2004: Föderalismus, Subsidiarität und Regionen in Europe* (Baden-Baden: Nomos), pp.123–46.

Thränhardt, Dietrich (1990): 'Bildungspolitik', in von Beyme, Klaus and Schmidt, Manfred G. (eds) *Politik in der Bundesrepublik Deutschland* (Opladen: Westdeutscher Verlag), pp.177–202.

Thurn, Susanna (2004): 'Leistung – was ist das eigentlich?', *Neue Sammlung: Veiltel-jahreszeitschrift für Erziehung und Gesellschaft*, Vol. 44.4, pp.419–35.

Traeger, Michael (2005): *Bildungspolitik in Deutschland: Eine ländervergleichende Netzwerkanalyse* (Marburg: Tectum).

Tsebelis, George (2002): *Veto-Players: How Political Institutions Work* (Princeton: Princeton University Press).

Tufte, Edward R. (1978): *Political Control of the Economy* (Princeton: Princeton University Press).

Vogel, David (2000): 'Environmental regulation and economic integration', *Journal of International Economic Law*, Vol. 3/2, pp.265–79.

Watts, Ronald L. (1999): *Comparing Federal Systems*, 2nd edition (Montreal and Kingston: McGill Queens University Press).

Webber, Douglas (1987): 'Eine Wende in der deutschen Arbeitsmarktpolitik?', in Abromeit, Heidrun, Blanke and Bernhard (1987) 'Arbeitsmarkt, Arbeitsbeziehungen und Politik in den 80er Jahren', *Leviathan: Zeitschrift für Sozialwissenschaften*, Sonderheft 8/1987 (Opladen: Westdeutscher Verlag), pp.74–85.

Weidenfeld, Werner and Korte, Karl-Rudolf (1999): *Handbuch zur Deutschen Einheit 1949–1989–1999* (Frankfurt: Campus).

Weingast, Barry R. (1995): 'The economic role of political institutions: Market-preserving federalism and economic development', *Journal of Law, Economics & Organization*, Vol. 11/1, pp.1–31.

Winkler, Jürgen (2000): 'Die saarländische Landtagswahl vom 5. September 1999: Die CDU erhält die Macht zurück', *Zeitschrift für Parlamentsfragen*, Vol. 30/1, pp.28–42.

Winkler, Jürgen (2005a): 'Die saarländische Landtagswahl vom 5. September 2004: Vom Zwei- zum Vierparteiensystem mit einer dominanten CDU', *Zeitschrift für Parlamentsfragen*, Vol. 35/1, pp.19–35.

Winkler, Michael (2005b): 'Bildungspolitik nach Pisa', in Opielka, Michael (ed.) *Bildungsreform als Sozialreform: Zum Zusammenhang von Bildungs- und Sozialpolitik* (Wiesbaden: VS Verlag), pp.23–43.

Wolf, Frieder (2006): *Die Bildungsausgaben der Bundesländer im Vergleich: Welche Faktoren erklären ihre beträchtliche Variation?* (Berlin: Lit Verlag).

Wolf, Frieder and Hildebrandt, Achim (2008): 'Sechzehn Länder, sechzehn Felder: Erträge des Vergleichs', in Hildebrandt, Achim and Wolf, Frieder (eds) (2008): *Die Politik der Bundesländer: Staatstätigkeit im Vergleich* (Wiesbaden: VS Verlag), pp.363–70.

Wollmann, Hellmut (2002): 'Local government and politics in East Germany', *German Politics*, Vol. 11.3, pp.153–78.

Zohlnhöfer, Reimut (2007): 'Öffentliche Bildungsausgaben im inter- und intranationalen Vergleich: Machen Parteien einen Unterschied?', in Schmidt, Manfred G., Ostheim, Tobias, Siegel, Nico A. and Zohlhöfen, Reinmut (eds) *Der Wohlfahrtsstaat: Eine Einführung in den historischen und internationalen Vergleich* (Wiesbaden: VS Verlag), pp.372–88.

Newspapers and magazines

Altmark-Zeitung

18th February 2006: 'Land setzt auf Niedriglohnjobs'

Berliner Morgenpost

13th July 2004: 'Hartz-IV: Ostdeutsche Länder lenken ein'

Berliner Tagesspiegel (Tagesspiegel)

20th August 2001: 'Hessische Landesregierung: Mehr als private Gründe'
25th June 2002: 'Bayern im Himmel, Bremen am Boden'

23rd March 2006: 'Bodenlos rechts'
19th September 2006: 'Made in Magdeburg'

Berliner Zeitung

27th November 1997: 'Die Lega Süd gibt sich geizig'
17th May 1999: 'Saar-CDU will bei Wahlen gewinnen'
29th March 2004: 'Sachsen-Anhalt will Löhne für Azubis senken'

Elbe-Report

12th March 2006: 'Reformen fortsetzen und ausbauen'

Focus

5th March 2008: 'Schüler als Versuchskaninchen'
6th May 2008: 'Bundesländer wollen Zahl der Sitzenbleiber senken'

Frankfurter Allgemeine Zeitung (FAZ)

2nd July 2004: 'Die größte Kürzung von Sozialleistungen seit 1949'
9th July 2004a: 'Massive Nachteile für den Osten'
9th July 2004b: 'Länder stimmen "Hartz IV" zu'
1st February 2005: 'Kritik an hessischer Familienpolitik'
25th February 2008: 'Eine lange Tradition'

Frankfurter Rundschau (FR)

20th March 1999: 'Mit "okay" besiegelt Koch den Regierungsbund'
6th May 1999: 'Grundsätzliches Ja zu Modellversuch'
7th May 1999: 'Kürzung bei Landesprogramm'
11th May 1999: 'Es ist noch Schonzeit'
15th May 1999: 'Eltern haben in der Schule weniger zu melden'
20th May 1999: 'Die SPD sieht einen Rückfall in die 70er Jahre'
3rd August 1999: 'Schon drei Interessenten für den Kombilohn'
14th September 1999: 'Lehrergewerkschaft auf Konfrontationskurs'
19th October 1999: 'Pädagogen gegen Ziffernoten'
11th February 2000: 'FDP über Hessen-Koalition zerstritten'
14th February 2000: 'Festhalten an der Koalition'
24th February 2000: 'FDP-Chefin droht mit Rücktritt'
9th August 2000: 'Kindergartenpläne erregen Unmut'
2nd September 2000: 'In der Hessen-CDU mehren sich die Signale von rechtsaußen'
26th October 2000: 'Mehr Breite statt Tiefe'
8th March 2001a: 'Kirchen und Fachleute warnen vor größeren Gruppen'
8th March 2001b: 'Bildungsauftrag ist nicht mehr zu erfüllen'
15th March 2001: 'Kita-Richtlinien: Ministerin kündigt Anhörung an'
27th March 2001: 'Leistungskurse bleiben bestehen'
31st March 2001: 'Hessen will Sonderzahlung für engagierte Lehrer'
3rd May 2001: 'Neues Programm gegen Stundenausfall geplant'
16th June 2001: 'Religionsunterricht bisher ohne Chance'
6th August 2001: 'Koch kent Fokus auf mehr Druck'
7th August 2001: 'Wisconsin Works'
21st August 2001: 'Die Werteorientierung lässt Hessens Sozialministerin zurücktreten'
8th September 2001: 'Kultusminister verhängt Strafen gegen Schulleiter'

13th September 2001: 'Der integrierten Gesamtschule nicht zu nahe treten'
4th December 2001: 'Pisa-Studie lässt Streit über Schulformen aufleben'
30th January 2002: 'Wolff will Pilot-Schulen mit Ganztagsbetreuung'
18th June 2002: 'GEW: Ergebnisse nicht aussagekräftig'
26th June 2002: 'Vernichtende Abschlussbilanz für Rot-Grün'
27th June 2002: 'Mit Pisa in die Ferien'
8th August 2002: 'Haupt- und Realschüler müssen 2004 in die Prüfung'
14th January 2003: 'Wolff will auf Turbo-Abi umstellen'
31st January 2003: 'Vorlaufkurse sind überstürzt eingeführt worden'
5th February 2003: 'Vorstand stützt Ruth Wagners Nein zur Koalition'
13th May 2003: 'Ganztagsschul-Vertrag perfekt'
4th October 2003: 'GEW-Chef Nagel empört sich über Karin Wolff'

Magdeburger Volksstimme (Volksstimme)

8th April 2002: 'Höppner lehnt PDS-geführte Koalition ab'
17th April 2002: 'Höppner lässt durchblicken: Mein Ziel ist SPD-PDS-Koalition'
18th April 2002: 'Höppner entfacht in der SPD einen neuen Richtungsstreit'
24th April 2002: 'Gemeinsmkeiten überwiegen: CDU und FDP wollen Mittelstand stärken und Ämter verschlanken'
25th April 2002: 'Böhmer: Vor Pfingsten steht die Regierung'
26th April 2002: 'Ludewig sagt ab'
27th April 2002: 'Innere Sicherheit ist Streitpunkt'
6th May 2002: 'Pieper will Kultusressort uebernehmen'
10th May 2002: 'Arbeitgeber zufrieden mit den neuen Ministern'
13th May 2002: 'Pieper wird doch nicht Ministerin'
14th May 2002: 'Koalitionsverhandlungen sind beendet'
17th May 2002: 'Böhmer erhielt sogar Stimmen von der Opposition'
31st May 2002: 'Ich bin kein Rohrstock-Minister'
1st June 2002: 'Als Frauenminister fuehle ich mich Wohl'
13th June 2002: '12-Jahre-Abitur wird schon 2005 möglich sein'
21stJune 2002: 'Protest gegen Schulpolitik'
26thJune 2002: 'Reform der Grundschule geplant – Schüler sollen schneller lesen lernen'
27th June 2002: 'Nach einem halben Jahr muss das Alphabet wirklich sitzen'
9th July 2002: 'Böhmer und Püchel streiten ueber Vorschläge der Hartz-Kommission'
10th July 2002: 'Olbertz verlangt von Abiturienten mehr Leistung'
19th September 2002: 'Böhmer kontra Minister: Es gibt keine Spar-Tabus'
28th September 2002: 'Kürzungen im Sozialbereich: CDU erwartet "heissen Herbst"'
30th September 2002: 'Püchel: Bei Kinderbetreuung darf nicht gespart werden'
2nd October 2002: 'Regierung will ab 2006 Abitur in zwölf Jahren'
7th October 2002: 'Kultusminister marschiert falsch'
8th October 2002: 'Anspruch auf Krippenplatz wackelt: Kritik kommt auch aus der CDU'
11th October 2002: 'Schulschliessung wegen freier Schulwahl?'
12th October 2002: 'Ab 2007 Abitur wieder nach zwölf Jahren'
23rd October 2002: 'Regierung verschiebt Vorlage für Kinderbetreuungs-Gesetz'
25th October 2002: 'Zuckerbrot und Peitsche: Mehr Freiheit, aber weniger Geld für die Gemeinden'
9th November 2002: 'Opposition lehnt den Einsatz von Sozialassistenten in Kitas ab'
13th November 2002: 'Land schränkt den Rechtsanspruch ein'
19th November 2002: 'Bündnis will im Februar Volksbegehren starten'

23rd November 2002: Ludewig und Spaeth im neuen Wirschaftsbeirat'
27th November 2002: 'Forum für Wirtschaft und Arbeit löst "Buendnis für Arbeit" ab'
5th December 2002: 'Disput um die Hauptschule – wird mit ihr selektiert?'
6th December 2002a: 'Scharf: GEW sollte ernsthafter Gesprächspartner bleiben'
6th December 2002b: 'Lehrer-Tarifvertrag: Gehaltsversicht, dafuer aber Kündigungs-schutz bis 2010'
11th December 2002: 'Sachsen-Anhalt drohen 20000 neue Arbeitslose'
13th December 2002: 'Nicht Leistung *oder* Chancengleichheit, sondern Leistung *und* Chancengleichheit'
8th January 2003: 'Zwei Kopfnoten im Zeugnis'
9th January 2003: 'GEW: Kopfnoten lösen nicht das Problem'
18th January 2003: 'CDU und FDP gehen auf SPD zu'
21st January 2003: 'Demonstration gegen Einschnitt bei der Kinderbetreuung'
29th January 2003: 'Eltern sollen bald für Schulbücher zahlen'
19th February 2003: 'Mini-Grundschulen haben bis 2006 Bestand'
21st February 2003: 'Rosskur für das Bildungswesen mit 150 Jahre alten Rezepten'
24th February 2003: 'CDU fordert Ausnahmen bei Schulschliessungen'
8th March 2003: 'SPD: Mehr Geld für Ganztagsschulen'
10th March 2003: 'Ganztagsschule nur in reichen Ländern?'
14th March 2003: 'Ganztagsschule ist kein Allheilmittel'
10th May 2003: 'Bürgermeister erklärt Rücktritt'
18th October 2003: 'SPD will kleine Schulen vor dem Aus bewahren'
27th August 2004: 'Ich empfehle jedem, sich mal in eine westdeutsche Kneipe zu setzen …'
4th January 2005: 'Jugendhilfe, Frauenhäuser und Sportförderung wären stark gefährdet'
8th January 2005: 'Volksentscheid am 23. Januar: Was sagen die Parteichefs?'
11th January 2005: 'Vom Rechsanspruch 1991 bis zur ersten großen Finanzkrise 1998'
12th January 2005: 'Höppner setzt Kürzung durch und nennt Volksinitiative verant-wortungslos'
13th January 2005a: 'SPD überrascht Regierung mit Kompromiss: Fünf Stunden für alle'
13th January 2005b: 'Ministerium: "Magdeburg schießt übers Ziel hinaus"'
14th January 2005: 'Schleichende Zerschlagung des gelobten Kita-Netzes'
25th January 2005: 'Böhmer: Gesetz auf Dauer sicher. Esche: Wir lassen das Thema ruhen'
2nd February 2005: 'Arbeits-Agentur streicht Zuschüsse für Beschäftigung'
5th February 2005: 'Olbertz: Lehrer sollten mehr bei Unterrichtsthemen verweilen'
17th February 2005: 'Gewerkschaften betrachten Niedriglohnjobs äußerst skeptisch'
7th April 2005: 'Wahl zwischen Eisdiele und Ethikstunde vorbei'
20th April 2005: 'Wer regiert bald? Hinter den Kulissen beginnt Gerangel um Ministerämter'
3rd May 2005: 'Immer wider wird ihm einer reingewürgt'
26th January 2006: 'Vom ewigen Streit ums Schulsystem und einem wackelnden Minister'
2nd February 2006: 'Arbeis-Agentur streicht Zuschüsse für Beschäftigung'
22nd March 2006: 'Vordenker und Tabubrecher bringt die SPD auf einen neuen Kurs'
27th March 2006: 'Nicht einmal die Hälfte ging wählen: Zeichen stehen auf Große Koalition'

Mitteldeutsche Zeitung

4th January 2005: 'Streit um Hürden auf dem Weg zum Gymnasium'
10th January 2005: 'FDP will Zentralabitur für Mitteldeutschland'

18th February 2005: 'Hoffnung paart sich mit Skepsis'
24th February 2005: 'Heftige Debatte zu Schul-Empfehlung'
13th March 2005: 'Kreisklasse oder Kreisfreiheit'
14th April 2005: 'Neue Pflicht zum Ethik-Unterricht'
27th April 2005a: 'SPD will zurück in die Schul-Zukunft'
27th April 2005b: 'Jetzt doch kleinere Schulen möglich'
4th January 2006: 'Bei Kombilohn geht Sachsen-Anhalt voran'
1st February 2006: 'Kritik ruft gemischte Reaktionen hervor'
22nd March 2006: 'Minister plant Rangliste für Schulen'

Das Parlament

31st January 2005: 'Duale Ausbildung wird flexibler'
20th February 2006: 'Weiter mit Schwarz-Gelb oder wieder ein rot-rotes Magdeburger Modell'
3rd July 2006: 'Machtpoker in den Amtsstuben'

Saarbrücker Zeitung (SBZ)

8th February 1996: 'Schulstrukturreform rückt näher'
19th January 1999: 'Saar-CDU gegen Islam-Unterricht'
8th February 2000: 'Noten schon ab der zweiten Klasse?'
6th June 2000: 'Ein Minister mischt die Schulen auf'
8th June 2000: 'Kein Beitrag für letztes Jahr im Kindergarten'
1st August 2001: 'Panne bei Schreiers Realschul-Erlass'
18th August 2001: 'Saar-Modell bisher ohne größere Erfolge'
8th October 2001: '"Recht auf Religion" für Muslime?'
2nd February 2002: 'Saar-Sozialministerin schlägt Erneuerung des "Diesnstmädchen-Privegs" vor – Länder-Initiative im Bundesrat gescheitert'
6th February 2002: 'Dem Ministerpräsidenten schmeckt kein Einheitsbrei'
16th February 2002: 'Für Mütter kaum Chances auf Jobs'
19th April 2002: 'Saarland für nationalen Lehrplan'
17th June 2002a: 'Sind Saarländer doofer?'
17th June 2002b: 'Schreier kündigt neue Grundschul-Offensive an'
8th August 2002: 'Das Fundament Grundschule'
30th December 2002: Saar-Schüler trainieren für Pisa-Test'
28th August 2003: 'Saar-Schüler büffeln für die zweite Chance'
30th August 2003: 'Initiative von Saar-Kultusminister Schreier ist richtig'
28th November 2003: 'Schreier streitet mt GEW-Chef Kessler'
15th September 2004: 'Nur eine Verwahranstalt für Kinder'

Der Spiegel/Spiegel Online

11th January 1961: 'Roter Stehaufmann'
15th February 1999: 'Der Mutmacher aus Hessen'
30th July 1999: 'Kombi-Lohn im Praxis-Test'
4th September 2000a: 'Verbale Stahlgewisser'
4th September 2000b: 'Was wusste Roland Koch?'
11th September 2000: 'Einsatz für den CDU-Konzern'
22nd November 2000a: 'Saar-Innenminister Meiser zurückgetreten'
22nd November 2000b: 'Die erste Innenministerin Deutschlands'
22nd November 2000c: 'Saarland: Abitur nach zwölf Jahren'
23rd April 2001: '12-Jahres Abitur: SPD will Schulen entscheiden lassen'

16th August 2002: 'Wir sind alle gefordert'
9th December 2002: 'Eisblock in Fahrt'
12th December 2002: 'Koch provoziert Sturm der Entrüstung'
17th January 2003: 'Kochs gewagte Zehlenakrobatik'
26th February 2003: 'Bund-Länder-Gezerre: Es lebe die Kleinstaaterei'
12th May 2003: 'Bund und Länder raufen sich zusammen'
29th July 2003: 'Saarlands Müller hat am meisten Erforg'
6th July 2004: 'Ostdeutsche Länder verweigern Zustimmung'
9th July 2004: 'Hartz-IV-Gesetz: Bundesrat billigt Arbeitsmarktreform'
12th July 2004: 'Schröder verteilt Bonbons an den Osten'
13th July 2004a: 'Neues Streitmaterial nach Krisengipfeln'
13th July 2004b: 'Kanzlerrunde war richtig und wichtig'
27th July 2004: 'Rechtschreibreform: Debatte ohne Punkt und Komma'
15th August 2004: 'Geradezu obszön'
17th August 2004: 'Lafontaine macht sich zum CDU-Wahlkämpfer'
20th December 2004: 'Die Blamage'
4th September 2006: 'Koch-Regierung will nachbessern'
13th October 2006: 'Schulskandal um Nazi-Parole schockiert Sachsen-Anhalt'
21st February 2007: 'Streit über Familienbild: Schönbohm wirft von der Leyen antiquiertes Männerbild vor'
22nd February 2007: 'Frauan als Gebärmaschinen: Bischof giftet gegen von der Leyen'
25th May 2007: 'Kinderbetreuung: Union streitet über Gutscheine und Herdprämie'

Süddeutsche Zeitung (SZ)

23rd October 1999: 'Im Profil: Karin Wolff'
19th November 2002: 'Streitnah: Hessen will Ganztagsmittel für Bücher'
2nd September 2003: 'Was soll dieser Vertrag, Herr Olbertz?'
16th March 2006: 'Schmusekurs im "Eisen-Karl"'

Die tageszeitung (taz)

5th July 2007: 'Gegen die Schöpfung?'
25th March 2008: 'Ganztagsschule light'

Die Welt

24th June 2004: 'Saarland beschließt Verbot'

Wochenspiegel

29th December 2004: '9. Schulgesetznovelle'
19th January 2005: 'Das Allerbeste ist immer noch: Kinder machen!'

Die Zeit

5th October 2000: 'Arbeitsplätze im Gepäck'
30th August 2001: 'Die Provokation aus Hessen'
2nd January 2006: 'Hoffnungsträger Kombilohn'

Appendix 2 List of Interviews

Personal interviews

A. 11th October 2006: Jürgen Scharf MdL, Chair, CDU-Fraktion, Landtag of Saxony-Anhalt

B. 11th October 2006: Norbert Bischoff MdL, Parliamentary Business Leader of the SPD-Fraktion, Social Policy Spokesperson of the SPD-Fraktion (bis 2006), Landtag of Saxony-Anhalt

C. 11th October 2006: Thorsten Wahl, Deputy Land Chair and Birgit Münchhausen, Deputy Land Chair, Verband Bildung und Erziehung, Saxony-Anhalt

D. 11th October 2006: Senior official, Ministry of Health and Social Affairs of Saxony-Anhalt

E. 12th October 2006: Udo Gebhardt, Chair, DGB, Saxony-Anhalt

F. 12th October 2006: Wolfgang Schuth, Land Business Leader, Arbeiterwohlfahrt, Landesverband Saxony-Anhalt e.V.

G. 12th October 2006: Dr. Peter Linde, Head of Section for cooperation with Land Politics, Bundesagentur für Arbeit, Regionaldirektion Saxony-Anhalt/Thüringen, Wolfgang Meyer, Leiter der Arbeitsagentur Magdeburg

H. 16th October 2006: Rita Mittendorf MdL, Education Policy Spokesperson, SPD-Fraktion, Landtag of Saxony-Anhalt

I. 16th October 2006: Markus Kurze MdL, Vice-Chair, CDU-Fraktion (from 2006), Child and Youth Affairs Spokesperson, CDU-Fraktion (until 2006), Landtag of Saxony-Anhalt

J. 16th October 2006: Eva von Angern MdL, Youth Affairs Spokesperson, PDS-Fraktion, Landtag of Saxony-Anhalt

K. 17th October 2006: Thomas Lippmann, Land Chair, Gewerkschaft Erziehung und Wissenschaft (GEW), Saxony-Anhalt

L. 17th October 2006: Dr. Bernd Kregel, Land Business Leader, Städte- und Gemeindebund, Saxony-Anhalt

M. 17th October 2006: Senior official, Ministry for Economy and Work, Saxony-Anhalt

N. 17th October 2006: Prof. Dr. Jan-Hendrik Olbertz, Minister for Education, Land Saxony-Anhalt

O. 18th October 2006: Petra Grimm-Benne MdL, Social Policy spokesperson of the SPD-Fraktion, Landtag of Saxony-Anhalt

P. 19th October 2006: Dr. Rosemarie Hein, Education Policy spokesperson of the PDS-Fraktion, Landtag of Saxony-Anhalt (until 2006)

Q. 19th October 2006: Detlef Gürth, Land Business Leader of the CDU-Fraktion, Labour Market Policy Spokesperson of the CDU-Fraktion (until 2006), Landtag of Saxony-Anhalt

R. 20th October 2006: CDU Landtag member, Saxony-Anhalt

S. 31st October 2006: Dr. Jürgen Borchert, Social Judge, Hesse Social Court, Darmstadt, Family Policy Advisor of the Hesse State Government (2000)

T. 1st November 2006: Karl-Christian Schelzke, Operations Director, Hessischer Städte- und Gemeindetag

U. 1st November 2006: Stefan Körzell, Land Chair, Deutscher Gewerkschaftsbund (DGB), Hesse

V.   2nd November 2006: Senior official, Social Affairs and Labour Ministry of Hesse (until 2005)
W.   3rd November 2006: Norbert Kartmann MdL, President of Landtag of Hesse (from 2003), Chair, CDU-Fraktion, Landtag of Hesse (until 2003)
X.   3rd November 2006: Petra Fuhrmann MdL, Social Affairs Spokesperson of the SPD Fraktion, Landtag of Hesse
Y.   3rd November 2006: Rolf Eifert, Head of the State School Office, Frankfurt-am-Main
Z.   6th November 2006: Dr. Regine Görner, Minister for Work and Social Affairs of the Saarland (until 2004)
AA. 7th November 2006: Jochen Nagel, Land Chair, Gewerkschaft Erziehung und Wissenschaft (GEW), Hesse
BB. 8th November 2006: Senior official, Ministry for Work and Social Affairs, Hesse
CC. 8th November 2006: Senior official, Kultusministerium, Hessen
DD. 9th November 2006: Dr. Stephan Hölz, Head of the Office of the Minister, Ministry for Work and Social Affairs, Hesse
EE. 9th November 2006: Dorothea Henzler MdL, Education Policy Spokesperson of the FDP-Fraktion, Landtag of Hesse
FF. 22nd November 2006: Heiko Maas MdL, Chair of the SPD Fraktion, Landtag of the Saarland
GG. 23rd November 2006: Senior official, Ministry for Economics, Saarland
HH. 23rd November 2006: Eugen Roth MdL, Chair of the DGB, Saarland, Labour Market Policy Spokesperson of the SPD-Fraktion, Landtag of the Saarland
II.   23rd November 2006: Richard Nospers, Managing Director, Saarländische Städte- und Gemeindetag
JJ.   23rd November 2006: Reiner Braun MdL, Education Policy Spokesperson of the SPD Fraktion, Landtag of the Saarland; Isolde Ries MdL, Women's Affairs Spokesperson of the SPD Fraktion (until 2004), Landtag of the Saarland, Petra Scherer, Women's Policy Spokesperson of the SPD Fraktion (from 2004), Landtag of the Saarland
KK. 24th November 2006: Senior official, Education Ministry of the Saarland
LL. 24th November 2006: CDU Member, Landtag of the Saarland
MM. 29th November 2006: Dr. Roland Märker, Land Director, Arbeiterwohlfahrt, Landesverband Saarland e.V.
NN. 30th November 2006: Annegret Kramp-Karrenbauer, Interior Minister of the Saarland (from 2001), Parliamentary Business Leader of the CDU-Fraktion, Landtag of the Saarland (1999–2000)
OO. 30th November 2006: Senior official, Ministry for Economics and Labour, Saarland
PP. 1st December 2006: Klaus Kessler, Land Chair, Gewerkschaft Erziehung und Wissenschaft (GEW), Saarland

Telephone interviews

Ia.   31st October 2006: Lothar Quanz MdL, Education Policy Spokesperson of the SPD-Fraktion, Landtag of Hesse
IIa. 1st November 2006: Senior official, Social Affairs and Labour Ministry of Hesse
IIIa. Karin Wolff: Education Minister of Hesse, 15th December 2006

Appendix 3   Commonly Used German Terms and Abbreviations

Abitur: German school-leaving examination for grammar school pupils
Abteilungsleiter: Head of Section
Angestellte: State employee without enhanced job status
Arbeiterwohlfahrt (AWO): Workers' Welfare Organisation
Arbeitsagentur: Job Centre
Beamte: State employee with enhanced job status
Bund: Federal government
Bundesagentur für Arbeit: Federal Labour Agency
Bundesanstalt für Arbeit: Federal Labour Organisation
Bundesrat: second chamber
Bundestag: Federal Parliament
Bürgerschaft: Assembly of the City State of Hamburg (equivalent to a Landtag)
BVerfG: Bundesverfassungsgericht (Federal Constitutional Court)
CDU: Christlich Demokratische Union (Christian Democratic Party)
CSU: Christlich-Soziale Union (Christian Social Union: the Christian Democratic Party in Bavaria)
DGB: Deutscher Gewerkschaftsbund (German Trade Union Confederation)
DVU: Deutsche Volksunion (German People's Union: a far right party)
Einstiegsgeld: Introductory payment (a form of wage subsidy)
Familienpolitik: Policy towards families
FDP: Freie Demokratische Partei (Free Democratic Party)
Förderstufe: Mixed-ability class for pupils in years 5 and 6
Fraktion: Party Group (in an assembly)
Fraktionsvorsitzender: Party Group Chair
Ganztagsschulen: all-day schools
Gemeinden: Districts
Gesamtschule: Comprehensive School
GEW: Gewerkschaft Erziehung und Wissenschaft (Trade Union for Education)
GVBl LSA: Gesetzes- und Verordnungsblatt Land Sachsen-Anhalt (Official Notice, Land Saxony-Anhalt)
Gymnasium: Grammar school
Hauptschule: Secondary school, lowest of three tiers of general-needs education
Jugendamt : Youth service
KMK: Konferenz der Kultusminister (Conference of Ministers of Education)
Koalitionsaussagen: Statements made about which coalition a party would join
Kombilohn: Wage top-up
KPD: Kommunistische Partei Deutschlands (Communist Party of Germany)
Land/Länder: State/states
Länderfinanzausgleich: Fiscal equalisation mechanism
Landesregierung: State government
Landesverband: Land-level party
Landesverfassung: Land constitution
Landkreis: County

Landkreise: Counties
Landrat (plural Landräte): directly-elected head of the administration of a county
Landtag: State parliament
Landtagsfraktion: Party group in the state parliament
LDP: Liberal Democratic Party (a previous name of the FDP in Hesse)
MdL: Member of a state parliament
MEP: Member of the European Parliament
Mittelschule: Middle-level school
NDP: National Democratic Party of Germany
Oberstufe: Final two years' of grammar school
Ostpolitik: Policy towards the east of Germany
PDS: Party of Democratic Socialism
Plenarprotokoll: Transcript of parliamentary debate
Politikverflechtung: interlocking policy-making
Radikalenerlass: Ban on employing potential extremists in public service
Realschule: Secondary school, middle of three tiers of general needs education
Rechtsstaat: state governed by the rule of law
Sekundarschule: Secondary school (below the level of grammar school)
Sozialstaat: social state
SPD: Sozialdemokratische Partei Deutschlands (Social Democratic Party of Germany)
Staatsgerichtshof: State Court
Staatskanzlei: State Chancellory (Office of the Minister President)
Städte- und Gemeindetag/Städte- und Gemeinbund: Association of towns and municipalities
VBE: Verband Bildung und Erziehung (Association of Schooling and Education)

Index